Veiled Power

LAW AND GLOBAL GOVERNANCE SERIES

Editors:
Andrew Hurrell, Benedict Kingsbury, and Richard B. Stewart

Global governance involves the exercise of power, beyond a single state, to influence behaviour, to generate resources, or to allocate authority. Regulatory structures, and law of all kinds, increasingly shape the nature, use, and effects of such power. These dynamic processes of ordering and governance blend the extra-national with the national, the public with the private, the political and economic with the social and cultural. Issues of effectiveness, justice, voice, and inequality in these processes are growing in importance.

This series features exceptional works of original research and theory—both sector-specific and conceptual—that carry forward the serious understanding and evaluation of these processes of global governance and the role of law and institutions within them. Contributions from all disciplines are welcomed. The series aims particularly to deepen scholarship and thinking in international law, international politics, comparative law and politics, and public and private global regulation. A major goal is to study governance globally, and to enrich the literature on law and the nature and effects of global governance beyond the North Atlantic region.

Veiled Power

*International Law and the Private
Corporation, 1886–1981*

DOREEN LUSTIG

OXFORD
UNIVERSITY PRESS

OXFORD
UNIVERSITY PRESS

Great Clarendon Street, Oxford, OX2 6DP,
United Kingdom

Oxford University Press is a department of the University of Oxford.
It furthers the University's objective of excellence in research, scholarship,
and education by publishing worldwide. Oxford is a registered trade mark of
Oxford University Press in the UK and in certain other countries

First Edition published in 2020

Impression: 1

Published in the United States of America by Oxford University Press
198 Madison Avenue, New York, NY 10016, United States of America

British Library Cataloguing in Publication Data
Data available

Library of Congress Control Number: 2019957399

ISBN 978–0–19–882209–7

Printed and bound by
CPI Group (UK) Ltd, Croydon, CR0 4YY

To my father

Acknowledgements

I would like to thank the individuals and institutions who helped me write this book.

I am indebted to my teacher and committed supervisor, Benedict Kingsbury, who taught me how to read, think and study history and international law. As I turn away from the keyboard I can almost see him at the other end of his office-desk, gently pressing me to look further, to think harder, to dare and explore. His rigorous mentorship defined my understanding of scholarly work. I am also deeply grateful to Martti Koskenniemi, who provided me with guidance, encouragement and close mentorship throughout the various stages of this project. His tireless motivation, intellectual curiosity and vitality proved wonderfully contagious and inspired me to pursue unintended angles of this work. I wish to thank him for the numerous conversations we had and for his unequivocal support during the writing of this project.

The earlier stages of the writing of this book were written as part of my J.S.D dissertation at NYU Law School. I'd like to thank the Hauser Global Legal Program and the Institute of International Law and Justice at NYU for their generous institutional support and funding. I'd like to thank the NYU vibrant community of international law for its kind friendship and collegial support. Amongst the members of that inspiring community I'd like to thank Joseph H. H. Weiler who was a close mentor to me throughout my studies at NYU and a dear friend in the years which followed. Joseph Weiler taught me lasting lessons on what it means to be a teacher. I can only aspire to follow his example.

Special thanks are owed to Lauren Benton who commented on earlier drafts of this project and examined the original thesis. I am grateful to the teachers and colleagues at NYU who read and commented on various parts of the project: Kevin Davis, Mattias Kumm, Jeremy Waldron, Guy Fiti Sinclair, Colin Grey, Arie Rosen, Eran Shamir-Borer, Nourit Zimmerman, Vanessa Casado, Lisa Kerr, Maria Varaki, Angela Delfino, and Galia Rivlin.

Much of the book was written while I was at Tel Aviv University Faculty of Law. My special thanks to my dear friends and colleagues Leora Bilsky, Ron Harris, Roy Kreitner, David Schorr, Assaf Likhovski, Hila Shamir, and Tami Kricheli-Katz for their valuable comments and support. I am grateful for the Cegla Center for Interdisciplinary Research of the Law, the David Berg Foundation Institute for Law and History and the Edmond J. Safra Center for Ethics at Tel Aviv University for their generous financial support.

I'd like to convey my thanks to Amanda Dale, who worked tirelessly on the editing of the book manuscript and to my research assistants Neli frost, Guy Priver, and Jasmin Wennersbusch. I'd like to thank the staff at the College Park Archives at Maryland, the Telford Taylor Papers Collection at Columbia University and the librarians at NYU Libraries and Tel Aviv University Libraries for their close guidance and assistance.

I would like to thank my dear friends Tami kricheli-Katz, Hila Shamir, Maytal Giloba, Natalie Davidson, Eliav Lieblich, Ori Goldberg, and Ilana Toren-Amit for their kind friendship and support.

Special thanks are owed to Yaniv Friedman, who was my companion and partner during the better part of this journey. I wish to thank my aunt, Gila Menachem, for her encouragement and good advice and to my grandfather, Avraham Blinder, who made sure his grandchildren would sustain their curiosity whatever they do. I'd like to thank the warmth and love of my mother and sisters Bella, Lian, and Shimrit Lustig. I am grateful to Eyal, my kindred spirit. My boys, Avner and Yotam, have always been my source of joy, faith and inspiration.

This book is dedicated to my father, Itzhak (Itzik) Lustig (1953–1998), who encouraged me to pursue an intellectual life and had faith in my dreams.

Contents

List of Abbreviations

A.G.	*Aktiengesellschaft*
AIOC	Anglo-Iranian Oil Company
APOC	Anglo-Persian Oil Company
ATS	Alien Tort Statute
BP	British Petroleum
BIT	Bilateral Investment Treaty
BSAC	British South Africa Company
CCL10	*Control Council Law No. 10*
CEO	Chief Executive Officer
CFAE	Compagnie Française de l'Afrique Équatoriale
CIA	Central Intelligence Agency
CSR	Corporate Social Responsibility
DITE	Division of Investment Technology and Enterprise Development
EEC	European Economic Community
ERP	European Recovery Plan
FCN	Friendship, Commerce and Navigation
FCPA	Foreign Corrupt Practices Act
GATT	General Agreement on Tariffs and Trade
GEP	Group of Eminent Persons
IBRD	International Bank of Reconstruction and Development
ICJ	International Court of Justice
ICSID	International Centre for Settlement of Investment Disputes
IDB	Inter-American Development Bank
I.G.	*Interessengemeinschaft*
ILO	International Labour Organization
IMF	International Monetary Fund
IMT	International Military Tribunal
ISDS	investor–state dispute settlement
ITO	International Trade Organization
ITT	International Telephone and Telegraph Company
JAG	Judge Advocate General
MAI	Multilateral Agreement on Investment
MFN	Most Favoured Nation
MNC	multinational corporation
NAC	National African Company
NGO	Non-governmental organization
NIEO	New International Economic Order
NIOC	National Iranian Oil Company
OECD	Organisation for Economic Co-operation and Development

OEEC	Organisation for European Economic Co-operation
OMGUS	U.S. Office of Military Government
OPEC	Organization of the Petroleum Exporting Countries
OSS	Office of Strategic Services
R&A	Research and Analysis
SEC	Securities and Exchange Commission
TSC	Temporary Slavery Commission
TNC	transnational corporation
TWAIL	Third World Approaches to International Law
UNCTAD	United Nations Conference on Trade and Development
UNCTC	UN Centre on TNCs
WTO	World Trade Organization

1

Introduction

It is widely accepted that corporations are hugely influential actors in international affairs. It is also often assumed that international law started to become relevant to this corporate phenomenon only relatively recently, after the end of the Cold War period. This book suggests an alternative way of thinking about the role of international law and its relevance to the private business corporation. It traces the emergence of the contemporary legal architecture for corporations in international law and shows how modern international law constitutes a framework within which businesses and governments allocate resources and responsibilities—a framework that began to operate as early as the late-nineteenth century and continued throughout the twentieth century.

Corporations have limited responsibilities in international law but enjoy far-reaching rights and privileges.[1] International legal debates often conceive of this issue in broad cosmopolitan terms, as a problem of business accountability for human rights violations.[2] This literature on corporations and human rights typically concentrates on the failure of international law to regulate corporations—that

---

[1] For a comprehensive book on this issue, *see* PETER T. MUCHLINSKI, MULTINATIONAL ENTERPRISES AND THE LAW (2007). *See also* Peter T. Muchlinski, *Corporations in International Law*, *in* MAX PLANCK ENCYCLOPEDIA OF PUBLIC INTERNATIONAL LAW (Rüdiger Wolfrum ed., 2009). For an analysis of this imbalance in the context of international investment law, *see* James Gathii & Sergio Puig, *Introduction to The Symposium on Investor Responsibility: The Next Frontier in International Investment Law*, 113 AM. J. INT'L L. UNBOUND 1 (2019).

[2] The literature on this issue is vast. *See*, for example, Steven Ratner, *Corporations and Human Rights: A Theory of Legal Responsibility*, 111 YALE L.J. 443 (2001); Paul Hoffman & Beth Stephens, *International Human Rights Cases Under State Law and in State Courts*, 3 U.C. IRVINE L. REV. 9 (2013); ANDREW CLAPHAM, HUMAN RIGHTS OBLIGATIONS OF NON-STATE ACTORS (2006); NON-STATE ACTORS AND HUMAN RIGHTS 141–350 (Philip Alston ed., 2005); John Ruggie, *Business and Human Rights: The Evolving International Agenda*, 101 AM. J. INT'L L. 819 (2007); Andrea Bianchi, *The Fight for Inclusion: Non-State Actors and International Law*, *in* FROM BILATERALISM TO COMMUNITY INTEREST: ESSAYS IN HONOUR OF BRUNO SIMMA 39 (Ulrich Fastenrath et al. eds., 2011); M.T. Kamminga, *Multinational Corporations in International Law*, *in* OXFORD BIBLIOGRAPHIES IN INTERNATIONAL LAW (Anthony Carty ed., 2013). Online: https://www.oxfordbibliographies.com/view/document/obo-9780199796953/obo-9780199796953-0049.xml ; PHILIP ALSTON & RYAN GOODMAN, INTERNATIONAL HUMAN RIGHTS 1464 (2012); David Weissbrodt, *Roles and Responsibilities of Non-State Actors*, *in* THE OXFORD HANDBOOK OF INTERNATIONAL HUMAN RIGHTS LAW 719, 726–27 (Dinah Shelton ed., 2013). For a global governance perspective on this issue, *see* BUSINESS AND HUMAN RIGHTS: BEYOND THE END OF THE BEGINNING (Cesar Rodriguez-Garavito ed., 2017). Some scholars have shifted their focus to global supply chains as their preferred conceptual framework for questions of corporate accountability. *See*, for example, BUILDING A TREATY ON BUSINESS AND HUMAN RIGHTS: CONTEXT AND CONTOURS (Surya Deva & David Bilchitz eds., 2017).

Veiled Power. Doreen Lustig, Oxford University Press (2020). © Doreen Lustig.
DOI: 10.1093/oso/9780198822097.001.0001

is, the accountability gap they create.[3] The shift to governance in international legal theory and socio-legal studies triggered greater attention to soft law mechanisms of corporate social responsibility (CSR), which are often criticized in comparison with conventional top-down regulatory measures.[4] Conceptually, the issue of corporations in international law has focused on whether or not they are, or ought to be, recognized as 'subjects' of responsibility in international law and on the adequate conceptual analogy to the corporation (the individual? the state? an institution?).[5]

This book challenges the 'failure' narrative and presents an alternative reading of the history of international law and business corporations. It does so by challenging the public/private distinction that animates the 'failure' argument in the context of business corporations in international law. Perhaps the most appropriate starting point for such an alternative reading is Morris Cohen's 1927 article, 'Property and Sovereignty'. Cohen opens the article as follows: 'Property and sovereignty, as every student knows, belong to entirely different branches of the law. Sovereignty is a concept of political or public law and property belongs to civil or private law. This distinction between public and private law is a fixed feature of our law-school curriculum.'[6]

This fixed feature is the target of Cohen's critique and the backdrop against which he developed his alternative account. In the context of public international law and the private business corporation, a similar understanding prevails. We often conceive of sovereign states and business corporations as entities belonging to entirely different fields of law. This distinction between public and private has long been a resilient feature of our international law teaching and, as the following

---

[3] For the analysis of the accountability gap in international law, *see* JEAN THOMAS, PUBLIC RIGHTS, PRIVATE RELATIONS (2015); ALSTON & GOODMAN, *supra* note 2, at 1467; OLIVIER DE SCHUTTER, INTERNATIONAL HUMAN RIGHTS LAW 395–98 (2d ed. 2014).

[4] The debate over corporate social responsibility is extensive. *See*, for example, DAVID VOGEL, THE MARKET AS VIRTUE: THE POTENTIAL AND LIMITS OF CORPORATE SOCIAL RESPONSIBILITY (2005); Ronen Shamir, *Capitalism, Governance, and Authority: The Case of Corporate Social Responsibility*, 6 ANN. REV. L. & SOC. SCI. 531 (2010); Tim Bartley, *Institutional Emergence in an Era of Globalization: The Rise of Transnational Private Regulation of Labor and Environmental Conditions*, 113 AM. J. SOC. 297 (2007); TIM BARTLEY, RULES WITHOUT RIGHTS: LAND, LABOR, AND PRIVATE AUTHORITY IN THE GLOBAL ECONOMY (2018); Stephen Brammer et al., *Corporate Social Responsibility and Institutional Theory: New Perspectives on Private Governance*, 10 SOCIO-ECON. REV. 3 (2012); TIM BÜTHE & WALTER MATTLI, THE NEW GLOBAL RULERS: THE PRIVATIZATION OF REGULATION IN THE WORLD ECONOMY (2011); CORPORATE SOCIAL RESPONSIBILITY IN A GLOBALIZING WORLD: GLOBAL DYNAMICS AND LOCAL PRACTICES (Kiyoteru Tsutsui & Alwyn Lim eds., 2015).

[5] Jose E. Alvarez, *Are Corporations 'Subjects' of International Law?*, 9 SANTA CLARA J. INT'L L. 1 (2011); MARKOS KARAVIAS, CORPORATE OBLIGATIONS UNDER INTERNATIONAL LAW (2014). For an analysis of competing conceptual accounts of the corporation in international law—individualism, statism, and institutionalism—*see* Fleur Jones, *Theorizing the Corporation in International Law*, in THE OXFORD HANDBOOK OF THE THEORY OF INTERNATIONAL LAW 635 (Anne Orford & Florian Hoffman eds., 2016). For an argument that conceives of the corporation as a sovereign and emphasizes regulatory failure, *see* JOSHUA BARKAN, CORPORATE SOVEREIGNTY (2013).

[6] Morris R. Cohen, *Property and Sovereignty*, 13 CORNELL L. REV. 8 (1927).

analysis will show, is particularly pertinent to the prevailing assumptions on corporations in international law.

Private business corporations began to feature as a human rights concern and potential subjects of international legal responsibility only towards the end of the twentieth century. But this does not mean that international law was irrelevant to their operation or failed in their regulation in previous decades. The limited attention to business enterprises rendered their marginality self-evident. In addition, the international legal doctrines, practices, and institutions that were central to international law-making constituted a facilitative legal order that was pivotal to the operation and flourishing of private business corporations. Intriguingly, post-colonial communities used the very same international legal building blocks that were implemented against them as a basis to oppose and resist the influence of private business corporations.

Thus, while private business corporations rarely appeared as a stand-alone issue in the international legal texts of the twentieth century, juxtaposing the conceptual approaches prevailing in international law throughout that period (such as the public/private distinction) and the practices of business corporations exposes the central role that international regulation actually played in their history.

This book is devoted to four in-depth case studies ranging from the interwar period to the 1980s: the case of The Firestone Company in Liberia; the Industrialist cases at Nuremberg; the Anglo Iranian Oil Company case; and the rise of the multinational corporation as a subject of 'regulatory concern' in international law in the 1970s. Though each of their time, these case studies all show how international lawyers engaged directly with private business corporations in a variety of regulatory contexts such as labour, international criminal law, antitrust, natural resources, human rights, and investment. Furthermore, they demonstrate that the power conferred by the international legal order on corporations cannot be fully appreciated if we think of corporations merely through the prism of private law. Indeed, the history of the international law of the business corporation is neither a history of the global corporate actor nor a distinct international law of the corporation, but rather the history of the interplay between these legal fields. The rights of corporations are supported by duties and arrangements on the part of states and international organizations, all of which are regulated by international law.

The building blocks of the international legal theory of corporations were borne out of the parallel development of the modern international legal order as an inter-state regime and the transition in corporate law from chartered to privately incorporated companies in the last third of the nineteenth century.[7] The point

---

[7] For further analysis on the transition between chartered and private corporations in colonial settings and its meaning for the modern international legal order, see Chapter 2 For an elaborate account on the rise and fall of British Chartered Companies and their meaning to the history and theory of international law, *see* Doreen Lustig, International Law and the Rise and Fall of Chartered Companies in Africa 1881–1923 (unpublished article, on file with author).

of departure for this history is the analogous emergence of international law as a modern legal discipline and the turn to free incorporation in corporate law during the last third of the nineteenth century. Private business corporations appear on the world scene during the globalization of markets of the 1880s, parallel to the emergence of international law as a professional field. The parallel emergence of these legal arenas reconfigured the relationship between businesses and governments and constituted an international regulatory space that facilitated, *inter alia*, the thriving of private corporations world-wide. The analysis offered in this book thus reveals how international law undergirds corporate action. The full relevance of the international legal architecture to corporations becomes visible only once the analysis penetrates 'the official statements or formal acts of governments and diplomatic chancelleries'[8] and addresses issues that were silenced, marginalized, or structured as irrelevant by formal sources.

In addition to the facilitative role of the international legal order in the operation of private corporations, the book demonstrates how the regulatory framework governing corporations in international law is shaped by the co-construction of the state and the corporation. It is constituted by the interplay between the legal theories and doctrines of the sovereign veil of the state and the corporate veil of the company. The veil of sovereignty in international legal theory and practice constitutes the state's internal affairs as a 'private realm' of non-interference. In the context of corporate law, the corporate veil constitutes the legal personality of the company and links it to the state—that is, the company is an entity incorporated under the company law of the state in question.

In this book, I demonstrate the consequences of the interplay between these two dimensions of the sovereign and corporate veils. Their co-construction often insulated companies from responsibility by conceiving of them as agents operating in the private domain, free from external intervention. I therefore explain how key features in the history of international legal thought and practice—particularly statism and formalism—limited outsiders' capacity to grasp the realities of private economic power and simultaneously sustained hierarchical economic and political power relations. These conceptual tendencies and limitations facilitated individual impunity at Nuremberg (Chapters 4 and 5) and contributed to the flourishing of multinational corporations (MNCs) (Chapters 3, 6, and 7).

However, the interplay between the state and the corporation in international law was not always beneficial to the powerful and, at times, it was utilized by those who hoped to challenge and undermine persistent power structures. Indeed, international lawyers' rigid attitudes to the veil of the sovereign and the private corporation also worked against the interests of powerful states and corporations. In the decades of decolonization, the corporate and sovereign veils served to *limit* the

---

[8] Martti Koskenniemi, *Expanding Histories of International Law*, 46 Am. J. Legal Hist. 104 (2016).

scope of diplomatic protection conferred on companies from the Global North, enhancing the prerogative of the new sovereign states to regulate assets and corporations within their jurisdiction. This rigid adherence to the principle of the corporate veil and the separation between ownership and control empowered decolonized nations in their struggle against the influence of foreign commercial and political power. Nevertheless, the fruits of these challenges did not remain ripe for long. As the last chapter of this book reveals, once the old international legal vocabulary proved itself favourable to the struggle of new states, capital-exporting countries sought an alternative international legal framework, and the new regime of international investment law gradually came into being.

The book also traces a history of impulses away from statism and formalism. The rising influence of corporations and their operations in post-colonial settings sparked a conceptual and normative debate: how should international legal doctrines and institutions address the corporate entity or its shareholders—as subjects of international law, as participants, or as nationals of the state? This debate drew inspiration from the policy-oriented theories of Myres McDougal and the New Haven School, Philip Jessup's concept of transnational law, and Hersch Lauterpacht's ideas on the access of individuals to international courts. The move away from international law to 'transnational law' did not initially lead to the revision of the legal norms applicable to corporations in public international law but did eventually serve as an important background to inform the transition of investment protection to a separate legal regime: international investment law (Chapters 6 and 7).

Contribution and Methodology

This book draws inspiration from scholarship on the history of international trade law[9] and international investment law,[10] from critical perspectives on the history of the international economic order,[11] and from political economic analysis of international law.[12] In it, I offer an original angle by connecting these specialized fields

---

[9] ANDREW LANG, WORLD TRADE LAW AFTER NEOLIBERALISM (2011); MICHAEL FAKHRI, SUGAR AND THE MAKING OF INTERNATIONAL TRADE LAW (2017).

[10] KATE MILES, ORIGINS OF INTERNATIONAL INVESTMENT LAW (2013); INTERNATIONAL INVESTMENT LAW AND HISTORY (Stephan W. Schill et al. eds., 2018); KENNETH J. VANDEVELDE, BILATERAL INVESTMENT TREATIES: HISTORY, POLICY, AND INTERPRETATION (2010); ANTONIO PARRA, THE HISTORY OF ICSID (2d ed. 2017); TAYLOR ST. JOHN, THE RISE OF INVESTOR–STATE ARBITRATION: POLITICS, LAW, AND UNINTENDED CONSEQUENCES (2018).

[11] ANTONY ANGHIE, IMPERIALISM, SOVEREIGNTY AND THE MAKING OF INTERNATIONAL LAW (2005); SANDHUYA PAHUJA, DECOLONIZING INTERNATIONAL LAW: DEVELOPMENT, ECONOMIC GROWTH AND THE POLITICS OF UNIVERSALITY (2011); SAMUEL MOYN, NOT ENOUGH: HUMAN RIGHTS IN AN UNEQUAL WORLD 91–117 (2018); Anne Orford, Law, Economics, and the History of Free Trade: A Response, 11 J. INT'L L. & INT'L REL. 155 (2015).

[12] See, e.g., Eyal Benvenisti & George W. Downs, The Empire's New Clothes: Political Economy and the Fragmentation of International Law, 60 STAN. L. REV. 595, 616–17 (2007).

in a single lens: the corporate form. This lens challenges a compartmentalized view of international law and its histories, and attunes us to broader power relations or ideological sensibilities that run through and between these different sub-fields.

Beyond this rich body of literature, this work engages with contemporary conversations on global governance. The thrust of much current governance scholarship is to look past formal legal categories and focus instead on norms and processes.[13] The book similarly draws attention to the realities of corporate conduct, but it also emphasizes the ongoing centrality of basic legal categories. It unravels the pivotal role of international law in the formation of the political economy for private business corporations, and particularly how international law constitutes the transnational regulatory space in which private business corporations were able to operate (and continue to do so). The book thus sits alongside other attempts to think synthetically about how (international) law has organized relations between public and private authority[14] and other critical approaches to current constellations of public and private authority and rights in international law.[15]

This work is inspired by a broader historical turn in international law, most famously associated with the publication of Martti Koskenniemi's *Gentle Civilizer* in 2001.[16] This turn to a critical history of international law was primarily a turn to *intellectual* histories of international law (as opposed to practices, doctrines, or events),[17] but it also included the introduction of a pluralist

---

[13] Benedict Kingsbury, *The Concept of 'Law' in Global Administrative Law*, 20 Eur. J. Int'l L. 23 (2009); J.H.H. Weiler, *The Geology of International Law: Governance, Democracy and Legitimacy*, 64 Zeitschrift für Ausländisches Öffentliches Recht und Völkerrecht [J. Foreign Pub. L. & Int'l L.] 547 (2004).

[14] *See, e.g.*, Private International Law and Global Governance (Horatia Muir Watt & Diego P. Fernández Arroyo eds., 2014). For a conceptual analysis of the concept of the 'public' in public international law, *see* Kingsbury, *supra* note 13.

[15] Anghie, *supra* note 11; Pahuja, *supra* note 11. For the role of private international law in forming the character of sovereignty or informing questions of legitimacy in situations of political conflict, *see* Karen Knop et al., *Foreword to 'Transdisciplinary Conflict of Laws'*, 71 L. & Contemp. Probs. 16 (2008).

[16] The historical turn in international legal historiography is owed to the publication of Martti Koskenniemi, The Gentle Civilizer (2001). Koskenniemi's book unravelled the history of international law through the eyes of its main interlocutors and exposed a rich seam of thought that challenged contemporary understandings of various aspects of international law. *See* George Rodrigo Bandeira Galindo, *Martti Koskenniemi and the Historiographical Turn in International Law*, 16 Eur. J. Int'l L. 539 (2005). This turn is often associated with the establishment of the *Journal of the History of International Law*, the work of scholars at the Max Planck Institute for European Legal History in Frankfurt, and the publication of the Oxford Handbook of the History of International Law (Bardo Fassbender & Anne Peters eds., 2012).

[17] Koskenniemi, supra note 16; Benedict Kingsbury, *Legal Positivism as Normative Politics: International Society, Balance of Power and Lassa Oppenheim's Positive International Law*, 13 Eur. J. Int'l L. 401 (2002); David Armitage, Foundations of Modern International Thought (2013); Jennifer Pitts, A Turn to Empire: The Rise of Imperial Liberalism in Britain and France (2005); Mónica García-Salmones Rovira, The Project of Positivism in International Law (2013). In addition, the *European Journal of International Law* has published a few symposia on the European tradition in international law, devoted to international legal thinkers such as Georges Scelle (Volume 1), Hersch Lauterpacht (Volume 8[2]), Hans Kelsen (Volume 9[2]), James Lorimer (Volume 27[2]), and others. Special attention has been paid to histories of international law, natural law, and human rights. *See, e.g.*, Annabel Brett, Changes of State: Nature and Limits of the City in Early Modern Natural Law (2011); Samuel Moyn, The Last Utopia (2010); Martti Koskenniemi,

historical lens and a layered understanding of imperial ordering,[18] a turn to the sociological history of international law as a discipline,[19] a history of international legal institutions,[20] a history of transnational networks,[21] and feminist histories of international law.[22]

Within the broader context of critical international legal history, the book joins the conversation of Third World Approaches to International Law (TWAIL)[23] and analyses the influence of international legal concepts, doctrines,

---

Rights, History, Critique, in HUMAN RIGHTS: MORAL OR POLITICAL? 41 (Adam Etinson ed., 2018). The emphasis on the history of ideas among international lawyers sparked a methodological debate. *See,* for example, Anne Orford, *On International Legal Method,* 1 LONDON REV. INT'L L. 166 (2013). For a brief overview of this debate, *see* Alexandra Kemmerer, *Völkerrechtsgeschichten: Histories of International Law,* EJIL: TALK! (Jan. 6, 2015). Online: https://www.ejiltalk.org/volkerrechtsgeschichten-histories-of-international-law/. GLOBAL INTELLECTUAL HISTORY (Samuel Moyn & Andrew Sartori eds., 2015).

[18] LAUREN BENTON & LISA FORD, RAGE FOR ORDER: THE BRITISH EMPIRE AND THE ORIGINS OF INTERNATIONAL LAW (2016); LAUREN BENTON, A SEARCH FOR SOVEREIGNTY: LAW AND GEOGRAPHY IN EUROPEAN EMPIRES, 1400–1900 (2010) and LAW AND COLONIAL CULTURES: LEGAL REGIMES IN WORLD HISTORY, 1400–1900 (2001); THE ROMAN FOUNDATIONS OF THE LAW OF NATIONS: ALBERICO GENTILI AND THE JUSTICE OF EMPIRE (Benedict Kingsbury & Benjamin Straumann eds., 2010); INTERNATIONAL LAW AND EMPIRE (Martti Koskenniemi et al. eds., 2017).

[19] David Kennedy, *The Move to Institutions,* 8 CARDOZO L. REV. 840 (1987); KOSKENNIEMI, *supra* note 16. For a reading of the GENTLE CIVILIZER as a history of the discipline, *see* Anne Orford, *International Law and the Limits of History, in* THE LAW OF INTERNATIONAL LAWYERS: READING MARTTI KOSKENNIEMI 297 (Wouter Werner et al. eds., 2017).

[20] MARK MAZOWER, GOVERNING THE WORLD: THE HISTORY OF AN IDEA (2012) (on the history of the UN); SUSAN PEDERSEN, THE GUARDIANS: THE LEAGUE OF NATIONS AND THE CRISIS OF EMPIRE (2015) (on the history of the Permanent Mandate Commissions of the League of Nations); PATRICIA CLAVIN, SECURING THE WORLD ECONOMY: THE REINVENTION OF THE LEAGUE OF NATIONS 1920–1946 (2013) (on the history of the predecessors of the World Bank during the League Period). GUY FITI SINCLAIR, TO REFORM THE WORLD: INTERNATIONAL ORGANIZATIONS AND THE MAKING OF MODERN STATES (2017) (examines the expansion of powers exercised by international organizations under international law); Megan Donaldson, From Secret Diplomacy to Diplomatic Secrecy: Secrecy and Publicity in the International Legal Order 1919–1950 (2016) (unpublished JSD Dissertation, NYU Law School, on file with author); Jan Klabbers, *The EJIL Foreword: The Transformation of International Organizations Law,* 26 EUR. J. INT'L L. 9 (2015).

[21] JUAN PABLO SCARFI, THE HIDDEN HISTORY OF INTERNATIONAL LAW IN THE AMERICAS: EMPIRE AND LEGAL NETWORKS (2017); MARCO DURANTI, THE CONSERVATIVE HUMAN RIGHTS REVOLUTION (2017).

[22] Deborah Whitewall, *A Rival History of Self-Determination,* 27 EUR. J. INT'L L. 719 (2016); Susan Zimmerman, *The Politics of Exclusionary Inclusion: Peace Activism and the Struggle on International and Domestic Political Order in the International Council of Women, 1899–1914, in* PARADOXES OF PEACE IN NINETEENTH CENTURY EUROPE 189 (Thomas Hippler & Miloš Vec eds., 2015).

[23] This critical historiography, championed in ANTONY ANGHIE's work (*supra* note 11), emphasized international legal history as a history of European domination. Anghie's work has been followed by a variety of studies inspired by postcolonial theory, focusing on the ideas and influence of international lawyers on the periphery: Third World Approaches to International Law (TWAIL). *See, e.g.,* B.S. Chimni, *The Past, Present and Future of International Law: A Critical Third World Approach,* 8 MELBOURNE J. INT'L L. 27 (2007); PAHUJA, *supra* note 11; ARNULF BECKER LORCA, MESTIZO INTERNATIONAL LAW: A GLOBAL INTELLECTUAL HISTORY 1842–1933 (2015); Liliana Obregón, *Between Civilisation and Barbarism: Creole Interventions in International Law,* 27 THIRD WORLD Q. 815, 820–24 (2006); UMUT ÖZSU, FORMALIZING DISPLACEMENT: INTERNATIONAL LAW AND POPULATION TRANSFERS (2015); LUIS ESLAVA, LOCAL SPACE, GLOBAL LIFE: THE EVERYDAY OPERATION OF INTERNATIONAL LAW AND DEVELOPMENT (2015); MAMADOU HEBIE, SOUVERAINETÉ TERRITORIALE PAR TRAITÉ: UNE ÉTUDE DES ACCORDS ENTRE PUISSANCES COLONIALES ET ENTITÉS POLITIQUES LOCALES (2015).

and institutions on the involvement of powerful corporate actors in post-colonial settings (Chapters 3 and 6). Following in the footsteps of earlier studies on international legal resistance and the rise of the New International Economic Order (NIEO),[24] it further explores the interaction between the rise of 'the multinational corporation' as a critical concept for civil society in the Global North and the NIEO struggle over the regulation of these corporations in the 1970s (Chapter 7).

The turn to history in international law has hitherto devoted little attention to the market and economic agents and institutions.[25] This book attempts to address this lacuna by offering a history of corporate regulation in international law. A possible explanation for the marginalization of corporations in international legal historiography lies in their marginality in international legal sources until quite late in the twentieth century. The methodological approach of the book is to discern the history of corporations in international law by juxtaposing the official perspectives of international lawyers with a better grasp of 'international law in practice'. The latter includes the ideas and practices of lower-ranking state officials and bureaucrats in international organizations, and legal officials affiliated with the company. While other scholars have studied international economic institutions or international legal attempts to formulate a vision for the global economy,[26] and exemplified how international legal doctrines and ideas distance economics from politics,[27] the focus here is not on international economic institutions per se, but on the possible role of public international law in shaping the regulation of the business corporation.

---

[24] MAZOWER, *supra* note 20; PAHUJA, *supra* note 11; Surabhi Ranganathan, *Global Commons*, 27 EUR. J. INT'L L. 693 (2016); Vanessa Ogle, *State Rights against Private Capital: The 'New International Economic Order' and the Struggle over Aid, Trade and Foreign Investment, 1962–1981*, 5 HUMANITY 211, 222–23 (2014); Nils Gilman, *The New International Economic Order: A Reintroduction*, 6 HUMANITY 1 (2015); Bret Benjamin, *Bookend to Bandung: The New International Economic Order and the Antinomies of the Bandung Era*, 6 HUMANITY 33 (2015); Antony Anghie, *Legal Aspects of the New International Economic Order*, 6 HUMANITY 145 (2015); Jennifer Bair, *Corporations at the United Nations: Echoes of the New International Economic Order?*, 6 HUMANITY 159 (2015); BANDUNG, GLOBAL HISTORY AND INTERNATIONAL LAW: CRITICAL PASTS AND PENDING FUTURES (Luis Eslava et al. eds., 2017); MOYN, *supra* note 11, at 91–117.

[25] As noted by Martti Koskenniemi, 'That the market is not, and has never been, independent from public power, but, contrarily, the effect of constant state intervention has not inspired international legal historians so far to examine how this cooperation has taken place.' Martti Koskenniemi, *Histories of International Law: Significance and Problems for a Critical View*, 27 TEMP. INT'L & COMP. L.J. 215, 235 (2013). For further analysis, *see* Doreen Lustig, *Governance Histories of International Law*, in OXFORD HANDBOOK OF LEGAL HISTORY 859 (Markus D. Dubber & Christopher Tomlins eds., 2018).

[26] *See*, for example, PEDERSEN, *supra* note 20, at 233–60; PAHUJA, *supra* note 11; CLAVIN, *supra* note 20; FAKHRI, *supra* note 9. PAHUJA, *supra* note 11; Vanessa Ogle, *Archipelago Capitalism: Tax Havens, Offshore Money, and the State, 1950s–1970s*, 122 AM. HIST. REV. 1431 (2017); Anne Orford, *Law, Economics, and the History of Free Trade: A Response*, 11 J. INT'L L. & INT'L REL. 155 (2015); Anne Orford, *Theorizing Free Trade*, in THE OXFORD HANDBOOK OF THE THEORY OF INTERNATIONAL LAW 701 (Anne Orford & Florian Hoffman eds., 2016).

[27] PAHUJA, *supra* note 11.

Chapter Outline

The period between 1870 and 1914 saw particularly rapid levels of private business corporation creation; from the 1880s, the numbers and size of multinationals grew rapidly. The 1880s mark the formative period of international law as a legal discipline and the turn to the privately incorporated business corporation as a global actor, and thus constitute the starting point for this book.[28] In Chapter 2, I set the scene for the following chapters by analysing the rise and fall of the chartered company during the 'Scramble for Africa'. The second chapter presents the parallel emergence of international law as a modern legal discipline and the turn to free incorporation in corporate law during the last third of the nineteenth century, and examines its implications for the regulatory influence of international law on companies' practices in the forthcoming decades.

Chapter 3 addresses an early example of the growing presence of American corporations in international relations: the interwar case of the Firestone Company in Liberia. The case is analysed against the backdrop of the League of Nations' attempt to regulate the abolition of slavery and forced labour as an inter-state regime. The Slavery and Forced Labour Conventions of 1926 and 1934 implicitly took for granted the capacity of states to exercise effective governance. This approach, which would later become the model of human rights treaties, shifted the impulse behind the abolition of slavery: away from its humanitarian logic as a fight to abolish the relationship of ownership between the slaveholder and the slave, and towards the positivist obligation of the (Liberian) state to abolish slavery and forced labour within its jurisdiction. That shift—from interpersonal relations to state/individual relations—assumed that sovereigns are equal and that each state party has the capacity to regulate and intervene against the inadequate labour practices of private actors. Paradoxically, as Chapter 3's analysis of Firestone in Liberia reveals, the presumption of equality sustained and accentuated global inequality and the subordination of weaker governments and their inhabitants to the unruly influence of commercial and governmental actors.

The Liberian case epitomizes a very early example of this shift from the legal ordering of inequality during the inter-imperial phase to the international legal ordering that undergirded the inequalities of the inter-state phase of the twentieth century. Liberia was, formally speaking, a free state, not directly governed by an imperial political power, but it was precisely the discrepancy between the formal insistence upon the independence of the Liberian state as a marker of its freedom and its actual capacity to secure the freedom of its citizens that rendered its government and its citizens enslaved for decades to come. Chapter 3 exposes this enduring

---

[28] For an overview of this period, *see* GEOFFREY JONES, MULTINATIONALS AND GLOBAL CAPITALISM: FROM THE NINETEENTH CENTURY TO THE TWENTY-FIRST CENTURY 18–29 (2005). Jones draws attention to the limited reliable data on this period.

dissonance between the vision of Liberia as the land of the freed former slaves and its economic and political fragility, tellingly nicknamed the 'Firestone Republic'. The chapter shows how a legal order that was designed to recognize states as the *only* responsible actors for conditions of slavery in international law marginalized the responsibility of the very private business actors that were directly engaged in such practices of slavery.

While Liberia differs from later post-colonial states in its unique history and early independent status, the case of Firestone in Liberia is a precursor to future relations between foreign companies and post-colonial states. Given the power balance between the company and Liberia, the government was not capable of introducing limitations on the private enterprise's labour policies. Liberia's engagement with the Firestone Company thus provides an intriguing prelude to the limitations of the emerging international legal order to abolish the enslavement of humans, and further demonstrates how this very limitation could facilitate the enslavement of political communities.

But the presumption of the regulatory capacity of the state to keep the corporate actor in check was not limited to post-colonial settings. Chapter 4 advances chronologically to the aftermath of the Second World War and addresses the debate over the Industrialists' responsibility in the subsequent trials at Nuremberg as a struggle between competing theories of the *totalitarian state*.[29] The greatest novelty of the International Military Tribunal (IMT) at Nuremberg was the recognition of *individual* responsibility under international law for the committing of international crimes.[30] According to this historical precedent, 'the screen between international law and the individual, normally constituted by state sovereignty, was pierced'.[31] Nevertheless, the legal reasoning in the *Industrialist* decisions failed to develop a theory of business responsibility in cases where businesses were not fully

---

[29] The story of the *Industrialist* cases is not usually included as a central feature in accounts of the first Nuremberg Trial. The proceedings against those known as 'major war criminals of the second rank' are usually referred to as the 'subsequent' Nuremberg proceedings. The *Industrialist* cases at the heart of Chapters 4 and 5 are: United States v. Friedrich Flick (*The Flick Case*), 6 TRIALS OF WAR CRIMINALS BEFORE THE NUREMBERG MILITARY TRIBUNALS UNDER CONTROL COUNCIL LAW No. 10 (1949–53) [hereinafter T.W.C] (1952); United States v. Krauch (*The Farben Case*), 7 T.W.C (1953) and 8 T.W.C. (1952); and United States v. Krupp (*The Krupp Case*), 9 T.W.C. (1950).

[30] The Treaty of Versailles (1919) was a prominent milestone in this process. Article 227 of the Treaty of Versailles established the individual criminal responsibility of the ex-German Emperor, Kaiser Wilhelm II; and Article 228 provided for the Prosecution of German Military personnel who committed war crimes. Despite these attempts, few trials were held and there were virtually no convictions. For an account of these failed national trials, *see* George Gordon Battle, *The Trials Before the Leipzig Supreme Court of Germans Accused of War Crimes*, 8 VA. L. REV. 1 (1921).

[31] Christian Tomuschat, *The Legacy of Nuremberg*, 4 J. INT'L CRIM. JUST. 830, 840 (2006). In Justice Robert H. Jackson's words, '[I]t is quite evident that the law of the charter pierces national sovereignty and presupposes that statesmen of the several states have a responsibility for international peace and order, as well as responsibilities to their own states.' ROBERT H. JACKSON, REPORT OF ROBERT H. JACKSON, UNITED STATES REPRESENTATIVE TO THE INTERNATIONAL CONFERENCE ON MILITARY TRIALS: LONDON, 1945 (1945). Online: http://avalon.law.yale.edu/subject_menus/jackson.asp .

governed or controlled by the state, or alternatively when the state did not influence their operations. Chapter 4 considers the influence of the Frankfurt School and Franz Neumann's theory of the Nazi state as 'Behemoth', according to which the Nazi regime comprised four ruling classes that governed Germany: the Nazi Party, the army, the state bureaucracy, and the industrialists that collaborated without systematic coherence. Despite Neumann's influence on the Prosecution's innovative theory of the Nazi regime, the Nuremberg judgments reduced the more complex aspects of Nazi operations to an assumed Hobbesian dictatorial regime. The Tribunals' insistence on a Hobbesian model and a hierarchical governing authority of the state over the operations of business actors failed to capture the complex business–state relations in Nazi Germany and, more fundamentally, did not develop a theory of responsibility for economic actors regardless of their relationship with the state. The *Industrialists'* judgments required the involvement of state agents or a state apparatus as a condition for the illegality of certain business practices. But the Nazi totalitarian state, as widely documented and explored by historians and philosophers, was often characterized by the very loss of a functioning legal system. Chapter 4 exposes the tension between the Tribunals' ill-suited theory of the Nazi state as a well-functioning governance regime and the reality of a total collapse and eventual loss of the rule of law. The chapter further shows how this very collapse benefited business actors twice over: first, as they took advantage of such realities, and later, when the Tribunals failed to recognize and develop a theory of international responsibility for those taking advantage of such conditions.

Chapter 5 focuses on the attitudes towards corporate responsibility and the 'corporate entity' that were developed by different actors in the U.S. Administration, the Prosecution teams, and the judges' decisions. This chapter further interrupts the narrative of 'sheer failure' by distinguishing between organizational features of corporations that were targeted by the U.S. occupation regime in post-war Germany directly (monopolies) and others that were not (the corporate entity of the business corporation as a subject of responsibility), and analyses different conceptions of legitimate corporate practice. While there are features in these cases that are unique to the anomalous circumstances of the Nazi regime, the tension between the findings of limited responsibility in the judgments of these trials, against the backdrop of the initial support of the U.S. Administration and the gravity of the violations addressed in these proceedings, renders this crisis of corporate impunity in the Industrialist cases at Nuremberg a crisis over international law's capacity to regulate corporations more broadly. The analysis of the possible influence of these competing conceptions of the corporate structure of authority provides a possible explanation to the unprincipled different treatment of corporate officials who were brought to trial in these cases. It further offers a normative critique on the decision not to engage with a rigorous analysis of corporate structures of authority in the industrialist trials as part of the legal reasoning required to establish the responsibility of corporate officials. This crisis had a lasting influence on the question of responsibility of economic actors in international law.

The Industrialist Trials at Nuremberg revealed how the corporate veil of the state and the company served as a shield against responsibility. In Chapter 6, I explore how this shield served, at least initially, *to support* the cause of the weaker party (the Iranian state) and the broader principles of self-determination, sovereignty, and perhaps even equality. This chapter is devoted to the Abadan Crisis and the circumstances surrounding the decision of the International Court of Justice (ICJ) in the famous dispute between Britain and Iran over the ownership of oil in Iran, known as the Anglo-Iranian Oil Company (AIOC) case. The AIOC case clarified that international legal doctrines conceive of corporations as entities separate from the state, even if the majority of their shares are owned by that state. This separation between public and private and between ownership and control hampered Britain's attempt to use international legal doctrines and the institution of the ICJ to protect its interests in Iran. Together with additional cases in which decolonized governments nationalized assets in their territories, the AIOC posed significant political and economic challenges to governments and companies in the Global North. The AIOC case was therefore an important marker of the threat decolonization represented for investors and the protection of their interests when they were operating in former colonial contexts.

Chapter 7 tells the story of an even greater threat to the economic hegemony of the Global North: the coalition between postcolonial states in the 1950s and 1960s that would form the renowned NIEO, and its struggle against foreign corporations' control over natural resources in the Global South. Intriguingly, the NIEO's critique of the influence of multinational corporations in their overseas operations was enhanced by similar concerns from within U.S. and European civil society and academia. Importantly, the ICJ decisions in two landmark cases involving corporations and their protection—the Anglo-Iranian Oil case I discuss in Chapter 6 and the Barcelona Traction case I analyse in Chapter 7—were favourable to post-colonial nations's interests. As mentioned earlier, the AIOC decision supported the Iranian argument against the jurisdiction of the ICJ and blocked the British Government from seeking an international remedy against the nationalization of the company's assets. In the Barcelona Traction case, the ICJ narrowed the protection of shareholders under the doctrine of diplomatic protection in international law.

In both cases, the Court based its analysis on domestic corporate law principles, most importantly the separation between ownership and control. Both decisions sent a clear supportive signal to post-colonial nations—indeed, Iranians rallied in the streets to celebrate their achievement. In the aftermath of the Barcelona Traction case, George Abi-Saab, a leading scholar of the NIEO, argued that the decisions of the Court in this case and that of the AIOC signified the end of the era in which the major powers dictated international law.[32] These circumstances paved the way for a rare moment of negotiation between North and South over the future regulation of global investment under the auspices of the United Nations (UN).

But this moment was to be short-lived. The ICJ decisions did not only send an empowering signal to the NIEO states. They also clarified to the U.S. and European countries that they could not entrust the interests of their investors in proceedings before the ICJ. Since oil-importing countries could not afford to lose control over Iranian oil, they turned to the last-resort measures of gunboat diplomacy, boycotting, and covert operations. These measures, however, were very costly and lacked the desired stability and security a global economic market required. When the second attempt to seek investors' protection in proceedings before the ICJ failed in the Barcelona Traction decision of 1970, capital-exporting countries found themselves with little choice but to seek alternative institutional and legal means to protect their investors. In the coming years, they would marginalize the United Nations as a regulatory arena for investment issues in favour of dispersing the question of corporate regulation under international law into different institutional sites and regimes. The terms of the emerging investment regime would henceforth be set in bilateral agreements that 'divided' the South and leveraged exporting nations to dictate rules that were compatible with their (investors') interests.

Indeed, while the private business corporation rarely appeared in international legal treatises and texts as a subject of enquiry or concern until the 1970s, this book exposes and explores how international legal doctrines, practices, and institutions constituted a regulatory framework for the operation of businesses throughout the twentieth century. Until now, this regulatory scheme has been embedded in a narrative of marginalization and failure, which this book now seeks to challenge. This challenge reaches its zenith in the final chapter (Chapter 7), which examines the first attempt to develop a treaty for direct corporate responsibility in the 1970s. This attempt was not to bear fruit. The end of the 1970s marks a shift towards a new phase in the private business corporation's relationship to international law: from an entity that operates 'behind the scenes' to a recognized participant with the right to sue governments for damages and to choose the forum in which to do so. The turn to this new phase in the history of the international regulatory architecture for corporations concludes this book.

Chapters 3–5 thus show how the assumptions of sovereign equality and the belief that the sovereign was able to regulate and control corporations rendered alternative relations between governments and corporate actors invisible to legal scrutiny. In the 1950s, decolonized nations would begin to turn the tables against powerful nations and business corporations by using the same formalist and positivist approaches to international law against unruly corporate power. Amid

---

[32] George Abi-Saab, The International Law of Multinational Corporations: A Critique of American Legal Doctrines 97, 122 (1971).

the menace of the old international legal vocabulary in the service of new states, capital-exporting countries would seek other means and eventually hold sway by introducing an alternative international legal framework—the new regime of international investment law. This book thus attempts to replace the unchallenged history of the irrelevance of international law to the question of business enterprises in the aftermath of the charter's dissolution with a history of its *facilitative* role in constituting a post-charter economic order that proved highly beneficial to economic interests in the Global North.

2

Setting the Scene

The Facilitative Failure of the Chartered Company

Free incorporation started to become a central feature of business organizations operating transnationally only towards the end of the nineteenth century. This shift in legislation towards free incorporation challenged the connection between an act of incorporation and political control. Britain led the impulse towards free incorporation, with the New Company Law of 1844.[1] Thereafter, freedom of incorporation was established in many countries in Europe (*e.g.* France, 1863–67,[2] and Germany, 1870),[3] in Japan (1899),[4] and in the United States (1860–75).[5] The grant theory (the idea that corporations are artificial creations of the state) that had informed the chartered companies of previous generations came to be considered an obstacle to economic growth and ineffective as a control mechanism,[6] and the long-established essence of the company as an organ of the state was destabilized.[7]

---

[1] Ron Harris, *Spread of Legal Innovations Defining Private and Public Domains, in* 2 The Cambridge History of Capitalism 127, 142–43 (Larry Neal & Jeffrey G. Williamson eds., 2014).

[2] The first public company law was contained in the French *Code de Commerce* of 1807. This code served as a model for all later European public company statutes. The French Company Acts of 1863 and 1867 provided for limited liability companies free of governmental restraint.

[3] German legislation of the late-nineteenth century resembled the French legislation as 'economic liberalism entered into German law'. However, this legislation embodied a strong presumption that firms would regulate themselves. This view derived from the corporate self-governance tradition more than it did from *laissez-faire* virtues. Morton Keller, *Public Policy and Large Enterprise: Comparative Historical Perspectives, in* Recht und Entwicklung der Grossunternehmen im 19. und Frühen 20. Jahrhundert [Law and the Formation of Big Enterprises in the 19th and Early 20th Centuries] 515 (Norbert Horn & Jürgen Kocka eds., 1979). The first German public company statute was the 1843 Prussian Act, established five years after the 1838 Prussian Act on railway enterprises.

[4] The Japanese Commercial Code (*Shôhô*), which contains most of Japanese corporate law, dates back to 1899.

[5] In the United States, company law was a matter of state law and has remained so to this day, although since the 1930s the Federal Government has asserted authority through federal securities regulation.

[6] For a ground-breaking account of these developments, *see* Morton Horwitz, The Transformation of American Law, 1870–1960, at 65–108 (1992).

[7] Writing on the U.S. context, James Willard Hurst referred to this development as the 'release of energy'—the process by which the control of the developing economy was put into private hands. James Willard Hurst, Law and the Conditions of Freedom in the Nineteenth-Century United States (1956). This transition coincided with attempts to decipher analytically what the corporate entity *was*. Scholars in Germany, Britain, France, and the United States were heavily engaged in essentialist inquiries on the meaning and nature of the corporate personality during this period and throughout the first quarter of the twentieth century. For an elaborate discussion, *see* Gregory A. Mark, *The Personification of the Business Corporation in American Law*, 54 Chi. L. Rev. 1441 (1987); William W. Bratton, Jr., *The New Economic Theory of the Firm: Critical Perspectives from History*, 41 Stan. L. Rev. 1471 (1989); Ron Harris, *The Transplantation of a Legal Discourse: Corporate Personality Theories from*

Veiled Power. Doreen Lustig, Oxford University Press (2020). © Doreen Lustig.
DOI: 10.1093/oso/9780198822097.001.0001

From the late-nineteenth century onward, the private business corporation as a privately incorporated entity was no longer conceived as a vehicle of the state but rather an entity separate and distinct from it. This period of the turn to free incorporation and its migration to different legal systems coincides with the history of the rise and fall of the charter as a colonization device in the course of the 'Scramble for Africa'. The revival of the chartered company for the colonization of Africa marks an important step in the gradual conceptual divide between public international law and private business corporations, and the starting point for this book.[8]

During the 1880s, imperial governments, most notably Britain, revived the chartered company, a central vehicle for colonial expansion and global trade in previous centuries,[9] to pursue their imperial endeavours in Africa. This late experimentation with the old charter device barely lasted a few years before it was replaced. International lawyers addressed the reviving charter in their commentaries as a skewed form of colonialism, and challenged its legitimacy. Their critical views, which echoed the tone of local parliamentary debates and popular commentary,[10] opposed the use of the chartered company since it undermined their understanding of sovereignty, enhanced monopolistic practices, and jeopardized the civilizing mission in colonial Africa.[11]

The dissolution of the charter mechanism towards the end of the nineteenth century was followed by a relative silence over the role and responsibilities of corporations in international law until decolonization gained momentum in

---

German Codification to British Political Pluralism and American Big Business, 63 WASH. & LEE L. REV. 1421 (2006).

[8]   For a detailed account, *see* Doreen Lustig, International Law and the Rise and Fall of the Chartered Company in Africa 1881–1923 (on file with author).

[9]   Philip Stern described the East India Company as a corporation and a government from its inception in 1600. By the second half of the seventeenth century, it had also become a colonial proprietor and was involved in governmental practices such as law administration, tax collection, punishment, and economic regulation. PHILIP J. STERN, THE COMPANY-STATE, CORPORATE SOVEREIGNTY AND THE EARLY MODERN FOUNDATIONS OF THE BRITISH EMPIRE IN INDIA (2011).

[10]   Bill to make provision for Payments in Connection with Revocation of Charter of Royal Niger Company H. C. Bill (1899), [370]. Online: https://api.parliament.uk/historic-hansard/commons/1899/jul/26/royal-niger-company-bill.

[11]   HENRY SUMNER MAINE, INTERNATIONAL LAW: A SERIES OF LECTURES DELIVERED BEFORE THE UNIVERSITY OF CAMBRIDGE, 1887, at 56–67 (1888); Gustave Rolin-Jaequemyns, *L'Année 1888 au Point de Vue de la Paix et du Droit International*, XXI REVUE DE DROIT INTERNATIONAL 189 (1889); CHARLES SALOMON, L'OCCUPATION DES TERRITOIRES SANS MAITRE 128–88 (1889); GASTON JÈZE, ÉTUDE THÉORIQUE ET PRATIQUE SUR L'OCCUPATION COMME MODE D'ACQUÉRIR LES TERRITOIRES, EN DROIT INTERNATIONAL 342–87 (1896); MARK F. LINDLEY, THE ACQUISITION AND GOVERNMENT OF BACKWARD TERRITORY IN INTERNATIONAL LAW 94–101 (1926); T.J. LAWRENCE, THE PRINCIPLES OF INTERNATIONAL LAW 79–82, 166–67 (1927); JOHN WESTLAKE, CHAPTERS ON THE PRINCIPLES OF INTERNATIONAL LAW 139–45, 159–60, 190–92 (1982). Not all international law stated a clear opposition to the chartered company. Travers Twiss held a more favourable position that was compatible with his support for King Leopold's use of a private organization in Belgium. *See* U.S. Congress, Senate, Committee of Foreign Relations, Travers Twiss in his opinion to the Committee of Foreign Relations, 48th Cong., 1st sess., 1884, S. Rep. No. 393, 33.

the 1960s and 1970s. This apparent hiatus could be erroneously conceived as a testament to the irrelevance of international legal ideas, institutions, and practices to the history of private business corporations in colonial and other global settings henceforth. This book argues against such an interpretation and unravels the relevance of international law to the regulation of business corporations. The following in-depth analysis of the case of the Royal Niger Company in Africa offers an interpretation of the meaning of the fall of the chartered companies as an important juncture in the history of corporate regulation in international law.

In the period between 1870 and 1914, international flows of goods, capital, technology, and people reached unprecedented levels. Industrialization increased and businessmen from the industrial economies were interested in gaining access to foreign markets to sell their products and buy raw materials.[12] These background factors informed the growing interest in the colonization of Africa but, more importantly, intensified the scale of trade with the region once the partition was underway. The economic engagement of Europeans with Africa also shifted—from building trade relations with Africans along the coastline, to fostering greater scale and scope of global trade and further intervention in the hinterland to establish plantations, railroads, infrastructure, and mines.[13]

This growing interest in the colonization of Africa and the high costs it involved led British businessmen and government officials to use the chartered company as a vehicle for the new colonial endeavour. Chartered companies of the sixteenth and seventeenth centuries had been characterized by a special relationship with the monarch, trade monopolies, and trading zones.[14] Conversely, the British charter of the late-nineteenth century neither incorporated the companies (they were freely incorporated) nor secured a formal monopoly for their commercial operations. The charter rendered company officials formal representatives of the British Government and granted them the authority to exercise functions such as trade governance, policing, and abolition of slavery. The British Government, in turn, sought to use the charter to establish its sovereign authority over African territories and resources at minimal cost.

---

[12] For data on the rise in manufacturing in Britain, Western Europe, and the United States during the nineteenth century, see Robert C. Allen, The Spread of Manufacturing, in 2 THE CAMBRIDGE HISTORY OF CAPITALISM, supra note 1, at 22, 22–23; on the growth in world agriculture, see Giovanni Federico, Growth, Specialization and Organization of World Agriculture, in 2 THE CAMBRIDGE HISTORY OF CAPITALISM, supra note 1, at 47, 47–52. Kevin H. O'Rourke & Jeffrey G. Williamson, Introduction: The Spread and Resistance to Global Capitalism, in 2 THE CAMBRIDGE HISTORY OF CAPITALISM, supra note 1, at 1; Kristine Bruland & David C. Mowery, Technology and the Spread of Capitalism, in 2 THE CAMBRIDGE HISTORY OF CAPITALISM, supra note 1, at 82, 86–88.

[13] Sidney Pollard, Free Trade and the World Economy, in THE MECHANICS OF INTERNATIONALISM: CULTURE, SOCIETY AND POLITICS FROM THE 1840S TO THE FIRST WORLD WAR 27, 28–29 (Martin H. Geyer & Johannes Laulmann eds., 2001).

[14] Fernand Braudel discussed these characteristics in greater detail. FERNAND BRAUDEL, THE WHEELS OF COMMERCE 445–47 (1982).

The British revival of the chartered company began with the North Borneo Company in 1881.[15] It was soon followed in Africa with the Royal Niger Company (1886–1900), The Imperial British East African Company (1888–96), and Cecil Rhodes's British South Africa Company (BSAC) (1889–1923). The historical accounts of these enterprises typically discuss their role in the development of governmental colonial rule in their respective areas of operations. The Royal Niger Company preceded the British rule over northern Nigeria, the Imperial British East Africa Company paved the way for British control over Kenya and Uganda, and the BSAC brought the Rhodesias and Bechuanaland under British rule. The charters of the British East Africa Company and the Royal Niger Company were dissolved in 1895 and 1900 respectively, but the BSAC was actively governing its territories until 1923. As the following history of the specific case of the Royal Niger Company suggests, these companies marked a turning point towards a new form of company–state relations towards the end of the nineteenth century.

The Royal Niger Company 1886–1900

Until the mid-1880s, British traders in West Africa were less interested in the British Empire having a strong political presence in the area than in obtaining free-trade guarantees against discriminatory tariffs rather than annexations[16] and pursued a somewhat equivalent policy to that of the 'Open Door'.[17] After 1850, the volume of trade in West Africa had increased the demand for improved harbours, offshore facilities, and railways and 'exerted a powerful hold on the imagination of explorers, geographers, military adventurers, and merchants in the 1870s and 1880s'.[18]

The history of the Royal Niger Company begins against the backdrop of intensified interest in control over trade routes in West Africa. The family of George Goldie Taubman, who later became Sir George Goldie, owned one of the smaller firms operating in the Niger basin in 1875. In 1879, he merged his family's firm with

---

[15] The North Borneo Charter did not grant governmental powers to the company, and prohibited a trading monopoly. Like the African chartered company, the North Borneo Company was incorporated under the Companies Act and could have operated in North Borneo independently of the royal charter. John Galbraith described how the British Government used the charter as 'an effective means of fencing off North Borneo from the intrusion of other powers without itself accepting direct responsibility, and the Company enabled it to do so.' John S. Galbraith, *The Chartering of the North Borneo Company*, 4 J. BRIT. STUD. 102, 125 (1965). Galbraith further argues that, while the founders of the British African chartered companies cited the North Borneo Company as a precedent, the company's charter conferred no governmental powers, and was therefore an unsatisfactory precedent.

[16] MARTIN LYNN, COMMERCE AND ECONOMIC CHANGE IN WEST AFRICA: THE PALM OIL TRADE IN THE NINETEENTH CENTURY 173 (1997).

[17] A.G. HOPKINS, AN ECONOMIC HISTORY OF WEST AFRICA (1973); Colin Newbury, *On the Margins of Empire: The Trade of Western Africa, 1875–1890, in* BISMARCK, EUROPE, AND AFRICA: THE BERLIN AFRICA CONFERENCE 1884–1885 AND THE ONSET OF PARTITION 5 (Stig Förster et al. eds., 1988).

[18] Newbury, *supra* note 17, at 35, 39.

three other firms to create the United African Company.[19] The company traded on the Niger and Benue rivers for several years and gained a virtual monopoly in its area of operation,[20] expanding at the expense of small traders and obtaining new concessions from local leaders.[21] But amalgamation soon proved insufficient to secure the company's position. Rivalry with French companies, most notably the Compagnie Française de l'Afrique Équatoriale (CFAE),[22] and further competition with Germany, which escalated with its declaration of protectorates over Togoland and the Cameroons in July 1884,[23] challenged the supremacy of Goldie's company. He began to seek government support for his endeavours by signalling his strategic value for British interests. In November 1884, Goldie wrote to the Foreign Office declaring that the two French trading houses had sold out and that Britain 'stood alone on the Niger'.[24] He then attended the Berlin Conference as an unofficial adviser to the British delegation. The Niger Act paved the way for the German chartered regimes in South-west and East Africa;[25] conditions were ripe for a British chartered company in Africa.

In the years leading up to the granting of the charter, Goldie worked to improve the company's balance sheet and extend its influence through the nomination of influential figures to the board of directors.[26] Establishing a charter in the 1880s raised tensions between the old and new forms of incorporation: could a privately incorporated company (under the British Companies Act) legally be granted a charter? And could the company accept such a charter under its present legal

---

[19] The United African Company resembled an alliance of firms. Each of the old firms received shares in the new company proportionate to the assets it sold. No single group had a controlling number of shares. Goldie emerged from the amalgamation with no financial control of the company, but remained its leader until his retirement. JOHN E. FLINT, SIR GEORGE GOLDIE AND THE MAKING OF NIGERIA 29–31 (1960).

[20] '[T]he formation of the United African Company was based on an agreement between all the Niger firms to cease competition, to pool their ships, stores and staff into one organization, and to share the resultant profits proportionately between themselves.' Id. at 32.

[21] Id. at 33.

[22] H. Laurens van der Laan, Modern Inland Transport and the European Trading Firms in Colonial West Africa, 21 CAHIER D' ÉTUDES AFRICAINES 547 (1981); JOHN D. HARGREAVES, PRELUDE TO THE PARTITION OF WEST AFRICA 275 (1963). The company became active on the Niger from 1880, supported by the French consular agent, Captain Mattei, and the arrival of French warships in 1883.

[23] For further details, see HARGREAVES, supra note 22, at 316–49.

[24] Minute by Granville, 3 November 1884. Quoted by W.M. ROGER LEWIS, ENDS OF BRITISH IMPERIALISM: THE SCRAMBLE FOR EMPIRE, SUEZ AND DECOLONIZATION: COLLECTED ESSAYS 100 (2006).

[25] For further discussion on the German Chartered companies, see W.O. HENDERSON, STUDIES IN GERMAN COLONIAL HISTORY 13–14 (1962). In an earlier episode, the Chancellor had tried to persuade key figures in the German financial community to establish a syndicate that would take over the assets of the merchant Adolf Lüderitz in South-west Africa. The Deutsche Kolonialgesellschaft für Südwestafrika (German Colonial Company for South-west Africa) was established for that purpose, but its managers refused the offer of a charter. They were concerned they lacked sufficient manpower and resources to administer the territory of South-west Africa as sovereigns. For this interpretation, see RICHARD A. VOELTZ, GERMAN COLONIALISM AND THE SOUTH WEST AFRICA COMPANY 1894–1914 (1988).

[26] FLINT, supra note 19, at 41–48.

constitution? To avoid these potential problems, Goldie reorganized the company in 1882. Carrying the telling name National African Company (NAC), the new entity was formed with clear intentions to govern the region with which it traded. The NAC signed multiple treaties with local leaders that were separate from, and independent of, those of the natives with the British Government.[27] The three main provisions of these treaties were as follows: (a) 'Cession to the company of the territories of the signatories'; (b) 'private property was not to be taken without compensation'; and (c) the company had the right to exclude foreign settlers. The latter provision conferred a monopoly and was inconsistent with the free-trade 'Clause 6' in the British protection treaties. Therefore, when the British Consul concluded a protection treaty *after* the company's treaty, Clause 6 ran thus: 'Permission to trade in ... shall be regulated by the terms of the agreement entered into with the National Africa Company'.[28]

Goldie and his NAC challenged the French companies and the French threat to British supremacy by dragging them into a price war they could ill afford. The French mechanism for expansion in Africa relied on the state's direct interference, as well as on companies whose actions were based on concessions and treaty-making power in the colonies.[29] Lacking alternative financial support, the Foreign Office grew increasingly close to, and more dependent on, the NAC.[30] In 1886, Goldie succeeded in his mission, securing a charter that matched the company's interests: no direct governmental control over its officials, their appointment, or dismissal, or over regulations or ordinances made by the company regarding the levying of custom duties, taxes, or licenses. The only possible threat of the government was to cancel the charter altogether and thus establish a direct administration.[31] Without the charter, the company would remain incorporated, but with the charter it retained sovereign rights, which were seen to have come from its treaties with Africans.[32] The chartered NAC became the Royal Niger Company, and its commercial officers became consular agents making treaties in the company's name, as a basis for territorial boundaries.[33]

---

[27] WILLIAM N.M. GEARY, NIGERIA UNDER BRITISH RULE (1927), at 179 (1965).

[28] *Id.* at 179–80. *See also* MURIEL E. CHAMBERLAIN, THE SCRAMBLE FOR AFRICA 51 (2d ed. 1999); H.L. WESSELING, DIVIDE AND RULE: THE PARTITION OF AFRICA 1880–1914, at 190 (1996).

[29] Important examples include the French trading companies that operated on the Niger prior to the Berlin Conference of 1884–1885, the Compagnie Française de l'Afrique Equatoriale (CFAE), and Compagnie du Sénégal et de la Côte Occidentale de l'Afrique. Although the companies stated they were operating out of patriotism, their motives were primarily commercial. A.S. Kanya-Forstner, *French African Priorities and the Berlin West Africa Conference, in* BISMARCK, EUROPE, AND AFRICA, *supra* note 17, at 171.

[30] Kanya-Forstner, *supra* note 29, at 171. *See also* CHAMBERLAIN, *supra* note 28, at 46.

[31] *See* the Royal Charter granted to the National African Company, later called the Royal Niger Company, in Appendix II, FLINT, *supra* note 19, at 330.

[32] John Flint, *Chartered Companies and the Transition from Informal Sway to Colonial Rule in Africa, in* BISMARCK, EUROPE, AND AFRICA, *supra* note 17, at 69.

[33] Newbury, *supra* note 17, at 35, 52.

The Royal Niger Company attempted to circumvent the influence of African brokers by forging direct contacts with producers in the interior and consequently undercutting their British competitors, the Liverpool merchants. Indeed, the company was prohibited from establishing a monopoly according to Article 14 of the charter, but it controlled the market by forcing producers' prices down, supplying imported goods to the African producers, and establishing relatively high customs duties and a licensing system that drove most of its competitors out. The chartering of the company led to an outcome paradoxically at odds with the aims of the Berlin Conference—namely, the establishment of a rather effective monopoly that excluded competitors from the Niger. Michael Hicks Beach, Chancellor of the Exchequer, summarized its monopolistic practices to members of the Cabinet in 1898:

> Their exaction of all persons, except their own members, of a 'trading license' of 50%; their prohibitions against vessels touching, even for fuel, at any but forty specified points within a river length of 800 miles; their acquisition of the sole right to strip of land along the river banks through the whole of its navigable course, giving them the power to compel outsiders to pay such a price as they may choose to fix for the establishment of trading stations ... [are] practically prohibitory of native trade on the Niger; and are not in accordance with the policy of freedom of commerce to which they are pledged by the Act of Berlin.[34]

Criticisms of the Royal Niger Company over its monopolistic practices were similarly voiced by members of parliament[35] and by foreign companies.[36] In a memorandum signed by the Brass Chiefs on 8 June 1895, they stated that: 'to carry out these Regulations and pay these duties means ruin to us'.[37] Sir John Kirk, who was asked to investigate these allegations, concluded that 'the Rules in force are practically prohibitory to native trade, and the Brass men are right in saying that this is so'.[38]

But the monopolistic objective—the main rationale for Goldie's choice of the chartered company mechanism in the first place—eventually led to its dissolution.

---

[34] Royal Niger Company (Confidential), British National Archives, CAB 34/46 (1898) No. 21. Sir Claude MacDonald similarly documented these monopolistic practices to the British Government. His findings were later published in a book, A.F. MOCKLER FERRYMAN, UP THE NIGER: NARRATIVE OF MAJOR CLAUDE MACDONALD'S MISSION TO THE NIGER AND BENUE RIVERS, WEST AFRICA (1892).

[35] See, e.g., Parl. Deb., 4th ser., Commons, 2, 24 March 1892, 1639–1788 ('MR. H. S. CROSS: I beg to ask the Under Secretary of State for Foreign Affairs whether Her Majesty's Government, before authorising increases of tariff on the part of the Royal Niger Company, Chartered and Limited, have communicated with merchants or Chambers of Commerce interested in the trade of the district; and, if not, by what means has it been ascertained that these increases ought to be approved?').

[36] France and the Niger Company, FIN. TIMES, Aug. 24, 1895.

[37] 'Africa. No. 3 (1896). Report by Sir John Kirk on the disturbances at Brass', Sessional Papers, 1896, LIX (361), 59.

[38] Sir John Kirk to the Marquis of Salisbury, Sevenoaks, Aug. 25, 1895, id.

The Royal Niger Company faced competition on four fronts: from French companies and merchants who often benefited from imperial support; from German companies and merchants who likewise enjoyed such support; from other British merchants, most notably the Liverpool Group that competed with the company in Africa and lobbied against it in London; and from African traders who served as brokers on the Niger coast and prevented direct exchange between the African producers and the European traders.

During the 1890s, the company suffered serious blows on all four of these fronts. The Liverpool merchants consolidated and formed the African Association, advocated for a charter, and lobbied against the Royal Niger Company in Parliament.[39] The British Government established the Oil Rivers Protectorate (from 1893, the Niger Coast Protectorate), which signalled the government's willingness to assert its control over the Niger Delta and its hinterland.[40] By 1895, the Administration's reach extended deep into the interior.[41] During that same year, central tribal groups that had suffered most from the company's exclusion took temporary control over port facilities. Sir John Kirk was called to investigate, and presented a plan to transform the company into an administrative body.[42] Almost parallel to these developments, the colonial governments of France and Germany changed their occupying strategy in favour of military conquest. From 1896, the French intensified their presence in the region. The occupation of the strategic city of Bussa in 1897, at the entrance to the Niger, posed a serious threat to the Royal Niger Company. These developments brought the conflict of interests between the imperial government and the company to the fore. As noted by Lord Stanmore in the Spring of 1897:

> The recent enlargement of the Niger Company's administrative area brought it into contact with the spheres of influence of other nations not less susceptible than ourselves. When such contact existed, occasions for friction must arise; and when they did, men who regarded above all things the maintenance of the rights and position of the local authorities would be not unlikely to act in a different manner from men with whom the importance of maintaining good relations between ourselves and other European states was a primary consideration.[43]

---

[39] *See, e.g.*, Parl. Deb., 3rd ser., Commons, 354, 9 June 1890–1891, 9–92; Parl. Deb., 3rd ser., Commons, 355, 2 July 1891, 190–300; Parl. Deb., 4th ser., Commons, 1, 3 March 1892, 1761–886.

[40] *British Protectorate over Uganda, London, June 18, 1894, in* 1 EDWARD HERTSLET, THE MAP OF AFRICA BY TREATY 395 (3d ed. 1909). In the following years, further agreements were concluded between the British Government and the Kabaka Chiefs (1900, 1901) in which the specific boundaries and administrative divisions were detailed and property relations altered.

[41] LYNN, *supra* note 16, at 173–74.

[42] For an early account of the circumstances leading to the report, *see* GEARY, *supra* note 27, at 197–207; *Africa. No. 3 (1896). Report by Sir John Kirk on the disturbances at Brass*, Sessional Papers, 1896, LIX (361), 59. For parliamentary discussions on Sir John Kirk's inquiries, *see* Parl. Deb., 4th ser., Commons, 33, 30 April 1895, 115–216; Parl. Deb., 4th ser., Commons, 39, 27 March 1896, 260–360. For a discussion on the suggested scheme, *see* FLINT, *supra* note 19, at 208–12.

[43] Parl. Deb., 4th ser., Lords, 49, 24 May 1897, 1109–16.

Eventually, treaties with local chiefs proved insufficient as a basis for British authority.[44] Towards the end of 1897, the West African Frontier Force was set up, under the command of Lord Lugard, and was soon entangled in a series of violent conflicts with the French and the indigenous population. The company was later accused of bringing 'the country to the brink of war with another nation'.[45] This was hardly the first violent confrontation between the company and its related officials but was rather part of a long and continuous series of conflicts with the indigenous population.[46] These conflicts were condemned by activists and discussed and criticized in parliamentary debates. The voice of these critics had intensified by the late 1890s.[47]

When the British Government asked Goldie to assist the British Frontier Force as part of its commitments under the charter, he seized the opportunity to negotiate a favourable settlement.[48] The British Government negotiated with Goldie but refrained from concluding a deal until the agreement with the French was settled.[49] Upon the signature of the Niger Convention of 1898 between Britain and France, which divided West Africa between the two countries and put an end to years of bitter rivalry,[50] all the conditions were in place for a new deal to be forged.

In June 1899, the Foreign Office instigated procedures to revoke the company's charter. In its letter to the company it stated that the government needed to control the Frontier Force in light of complaints by other firms against the company's monopoly and the effect it was having on African traders.[51] The company's charter was

---

[44] The Secretary of State for Foreign Affairs and Prime Minister Salisbury addressed the competition with the French and conceded that 'the rights to territory are not sufficiently defined to exclude the possibility of contest, and that matters may even come to such a point as they have done in the case ... of Broussa, where a French force marched in and taken a territory which the Niger Company imagined to be their own', Parl. Deb., 4th ser., Lords, 49, 24 May 1897, 1109–16.

[45] Parl. Deb., 4th ser., Commons, 73, 3 July 1899, 1263–1388; see also Parl. Deb., 4th ser., Commons, 73, 4 July 1899, 1402–1512.

[46] For an early account of such frequent confrontations, see MOCKLER FERRYMAN, supra note 34.

[47] Parl. Deb., 4th ser., Commons, 17, 7 September 1893–94, 453–560: 'it seemed pretty clear that some very questionable things had been done by agents of the Company ... It was stated in the paper [THE LIVERPOOL DAILY POST] that natives endeavoring to run a gauntlet through the territory of the Company had been shot at.' Further incidents are discussed in the Parl. Deb., 4th ser., Commons, 17, 15 September, 1893–94, 1265–1404; Parl. Deb., 4th ser., Commons, 30, 19 February 1895, 1066–4188; and Parl. Deb., 4th ser., Commons, 31, 28 February 1895, 4–144. In the aftermath of Kirk's report, members of parliament demanded better supervision of the Royal Niger Company, and further allegations were made regarding its involvement in violent incidents involving the indigenous population. See Parl. Deb., 4th ser., Commons, 39, 27 March 1896, 260–360; and for demands to admit the Brass men into markets hitherto closed to them by the Royal Niger Company, see Parl. Deb., 4th ser., Commons, 41, 11 June 1896, 827–932.

[48] FLINT, supra note 19, at 270–312.

[49] In a confidential memo, Michael Hicks Beach, Chancellor of the Exchequer, circulated to the Cabinet the pros and cons of different conditions for revoking the charter and its preferable timing. Royal Niger Company (Confidential) CAB 34/46 (1898) No. 21 British National Archives.

[50] Convention Between Great Britain and France for the Delimitation of their Respective Possessions of the West of the Niger, and their Respective Possessions and Spheres of Influence to the East of that River, June 14, 1898. HERTSLET, , supra note 40, at 785–97.

[51] 'Royal Niger Company. Papers with respect to revocation of the charter of the Royal Niger Company, and the taking over by H. M. Government of the rights and powers of the Company; Notes on the Niger District and Niger Coasts Protectorates, 1882–93; the Royal Charter of National African

formally revoked as of 1 January 1900, and the Royal Niger Company, Chartered and Limited, became the Niger Company, Limited. The government agreed to pay the company a half of all royalties on minerals produced in much of the former Niger Territory for a period of ninety-nine years. The company was relieved of all its administrative powers and duties, and assigned the government all the benefits of its treaties, with the exception of 'its plant and trading assets, and its stations and waterside depots, with customary rights of access, building, wharves, workshops and the sites thereof'.[52]

The tension between the company and the imperial government that culminated in the revocation of the charter was not simply a matter of conflict between political and economic interests. The imperial government sought to work for the benefit of additional or broader economic objectives that were not necessarily compatible with those of Goldie's company (the interests of the Liverpool merchants, for instance). It was also committed to putting an end to competition with other imperial powers. The British Government itself experienced conflicting interests and competing agendas that resulted from its commitment to different local constituencies and bureaucratized decision-making processes. In addition, the revocation could be attributed to the growing influence of Joseph Chamberlain, who became Secretary of State for the Colonies in 1895 and advocated a robust governmental colonial administration in West Africa.[53]

The terms of the revocation of the charter were quite favourable to the company's interests and harshly criticized in parliamentary debates.[54] The *Economist* noted in 1899 that the terms of the charter's revocation reduced the company's risks 'by the certainty that if they fail the British Government will help them out of their scrape, and if they succeed will buy their possessions at twice the value of the capital invested'.[55] It is therefore not surprising that '[i]nstead of falling like a house of cards after 1900, the Niger Company turned advantages obtained and secured during the chartered period into a near monopolistic control of trade under early British colonial administration'.[56] By contrast, the revocation had a detrimental effect on the coastal African brokers.[57]

Company, 1886; List of treaties with native chiefs, 1884–92; Balance sheets and statements of revenue and expenditure of the Niger Government, 1887–98, Sessional Papers, 1899, LXIII (417), 63. Parl. Deb., 4th ser., Commons, 73, 3 July 1899, 1263–388.

[52] Bill to make provision for Payments in Connection with Revocation of Charter of Royal Niger Company (H.C.), 1899, 260.
[53] TRAVIS CROSBY, JOSEPH CHAMBERLAIN: A MOST RADICAL IMPERIALIST 120–21 (2011).
[54] Parl. Deb., 4th ser., Lords, 73, 4 July 1899, 1389–1401; Parl. Deb., 4th ser., Lords, 74, 14 July 1899, 861–63; Parl. Deb., 4th ser., Commons, 74, 19 July 1899, 1269–1344; Parl. Deb., 4th ser., Commons, 75, 26 July 1899, 365–432; Parl. Deb., 4th ser., Lords, 75, 1 August 1899, 965–1013.
[55] *Nigeria*, ECONOMIST, July 8, 1899.
[56] Scott R. Pearson, *The Economic Imperialism of the Royal Niger Company*, 10 FOOD RES. INST. STUD. 69 (1971).
[57] LYNN, *supra* note 16, at 187.

In the forthcoming years, the Niger Company flourished. Its business consisted of buying local produce (primarily palm oil and palm kernels) and importing whatever was demanded by local markets. It conducted its business from a growing number of trading stations, while production remained in the hands of local cultivators.[58] It engaged in agreements, contracts, and negotiations with colonial governments and shippers to defend its monopoly over the river communications secured pre-1900.[59] Its agents also expanded the geographical areas and commercial operations with which it was involved (to include, *inter alia*, mining). In 1920, the company was taken over by the Lever brothers.[60] In 1929, it was re-formed as the United African Company, a merger between the Niger Company and the African and Eastern Corporation, and became by far the largest single commercial organization in West and Equatorial Africa—and thus central to modern African economic history. It was later absorbed into Unilever.[61]

The Post-Charter International Legal Order

By the end of the nineteenth century, Africa was partitioned by new political boundaries, with economic boundaries not far behind. In the post-charter era, the international legal order would facilitate the rise of inter-state arrangements that bore coordination and governance costs, to the benefit of business corporations' global operations. This functional division of labour corresponded with a conceptual private/public divide that regarded states as the central accountable actors in international law and assumed that states were, like colonial governments of the past, powerful enough to regulate everything within their jurisdiction. Business corporations, in turn, were not subject to a deep theoretical discussion in international law until at least the late 1960s.

In the post-charter era, most international lawyers conceived the colonial encounter as a confrontation between a sovereign European state and a non-European society that was mostly regarded as lacking sovereign status, while they ignored the role and involvement of private business corporations and other modalities of business organizations. Initially, the concessions agreed between chartered companies and indigenous leaders provided a basis for European claims to sovereignty. In this later post-chartered company phase, concessionary agreements had two objectives: first, to provide the basis for imperial

---

[58] A.G. Hopkins, *Imperial Business in Africa. Part II. Interpretations*, 17 J. Afr. Hist. 267, 277 (1976); Geoffrey Jones, Merchants to Multinationals: British Trading Companies in the Nineteenth and Twentieth Centuries 77 (2000).

[59] Colin Newbury, *Trade and Technology in West Africa: The Case of the Niger Company 1900–1920*, 19 J. Afr. Hist. 551 (1978).

[60] Newbury attributes this development to slow organizational adjustments. *Id.* at 551, 553.

[61] For a comprehensive study, *see* David K. Fieldhouse, Merchant Capital and Economic Decolonization: The United Africa Company, 1929–1987 (1994).

sovereignty; and second, to establish the authority of the latter to confer economic rights on commercial actors through commercial concessions. The new concessionary arrangements that were built on the previous charter device and endowed businesses with control over vast territories and natural resources were now effectively invisible as sources of law, rendering their beneficiaries invisible as subjects of scrutiny. Under these new arrangements, the former chartered companies were able to use their former status to retain new advantages. In particular, the vast tracts of land, resources, and trading routes that were previously assigned to companies through the old system of concessionary relations and provided a basis on which to declare imperial sovereignty remained subject to the post-charter companies' economic ownership and control. Now relieved of their sovereignty-related responsibilities, these post-charter businesses could concentrate their efforts on what had driven most of them to Africa in the first place: commercial (rather than governance) endeavours. Thus, with the demise of the charter and of the quasi-sovereign status of these private business corporations, so too came to an end international lawyers' attempts at holding them to account under international law, for decades to come.

International lawyers of the late-nineteenth century may have sought to bring order to the messy legal landscape in Africa by dictating who was to be considered a sovereign (the imperial government) and who was not (the company); what was *legitimate* monopoly (sovereign monopoly over violence) and what was not (monopoly over trade); or who was the harbinger of humanity (the civilizing imperial government) and who was not (the company men, with their devotion to profit).[62] But reading their commentaries alongside the experience of post-charter companies challenges this tidying-up endeavour. Similar to the interplay between the recognized and the non-recognized agreements that constituted a legal space of manoeuvring away from responsibility and costs while enabling exploitation, a similar legal tension arose between the rigidity of the public/private divide in the books and its far less stable meaning for colonial and commercial agents operating in Africa.

Thus, the move away from the chartered company to the post-charter business enterprise did not necessarily result in the resumption of responsible governance on the part of the imperial state. Nor did business enterprises make a radical shift away from the practices associated with the charter era. Rather than a history of a clear rupture from informal to formal empire or a move to a clearer distinction between public and private, the shift from chartered to private business corporations was not a transition from informal empire (through the chartered company) to formal empire (governmental colonial rule), but rather a transition to a different

---

[62] *See, e.g.,* MAINE, *supra* note 11, at 56–67; Rolin-Jaequemyns, *supra* note 11, at 189–92; SALOMON, *supra* note 11, at 128–88; JÈZE, *supra* note 11, at 342–87; LINDLEY, *supra* note 11, at 94–101; LAWRENCE, *supra* note 11, at 79–82, 166–67; WESTLAKE, *supra* note 11, at 139–45, 159–60, 190–92.

modality of informal and flexible alliance between governments and private corporations. We now turn to the history of the development of different modalities of this unruly alliance, which continued despite the formal dissolution of the charter and would later be challenged by postcolonial communities and human rights activists alike.

3

Liberia, Firestone, and the End of Slavery as a Political Cause

Between the Weak State and the Unruly Corporation
1926–1934

Introduction

The previous chapter traced the origins of the international legal architecture for corporate regulation as it was institutionalized in the early decades of the twentieth century against the backdrop of the 'Scramble for Africa'. While most of Africa remained under colonial control during the interwar years, Liberia was different. It was formally independent from colonial rule but acutely dependent on the economic assistance of the United States and other colonial powers. In addition to its economic fragility, members of its government were involved in dubious practices of slave trading and forced labour. The 1920s case of Firestone's arrival in Liberia prefigured a broader postcolonial pattern of an economically and politically powerful multinational corporation (MNC) operating in the territory of a weaker (and at times unwilling) government. The Firestone Company was a privately owned U.S. firm specializing in rubber products. Operating in overseas rubber plantations, it represents an early case of an MNC active in postcolonial settings.[1] Reading this case against the backdrop of the newly institutionalized slavery and forced labour international regulation (the Slavery Convention of the League of Nations and the International Labour Organization's Forced Labor Conventions) demonstrates how the pretence of the international legal order as an inter-state order embodied in these documents masked economic subjection. The Anti-slavery and Forced Labor Conventions were tailored to address colonial settings and thus presumed a colonial regime that could effectively abolish slavery practices and avoid using forced labour. The Liberian case, as the following analysis suggests, exposes how these assumptions were ill-suited from the outset to address the regulation of labour relations in the context of a fragile state (rather than an empire) and a powerful private foreign corporation (rather than a colonial bureaucracy) backed by a strong powerful state.

---

[1] For the history of the concept of the MNC and the international attempts to regulate MNCs, *see* Chapter 7.

Veiled Power. Doreen Lustig, Oxford University Press (2020). © Doreen Lustig.
DOI: 10.1093/oso/9780198822097.001.0001

Enslavement and exploitation appear in various layers of the Liberian case. Liberia was, to a great extent, economically and politically enslaved to the foreign assistance of imperial governments or private investors, and Liberian society was entangled in complex relations of exploitation between the settler and indigenous communities. Practices of forced labour, *de facto* slavery, and even slave trading were integral to the Liberian social and economic reality of the interwar period.

The case of Firestone in Liberia was a precursor to future relations between foreign companies and postcolonial states. Firestone did not immediately resemble the MNC model of the second half of the twentieth century. Its corporate structure was similar to other nineteenth-century companies. It was privately owned and was, in its early days, limited in size. Similar to the Ford Motor Company, in the period covered by this case study, Firestone remained owned and directed by Harvey Firestone and his immediate associates. However, it nonetheless epitomized important changes in the economic organization of its era. 'The factory system, the basis of the industrial revolution, brought an increasingly large number of workers directly under a single management ... [t]he independent worker who entered the factory became a wage laborer surrendering the direction of his labor to his industrial master.'[2] In his pioneering work on the managerial revolution, Alfred D. Chandler identifies the turning point in the U.S. rubber industry: the invention of the car. Chandler further attributes the success of Firestone and other rubber companies to their integrated organization of production and distribution.[3]

Firestone not only developed a sophisticated production chain that positioned its business as a model for the managerial revolution, it also pioneered a global supply chain in its quest to source raw materials beyond U.S. borders. Harvey Firestone arrived in Liberia in 1924, looking for new sources of rubber. And while he was not alone in looking abroad for industrial purposes, despite clear linkages to previous generations, his arrival in Africa marked a shift in the role of merchants and traders outside Europe.[4] By the 1870s, the rapid development in manufacturing and industrialization in Europe and North America had fundamentally altered the needs of core economies and led to a new wave of expansion at the periphery.[5] Factories in need of raw materials and urban populations in need of food reshaped Europe's

---

[2] ADOLF A. BERLE & GARDINER C. MEANS, THE MODERN CORPORATION AND PRIVATE PROPERTY 3 (1932).

[3] ALFRED D. CHANDLER, THE VISIBLE HAND 350–53 (1977).

[4] In DECOLONIZATION AND AFRICAN SOCIETY, Frederick Cooper explores the encounter between French and British colonial authorities, their normative framework of free labour, and the reality of official forced labour in Africa of the early decades of the twentieth century. Africans were not considered workers—strikes were initially considered detribalizations. In the coming decades, the colonial reality of the growing wage-earning class of Africans would slowly undermine these ideas. FREDERICK COOPER, DECOLONIZATION AND AFRICAN SOCIETY: THE LABOR QUESTION IN FRENCH AND BRITISH AFRICA (1996).

[5] For further discussion, *see* Colin Newbury, *Great Britain and the Partition of Africa, 1870-1914,* *in* 3 THE OXFORD HISTORY OF THE BRITISH EMPIRE, THE NINETEENTH CENTURY 624, 629 (Andrew Porter ed., 1999).

relations with overseas economies, stimulating 'rapid territorial expansion and economic growth in those regions where European settlers, capital, and commodities could most easily be employed.'[6] The increased use of plantation labour was a direct result of these developments. A 1950 report issued by the International Labour Organization (ILO) on 'Basic Problems of Plantation Labor' described how the economic life of plantation communities was brought into contact with world trade and became dependent on the most sensitive commodity markets, this being especially evident during the Great Depression of 1929.[7] The report further described the influence of capital investment and technology on the agriculture of certain underdeveloped countries, often called 'plantation economies.'[8] But the turn to plantation economies and the decline of the slave trade did not put an end to enslavement and forced labour in Africa. The growing demand for labour to construct roads, railways, buildings, and plantations led to the expansion of *domestic* slavery and forced labour for public and private purposes.[9] But the continuation of slavery led to strong public criticism. The public campaign influenced the British and the French to end the legal status of slavery in most of Africa by the end of the first decade of the twentieth century.[10]

The story of Liberia begins at this very crossroads of the turn from the slave trade to global trade in raw materials and the growing involvement of European powers in the administration of African territories. Liberia was established at the dawn of the nineteenth-century campaign to outlaw slavery. In 1816, the American Colonization Society was founded in the United States for the purpose of promoting the welfare of some 200,000 slaves who had become free, for the most part through the voluntary action, or the death, of their owners. It was decided that the freed slaves would be returned to Africa, with the idea of forming a state, a 'free negro republic in their land of origin.'[11] Most historical accounts of

---

[6]   B.R. Tomlinson, *Economics and Empire: The Periphery and the Imperial Economy, in* 3 THE OXFORD HISTORY OF THE BRITISH EMPIRE, THE NINETEENTH CENTURY, *supra* note 5, at 53.

[7]   International Labor Organization, Committee on Work on Plantations, *Basic Problems of Plantation Labor* 8–9 (1950).

[8]   *Id.* at 9.

[9]   Frederick Cooper, *Conditions Analogous to Slavery: Imperialism and Free Labor Ideology in Africa, in* BEYOND SLAVERY: EXPLORATIONS OF RACE, LABOR, AND CITIZENSHIP IN POSTEMANCIPATION SOCIETIES 105, 113 (Frederick Cooper et al. eds., 2000); Suzanne Miers, *Slavery and the Slave Trade as International Issues 1890–1939*, 19 SLAVERY & ABOLITION 16, 22 (1998).

[10]   'The colonial system made it possible for slaves to flee a harsh master, to transfer their dependence to other groups or individuals, to redefine relations of dependence, or to take their chances finding jobs in colonial cities, colonial armies, colonial railways, or colonial schools and mission stations. By the end of the first decade of the new century, the British and the French—and, at least on paper, the Portuguese, Belgians, and Germans as well—had ended the legal status of slavery in most [of] Africa, and the practices of enslavement, of the reproduction of slave populations, and of the large-scale economic exploitation of slaves were in rapid decline.' Cooper, *supra* note 9, at 119. For further analysis, *see* THE END OF SLAVERY IN AFRICA (Suzanne Miers & Richard Roberts eds., 1988). The normative distinction between slave-trading and slavery later resonates in some of the wording chosen by members of the League for the Slavery Convention.

[11]   M.D. Mackenzie, *Liberia and the League of Nations*, 33 J. ROYAL AFR. SOC'Y 372 (1934).

nineteenth-century Liberia describe a nation divided into two classes: a settlers' society that interacted with European traders, and a native African population that produced many of the goods that were bought and sold by more recent immigrants. Despite continuing struggles between the new settlers and the local population, a Declaration of Independence was made in 1847 and a constitution was drafted on the lines of the U.S. constitution. Liberia differs from later postcolonial states in its unique history and early independent status. And yet, as the following analysis suggests, its engagement with the Firestone Company provides an intriguing prelude to the limited capacity of the emerging international legal order to abolish the enslavement of humans and further demonstrates how this very limitation could facilitate the enslavement of political communities.

By the late-nineteenth century, the slave trade was abolished, followed by a fierce campaign against domestic slavery that marked its final days. In 1926, the League of Nations codified the prohibition of slavery in its Slavery Convention. These measures were reinforced by the ILO Convention on Forced Labor in 1930. These decisive acts are often alleged to conclude the history of the international abolition of slavery. But Liberia's story of its relationship to Firestone—of almost a century of enduring practices of slavery, and the struggle against it—clearly problematizes this narrative. When Firestone's men arrived in Liberia to negotiate the terms of a concession with the local government, League officials were labouring over the terms of the Convention on Slavery. Liberian officials signed the concession in 1926, the same crucial year in the history of slavery. It is to a very brief introductory note on the history of the Slavery Convention that we now turn.

The League of Nations and the Abolition of Slavery

Historical perspectives on the abolition of slavery

The formalization of imperial rule suffered considerable blows after the Boer Wars,[12] the aftermath of King Leopold's intervention in the Congo,[13] and other humanitarian disasters.[14] But, though grave, they were not radical enough to change

---

[12] M. van Wyk Smith complicates the narrative of humanitarian outrage, pacifism, and anti-imperialism that developed in reaction to the Boer Wars by illuminating its racist aspects. *See* M. van Wyk Smith, *The Boers and the Anglo-Boer War (1899–1902) in the Twentieth Century Moral Imaginary*, 31 VICTORIAN LITERATURE & CULTURE 429 (2003).

[13] From the 1890s until the end of the century the King Leopold's rule of terror in the Congo became well known and led to fierce public criticism. The political pressures eventually compelled the King to transfer the territory to Belgium in 1908. For a detailed account, *see* ADAM HOCHSCHILD, KING LEOPOLD'S GHOST 115–81 (1999). On the silence of international lawyers during the years of the Congo controversy, *see* MARTTI KOSKENNIEMI, THE GENTLE CIVILIZER 155–66 (2001).

[14] *See*, for example, the discussion of Thomas Pakenham on the German South-West Africa extermination policy. THOMAS PAKENHAM, THE SCRAMBLE FOR AFRICA 602–15 (1991).

the tradition of the European Great Powers overnight. The anti-slavery campaign was hierarchical and reserved the competence of treaty-making to the 'civilized states' alone.[15] The failure to include racial equality in the Covenant of the League of Nations is another testament to the League members' complicated position on questions of racism and equality.[16] The attitudes and involvement of the League officials in regulating business enterprises in contexts such as labour and trade tell a complex story of its members' ethos, initiatives, and use of its institutional setting.[17] I will devote more attention to its policies on trade and investment in Chapter 6.

Intriguingly, Ethiopia's attempt to become a member of the League of Nations coincided with the British anti-slavery Society's campaign to internationalize the repression of slavery.[18] Sir Steel-Maitland, Delegate for New Zealand, submitted two resolutions to the Assembly of the League of Nations, the first requesting an inquiry into slave-trading in Ethiopia, and the second requesting a general inquiry into slavery in Africa. Only the latter was adopted.[19] Consequently, Ethiopia was admitted to the League of Nations, and the attention of the Slavery Convention turned to the international arena. In 1924, the League's Assembly decided to appoint a competent body to inquire into slavery, the Temporary Slavery Commission [hereinafter: the TSC].[20]

---

[15] Edward Keene, *The Construction of International Society: A Case Study of British Treaty-Making Against the Slave-Trade*, 61 INT'L ORG. 311, 314 (2007). Keene described in his article the convergence between ideas about civilization and the shift to positivism in international law. 'At roughly the same time that international legal discourse was beginning to move away from the discourse of "natural rights", in other words, Europeans were also beginning to think of themselves and their societies in a novel way, using the term 'civilization' to describe what they saw as their unique political, cultural, social, economic, and technological achievements ... The Eurocentric focus of the early positivist treaty collections coincided with the growing belief that "barbarians" lacked the competence of "civilized" states to make law, or at least to make acceptable laws, and each discriminatory tendency reinforced the other.' *Id.* at 318–19.

[16] NAOKO SHIMAZU, JAPAN, RACE AND EQUALITY: THE RACIAL EQUALITY PROPOSAL OF 1919 (1998).

[17] Key challenges to the narrative of failure were championed by Susan G. Pedersen, *Back to the League of Nations: Review Essay*, 112 AM. HIST. REV. 1091 (2007); SUSAN PEDERSEN, THE GUARDIANS: THE LEAGUE OF NATIONS AND THE CRISIS OF EMPIRE (2015). *See also* PATRICIA CLAVIN, SECURING THE WORLD ECONOMY: THE REINVENTION OF THE LEAGUE OF NATIONS, 1920–1946 (2013); Natasha Wheatley, *Mandatory Interpretation: Legal Hermeneutics and the New International Order in Arab and Jewish Petitions to the League of Nations*, 227 PAST & PRESENT 205 (2015).

[18] Jean Allain, *Slavery and the League of Nations: Ethiopia as a Civilized Nation*, 8 J. HIST. INT'L L. 213, 219 (2006).

[19] League of Nations, Motion Proposed by Sir Arthur Steel-Maitland, Delegate for New Zealand, on Sept. 7, 1922, Third Assembly of the League of Nations, Sept. 7, 1922 LofN Doc. 23253 (A/47/1922).

[20] The Commission was composed of three members of the Mandates Commission, two former Colonial officials, the Secretary General of the Italian Geographical Society, a Haitian delegate, and an official from the International Labor Office who was an expert on 'native labor questions'. Temporary Slave Commission—Minutes of the First Session, League of Nations Doc. A.18 1924 VI.B (1924). Parallel to the work of the Assembly, the Secretary General of the League of Nations asked member states to supply the Council with any information on the existing situation regarding the matter of slavery and, later on, regarding 'colonial possessions'. *See* League of Nations Memorandum by the Secretary General, *The Question of Slavery*, Aug. 4, 1924, LoN Doc. 38385 (A/25/1924).

Since colonial governments were unwilling to open the door to outside scrutiny of their policies, the TSC had to narrow the scope of its recommendations.[21] In light of its findings, the TSC proposed the establishment of an international convention meant to suppress slavery in all its forms.[22]

The Slavery Convention was adopted on 25 September 1926 and came into force on 9 March 1927. The Convention was intended to bring about 'the disappearance from written legislation or from the customs of the country of everything, which admits the maintenance by a private individual of rights over another person of the same nature as the rights which an individual can have over things'.[23] The Rapporteur of the Sixth Committee of the Assembly of 1925 pointed out the status of the provisions of previous conventions in light of the newly established draft:

> I would like to emphasize the fact that the Committee does not hold up this document as the ultimate aim to be achieved in the international effort to do away with such abuses as the slave trade, slavery and conditions analogous thereto. *It represents merely what the Committee considers to be the highest minimum standard which can be set forth in formal international arrangements at the present time.* It is recognized that the standard already existing in certain colonial areas is considerably higher and *it is hoped that no States will be satisfied with compliance with the minimum standard which is now proposed.*[24]

Article 1(1) of the 1926 Slavery Convention defined slavery as 'the status or condition of a person over whom any or all of the powers attaching to the right of ownership are exercised'.[25] Article 2 of the Convention sought to establish the obligations of the contracting parties—that is, states—to their territories and to territories placed under their 'sovereignty, jurisdiction, protection, suzerainty or

---

[21] Suzanne Miers, *Slavery and the Slave Trade as International Issues 1890–1939*, 19 SLAVERY & ABOLITION 16, 28 (1998).

[22] *See* Letter from the Chairman of the Commission to the President of the Council and Report of the Temporary Slavery Commission, League of Nations Doc. A.19 1925 VI.B (1925).

[23] League of Nations, Question of Slavery, Slavery Convention: Report Presented to the Assembly by the Sixth Committee, Sept. 24, 1926, LofN Doc. A.104 1926 VI, as found in League of Nations, *Publications of the League of Nations*, VI.B. Slavery, 1926, VI.B. 5, p. 2, *Microfilm* 11653, Reel 180 [hereinafter: LofN, Question of Slavery, 1926 Report].

[24] The Suppression of Slavery, Memorandum submitted by the Secretary General, U.N.—ESCOR, Ad Hoc Committee on Slavery, 14 (July 11, 1951).

[25] The Slavery Convention Art. 1(1), Sept. 25, 1926, 60 L.N.T.S. 254 [hereinafter The Slavery Convention]. The Report of the Sixth Committee to the Assembly in 1926 sought to clarify the scope of the definition of slavery: 'This applies not only to domestic slavery but to all those conditions mentioned by the Temporary Slavery Commission ... i.e. debt slavery, the enslaving of persons disguised as the adoption of children and the acquisition of girls by purchase disguised as payment of dowry. Even if these last practices do not come under the definition of slavery, as it is given in Article 1, the Commission is unanimously of the opinion that they must be combated.' The Suppression of Slavery, Memorandum submitted by the Secretary General, *supra* note 24. at 14.

tutelage'.[26] Concerns over the difficulties that might arise from suppressing slavery by 'one stroke of the pen' led the Committee to adopt more circumspect wording. Hence, the Convention distinguished between a complete obligation to 'prevent and suppress the slave trade' and an obligation progressively to bring about a complete abolition of slavery. These definitions were originally proposed in the 1925 British Draft Protocol and subsequently incorporated into the Convention itself. Viscount Cecil, the British minister responsible for League affairs, explained the cautious nature of the wording of Article 2(b): '[it] must be left to the *judgment of the Government responsible*', as circumstances varied from state to state; and the Sixth Committee was ready to concede that 'in certain cases there could be an arrangement whereby freed slaves in possession of all their natural and civil rights might be obliged to continue to serve their former masters for a certain time, but only subject to the obligations and rights consequent upon a labour contract'.[27]

Most contentious of all was the issue of forced labour.[28] The discussion in the TSC and the later reports of the Sixth Committee suggest that forced labour was primarily conceived as a *colonial concern*.[29] It was finally decided to distinguish between the obligations that derived from a colonial regime and those applicable to the Mandate system, and to adopt a wording that conveyed a less demanding standard in colonial settings than in Mandates.[30] The Convention distinguished

---

[26] The High Contracting Parties undertake, each in respect of the territories placed under its sovereignty, jurisdiction, protection, suzerainty or tutelage, so far as they have not already taken the necessary steps:

(a) To prevent and suppress the slave trade;
(b) To bring about, progressively and as soon as possible, the complete abolition of slavery in all its forms. The Slavery Convention, Art. 2.

[27] 'The Sixth Committee', Lord Cecil wrote, 'interprets Article 2 as tending to bring about the disappearance from written legislation or from the custom of the country of everything which admits the maintenance by a private individual of rights over another person of the same nature as the rights which an individual can have over things', a framing 'which at first sight might seem rather weak'. The Suppression of Slavery, Memorandum submitted by the Secretary General, *supra* note 24, at 16. Another amendment proposed to add a paragraph (c): 'To endeavor, as far as possible, to bring about the disappearance of conditions resembling slavery, e.g., debt slavery, sham adoption, childhood marriage, traffic in women, etc.', but League member states failed to reach agreement on this addition as well. *Id.*

[28] As stated in the Sixth Committee's Report to the Assembly in 1926: 'In drafting this article, the Committee confronted perhaps the most difficult of the problems before it.' LofN, Question of Slavery, 1926 Report, *supra* note 23, at 2.

[29] The TSC considered three main sources from which to draw analogies in this context: the principles applied to B and C mandates, Article 23 of the Covenant ('fair and humane conditions of labour for men, women and children') and the recommendation made by the Assembly on the protection of minorities. Temporary Slavery Commission, Minutes of the Second Session, held in Geneva, from July 13–25, 1925, *The League of Nations Documents and Publications* 1919–1946. *Microfilm* 11653 Reel 180, pp. 72–74 [hereinafter TSC, Minutes of the Second Session].

[30] As noted by the Rapporteur: 'its [the Convention's] provisions do not go so far as those contained in the B and C mandates; but the Committee felt that it was wiser to set up a minimum standard which was clearly understood and accepted'. League of Nations, Question of Slavery: Report presented to the Sixth Assembly by the Sixth Committee, Sept. 26, 1925, LofN Doc. A.130.1925.VI.B as found in League of Nations, *Publications of the League of Nations*, VI.B. Slavery, 1926, VI.B. p. 3, Microfilm 11653, Reel 180 [hereinafter LofN, Question of Slavery, 1925 Report].

between public and private compulsory labour, indicating that, under certain conditions, compulsory labour would be allowed if required for *public purposes*:[31]

> In principle, the committee [the TSC] was most decidedly opposed to the use of forced labour for other than public purposes, but at the same time it recognized that, owing to special conditions in certain colonies, it might be necessary to call upon the population for this kind of labour in exceptional cases.[32]

These so-called exceptional cases were only permitted in situations of 'imperious necessity'; workers had to be 'adequately remunerated', and 'in no case must it involve the removal of labourers from their usual place of residence'.[33] The discussion of private forced labour is particularly important for our purposes. In the TSC report, forced labour for private enterprises was strictly forbidden.[34] However, the TSC reported that, although no legislation authorized such compulsory labour, it did *in fact* exist in the colonial world.[35] The TSC's proposal to prohibit private forced labour was strongly worded: 'The Commission considers that the forms of direct or indirect compulsion the primary object of which is to force natives into private employment *are abuses*' (my emphasis).[36] The TSC considered what it termed 'the vicious circle argument' in which the introduction of an advanced labour system and economic progress initially required the use of compulsory labour, and 'called for prudence in the part of the administration' in such instances.[37]

The categorical language used by the TSC in reference to private forced labour was not, however, echoed by the Rapporteur.[38] No clear prohibition of private forced labour was articulated in the Rapporteur's report, nor was there any clear obligation on the part of private enterprise to abstain from forced-labour practices. Governments were positioned as the sole authorities held responsible under international law for forced-labour practices, both public and private. In a later report, Lord Cecil used more restrictive language referring to this issue, but maintained the possibility of lawful *private* forced labour:

[31] It was agreed not to use the Mandates' wording, 'essential public works and services', due to concern that 'services' might include the payment of taxes. A more general wording was then chosen—'public purposes'. LofN, Question of Slavery, 1925 Report, *supra* note 30, at 3.

[32] *Id.*

[33] *Id.*

[34] Temporary Slavery Commission, Report of the Temporary Slavery Commission Adopted in the Course of its Second Session, 13–25 July, 1925, *The League of Nations Documents and Publications 1919–1946*, A.19.1925.VI.B, 25 July, 1925, *Microfilm* 11653, Reel 180, p. 12 [hereinafter TSC, Report].

[35] 'Practices, however, apparently based on the principle of forced labour for private employers but not sanctioned by law have actually existed in some countries.' TSC, Report, *supra* note 34, at 12.

[36] *Id.* at 13.

[37] 'The Commission considers also that indirect or "moral" pressure, if exercised by officials to secure labour for private employment, may, in view of the authority of such officials over the minds of natives, be in effect tantamount to compulsion and calls therefore for prudence on the part of the Administration.' *Id.* at 13.

[38] LofN, Question of Slavery, 1925 Report, *supra* note 30, at 3.

it [the committee] has agreed that forced labour should only be resorted for public purposes, apart from purely transitory arrangements designed to make the progressive abolition of forced labour for private purposes both just and practicable. In this connection it will be observed that stringent conditions are imposed on forced labour for private purposes even during the transitory period. Among these conditions is the requirement that adequate remuneration should be paid to those subjected to forced labor. In the case of forced labour for public purposes, this condition is not repeated.[39]

These ideas are clearly stated in the final wording of Article 5:

The High Contracting Parties recognize that recourse to compulsory or forced labour may have grave consequences and undertake, each in respect of the territories placed under its sovereignty, jurisdiction, protection, suzerainty or tutelage, to take all necessary measures to prevent compulsory or forced labour from developing into conditions analogous to slavery.

It is agreed that:

(1) Subject to the transitional provisions laid down in paragraph (2) below, compulsory or forced labour may only be exacted for public purposes.
(2) In territories in which compulsory or forced labour for other than public purposes still survives, the High Contracting Parties shall endeavour progressively and as soon as possible to put an end to the practice. So long as such forced or compulsory labour exists, this labour shall invariably be of an exceptional character, shall always receive adequate remuneration, and shall not involve the removal of the labourers from their usual place of residence.
(3) In all cases, the responsibility for any recourse to compulsory or forced labour shall rest with the competent central authorities of the territory concerned.[40]

According to paragraph 3 of Article 5, the recourse to compulsory or forced labour would be the responsibility of the *competent central authorities* of the *territory concerned*. The drafters' main subject of regulation in this scheme was the colonial regime that was the competent authority in its territory. But what of those cases in which the state was not governed by a colonial authority and yet was not competent to exercise authority in its own territory?

In a TSC discussion entitled 'Consular Reports and Investigation', Sir Frederick Lugard suggested that commercial companies registered in civilized countries that

---

[39] LofN, Question of Slavery, 1926 Report, *supra* note 23, at 2.
[40] The Slavery Convention, Art. 5.

employed 'coloured labour' in territories not under the control of their own nation should be bound to notify their consul of the fact and forward to him their prospectus. The consul should from time to time visit their societies and factories and verify that no abuse was taking place.[41] Some committee members raised the concern that '[t]he consul couldn't intervene in the maintenance of the public order in a country where he carried out work. This duty belonged only to the authority of the country concerned.'[42] Lugard's answer was that:

[t]he obligation to see that employees are properly treated by employers lies, of course, primarily on the local government. But the fact that the consul had knowledge of the existence of a company whose operations were controlled by his fellow countrymen in the foreign country to which he was accredited and his occasional visits would be a safeguard against abuses in case the local government took no action.[43]

Not all Commissioners objected to Lugard's suggestion. Envisioning primarily an imperial setting, Mr. H.A. Grimshaw justified the suggestion: 'The British Government, for example, would merely instruct the consul to report cases where British citizens, as owners of factories, were using forced labour. This was no infringement of national sovereignty.'[44] Others, however, pointed to the potential diplomatic hurdles multiple inspections of this sort might create.[45] Eventually it was decided to suppress this paragraph.[46] This discussion shows that some Commissioners were inclined towards some form of home-state regulation over corporate bodies, but retreated because of strong opposition.

While holding the administrative authorities responsible, the TSC conceded that their power to regulate private enterprises was rather limited: 'The supply of labour desired by European industrialists and planters and the willingness to provide that labour will increase with the increasing needs of the natives and also with the improvements in pay, food and treatment.'[47]

The Commission regarded this issue to be 'beyond the scope of this report', but noted that, while '[t]he administrative authorities are powerless as regards to the first point [the supply of labour desired by European industrialists and planters] it is the duty of these authorities to give their closest attention to the

---

[41] Lugard noted that this suggestion was based on an official White Paper issued by the British Government in 1913 as a result of the Putumayo enquiry. TSC, Minutes of the Second Session, *supra* note 29, at 79.

[42] *Id.*

[43] *Id.*

[44] *Id.* at 80.

[45] One of the Commissioners raised the following hypothetical: what would happen if the British counsel were to report on a British enterprise operating in Cuba and the Counsel of Haiti initiated his own report, as Haitian workers were involved? *Id.* at 80.

[46] *Id.*

[47] *Id.* at 81.

second point [the needs of the natives, their payment, food, and treatment]'.[48] It further noted: 'it is quite clear that they [the administrative authorities] are doing their best and that any advice which might be given to them on this point would be, to say the least, superfluous'.[49] Legal historians rarely dwell on the approach chosen by the Slavery Convention to address *private* enterprises. One rare exception was the American Margaret Burton, one of the early League historians, who mentioned it in passing:

> [t]hat forced labor for private profit had not been categorically prohibited was due to the fact that certain states would not have adhered to a convention including such a provision. It had seemed wiser, therefore, to make concessions to secure the adhesion of these governments, in the hope that it would later be possible to go further.[50]

Despite the dramatic tone sometimes employed in narrating its history,[51] the normative content of the 1926 Slavery Convention committed European powers only to what they had already been legally bound to do: to suppress the last vestiges of the slave trade entirely and gradually abolish slavery.[52] The Convention thus embodied a delicate, yet disturbing, tension between the egalitarian essence on which the abolition of slavery was premised and a discriminatory notion of a 'civilized' versus a 'non-civilized' world.[53]

In 1931, the Council of the League of Nations appointed a Committee of Experts on Slavery to study the effects of the Slavery Convention.[54] One of its most remarkable, yet often forgotten, achievements was its detailed and

---

[48] *Id.*

[49] As an example, they mentioned a Decree enacted by the French-mandated territory of the Cameroons in 1922. *Id.*

[50] MARGARET ERNESTINE BURTON, THE ASSEMBLY OF THE LEAGUE OF NATIONS 256 (1941).

[51] 'The discussions in the Assembly and Council with regard to slavery, and the investigations of the International Labor Office on forced labour, have been echoed and re-echoed in the press of the world.' Ursula P. Hubbard, *The Cooperation of the United States with the League of Nations and with the International Labour Organization*, 14 INT'L CONCILIATION 675, 744 (1931). For press coverage, *see Slavery*, TIME MAGAZINE, June 14, 1926 [reporting the discussions in the League of Nations over the report of the TSC].

[52] For a critical discussion, *see* COOPER, *supra* note 4, at 28.

[53] Commentators usually refer to the lack of enforcement mechanisms as the main weakness of the 1926 Slavery Convention; it failed to establish either formal procedures for reviewing the existence of slavery within the territories of signatory states or an international body that would evaluate and investigate allegations of violations. Some attempts were made to establish an impartial body to gather information and prepare reports. However, the lack of an enforcement mechanism, inability to review questions relating to forced labour, and the confidentiality of its proceedings weakened its influence and effect. *See* Kathryn Zoglin, *United Nations Actions Against Slavery: A Critical Evaluation*, 8 HUM. RTS. Q. 306, 309–10 (1986).

[54] BURTON, *supra* note 50, at 260. For a detailed account of the reports of the Advisory Committee on Slavery between 1932 and 1938, *see* Renee Colette Redman, *The League of Nations and the Right to Be Free from Enslavement: The First Human Right to Be Recognized as Customary International Law*, 70 CHI.-KENT L. REV. 759, 781–82 (1994).

exhaustive investigation into slavery and forced labour in Liberia. The analysis of its work in Liberia is at the core of this chapter. As its research spanned the entire 1930s, we need to consider also the relevance and application of the 1930 ILO Convention concerning Forced or Compulsory Labour, also known as the Forced Labour Convention.

The ILO and the regulation of forced labour

After approving the Slavery Convention on 25 September 1926, the League of Nations Assembly asked the ILO to take further steps to prevent forced and compulsory labour.[55] After a period of deliberation, the ILO General Conference adopted the Forced Labour Convention in June 1930. As noted earlier, its objective was to suppress the use of forced or compulsory labour in all its forms within the shortest possible period. Article 2 of the Convention defines forced labour as 'all work or service which is exacted from any person under the menace of any penalty and for which the said person has not offered himself voluntarily'.

ILO policies of the interwar period were characterized by a clear distinction between the colonial and the non-colonial world. [56] Frederick Cooper observed how 'the discourse focused on the conduct of European governments as the most relevant issue in colonial societies. The labor process, and the ways in which workers built their lives as they labored, were not yet amenable to international discussion and regulation.'[57]

During the interwar period, colonial powers gradually changed their labour policies from direct exploitation to indirect rule, which included complex

[55] It requested the council, 'to inform the Governing Body of the International Labour Office of the adoption of the Slavery Convention, and to draw its attention to the importance of the work undertaken by the Office with a view of studying the best means of preventing forced or compulsory labour from developing into conditions analogous to slavery'. Further, 'The Assembly ... taking note of the work undertaken by the International Labour office in conformity with the mission entrusted to it and within the limits of its constitution; *Considering* that these studies naturally include the problem of forced labour; *Request* the Council to inform the Governing Body of the International Labour Office with a view of studying the best means of preventing forced or compulsory labour from developing into conditions analogous to slavery....' A.123.1926.VI quoted in The Suppression of Slavery, Memorandum submitted by the Secretary General, UN-ESCOR, Ad Hoc Committee on Slavery, 36 (1951).

[56] Daniel Roger Maul, *The International Labour Organization and the Struggle Against Forced Labour from 1919 to the Present*, 48 LAB. HIST. 477, 479 (2007). 'The increased need for manpower during the economic expansion of the 1920s was at no point met by the free local labour markets. The building of railways, roads and harbours for the expanding mining industry in southern Africa and for the plantation industries of South East Asia or West Africa required a level of manpower that was simply not to be had on a voluntary basis.'

[57] COOPER, *supra* note 4, at 56. *See also* JOHN A. JOHNSTON, THE INTERNATIONAL LABOR ORGANIZATION 232–33 (1970); ANTONY ALCOCK, HISTORY OF THE INTERNATIONAL LABOR ORGANIZATION 81–98 (1970).

systems of recruitment and taxation, and the joint interests of industry and government that made the distinction between public and private coercion hard to discern.[58] Colonial development in this period was dependent primarily on private enterprise, but 'private enterprise could not flourish without the support of colonial Government. It was the Administration which channeled private initiatives, organized transport, and arranged for native labour.'[59] Despite the established practices of private compulsory labour, French officials insisted they did not exist: such practices were defined as taxation or military recruitment rather than labour. In the British context, historians describe a similarly complex relationship among colonial officials, labourers, indigenous leaders, and private enterprise.[60] In Liberia, the administrative system introduced during the administration of President Arthur Barclay (1904–1912) followed a similar pattern of 'indirect rule'.[61] J. Gus Liebenow described how indirect rule perpetuated the social division of the hinterland into more than sixteen ethnic groups and capitalized on the existing political fragmentation of most of these indigenous collectives. The integrity of the tribe as a political unit was disregarded as district boundaries were formed regardless of existing notions of territorial units.[62]

Amid these developments, the ILO and the Permanent Mandate Commission (on which the ILO secured permanent representation) received reports of the harsh treatment of indigenous workers engaged in forced labour, and of floggings, deportations, suicides, and the desperate lack of medical services. In the 1930 Convention, ILO officials sought to address the challenge of compulsory labour. Article 6 addressed the issue of cooperation between public officials and private individuals or companies: 'Officials of the administration ... shall not put constraint upon the said populations [under their charge] or upon any individual members thereof to work for private individuals, companies or associations.'

---

[58] COOPER, *supra* note 4, at 11. As further noted by Cooper, the policy of indirect rule—through alliances with the old elites who had been previously portrayed as an obstacle to universal progress—became dominant in British and French Africa. It represented an attempt to make retreat sound like policy. *Id.*

[59] ALCOCK, *supra* note 57, at 82.

[60] 'Unwilling to spend metropolitan funds in any significant initiative to restructure colonial economies, frustrated in its hope that African slaves and peasants would turn themselves into wage laborers, the government in London—like that in Paris—became increasingly absorbed in the 1920s in the myth that Africa was and must remain a continent of tribes and tradition....' COOPER, *supra* note 4, at 49.

[61] These practices of indirect rule perpetuated the social division of the hinterland into more than sixteen ethnic groups and capitalized upon the existing political fragmentation of most of these indigenous groups. The integrity of the tribe as a political unit was disregarded as district boundaries were formed regardless of existing notions of territorial units. 'In return for maintenance of peace in their area and the payment of taxes collected from their tribal constituents, traditional authorities were given regular salaries, assured prestige and license to use of abuse the persons and services of their own subject without the customary constraints on their actions.' J. GUS LIEBENOW, LIBERIA: THE QUEST FOR DEMOCRACY 54 (1987).

[62] *Id.* at 55.

Other articles of the Convention proscribed specific practices commonly used under colonial rule.[63]

A transition period was provided in the Convention, during which forced labour could be used as an exceptional measure, under specific conditions, for public purposes only. Article 5 addressed the issue of concessions:

> No concession granted to private individuals, companies or associations shall involve any form of forced or compulsory labour for the production or the collection of products which such private individuals, companies or associations utilize or in which they trade.
>
> Where concessions exist containing provisions involving such forced or compulsory labour, such provisions shall be rescinded as soon as possible, in order to comply with Article 1 of the Convention.

Article 5 of the ILO Convention raised important questions. The inclusion of a formal authorization for forced labour was prohibited: such provisions, if they were to exist, should 'be rescinded as soon as possible'. What would happen if no formal authorization was mentioned in the concession agreement, but *de facto* forced labour practices were exercised by private companies? Could a company practising forced labour be held directly accountable under international law according to the ILO Convention?

'Slavery, when the League took it up', concluded Margaret Burton, 'had by no means been entirely abolished, but it had been successfully eliminated from large areas of the world ... [the Assembly] was taking a logical next step in an international effort begun more than a century earlier.'[64] However, this next step was resolved by assigning the duty to abolish and outlaw slavery and forced labour to states. As the following analysis suggests, the statist inclination was ill-suited to address the practices of slavery and forced labour of a foreign private business enterprise that could not be regulated or tamed by Liberian authorities. The shortcomings of the statist regulation of slavery and forced labour will be examined in the particular case of the League of Nations' investigation of allegations against Firestone's involvement in slavery and forced labour in Liberia.

---

[63] Article 7 discusses the authority of chiefs who exercise administrative functions to recourse to forced or compulsory labour. Article 8 deals with instances in which the civil authority in a territory is delegated to local authorities and their responsibilities therein. Article 10 stipulates that 'Forced or compulsory labour? Exacted as a tax and forced or compulsory labour to which recourse is had for the execution of public works by chiefs who exercise administrative functions shall be progressively abolished.' It then defines the conditions under which such forced labor for public purposes could be exercised. A similar approach was applied in the context of forced or compulsory labour for the transport of persons or goods, such as the labour of porters or boatmen. Convention concerning Forced or Compulsory Labour Article 18, June 28, 1930.

[64] BURTON, *supra* note 50 at 264.

Firestone: Harbinger of Turmoil

Firestone enters Liberia: Private entrepreneurship beyond state borders

Harvey S. Firestone established the Firestone Tire & Rubber Company in 1900. In the early years, Firestone relied on other companies to manufacture the rubber and focused on fitting it to steel carriage wheels.[65] In 1903, the company began to manufacture its own rubber, and, a year later, it developed pneumatic tyres for cars. Around that time, Henry Ford, who was barred from joining the Association of Licensed Automobile Manufacturers, identified Firestone as a potential partner. In 1906, the Ford Motor Company began mass production of four-cylinder Model N runabouts on 2.5 inch Firestone tyres. By 1908, with orders for 20,000 sets of tyres to fit the new Ford Model T as well as sales to other carmakers, Firestone had established itself in the rubber industry.[66] Ford and Firestone soon became close friends, sharing similar visions. As noted in a U.S. Government study, '[b]oth were early advocates of mass production for mass consumption; they believed in supplying as large a market as possible with the most efficient product sold at the cheapest price.'[67] When the United States entered the First World War in the spring of 1917, Firestone offered President Woodrow Wilson the use of his factory for government service. This cooperation elevated the Firestone Company to new heights in terms of sales. In the early 1920s, Harvey Firestone's company was a distinguished member of what was known as the Big Four, the four giant corporations that dominated decision-making in the rubber industry worldwide.[68]

While producing most of the world's cars in the early 1920s, U.S. manufacturers created rapidly growing demand for rubber, heightening their dependency on the suppliers of rubber in British colonies in Asia.[69] The brief depression after the First World War led rubber production to exceed consumption, triggering a price collapse. The British Government responded with a plan to stabilize rubber prices, known as the Stevenson Rubber Restriction Act. The plan limited British

---

[65] As described on the company's website: 'On August 3rd, 1900, the Firestone Tire & Rubber Company was founded in Akron, Ohio ... Firestone began manufacturing its own tires for the first time in 1903, and by late summer of the next year, they'd developed the first mechanically-fastened, straight-sided pneumatic automobile tire ... Firestone delivered 2,000 sets of tires to the Ford Motor Company. It was the largest single order for tires place[d] by the auto industry to date, and would start a business partnership that would last for decades.' Online: www.bridgestoneamericas.com/en/corporation/history (last visited October 9, 2019).

[66] ALFRED LIEF, THE FIRESTONE STORY 86–90 (1951).

[67] WAYNE CHATFIELD TAYLOR, THE FIRESTONE OPERATIONS IN LIBERIA (UNITED STATES BUSINESS PERFORMANCE ABROAD) 38–39 (1956).

[68] The other three corporations were the United States Rubber Company, the B.F. Goodrich Company, and the Goodyear Tire and Rubber Company.

[69] Frank Chalk, *The Anatomy of an Investment: Firestone's 1927 Loan to Liberia*, 1 CAN. J. AFR. STUD. 12, 14 (1967).

colonial rubber production to a level below demand, thereby creating artificially high prices. Despite gradually raising prices in the following years, the British planters demanded continued government intervention on their behalf.[70] The British act imposed a great burden on U.S. industry. Firestone sought to enlist the U.S. Government to fight the Stevenson Act, with limited success,[71] and began a search for sources of rubber not under British control. Eugene Staley describes how Firestone's initiative was aided by the U.S. Government and is thus an example of the close interaction between private foreign investment and foreign policy: 'The most conspicuous example of this sort was the plan of Mr. Harvey Firestone for establishing rubber plantations in Liberia, undertaken in connection with the campaign of Secretary of Commerce Herbert Hoover against the Stevenson Plan, in which British producers sought to "valorize" rubber.'[72]

While government agencies were investigating possible solutions to the limited rubber supply, Firestone launched independent attempts to locate new (cheaper) areas suitable for rubber plantations. Among the various locations surveyed by his experts, only Liberia proved feasible.[73]

The Liberia of the 1920s

The Liberia of the 1920s and early 1930s covered 40,000 square miles and was home to just over 1 million inhabitants. After a century of existence, its population was still divided into two classes. The acute racial discrimination prevalent there during those years was lucidly captured in one of the League of Nations reports:

> There are, on the one hand, the so-called Americo-Liberians, descendants of former slaves in the United States, freed and sent back to Africa, and, on the other hand, the aboriginal natives. The native population, largely isolated from the outer world, have preserved, to a great extent, their primitive customs, and are called by the Americo-Liberians 'uncivilized'. The 'civilized', however constitute only one-hundredth part of the total population, with the result that Liberia, the only case of a free nation deliberately formed from the black race, presents

---

[70] For a detailed analysis, see CHARLES R. WHITTLESEY, GOVERNMENTAL CONTROL OF CRUDE RUBBER: THE STEVENSON PLAN (1931).

[71] A buying pool was set up in the rubber manufacturing industry, with the encouragement of Secretary of Commerce Hoover, to combat the Stevenson Act. A bill was introduced in Congress to legalize this and similar buying pools by exempting them from the antitrust laws. The bill was not passed. EUGENE STALEY, RAW MATERIALS AND PEACE AND WAR 131 (1976).

[72] EUGENE STALEY, WAR AND THE PRIVATE INVESTOR 108 (1935).

[73] The production and export of rubber in Liberia began prior to Firestone's arrival. It started in the late 1880s with the collection of wild rubber by a British company, which led to the establishment of a rubber plantation in the early 1900s by yet another British company, the Liberian Rubber Corporation. F.P.M. VAN DER KRAAIJ, THE OPEN DOOR POLICY OF LIBERIA: AN ECONOMIC HISTORY OF MODERN LIBERIA 46 (1983).

the *paradox of being a Republic of 12,000 citizens with 1,000,000 subjects*. The distinction between citizens and subjects is not merely a question of the suffrage.
Liberian citizens live under a legislative régime modeled more or less on that of
white countries, a 'civilized' system, while the Liberian subjects live in accordance
with their tribal customs.[74]

During the 1880s, Liberia had been increasingly subjected to territorial pressures by European colonial powers.[75] This period was characterized by military
attempts to control the country and growing economic activity on the part of
foreign traders, bankers, and investors, who showed increasing interest in the
country. In 1871, it entered into a series of loan agreements with British banking
firms, which led to disputes between the two nations, accompanied by British demands that Liberia strengthen its customs administration by appointing British
officials and establish an adequate frontier force under European officers. While
these demands were complied with, the plan for economic improvement was a
failure.[76] Moreover, some commentators describe how the Liberian Government
lost faith in the British as an ally, and turned to the United States for help.[77] In
1912, the U.S. Government facilitated a loan agreement between Liberia and a
group of foreign bankers.[78] The U.S. Administration also intervened to assist
Liberia against a revolt of the Kru tribe in 1915.[79] Partly because of conditions
created by the First World War, the economic situation in Liberia deteriorated.
The government soon became heavily indebted to the local branch of the Bank of
British West Africa and was asked to give the Bank a share in its internal administration to protect its interests. The threat to the country's independence prompted
it, yet again, to seek U.S. assistance. To the Liberian Government's dismay, the
detailed loan agreement signed by the two governments in 1921 failed to meet
the U.S. Senate's approval.[80] When Harvey Firestone's experts arrived in Liberia

---

[74] The Brunot Report as it was published in GREAT BRITAIN, FOREIGN OFFICE, PAPERS CONCERNING
AFFAIRS IN LIBERIA, DECEMBER 1930–MAY 1934, at 54–80 (1934) [hereinafter The Brunot Report].

[75] The 1903 settlement, which defined the Mano River as the boundary with Sierra Leone, reflected
the British annexation of Liberian territories in the years that preceded it. Similarly, France annexed the
area east of the Cavalla River over which Liberia claimed jurisdiction. *See* VAN DER KRAAIJ, *supra* note
73, at 27–37.

[76] Cuthbert Christy, *Liberia in 1930*, 77 GEOGRAPHICAL J. 515, 526 (1931).

[77] 2 RAYMOND LESLIE BUELL, THE NATIVE PROBLEM IN AFRICA 787–89 (1928) described how this
revolt, also known as the Cadell Incident, led the Liberians to distrust the British Government.

[78] As a guarantee that Liberia would meet interest charges and would not fall into the hands of any
single power, the loan agreement provided that Liberian customs should be collected by a General
Receiver, designated by the United States, Britain, and France. The agreement also authorized American
officers to drill the Liberian Frontier Force.

[79] This sequence of affairs is described in Raymond Leslie Buell, *The Reconstruction of Liberia*, 8
FOREIGN POL'Y REP. 120, 121 (1932).

[80] 'As Firestone must have viewed Liberia's finances in 1924, the net result was that the British and
French had been eliminated from the Receivership but controlled a sizable and potentially troublesome
share of the 1912 bonds.' Chalk, *supra* note 69, at 18.

in 1924, the country was submerged in economic instability and threatened by the colonial interests of neighbouring European powers. This precarious set of circumstances paved the way for the agreement between the foreign entrepreneur and the fragile African state.

Negotiating the investment in Liberia

'Everything looks wonderfully favorable for a great development', wrote Firestone to Ford in 1924.[81] In April that year, he sent his personal secretary, William D. Hines, to Washington to inform the State Department of his findings and plans to invest in Liberia.[82] In June, Hines travelled to Monrovia and won the Liberian Government's approval for the drafts of three interconnected agreements. The first agreement concerned the lease of an old rubber plantation; the second gave the company the right to lease up to 1 million acres of rubber-growing land for ninety-nine years; and the third provided that the company would give Liberia $300,000 for the leases.[83]

These initial agreements made no mention of a loan.[84] After obtaining the Liberian principals' consent to the draft agreement in January 1925,[85] Firestone went to Washington to discuss the need for guarantees to protect his large investment in Liberia. His suggestion to the State Department was to gain U.S. control by offering Liberia a loan with conditions similar to those set forth in the unratified 1921 agreement.[86] Following the 1921 pattern, this addition meant assigning all the government's revenues to the service of the $5 million loan, and permitted the U.S. president to name Americans as collectors and disbursers of Liberian Government funds. Firestone personally wanted this control over the administration to secure his large investment. Concerned that Firestone assumed the United States would provide his firm with military support upon request, State Department officials emphasized that no special assurances would be provided: 'It should be clearly understood that there was no question of resort to force. It was a

---

[81] Quoted by LIEF, *supra* note 66, at 242–43.

[82] W.R. Castle Jr., Chief, Division of Western European Affairs, Department of State to Secretary of State, Apr. 8, 1924, 2 USFR, 1925 367.

[83] *See* draft agreements of June 1924, 2 USFR, 1925 369–79.

[84] The addition of a loan agreement might have resulted from pressures exerted by two American officers of the General Receivership who sought to achieve greater power by convincing Firestone to issue a new loan to Liberia. Campaigning for their cause, they met with State Department officials and with Harvey Firestone himself, conveying the need for close political supervision of the Liberian administration, with a view to securing Firestone's investment. Chalk, *supra* note 69, at 18–22.

[85] Raymond L. Buell, *Mr. Firestone's Liberia*, THE NATION, Feb. 2, 1928, at 521.

[86] '[T]he Company felt that in order properly to protect its proposed concessionary interests and the service of the loan, provisions similar to those set forth in the American-Liberian loan agreement of 1921 should be incorporated in their proposed loan agreement and accepted by the government of Liberia.' Memorandum by the Assistant Secretary of State, Harrison, July 8, 1924, 2 USFR, 1925 380.

matter of appropriate diplomatic support.'[87] It is interesting to note that, during the correspondence and meetings between Firestone and State Department officials, Firestone's managers made frequent mention of the involvement of private corporations (such as the United Fruit Company) in Latin America and the Caribbean and expressed the concern that there was not even the protection of the Monroe Doctrine in Liberia.[88]

According to the addition to the loan agreement, known as Clause K, Firestone would lend Liberia $5 million and appoint twenty-two Americans as officials to administer the country's financial, military, and legislative affairs. The addition of Clause K came as a bitter surprise to the Liberian Government. The government's main objection was that it was subjecting itself to the directives of a private firm, since it was the Firestone Company that had issued the loan. The Liberian objections led Firestone to ask for the U.S. Government's assistance. In a telegram to President Coolidge, he wrote: 'I am having difficulty in securing signature of Liberian Government to the rubber planting agreements which were approved by the State Department. I am asking Mr. W. R. Castle for assistance. Knowing your interest in this rubber development I am taking liberty of advising you of the situation.'[89]

In response, the Secretary of State wrote on May 1, 1925, to Solomon Porter Hood, the Minister to Liberia:

> The Department awaits with sympathetic interest the conclusion of the Firestone contracts ... the Department will be willing to give appropriate assistance and at the request of Liberia and of the American interests concerned would be prepared again to assist in the selection of a Receiver General of Customs.[90]

The Liberian government's correspondence with U.S. officials discloses that it was not in favour of an additional loan agreement and preferred to invest in financial rehabilitation. Its initial doubts and hesitations were supported by growing criticism of the Pan African Movement in the United States.[91] British officials also speculated over Firestone's intentions, mostly due to the potential to undermine the already dwindling British interests in Liberia.[92]

The Liberian Government eventually requested that the money for the loan be secured from sources other than a corporation operating in the country.[93]

---

[87]   Memorandum by Leland B. Harrison, Assistant Secretary of State, on a conversation held between Leland B. Harrison, Harvey S. Firestone Sr., and Amos C. Miller on Dec. 12, 1924, 2 USFR, 1925, 386.

[88]   Chalk, *supra* note 69, at 22.

[89]   Mr. Harvey S. Firestone to President Coolidge, April 30, 1925, 2 USFR, 1925 426.

[90]   The Secretary of State to the Minister in Liberia, May 1, 1925, 2 USFR, 1925 427.

[91]   BUELL, *supra* note 77, at 823.

[92]   J. Pal Chaudhuri, *British Reaction to Firestone Investment in Liberia*, 5 LIBER. STUD. J. 25 (1972–74).

[93]   RAYMOND LESLIE BUELL, LIBERIA: A CENTURY OF SURVIVAL, 1847–1947, at 30–31 (1947). As recorded in a telegram from the Minister to Liberia (Hood), May 1, 1925: 'The basic position taken by the Liberian Government on this question is that it is not politically advisable in their opinion to place the

Mr. Firestone solved this problem by setting up a subsidiary called the Finance Corporation of America. Secretary of State Frank B. Kellog urged the Liberian Government to accept Firestone's contracts,[94] and it eventually accepted a narrower version of his proposal.[95] Raymond Leslie Buell, an assistant professor from Harvard University's Department of Government, later attributed the Liberians' final agreement to the growing tensions with the French over the border and the government's fear of losing U.S. support.[96] Three draft agreements with Firestone were submitted to the Liberian legislature in 1925. The agreements and their subsequent amendments established the basic terms and conditions under which the Firestone Company has operated in Liberia for almost a century. In 1926, the Liberian Government entered into a 7 per cent loan agreement of $5 million from the Finance Corporation of America (the Firestone subsidiary). The agreement provided for the liquidation of previous loans and stipulated that no other loan should be accepted by the Liberian Government for twenty years.[97] The agreements provided for the development of Liberia by the construction of a harbour at Monrovia, new hospitals, and communication infrastructures, and for the maintenance of the frontier force.[98]

Republic of Liberia under financial obligations to private interests operating in Liberia under grants from the Liberian government.' 2 USFR, 1925 430. In a subsequent letter, Hood explained the concern of the Liberian Government that changes in the personnel of the Firestone company might take place and the 'Liberian government might have to deal with a very different condition of things than now exists in the Firestone Company.' Letter from Solomon Porter Hood to Frank B. Kellogg, Secretary of State, June 5, 1925, 2 USFR, 1925, 437.

[94] 'Mr. Firestone assures the Department that the company advancing the money for a loan will be separate from the corporation which will be formed to promote rubber development in Liberia ....' Letter from Frank B. Kellog to Solomon Porter Hood, May 22, 1925, 2 USFR, 1925, 432. Kellog reminded the Liberian Minister of the 'traditional policy of good will' that had guided relations between the two governments and mentioned that Firestone had been already negotiating for rubber plantations in other locations.

[95] 'Accordingly, as finally and most reluctantly approved by the Liberian Legislature, the 1926 Loan Agreement provided for an American financial advisor, to be nominated by the President of the United States and appointed by the President of Liberia, and a number of subordinate advisors who were also Americans. These supervisors, though fewer in number and with more limited powers than proposed in 1922, were granted extensive powers over the whole Liberian financial establishment.' TAYLOR, *supra* note 67, at 54.

[96] Buell, *supra* note 85, at 521. 'A tentative agreement on the basic concession was ready by January 1925, but its ratification by the Liberian Legislature was delayed until November 1926 owing to the difficult financial situation confronting Liberia at the time and other matters.' TAYLOR, *supra* note 67, at 47.

[97] Buell critically notes this provision as contradictory to the American Open Door policy. The Open Door policy that envisioned equal economic opportunity for businesses around the world was interpreted as prohibiting exclusive concessions. This was the prevailing perception of American foreign policy at the time. 'The fact that the American Government has encouraged this concession', argues Buell, 'therefore may increase the belief of European governments that the United States is interested in the open door doctrine only when it works to the advantage of American capital.' BUELL, *supra* note 77, at 830–31.

[98] Christy, *supra* note 76, at 527.

Rumours of slavery practices in Liberia

The year 1926 was a crucial one for Liberia. It was during this year that Firestone signed the concession agreement with the Liberian Government, and the Slavery Convention on which the League of Nations had been working since 1922 was completed and signed:

> These two events brought the affairs of Liberia into unaccustomed prominence, for on the one hand the terms of Firestone loan were much attacked by organs of the American press, and on the other hand discussions on African conditions which had preceded the final drafting of the Anti-Slavery Convention had indicated that evil practices were prevalent in Liberia.[99]

In the course of the discussions of the commission deliberating over the Covenant of the League of Nations, 'the government of Liberia had been cited as one of the countries in which conditions of a highly questionable nature existed ... Most of the information was drawn from fragmentary evidence of participating members, from books and other accounts of travelers and students coming to their attention.'[100]

One of the most influential sources for criticism on Liberia was the previously mentioned Harvard professor, Raymond Buell and his two-volume *The Native Problem in Africa*. During 1925 and 1926, the period in which the negotiations over the loan agreements with Firestone were taking place, Buell, carried out fifteen months' research in Africa on the administration in the colonial dependencies south of the Sahara. The results of this investigation were published in 1928. Buell's purpose was not merely descriptive but also to 'teach policy makers how to avoid the development of the acute racial difficulties which have elsewhere arisen'.[101] Although other publications throughout the 1920s reported on the disturbing practices of slavery in Liberia,[102] it was the publication of *The Native Problem in Africa* that triggered international political turmoil.[103] Buell's statements portrayed Firestone and the United States as promoters of forced labour:

---

[99] F.P. WALTERS, A HISTORY OF THE LEAGUE OF NATIONS 568 (1952).

[100] Report of the International Commission of Inquiry into the Existence of Slavery and Forced Labor in the Republic of Liberia, 8 Sept. 1930, Publications of the Department of State, Publication No. 147, at 3-4 (1931) [hereinafter The Christy Report].

[101] Colin Newbury, Book Review, *The Native Problem in Africa by Raymond Leslie Buell*, 8 RACE CLASS 299 (1967).

[102] The Christy Commission mentions other sources with findings similar to Buell's, such as HENRY FENWICK REEVE, THE BLACK REPUBLIC: LIBERIA: ITS POLITICAL AND SOCIAL CONDITIONS TODAY (1923). It further notes that Reeve's account is 'a notable example of the open charges, although it should be stated that the conditions described were founded upon observations made about 25 years ago'. The Christy Report, *supra* note 100, at 4. The report also mentions LADY KATHLEEN SIMO, SLAVERY (1929) but quickly dismisses its findings as cited from second-hand accounts.

[103] According to John Stanfield, State Department officials attempted to discredit Buell by preparing an immediate rebuttal through the Associated Press when Buell's book reached the public. Most of their

Mr. Firestone pays the government and the chiefs for each man recruited one cent per day. While there is no enactment obliging the men to work, the order of the chief is, in fact, law and few dare disobey it. As long as [the] Firestone company makes it financially profitable for the chiefs to supply labor, the available men must work whether they like it or not... It is one of the ironies of history that the Government of the United States should cast the weight of its influence in favor of a system which the French and the British have discarded as harmful to native interests.[104]

But academic publications were not the only catalysts leading to international intervention. Similar accusations were made by Thomas Faulkner, the Liberian presidential nominee, after his defeat in the 1927 presidential election.[105] These challenges were soon echoed in the League, and the allegations against Liberia led to the establishment of a commission of enquiry: the Christy Commission. We will now turn to its report.

Firestone and the League of Nations

The establishment of the Christy Commission

The Christy Commission comprised three members. The chairman (the choice of the president of the Council of the League of Nations) was Dr. Cuthbert Christy, from Britain. Christy, a 'well known naturalist and explorer', was educated in medicine and had extensive experience in the study of diseases in South America, the West Indies, and Africa.[106] His obituary would later describe the importance

efforts to deny the accuracy of Buell's perspective were published in the *New York Times*. John Stanfield, *Introductory Essay: Bitter Canaan's Historical Backdrop, in* CHARLES S. JOHNSON, BITTER CANAAN: THE STORY OF THE NEGRO REPUBLIC, at xi, xix (2000).

[104] Buell, *supra* note 85, at 521–24.
[105] In June 1929, Faulkner not only accused Charles King, the elected president, of allowing slavery to exist in Liberia, but also claimed that government officials were engaged in the forced shipping of labourers to Fernando Po. In July 1929, Faulkner repeated his charges in *The Baltimore Afro-American*. The U.S. Secretary of State wrote to the chargé in Monrovia that further pressure should be put on the Liberians 'for it is likely that this article will be followed by other public discussion in this country'. Quoted by I.K. SUNDIATA, BLACK SCANDAL: AMERICAN AND THE LIBERIAN LABOR CRISIS, 1929–1936, at 47 (1980).
[106] Christy's experience encompassed roles including that of senior medical officer in Northern Nigeria (1898–1900); member of the Uganda Sickness Commission (1902); assistant lecturer at the Liverpool School of Tropical Medicine (1903); and researcher on sleeping sickness in the Congo (1903–1904). He worked in Ceylon (1906), in Uganda and East Africa (1906–1909), and in Nigeria, the Gold Coast, and the Cameroons (1909–1910). IBRAHIM SUNDIATA, BROTHERS AND STRANGERS: BLACK ZION, BLACK SLAVERY 1914–1940, at 132 (2003). Christy published a technical book on the African rubber industry in 1911 and worked on natural history for the Belgian Government in the Congo. During the First World War, he researched malaria and sleeping sickness in Mesopotamia, the Sudan, and the Congo. At the end of the war, Dr. Christy was awarded the Royal Geographical Medal for

of the Commission to Christy's lifelong work in Africa: 'It can safely be said that, of all public work performed by Mr. Christy, there was none more useful than his chairmanship of the Liberian Commission, and those who knew him realized the great importance he attached to his work in this connection.'[107] The Liberian appointee to the Commission was Sir Arthur Barclay, ex-President of Liberia, who was deeply immersed in Liberian politics.[108] On his retirement, Barclay practised law and counted Firestone among his clients.[109] The United States appointed Dr. Charles Spurgeon Johnson, an African-American sociologist and expert in race relations who had headed Fisk University's department of social research since 1927. Johnson's service on the Commission was the impetus behind an intellectual endeavour that would hold his attention for nearly twenty years: the writing of *Bitter Canaan*.[110]

In 1930, the Commission members travelled to Liberia, where they heard witness testimonies by indigenous people and government officials and were able to examine public and private documents to contribute to their findings. The Commission's mandate was broader than the investigation of the slave trade. The members defined their assignment as part of a greater involvement on the part of the League of Nations in outlawing slavery and forced labour. Accordingly, their concluding report, published on 8 September 1930, was divided into two main sections: 'Slavery and Analogous Practices' (subdivided into 'Common or classic slavery' and 'Oppressive practices restrictive of the freedom of persons, constituting conditions analogous to slavery and tending to acquire the status of classic slavery'); and 'Forced and Compulsory Labor' (subdivided into 'Forced labor for public purposes' and 'Forced labor for private enterprise').

In its discussion of common or classic slavery, the Commission found that this practice, as defined in the Slavery Convention, existed in Liberia in many forms of inter- and intra-tribal relationship, but distinguished such relationships from 'classic' slavery.[111] The Commission dedicated most of its discussion to the system

---

his explorations in Central Africa. In the years preceding his service in Liberia, he was employed in Tanganyika (1925–1928) and in French Equatorial and West Africa (1928–1929). *Id.*

[107] Obituary, *Dr. Cuthbert Christy*, 31 J. ROYAL AFR. SOC. 339 (1932).

[108] Sir Arthur Barclay was the father-in-law of President King and the uncle of Secretary of State Edwin Barclay, later to be appointed president in the aftermath of the Christy Report.

[109] SUNDIATA, *supra* note 106, at 132.

[110] Johnson was not the first choice of the State Department. Initially, the State Department asked Howard University treasurer Emmett Scott to serve on the Commission. Scott refused the assignment. Some attribute his refusal to his alleged involvement in lobbying for the U.S. Government on behalf of the 1921 Liberian loan. In 1926, Johnson accepted the position of the Chair of the Sociology Department at Fisk University at Nashville. Twenty years later he became the first African American President of that university. For further discussion, *see* Personal, *Charles Spurgeon Johnson*, 42 J. NEGRO HIST. 149 (1957); Andrea Jackson, *Bibliographical Note, in* A GUIDE TO THE CHARLES S. JOHNSON COLLECTION (1–27), 1935–1956, FISK UNIVERSITY ARCHIVES 2–3 (2004). Stanfield, *supra* note 103, at iv. The book was written intermittently between 1930 and 1948, but not published until 1987.

[111] The Christy Report, *supra* note 100.

of enslavement exercised by the Americo-Liberians through the native system of pawning. The report further described the slave trade from Liberia to the Spanish colony of Fernando Po.[112] The Commission concluded that:

> it is quite clear that force has been relied upon for numbers; that the blind eagerness for private profit has carried the traffic to a point scarcely distinguishable from slavery; and that only by help of the instruments and offices of government could the traffic have reached such tragic effectiveness.[113]

For our purposes, it is important to note that, although initially a governmental endeavour, the slave trade was an enterprise involving both public officials and private interests (the *Syndicate Agricola de Guinea*).[114]

The last part of the report dealt with forced labour. The Commission found that the Liberian Government was using native forced labour to build an extensive network of roads and for construction and maintenance of government buildings. As regards forced labour for private enterprise, the report divided discussion into two sub-topics: labourers who were forced to work for high government officials who owned plantations producing rubber, coffee, cocoa, rice, or vegetables; and labourers who worked for the Firestone Plantation Company.

As later records show, the Christy Commission's report was mostly written by Johnson; his views are therefore particularly important in deciphering its underlying assumptions. Johnson was critical of Christy's naïve stance towards the indigenous population in Liberia and his anti-Firestone, anti-American point of view.[115] As the reading of *Bitter Canaan* reveals, Johnson believed that the primary problems of Americo-Liberians were economic in nature, and suggested their economic dependence was the main cause for their use of forced labour. Johnson did not question either Firestone's or the U.S. Government's motives in the region. His main focus was on Firestone's impact on Liberian labour policies and the Republic's

---

[112] The Christy Commission calculated that averaging 600 slaves shipped per year from 1914 to 1927. The serious need for labour in Fernando Po led two representatives of private interests on the island, Edward Baticon and Emanuel Gonzerosa, to offer a generous contract to interested parties in Liberia. A Mr. Samuel A. Ross was sought as the principal party to the new contract. The result was a private agreement between the Sindicato Agrícola de Guinea and a group of Liberian citizens. *Id.* at 22–70.

[113] *Id.* at 69.

[114] The Christy Commissioners reported on their encounter with Mr. Ross, writing: 'Mr. Ross said to me, this year I am going to make some money. I asked him in what way. He said I am going to do so by shipping some boys to Fernando Po. Mr. Ross said that the Spanish needed 3,000 boys but that the President [of Liberia] told him to share the number with Mr. Yancy [a public official].' *Id.* at 55.

[115] Johnson wrote that 'Christy manifested negative attitudes about American interests. In particular, he posed questions for the express purpose of uncovering Firestone involvement in encouraging the use of slave labor.' CHARLES S. JOHNSON, AFRICAN DIARY 205–07 (1947). For further discussion, *see* Philip James Johnson, Seasons in Hell: Charles S. Johnson and the 1930 Liberia Labor Crisis (2004) (unpublished PhD dissertation, Graduate Faculty of the Louisiana State University and Agricultural and Mechanical College, on file with author).

political economy.[116] In general, *Bitter Canaan* put forward a new approach to the problems of Liberia. It was unsympathetic to the Americo-Liberian elite and urged that the structure of Americo-Liberian leadership be reformed, allowing the indigenous population greater participation and voice. Johnson argued that the planned return of displaced sons and daughters to Liberia had failed. The country had not fulfilled its promise of becoming 'Black Zion', a destination of return for the population of African black slaves who were now free. The freed slaves turned into settlers and soon replicated the oppressive measures used against their ancestors to dominate the African indigenous communities they encountered in Liberia:

> Since the coming of the Black Americans, the Webbos' guns had been taken away, their age-old methods of settling their differences stiffly penalized, and their proud chiefs humbled and confused by strange courts of law. With each insult they had appealed to these new laws and, just as often, got impatient replies about being weaklings and eternal nuisances to civilized government.[117]

Johnson's views, as they were articulated in his publications, echoed the general argument conveyed by the Christy Report. The report focused on the complicity of the Liberian Government in the slave trade in Fernando Po and its involvement in forced labour. It harshly criticized the Liberian elite and their methods of governance, while giving a voice to the indigenous population who suffered under them.

Firestone and the Christy Report

How did Firestone's involvement in Liberia reach the corridors of the League of Nations and find itself subject to the investigations of the Christy Commission? One explanation can be found in Raymond Buell's writings on the Liberian Republic. Buell devoted three long chapters in *The Native Problem in Africa* to the involvement of the Firestone Company in the region. Buell attacked the State Department for compromising its open-door policy in favour of Firestone's interests, and suggested U.S. policies were equivalent to those of other imperial powers: 'In encouraging the Firestone activities in Liberia ... [i]n this struggle between the European plantation and the native small-farm school the United States has apparently thrown its influence against the native farmer in favor of the outside capitalist.'[118]

Whether Buell's detailed descriptions of the compulsory labour practices associated with the Firestone plantations led to the firm's inclusion under the

---

[116] Stanfield, *supra* note 103, at liv–lv.
[117] JOHNSON, *supra* note 103, at 6.
[118] BUELL, *supra* note 77, at 831.

Commission's jurisdiction is hard to determine. Some argue that Firestone had an interest in the investigation, since the private trade in Liberian labour 'competed with Firestone's access to workers and, more important, diluted its influence in Liberian politics'.[119] However, even without Firestone's direct interest in the investigation, its inclusion under the jurisdiction of the Commission, at least as 'subject matter', seems logical. The concession and the loan agreement made the Firestone Company a (if not *the*) prominent factor in the Liberian economy. In addition, the presence of the U.S. corporation created the public impression of a strong U.S. involvement in Liberian affairs. This impression was a valid one, given the concession's requirement that U.S. officials oversee the governance of the Liberian economy and the close relationship between Firestone and the State Department.

In the section of the Commission's report dealing with the Firestone Company, it followed the normative framework established in the Slavery Convention. Hence, it investigated the extent to which compulsory labour existed as a factor in the social and industrial economy of the state, either for public or private purposes, and, if it did, in what manner it was recruited and whether it was employed for public or private purposes. In its findings on 'Forced Labour for Private Enterprise', the Commission's emphasis was on the fact that most instances of slavery and abuse of labour it witnessed derived from the involvement of public, rather than private, actors. The Commission noted that the Firestone Company was the only large private enterprise in Liberia, and its account of Firestone's initial operations in Liberia was critical: 'The precipitous character of the company's pioneering operations in Liberia, the unfamiliarity of its employees with African conditions, the unsuitableness of its equipment and outfit, and the inexperience in the control of primitive labor all created difficulties which it took many months to get in front of.'[120]

The report further described Firestone's 1926 reinterpretation of the parts of the agreement dealing with the labour supply. The Commission's criticism was aimed at recruitment methods, specifically the change in recruitment policy from direct to indirect control.[121] The Commission supplied evidence that labourers who were on their way to work for the Firestone Company were turned back by interior officials or retained to carry out government projects instead. '[T]here was no choice given to the labourer for selecting his work, or to the Company for selecting its workers.'[122] The report cited the reply of a worker who was asked whether he liked

---

[119] Aric Putnam, *'Modern Slaves': The Liberian Labor Crisis and the Politics of Race and Class*, 9 RHETORIC & PUB. AFF. 235, 238 (2006).

[120] The Christy Report, *supra* note 100, at 122.

[121] In 1927, the government restricted the number of labourers who might be employed from each of the hinterland districts. 'The most serious aspect of this new policy', argued the Commission, 'was the shifting of direct control of labour registration and the Company's recruiting efforts from the Labour Bureau to the remote and out-of-hand District Commissioners. These Commissioners required, and with Government approval, a fee of one-half cent per man per day, and this principle became the focus of one of the most serious complaints of the natives.' *Id.* at 79.

[122] *Id.* at 80.

working for the Firestone Company: We like working for Mr. Firestone and any man who pays us for our labour. The reason we do not like to go to Firestone is if Mr. ___ (an official) hears you are [working] on the Firestone [plantation,] he goes there and get the money you worked for.'[123]

The Commission further noted labourers' frequent assertions that, when they were recruited and sent to work on the plantation, they received no pay, while the company's payroll sheets indicated each labourer received his monthly wages. The Commission described the difficult conditions and pressures the Firestone Company faced in sourcing labour.[124] Harvey S. Firestone Jr., who was appointed by his father to administer the plantation in Liberia, wrote to the President of Liberia of the company's desire to employ any labourers it deemed necessary, without first having to obtain the government's permission. 'Such labor so employed shall be free to bargain for its terms and conditions of employment with the company.'[125] His wishes, however, were not fulfilled. The Commission concluded that '[t]here is no evidence that the Company forcibly impresses labour or consciously employs labour which has been forcibly impressed. Contracts are no longer given out to independent contractors, and there is no contract arrangement between the company and the labourers who are free to terminate their service at will.'[126]

In an academic essay published simultaneously with the Christy Report, Cuthbert Christy discussed more openly his views on the responsibility of the Firestone Company:

Lack of knowledge of the special conditions existing in tropical Africa led the employees of the Firestone Plantations Company into difficulties both with the Government and the Natives during their early operations, but when experience was gained better conditions prevailed, and no compulsory or unpaid labor was allowed on their plantations. The Company has not been in any way responsible for the serious labour conditions which have recently been exposed in connection with road and other works in Liberia.[127]

Other, less favourable, accounts followed a different line. An investigation carried out by the ILO Conference in Geneva in 1929 reported that the Firestone plantations used forced labour 'in practice'.[128] Raymond Buell pointed out the

---

[123] *Id.* at 81.

[124] Commentators suggest that the company maintained an annual rate of employment of about 8,000 men in the period 1926–1930. Arthur J. Knoll, *Firestone's Labor Policy, 1924–1939,* 16 LIBER. STUD. J. 49, 55 (1991).

[125] Letter from Harvey S. Firestone, Jr. to C.T.O. King, Dec. 2, 1926, quoted in R. EARLE ANDERSON, LIBERIA: AMERICA'S AFRICAN FRIEND 136 (1952).

[126] The Christy Report, *supra* note 100, at 83.

[127] Christy, *supra* note 76, at 527.

[128] Quoted by Jules Charles Horwitz, A Case Study of the Firestone Tire and Rubber Company in Liberia 46 (1959) (unpublished M.A. Thesis, Faculty of the Division of the Social Sciences in Candidacy

unreasonableness of Firestone's requirement (in its agreement with Liberia) to employ 350,000 men, when 'the total able-bodied male population of Liberia [was] only between three hundred thousand and four hundred thousand'.[129] Moreover, Buell quoted a report by the labour bureau (the entity responsible for recruiting labourers for Firestone), according to which Firestone paid directly to the chiefs 'one cent a day for each boy, and the same sum to the Government Bureau'. He concluded:

> Thus, under this system, which is similar to that which produced wholesale compulsory labor in other parts of Africa, the Firestone Plantations Company is making it financially worth while for the government and for the chiefs to keep the plantations supplied ... As Liberian officials and chiefs are already accustomed to imposing compulsion ... there is no reason to believe that they will employ different methods in obtaining labor for the Firestone Plantation.[130]

The Christy Report was later criticized in the journal *International Labour Review* for its reluctance to fully investigate the impact of Firestone's large-scale operation on the Liberian population:

> At present the number of labourers required by Firestone Rubber Plantations is not large ... But the situation will need careful watching when the progress in development leads to a considerable increase in the demand for labour, and the future labour policy of Liberia should not be definitely laid down until the labour possibilities of the country have been fully and scientifically investigated from the point of view of the welfare of the Native inhabitants.[131]

From slavery to forced labour, from private to public: Firestone's responsibility dwindles

In less than half a decade, international legislation shifted its lens from the abolition of slavery to the Convention on Forced Labor. It was during this transition that the Christy Commission launched its investigation and report. The distinction between public and private practices was central to the Commission's analysis.

---

for the Degree of Master of Arts, Committee on International Relations, University of Chicago) (on file with author).

[129] Buell concluded, 'it is difficult to believe that despite the persuasive powers of Firestone recruiters and of the Liberian government, Mr. Firestone will be able to place under his employ—to the exclusion of other employers of the entire adult male population of the country'. BUELL, *supra* note 77, at 833.

[130] BUELL, *supra* note 77, at 834.

[131] Anonymous, *Slavery and Forced Labour in Liberia*, 26 INT'L LAB. REV. 417, 419–20 (1932).

Classification as either public or private marked who was to be held responsible. In fact, it was the Christy Commission members who clearly stated that:

> A very wide distinction is everywhere drawn between forced labour for public purposes and forced labour for private employers, and the Slavery Convention accentuates this difference. Moreover, it seems universally agreed that the latter is not permissible. Almost all legislation on the subject of forced labour forbids it. In Liberia, however, it seems still to be freely made use of.[132]

While conceding there was a complete prohibition on private forced labour, the Commission focused on the responsibility of *public* officials for such practices, without implying any responsibility on the part of private employers.[133] Firestone was not the only private enterprise excluded from the discussion. Private firms created by Liberian Government officials and private entrepreneurs who governed the slave trade through Fernando Po were also conspicuously absent.[134]

The Christy Commission attributed the Liberian Government's difficulties in meeting the administrative requests made by the Firestone Company to its being a young country.[135] In presenting this particular interpretation, the Commission positioned the Liberian Government as the responsible actor in dealing with

---

[132] The Christy Report, *supra* note 100, at 74.

[133] Firestone's managers' struggle over recruitment policies was accompanied by a serious fall in the price of rubber in 1929. The latter led the company to curtail its activities in Liberia during that year. Buell, *supra* note 79, at 123. As noted by the Christy Commission: 'Present operations require about 10,000 laborers, but during the past year the company has reduced its force, including both native workers and Americans. One fact of possible significance in this connection is the extraordinary decline in the price of rubber-growing areas … it is not so evident at present that the gigantic new acreage will yield either the profits or savings at first anticipated.' The Christy Report, *supra* note 100, at 131. In addition, once the ground had been cleared and the rubber trees planted, there was a period of relative inactivity until the crops grew, which also contributed to reducing the number of workers needed for the plantation: 'It is now only a question of keeping the ground clear and letting trees grow normally; very little labour, is therefore, required.' The Brunot Report, *supra* note 74, at 64. It nonetheless warned: 'The plantation, however, will soon be ready for tapping, and the labour problem will then become serious, as a large number of trained gatherers will be regularly required.' *Id.*

[134] According to the Commission's historical account, practices of forced labour were abolished as a result of Europeans' realization of their failure to settle and colonize Africa: 'Almost all legislation on the subject of forced labour forbids it. In Liberia, however, it seems still to be freely made use of. Twenty years ago the issue was one of daily discussion in tropical African administrative circles, and not Africa alone … Cases of abuse and ill-treatment accumulated to such an extent and the government became so frequently involved that the whole policy had to be studied afresh and revised. Then came the realization of the vital fact that Europeans could not themselves settle permanently in and colonize tropical Africa, even at considerable altitudes; nor could they succeed at all in any undertaking of the development of the interior, without the willing cooperation of the native population.' The Christy Report, *supra* note 100, at 74.

[135] '[T]he parental relations of the American Government to the Republic [of Liberia] since its founding through the efforts of the American Colonization Society afforded an added reason for Liberia being of this small independent Negro state, its undeveloped resources, its burden of loans from which little public benefit had been derived and its struggles to prevent territorial aggression, all reflected themselves in early days of company in safeguard required by the Government of the Republic against undue control over the administrative affairs….' *Id.* at 121.

violations of international law in its territory, thus confirming its status as a sovereign entity and a subject of international law. Nevertheless, Liberia was viewed as a state in transition, not yet developed and needing to 'endeavor progressively and as soon as possible to put an end to the practice'.[136] The country is thus portrayed as something of a hybrid in the Commission's account: both a colonial state exercising its power illegitimately against the local communities under its rule and simultaneously a not-yet-developed state.

The colonial setting that informed both conventions proved problematic in attempts to address the Liberian circumstances. The conventions presumed a strong colonial power capable of intervening in the inappropriate practices of private enterprises. But the Liberian context introduced a shift from the previous triangle of empire, chartered company, and local communities to that of a strong state, a private company, and a weaker state. The differences in the shift from informal imperialism to this new modality are not overly dramatic. The U.S. Government officials involved in the case were mostly supportive of Firestone. Many considered the penetration of U.S. businesses into overseas raw material markets an important element in U.S. foreign policy and actively welcomed Firestone's African endeavour. Yet despite this support, not all Firestone's wishes were fulfilled. The administration cautiously abstained from engaging in gunboat diplomacy. More importantly, the symbolic importance of Liberia to Americans and the notion of United States responsibility for its fate put the U.S. Government in a complicated position, between its sympathy towards Firestone and its commitment to Liberia. As for the relationship between the Liberian Government and Firestone, given the power balance between them, it is doubtful that the government was capable of introducing limitations on the private enterprise's labour policies. The Christy Commission's conclusions indicated that the government was not merely unable but also unwilling to so exercise its authority.

The sense of a shifting modality is furthered by the growing importance of the concession agreement to the relationship between political and economic actors. This was not an agreement between a chartered company and an indigenous leadership. Rather, it involved an American corporate actor, operating as a private enterprise, morally and politically supported by its government, in the territory of another, fundamentally weaker, sovereign state. Indeed, the Liberian Government itself was involved—both directly and indirectly—in forced labour, slave trade, and practices of slavery. To these features we may add the bureaucratization of the labour process (*i.e.* the administration of labour in the company's records) and the Christy commissioners' reliance on these items as evidence. It was precisely these features—the indirect recruitment and the absence of the recruited labourers from the records of the company—that rendered slavery invisible.

---

[136] The Slavery Convention, Art. 5.

The Christy Commission's report put an end to the slave trade to Fernando Po. Other practices, however, especially the troubling methods used for labour recruitment, continued to be an integral part of life in Liberia. In particular, Firestone's choice to accede to the dubious recruitment policies would impact the inhabitants of Liberia in the following decades. The Christy Report and the investigations that followed revived the debate over Firestone's investment in Liberia, and they complicate our understanding of its role. As the Firestone plantation took root in Liberian soil, the seeds of a lasting relationship between Firestone and the Liberian people were sown.

From the Regulation of Labour to the Regulation of the Concession

'Liberia was, financially speaking, a slave.'

The Brunot Report

An article in the *Economist*, published on 17 January 1931, concluded:

It is an ironical fact that when the League first took up the question of slavery several years ago, there was the customary accusation that it was looking for things that did not exist. Few, however, could have realized the appalling conditions which the International Commission has now made known, and the miserable natives are entitled to expect international protection. The United States Government evidently intend[s] to take energetic action, and the Members of the League will surely do likewise.[137]

As a direct outcome of the Christy Report, Vice-President of Liberia, Allen N. Yancy, and several Cabinet members were impeached. President King resigned, though his party—the True Whig Party—remained in power. Secretary of State Edwin Barclay (nephew of ex-president and Christy Commission member Arthur Barclay) was made interim president in December 1930. The criticism of the Christy Commission over the Liberian Government's involvement in slavery and forced labour practices was followed by a revolt against the Barclay administration, which, while suppressed, severely shook the latter's authority.[138]

Following the publication of the report in Geneva and simultaneously in America, the British Foreign Office requested that the matter be placed on the agenda of the January 1931 League Council. A Council committee was established

---

[137] ECONOMIST, Jan. 17, 1931, at 105–06.
[138] Buell, *supra* note 79, at 127.

to effect the Christy Commission's recommendations. The committee consisted of government representatives of eight member countries, and it authorized a non-member, the United States, to take part in its meetings.[139] The committee met in London and Geneva under the chairmanship first of Mr. Arthur Henderson (then British Foreign Secretary) and later of Lord Robert Cecil. At the London meetings, a committee of experts was appointed, headed by Mr. Henry Brunot, a French lawyer. Its recommendations, set out in what was known as the Brunot Report, were completed in September 1931, approved in principle in Geneva,[140] and published in May 1932. The cooperation between the League and the United States was considered 'very close' by scholars and diplomats familiar with the committee's work.[141]

U.S. involvement in Liberia was not limited to formal efforts under the auspices of the League of Nations. Behind the scenes, the U.S. State Department was considering different policies, while handling increasing demands on the part of Harvey Firestone Sr. for further intervention in Liberian policy-making. In a memorandum summarizing his conversation with the elder Firestone, Henry L. Stimson, the American Secretary of State, alluded to Firestone's concerns over the Liberian Government's competence in managing its affairs, and his expectations of U.S. intervention:

> Mr. Firestone ended up saying that the Liberian people were unable to handle their own affairs; that they must be controlled; that they were sinking down and down and there was nothing but anarchy ahead of them. He said the responsibility was always recognized to be ours and the time would probably come when Barclay would make a proposal to compromise and he hoped we would not accept it. I said I should not be in favor of accepting any compromise that did not have as its condition absolute authority commensurate with the responsibility, but I told him frankly I saw no likelihood of the American government being willing to assume responsibility in Liberia, across the Atlantic; that I thought that would have to be eventually handled by the League of Nations with such advice or help as we can give them, whatever that might be.[142]

---

[139] The invitation was accepted by Secretary of State Henry Stimson on 3 February. League of Nations Doc. C. L. 3, 1931, VI, at 582. Mr. Samuel Reber Jr., then the American chargé d'affaires in Liberia, was named the representative of the United States and was instructed to proceed at once from Monrovia to Geneva. He sat on an equal status with the members of the Council thus constituted into a special committee of inquiry. Clarence A. Berdahl, *International Affairs: Relations of the United States with the Council of the League of Nations*, 26 AM. POL. SCI. REV. 497, 502 (1932). The committee was initially composed of representatives from Great Britain, France, Germany, Italy, Spain, Poland, Venezuela, and Liberia. After Venezuela withdrew from the Council, it was replaced by Panama.

[140] Mr. Reber attended the meetings of the Council committee and 'expressly approved the plan, on behalf of the United States, and indicated that he expected to continue his collaboration with the committee until its work should be completed.' Berdahl, *supra* note 139, at 503.

[141] *Id.*

[142] Memorandum of an interview with Harvey Firestone, Dec. 10, 1930, 3 USFR, 1930, 387–88.

The aftermath of the publication of the Christy Report saw a gradual transition in the League's approach to the problems confronting Liberia. The need for change, clearly captured in the findings and recommendations of the Brunot Report, had also been conveyed by Liberia's permanent delegate to the League, Mr. Antoine Sottile, who argued:

> Liberia was, financially speaking, a slave ... The energies of the Liberian people are paralyzed—not by the Government of Liberia—not by the Liberian people, not by the world economic situation, and not by the soil of Liberia ...The cause is due to other factors ...[143]

The Brunot Report soon defined these 'other factors' as the conditions of the 1926 concession agreements with Firestone.[144] The second committee of investigation into Liberia under Dr. Brunot's chairmanship recommended 'the abolition of the Liberian Government's obligation under the 1926 contracts to recruit labor for the Firestone plantations'.[145] In addition, it suggested a system of far-reaching administrative and financial assistance to Liberia, to be implemented through advisors appointed by the League, amounting to virtual temporary control of Liberia by the League.[146]

While the Christy Report did not find Firestone directly responsible for practices of forced labour, the execution of the proposed reforms was very much dependent upon the firm's cooperation. The Brunot Report shifted the focus from the issue of slavery and forced labour to the economic situation in Liberia in general. 'Liberia's financial situation is tragic', it noted; '[s]he has no budget, no accounts, no money ... economically and financially, Liberia is *in imminent danger*.'[147] It concluded that the main problems arose from the centrality of the Firestone plantations in the Liberian economy and the conditions of the loan contract. The Brunot Committee acknowledged that '[n]o financial group, it is true, would have agreed to lend money to Liberia at a cheaper rate, but the advantage of the loan to the lenders was undoubtedly that they secured a large concession on very favourable terms'.[148] The report continued: 'Naturally, such a level could be reached only when Liberia has recovered economically, and it cannot do so without financial aid from abroad. *The result is a vicious circle*, from which there is no escape except by modifying the terms of the loan.'[149]

---

[143] 12 LEAGUE OF NATIONS O. J., no. 2, 1931, at 192.
[144] The Brunot Report, *supra* note 74.
[145] Ursula Phalla Hubbard, *The Cooperation of the United States with the League of Nations 1931–1936*, 18 INT'L CONCILIATION 295, 350, 355 (1937).
[146] Berdahl, *supra* note 139, at 502–03.
[147] The Brunot Report, *supra* note 74, at 65.
[148] *Id.*
[149] *Id.* at 66.

In short, the Committee held the League of Nations responsible for solving the problems raised by the presence of the Firestone plantations in Liberia. Its main concern, however, was not the labour conditions per se but the credit conditions that posed grave difficulties for the Liberian Government. In particular, it noted that the Firestone Concession required the Liberian Government to adapt itself to the company's needs:

> In the opinion of certain members of the Committee, the coexistence in Liberia of a weak State and a powerful foreign undertaking gives rise to disadvantages … It seems to those members of the Committee that it is the duty of the League of Nations to use all means at its disposal in order to find a solution of the problem on a sound basis, taking into account of the fact that the loan contract and the Firestone concessions form an important element in the difficulty.[150]

The strongest criticism was made by the Spanish committee member Salvador de Madariaga. Madariaga first criticized the Christy Report for its bias: 'Had the report been more impartial, it would have greatly facilitated the preparation of the second report and the Committee's work.'[151] He further criticized the involvement of Firestone in Liberia:

> Whenever a powerful private commercial undertaking interfered in a country which was particularly weak economically and politically there occurred between the economic entity and the political entity a symbiosis which clearly was a very bad thing .[152]

The Brunot Report noted that the rubber contract was very favourable to the lessees. 'At the end of the next five years the Liberian Government will probably receive from the rubber export tax and land rent, only $40,320, an amount which is not sufficient even to pay the officials responsible for the service of the loan.' It thus recommended the conclusion of new agreements between the Liberian Government and Mr. Firestone.[153] In reference to practices of forced labour, the recommendations of the Brunot Report were mostly reminiscent of the normative approach adopted in the 1930 ILO Forced Labour Convention. It noted that the Liberian Government had passed the necessary laws and was now required to put them into force. It recommended that action be gradual, but '[i]t must … be

---

[150] 13 LEAGUE OF NATIONS O. J., no. 3, 1932, at 523, 524.

[151] Id. at 526.

[152] Id. As noted in the Official Journal, 'M. de Madariaga was anxious that his observations should not be regarded as a reproach or criticism, or as indicating any hostility whatever to the firm in question. On the contrary … Nevertheless, in taking action with regard to Liberia, the League of Nations should accept as an essential principle of its work the fact that it was necessary to adapt the firm to Liberia and Liberia to the firm.' Id. at 527.

[153] Buell, supra note 79, at 129.

understood that this period of compromise should not last longer than the time necessary for exploring and penetrating the hinterland.'[154]

It further called for the abolition of all compulsory labour except in the case of communal work on roads and only 'in the territory of the tribe in question. This corresponds both with the customs of the natives and with the provisions of the Convention on forced labour which Liberia has ratified.'[155] It stressed that the rights of the indigenous population to its land and the products of its labour should be guaranteed.[156] In considering Firestone's involvement in the Liberian economy, the report stated that it was a great achievement 'due to the large capital and the really remarkable energy and effort displayed'. Nonetheless, it warned that, when the plantations became ready for tapping, the labour problem would become serious.[157]

The Council Committee's report addressing the Brunot Report drew up a plan of assistance. The execution of the plan required primarily the initiation of new negotiations over the loan agreement, without which none of the suggested reforms could be executed. The Brunot Committee stressed the need to ensure that the proper financial administration would be invested with the power to provide practical assistance and not merely advice.[158] The loan contract between the Liberian Government and the American Finance Corporation (controlled by Firestone) forbade the former to borrow elsewhere without the lender's permission. As F.P. Walters (a high-ranking official of the League of Nations who later wrote a book on its history) observed:

> [r]eforms could not be carried out without money ... [t]he only chance was to try and reach a new agreement with the Corporation; more than half of the loan was still unissued, and the residual sum would easily meet the need ... [however] negotiations with the Finance Corporation had hung fire: neither the Corporation, nor the government, really wished to see the plan put into effect.[159]

In response to the deadlock, the Liberian Government made its strongest protest thus far: it enacted a moratorium on Firestone's loan.[160] As for Firestone, it took the corporation until the summer of 1933 to agree to the modifications in the contract that the Brunot Report had proposed nearly two years earlier.[161]

---

154 The Brunot Report, *supra* note 74, at 66.
155 *Id.*
156 *Id.* at 67.
157 Buell, *supra* note 79, at 129.
158 The Brunot Report, *supra* note 74, at 78–80.
159 WALTERS, *supra* note 99, at 570.
160 Until its revenues reached $650,000 annually for two consecutive years.
161 Another example was the U.S. requirement to appoint an American as a chief advisor who would have the power to arbitrate disputes between the Liberian Government and the Firestone Company. This requirement was eventually abandoned.

The League's limited capacity to intervene exposed

The political initiatives that followed the publication of the Brunot Report were not limited to the formal attempts of the League to institute reforms in Liberia. Behind the scenes, another controversy ensued regarding the possibility of extending the power of the League to control Liberia still further. Some historical records suggest a lively debate over the possibility of making Liberia a League mandate, perhaps administered by the United States, Italy, or Germany.[162]

Similarly complex was the U.S. position throughout this period. The State Department, for example, found itself caught between the League and the Firestone Company. Its willingness to cooperate with the League was not unconditional. Mostly due to British pressure, the Department gradually withdrew its insistence on certain aspects of the suggested reservations (such as an American advisor). However, its agents hesitated to exert pressure on Firestone to comply with the League's requirements. Stimson asked his British colleague whether:

> if the situation were reversed, you would not find great difficulty in putting pressure on a British corporation that was the only real influence for civilization in an ill-governed tropical community to modify its contracts and advance yet further money in support of a plan until they were fully satisfied that their interests would be adequately protected.[163]

Accordingly, despite its final endorsement of the League of Nations plan, the U.S. Administration collaborated with Firestone to postpone his initiation of new negotiations. Nevertheless, while reluctant to pressure Firestone to cooperate with the League, the State Department maintained its objection to Firestone's pressure for a military intervention in Liberia.[164] The inability of the League to influence Firestone's Finance Corporation was quite evident:

---

[162] For a detailed account of the discussions in the British parliament and foreign ministry and the League, *see* MICHAEL D. CALLAHAN, A SACRED TRUST: THE LEAGUE OF NATIONS AND AFRICA 1929–1946, at 52–62 (2004). In addition to these private governmental discussions paralleling the League's formal debate, non-governmental organizations also tried to influence the course of affairs. The involvement of these groups in lobbying in the League is carefully documented in SUNDIATA, *supra* note 105, at 151.

[163] Henry L. Stimson, the American Secretary of State, to Gibson, Sept. 25, 1932, USFR (The British Commonwealth, Europe, Near East, and Africa), 1932, 758.

[164] In the concluding days of the Hoover administration, Firestone tried to convince the State Department that a British conspiracy was being orchestrated against him, attempting to do away with rubber plantations in Liberia. In a series of meetings with officials at the State Department, Harvey Firestone and his son Harvey Firestone Jr. demanded U.S. military intervention to Liberia to show its administration that 'America was prepared to stand for its rights'. Despite the sympathy of President Hoover to his plea, the State Department maintained its objection and tried to convince Firestone to collaborate with the League. Its efforts were of limited success. SUNDIATA, *supra* note 105, at 165–69.

The members of the Council were disappointed when advised later that the Finance Corporation would not begin negotiations until November, Viscount Cecil having said that this was a strange attitude for a commercial body to assume towards the League of Nations, and he thought that the Committee of the Council was surely entitled to more courteous treatment.[165]

The Finance Corporation eventually agreed to the League's suggested modifications in October 1933. The Liberian Government refused to concede, requesting further consideration of certain points. At its next session, in May 1934, the Council formally resolved that Liberia had rejected the plan of assistance and that its offer was therefore withdrawn: 'Thus, the three-year effort of the League of Nations and the United States to put Liberia on its feet came to naught. Liberia had succeeded in playing off the League, the United States and Firestone against each other, and the Liberian governing class had won.'[166]

A member of the Council:

took the occasion and declared that Liberia had grossly failed to honour the obligation laid on all Members of the League by Article 23(b) of the League, to secure the just treatment of the native inhabitants of territories under their control: and that the League would be quite entitled to expel her from membership.[167]

Liberia assured the Council of its intention to execute at least part of the plan: 'These efforts were not sustained for long but no further appeal appeared upon the agenda of the League.'[168] By 1934, the League's initiatives had completely waned; its inability to achieve reforms in Liberia remained a great disappointment in the eyes of many. But was it a total failure for Liberians? In fact, Liberia's membership in the League bought it time and rendered the country insusceptible to direct control by other countries and immune from attempts to compromise its sovereignty. Intriguingly, the League of Nations' relationship with Ethiopia was similarly caught between dialectic forces. However, for Ethiopia, unlike Liberia, this dialectic resulted in a trap rather than a safe haven.[169]

As the international chapter in their relationship came to an end, the Firestone Company and its host state began to acknowledge the need to combine efforts. In

---

[165] Hubbard, *supra* note 145, at 358.

[166] BUELL, *supra* note 93, at 41.

[167] WALTERS, *supra* note 99, at 571.

[168] *Id.*

[169] The standard of civilization, which was applied to Ethiopia as a condition for its admission to the League of Nations, was that of the suppression of slavery and the slave trade. The admission of Ethiopia had the unintended consequence of leading to the drafting of the 1926 Slavery Convention. In allowing for a transitional period, the Convention, through which abolition of slavery and slave-trading could be sought, provided Ethiopia with the necessary space to suppress these practices. Ironically, it was this identification that Ethiopia was undergoing transition that later served the Italians in justifying their aggression against it and the occupation of its territory in 1936. Allain, *supra* note 18, at 238–43.

1934, Barclay's administration adopted a three-year plan and came to terms with Firestone's interests. By the end of 1935, the United States had recognized President Barclay as the head of the Liberian state, and the British Government followed suit the next year.[170] Exploitation of labour in Liberia, mostly orchestrated by government officials, persisted in the years that followed the Christy investigation, with little redress. Firestone managers continued to cooperate with the Liberian Government in dealing with questionable labour arrangements. According to the arrangement between the government and the company, Firestone's recruiters were to work with district commissioners and local authorities in the procurement of labour.[171] This recruitment system was further institutionalized after the Second World War.[172]

Conflicting African-American voices

Charles Johnson, one of the three members of the Christy Commission, emphasized the responsibility of the Americo-Liberians for the fate of the indigenous peoples in the hinterland and reiterated the capacity of the Liberian people to govern, and in doing so, liberate themselves. As noted earlier, these views were incorporated into the Christy Report that eventually led to the resignation of key political officials. Johnson's insistence on the principle of a government's responsibility for the rights of labourers in its country emphasized the role of the Liberian Government in securing its citizens' freedom from slavery. That choice called on (and perhaps empowered) Liberia, the state of free slaves, to live up to its founders'

---

[170] BUELL, *supra* note 93, at 42–43.

[171] RUSSELL U. MCLAUGHLIN, FOREIGN INVESTMENT AND DEVELOPMENT IN LIBERIA 93–94 (1966). 'The pattern of recruitment developed by Firestone reached its classic form in the 1930s and persisted to the 1960s. Firestone went directly to the source, the villages for manpower. Here company labor recruiters ... dealt directly with clan and paramount chiefs. [Firestone's managers] compensated chiefs through a gift in either coin or kind. The company, employing Liberian English, called the gift "dash." If tendered in coin, "dash" amounted to 1 cent per man per day to chiefs by the company. Firestone advanced a similar sum to the Liberian Labor Bureau.' Knoll, *supra* note 124, at 62. *See also* CHARLES MORROW WILSON, LIBERIA 134 (1947).

[172] As documented in a National Planning Association case study on Liberia, 'Firestone soon discovered that, though Liberians might be attracted to work on the plantations, they often could not leave their native villages without the prior permission of their town, clan, or tribal chiefs. The chiefs were reluctant to consent because they did not wish to lose the unpaid labor ... [t]hus, Firestone was forced to develop a system of compensating the chiefs for lost labor and services.' TAYLOR, *supra* note 67, at 67. The new system required records to be kept of each chief's name, district, section, tribe, and the number of workers he sent to Firestone. This provided further information for recruiters and for tax purposes and involved coercion on the part of local recruiters. Deteriorating health and unpopular housing conditions led Firestone's managers to hire more doctors and provide the workers with the opportunity to conduct their own farming adjunct to their dwellings. Despite these attempts, working conditions were a continuing source of complaint and suffering amongst Firestone's workers. These complaints led the Liberian Government to exert pressure on the company, to little avail. Time and again the Liberian Government backed off from its attempts to persuade Firestone to improve its workers' conditions. Knoll, *supra* note 124, at 61–67.

dream. Johnson's special compassion for the plight of the indigenous communities he had met as a Commission member in Liberia had a lasting impact on his work. Their voices carry significant weight in his later publications, *Shadow of the Plantation*, his 1934 study of black sharecroppers in Alabama, and *Growing Up in the Black Belt* (1941). In a PhD thesis on Johnson's life and work, his grandson sought to correct the historical understanding of his grandfather's mission in Liberia.[173]

Some African-American leaders, such as W.E.B. Du Bois, were more sympathetic towards the Liberian elite and Government than Johnson; they identified the colonial power with the external powers of capital and empire rather than with internal political elites.[174] Du Bois' main published criticisms were aimed initially at the U.S. Administration and later at the Firestone Company:

> I remember standing once in a West African forest where thin, silver, trees loomed straight and smooth in the air. There were two men with me. One was a black man. Solomon Hood, United States Minister to Liberia; a man of utter devotion whose solicitude for the welfare of Liberia was like a sharp pain driving him on. And he thought he had found the solution. The solution was the white man beside us. He was a rubber expert sent by the Firestone corporation.[175]

Writing in *Foreign Affairs*, in 1933, he concluded:

> Liberia is not faultless. She lacks training, experience and thrift. But her chief crime is to be black and poor in a rich white world; and in precisely what portion of the world where color is ruthlessly exploited as a foundation for American and European wealth. The success of Liberia as a Negro Republic will be a blow to the whole colonial slave labor system.[176]

Firestone was not invisible in this account, but the responsibility for curtailing the company's influence was the responsibility of the state. If the Christy Report

---

[173] 'Although Johnson risked his life in Liberia, his role in the League of Nations inquiry met with mixed feelings among fellow African Americans unable to recognize the similarities between their second-class status in the United States and the plight of Liberia's tribal citizens. But as entries in his African journal amply demonstrate, there was much that churned beneath the surface in Johnson that contradicts the image of a self-centered, essentially weak-willed scholar afraid to raise his voice on behalf of society's underdogs. His 1930 League of Nations mission to Liberia, a significant event in African American history during the interwar years, must be viewed as central in shaping the thought of an important but often overlooked African American thinker and scholar.' JOHNSON, *supra* note 115, at 287.

[174] For a critical analysis of DuBois and other African-American leaders' reactions to the Liberian plight in the 1930s, *see* Cedric Robinson, *DuBois and Black Sovereignty: The Case of Liberia*, 32 RACE & CLASS 39 (1990); Tamba E. M'Bayo, *W.E.B. Du Bois, Marcus Gravey, and Pan Africanism in Liberia, 1919-1924*, 66 HISTORIAN 19 (2004).

[175] W.E.B. Du Bois, *Liberia, the League and the United States*, 11 FOREIGN AFF. 682 (1932-1933).

[176] *Id.* at 695.

was a toned-down version of Johnson's views on the Liberian crisis, the League's further involvement in Liberia through the Brunot Report marked a change of sensibility, closer to that conveyed by Du Bois. Firestone's concession with Liberia was a central target for reform alongside the numerous suggestions of governance reforms. On slavery, the Brunot Report concluded: 'the experts on their arrival in Monrovia found that the Liberian Government had already passed laws forbidding slavery and forced labour, and actually the experts found that the exportation of forced labour had been suppressed'.[177] At the same time, the Brunot Report exposed how the abolition of slavery was lost as a political cause at the very moment it was constituted an *inter-state* obligation by the League. 'It is notable', wrote Du Bois, 'that of the 50 pages of report and appendices, only one-third of a page is devoted to the question of slavery, practically the whole report being on economic conditions and the Firestone contract.'[178]

The loss of the abolition of slavery as a political cause

The Slavery and Forced Labour conventions between 1926 and 1934 reflected a denser and more sophisticated regulation of slavery and forced labour than had gone before. Their emphasis on state responsibility implicitly took for granted the capacity of states to exercise effective governance. Although coerced labour for private ends was more rigorously prohibited than forced labour for public ends, there was only the most marginal direct engagement with private actors and their responsibilities. This was particularly devastating where the states charged with responsibility for supervising private actors were largely powerless to do so. Liberia, in this sense, prefigured a broader postcolonial pattern in which the inter-state order rendered the economic exercise of coercion invisible in legal terms.

International lawyers recognized this dilemma, of the mutual interdependence of weak state and unruly corporation, as well as how this relation was enmeshed with other inter-state hierarchies, but had no meaningful way to address it. Some of the voices that might otherwise have been expected to express concern over the suffering of forced labour, such as African-American activists, were preoccupied with dual strategies of propping up Liberia as a black republic and preserving a vessel for political sovereignty, however compromised.

The redefinition of the commitment to combat slavery as an inter-state obligation did not do away with slavery. Indeed, the inter-state regulatory mode of the League introduced a new modality of emancipation and liberation, one that was critically aligned with nationalization movements. However, as the story of

---

[177] Sixty-Sixth Session of the Council (League of Nations). Minutes of 9th Meeting, Feb. 6, 1932 (O.J., March 1932, Part II, p. 525).

[178] Du Bois, *supra* note 175, at 689.

Firestone demonstrates, its normative force came at a price: a certain loss of humanitarian sensibility regarding personal and private obligations. The tension between the two would continue to haunt the colonial and postcolonial world in the following decades. We will revisit this tension in Chapter 6, in our discussion of the history of oil concessions after the Second World War, and in that chapter's analysis of the failing struggle of postcolonial countries to establish a new economic order in which the power relations between corporations and fragile host economies are subject to international legal scrutiny.

4

The Nature of the Nazi State and
the Responsibility of Corporate Officials
at Nuremberg

Introduction

If there is a known history of corporations in international law, it is the history of
the Industrialist Trials at Nuremberg. The history of these cases has been well documented, raising a series of controversies over the question of corporate criminal
liability in international law. Farben and other major Nazi-era corporations presented just about the clearest picture one could imagine of corporate culpability,
with devastating human consequences and major geopolitical implications. Perhaps
the most notable feature of these cases is that putting these infamous companies of
the Nazi era on trial resulted in the most alarming precedent exposing international
law's incompetence in regulating business corporations.

In the early 1940s, many in the U.S. Administration regarded German industry as a
primary factor in Hitler's rise to power and in the advancement of Germany's imperialistic policy. The controversy was not about the Industrialist's responsibility but about
what should be done about it. As the U.S. Administration moved to the reconstruction
phase it continued to address the breaking up of cartels as pivotal for a peaceful inter-
state order; the corporation was thus seen as politically salient for international law.

But the attempts to 'break down' German industry and especially its major cartels
were only partially successful.[1] None of the Industrialists was eventually tried by the

This chapter contains parts of the following article which have been reproduced with the kind permission of the New York University Journal of International Law and Politics. Doreen Lustig, The Nature of the
Nazi State and the Question of International Criminal Responsibility of Corporate Officials at Nuremberg:
Revisiting Franz Neumann's Concept of the Behemoth at the Industrialist Trials, 43 N.Y.U. J. Int'l L. & Pol.
965 (2011).

[1] The impunity gap at Nuremberg is manifested, inter alia, by the mild judgments and lenient sentences in
the Industrialist Trials. On January 31, 1951, John McCloy, the High Commissioner of occupied Germany,
freed one-third of the Nuremberg prisoners immediately and commuted most of the outstanding death
sentences to prison terms. The Industrialists were prominent beneficiaries of the High Commissioner's
decisions. See Office of the U.S. High Commissioner for Germany, Landsberg: A Documentary Report,
January 31, 1951, Frankfurt Germany. Record Group 466, High Commissioner for Germany, General
Records 1949–1952 Decimal 321.5–321.6 466/250/68/10/5 box 12 'German War Criminals' file. Other au-
thors share this critical view of the Trials. See, for example, PETER MAGUIRE, LAW AND WAR 206–08 (2000)
(explaining why the Nuremburg trials often failed to reach a just result); Florian Jessberger, On the Origins of
Individual Criminal Responsibility Under International Law for Business Activity, 8 J. INT'L CRIM. JUST. 783,
799 (2010) (attributing the lenient sentences received by Industrialists to the political climate).

Veiled Power. Doreen Lustig, Oxford University Press (2020). © Doreen Lustig.
DOI: 10.1093/oso/9780198822097.001.0001

first Nuremberg Tribunal (the International Military Tribunal, or IMT). In the subsequent Nuremberg Trials, the judges chose to narrow the scope of the Industrialists' responsibility significantly, and soon after their sentencing they were all pardoned and released. While the Industrialist cases did put German businessmen and corporate officials on trial, they would be later criticized for not including the corporate entities—the companies these individuals owned and/or managed—as subjects of responsibility in the proceedings, and for failing to hold the corporate officials they *did* try accountable for the gravity and scope of their actions.[2]

History provides several explanations for this process of marginalization of the responsibility of German (and American and other) businesses in the aftermath of the Second World War. On 19 April 1947, the first Industrialist Trial began: that of Friedrich Flick. On 5 June 5, 1947, U.S. Secretary of State George C. Marshall announced the European Recovery Plan (ERP) to a commencement audience at Harvard University. By the time the Marshall Plan was approved by the U.S. Congress in March 1948, the three Industrialist Trials were almost over. While the Industrialists stood trial, the political atmosphere had changed dramatically. It is hard to assess accurately the influence of the geopolitical, social, and economic context on the judicial proceedings and their aftermath. Nevertheless, it seems reasonable to assume these developments found their way into the courtroom, the judges' considerations, and the minds of administrators who handled the review of the trials and the execution of their verdicts. They most notably found their way into the judges' decisions and the clemency they ultimately granted.

This chapter addresses the debate over the Industrialists' responsibility as a struggle between competing theories of the *totalitarian state*. I will look at the influence of the Frankfurt School and Franz Neumann's theory of the Nazi State as *Behemoth* on the

---

[2] For a discussion of various historical explanations for the absence of the corporate entity as a subject of responsibility at Nuremberg, *see*Jonathan A. Bush, *The Prehistory of Corporations and Conspiracy in International Criminal Law: What Nuremberg Really Said*, 109 COL. L. REV. 1094, 1130–49 (2009). For interpretations that view corporate entity as *de facto* included as a subject of responsibility in the Industrialist Trials, see, for example, Anita Ramasastry, *Corporate Complicity: From Nuremberg to Rangoon—An examination of Forced Labor Cases and Their Impact on the Liability of Multinational Corporations*, 20 BERKELEY J. INT'L L. 91, 108 (2002). The debate over the Nuremberg precedent in this context arose in the context of Kiobel v. Royal Dutch Petroleum Co., 569 U.S. 108 (2013). Those who supported the recognition of direct corporate liability and relied on international law argued that both the Nuremberg jurisprudence and the policies governed by the Allies recognized the corporation as a subject of responsibility under international law. According to this view, it was understood that corporations could be 'made to pay' for their complicity. *See* Brief Amici Curiae of Nuremberg Scholars, December 21, 2011, in the case of Esther Kiobel et al. v. Royal Dutch Petroleum Co., et al., No. 10-1491. The opposing view argued against inferring a precedent from the various laws governing the former Germany after the war. According to this argument, the policies directed at businesses were 'for political and security reasons only, and the authority was not law, but Potsdam agreement or principles of peace and democracy'. *See* Brief Amici Curiae of Nuremberg Historians and International Lawyers in Support of Neither Party, December 21, 2011, in the case of Esther Kiobel et al. v. Royal Dutch Petroleum Co., et al., No. 10-1491. *See also* Jonathan Kolieb, *Through the Looking-Glass: Nuremberg's Confusing Legacy on Corporate Accountability Under International Law*, 32 AM. U. INT'L L. REV. 569 (2017); Henry Korn, *International Military Tribunals' Genesis, WWII Experience, and Future Relevance*, 2017 UTAH L. REV. 731 (2017).

Prosecution's innovative theory of the Nazi regime and the opportunity it provided to hold corporate entities *and individuals* accountable for international legal crimes. The Behemoth model was rejected by the Tribunals in favour of a more traditional, monolithic notion of the state famously celebrated in Hobbes's *Leviathan*. The challenge presented by the Behemoth alternative was a reality that failed to correspond with the Leviathan model. By insisting on the Hobbesian model, the Tribunals failed to acknowledge its contingency and role as an ideal against which regimes should be scrutinized. The Prosecution was caught in a different bias: one that equated Neumann's critique of the Nazi State as a model of responsibility. Their conception of the Nazi businessmen as part of an anomaly—a 'non-state'—prevented them from developing a theory of responsibility of businessmen operating as such. Furthermore, the judgments did not develop a theory of responsibility for economic actors regardless of their relationship with the state. They further insisted on the violence of the Nazi state as the criterion for the illegality of certain business transactions. In addition, their focus on direct violence rather than the loss of a functioning legal system significantly limited the protection of private rights of the occupied population and ultimately undermined its sovereignty.

The implications of the Tribunals' epistemological biases were significant. Rather than insisting on the Nazi state as a mega-Leviathan, they could have exposed the industrialist crimes as being a result of the collapse of the previous state apparatus and the loss of the rule of law. Furthermore, the judges of the Industrialist Trials at Nuremberg did not recognize the implications of the organizational structure of the modern company for individual responsibility, as I discuss in Chapter 5. Their failure to do so had an effect that lasted into this century on the question of responsibility of economic actors in international law.

Introducing the Industrialist Cases

After Germany's defeat in the Second World War, the Allied powers formed a control council consisting of representatives from the four victorious powers: the United States, the United Kingdom, France, and the Soviet Union. The Allies convened their London Conference in August 1945 to decide on the means by which to punish high-ranking Nazi war criminals. At this point, the question of who might be included in this group of criminals was still unsettled. The result was the most well-known of all war crime trials, the Trial of the Major War Criminals before the IMT. The formal agreement produced at the London Conference defined the IMT Charter, set out the court's procedural rules, and enumerated the charges to be adjudicated.[3] The Nuremberg Charter enabled the IMT to prosecute individuals for

---

[3] The Charter of the International Military Tribunal at Nuremberg, Aug. 8, 1945, 59 Stat. 1544, 82 U.N.T.S. 279 [hereinafter: Nuremberg Charter].

crimes against peace, war crimes, and crimes against humanity. The IMT convened from 14 November 1945 to 1 October 1946.[4]

On 8 December 1945, merely four months after the establishment of the Nuremberg Charter, the four major Allies in occupied Germany enacted a somewhat modified version of the Charter, known as *Control Council Law No. 10* [hereinafter: 'Control Council' or 'CCL10'].[5] CCL10 provided the legal basis for a series of trials before military tribunals as well as for subsequent prosecution by German tribunals that continued for several decades.[6] These proceedings against those known as 'major war criminals of the second rank' are usually referred to as the 'subsequent' Nuremberg proceedings. They were not the trials of primary suspects but rather trials of doctors, lawyers, industrialists, businessmen, scientists, and generals. The U.S. Prosecutors generally targeted defendants who represented the major segments of the Third Reich, divided into four categories: SS; police and party officials; military leaders; and bankers and industrialists. The judges on the U.S. tribunals were rarely, if ever, prominent jurists. They included U.S. state judges, law school deans, or practising attorneys.[7] Since the trials were conducted under military law, their verdicts were subject to the Military Government's review and confirmation. The twelve U.S. Nuremberg Trials comprised 185 defendants.[8]

The subsequent trials—and the indictment of the leading German industrialists—soon became a U.S. endeavour, although the U.S. Prosecution team depended on British cooperation to retrieve evidence.[9] 'So far as Sam Harris

---

[4] For secondary sources on the IMT, *see*, for example, DONALD BLOXHAM, GENOCIDE ON TRIAL (2001); ROBERT E. CONOT, JUSTICE AT NUREMBERG (1983); WAR CRIMES: THE LEGACY OF NUREMBERG (Belinda Cooper ed., 1999); BRADLEY F. SMITH, REACHING JUDGMENT AT NUREMBERG (1997); LAWRENCE DOUGLAS, THE MEMORY OF JUDGMENT 1–65 (2001); BRUCE M. STAVE ET AL., WITNESSES TO NUREMBERG: AN ORAL HISTORY OF AMERICAN PARTICIPANTS AT THE WAR CRIMES TRIALS (1998); TELFORD TAYLOR, THE ANATOMY OF THE NUREMBERG TRIALS (1992); ANN TUSA & JOHN TUSA, THE NUREMBERG TRIAL (1983); NORMAN E. TUTUROW, WAR CRIMES, WAR CRIMINALS, AND WAR CRIMES TRIALS: AN ANNOTATED BIBLIOGRAPHY AND SOURCE BOOK (1986); ROBERT K. WOETZEL, THE NUREMBERG TRIALS IN INTERNATIONAL LAW (1962); KEVIN JON HELLER, THE NUREMBERG MILITARY TRIBUNALS AND THE ORIGINS OF INTERNATIONAL CRIMINAL LAW (2011).

[5] TELFORD TAYLOR, FINAL REPORT TO THE SECRETARY OF THE ARMY ON THE NUERNBERG WAR CRIMES TRIALS UNDER CONTROL COUNCIL LAW NO. 10 app. D, at 250 (1949).

[6] The American regulation that was established to provide procedural guidelines for the military tribunals was Military Government Ordinance No. 7. *See* Mil. Gov't Ordinance No. 7, art II (b) (Oct. 18, 1946). For a general discussion of CCL10, Military Government Ordinance No. 7, and the Nuremburg Tribunals, *see* Telford Taylor, *The Krupp Trial: Fact v. Fiction*, 53 COLUM. L. REV. 197, 201 (1953).

[7] TAYLOR, *supra* note 5, at 35.

[8] The twelve war crime cases tried in the American Zone under the authority of Control Council Law No. 10 were substantially abbreviated in the legally official edition that was published in the fifteen massive volumes entitled TRIALS OF WAR CRIMINALS BEFORE THE NUREMBERG MILITARY TRIBUNALS UNDER CONTROL COUNCIL LAW NO. 10 (1949–1953) [hereinafter T.W.C.]. This work is popularly termed the 'Green Series'. Unless otherwise specified, all citations vis-à-vis these cases hereinafter refer to the Green Series.

[9] In a letter to the British Property Control, Fred Opel, the U.S. Chief of Counsel for War Crimes expressed the office's interest in 'material supplying evidence against Krupp and his associates', and asked for 'permission to visit the former Krupp office located in the British sector'. Letter from Fred M. Opel, Office of Chief Counsel for War Crimes (OCCWC), to O'Grady, British Property Control

[one of the legal counsels at the Nuremberg proceedings] knows', reads one internal memo, 'the British are doing nothing on further investigations concerning war crimes of Nazi industrialists in their area.'[10] Despite limited cooperation with the other allies, the Industrialists of three companies were finally chosen to be put on trial from many other potential candidates.[11] Amongst those who were often mentioned but eventually not chosen to be tried by the U.S. Tribunals were Fritz Thyssen[12] and Hermann Röchling.[13] The Industrialist cases I have selected as the focus of this chapter and Chapter 5 are *United States v. Friedrich Flick* ('Flick'),[14] *United States v. Carl Krauch* ('I.G. Farben'),[15] and *United States v. Alfried Krupp* ('Krupp').[16]

This preparatory work to establish a case against the three Industrialists began while the first Nuremberg Tribunal was underway.[17] The magnitude of the work

(Dec. 9 1946), OCCWC Berlin Branch, Group 238, no. 202, 190/12/35/01-02, National Archives and Records Administration (NARA).

[10] Memorandum from Drexel Sprecher, Dir., Econ. Div., OCCWC, to Staff, 'Conference of Feb. 1, 1946: Some Tips Concerning Work on Subsequent Case against Nazi Industrialists' (Feb. 4, 1946), OCCWC 1933–1949, Group 238, No. 159, 190/12/13/01-02, NARA. This memo further describes how a British and American group arrives at Essen and successfully imprisoned about twelve of the principal Krupp leaders as, *inter alia*, material witnesses and potential criminals.

[11] *See, e.g.*, Letter from Benjamin Ferencz to Drexel Sprecher, Dir., Econ. Div., OCCWC, 'Target List of 72' (Nov. 1, 1946), World War II War Criminals Records, OCCWC 1933–1949, Group 238, No. 159, 190/12/13/01-02, NARA (requesting that a list of financiers and industrialists subject to prosecution be forwarded to his office); Letter from Charles Winick, Chief of Documents Control Sec. Headquarters of the U.S. Forces, European Theater, to Telford Taylor, OCCWC, Subsequent Proceedings (June 19, 1946), Correspondence and Reports, World War II War Criminals Records, OCCWC 1933–1949, Group 238, No. 159, 190/12/13/01-02, NARA (providing information regarding twenty-six leading German industrialists chargeable with war crimes).

[12] Fritz Thyssen (1873–1951) was a prominent German industrialist who initially supported Hitler but later opposed the war and subsequently fled to Switzerland. He was caught by the Vichy authorities and imprisoned in a number of different concentration camps until the end of the war. In July of 1947, Sprecher advised Taylor to release Thyssen because '[i]t is now clear that (a) OCCWC cannot consider his role from 1923 to 1939 as a crime against peace; and (b) his utility as a witness to the truth is highly dubious'. Memorandum from D.A. Sprecher, Dir., Econ. Div., OCCWC, to Telford Taylor, Brigadier Gen., Chief of Counsel for War Crimes, US-OMGUS, 'Fritz Thyssen: Recommended Handling of the Case' (July 1, 1947), Correspondence and Reports, World War II War Criminals Records, OCCWC 1933–1949, Group 238, No. 159, 190/12/13/01-02, NARA.

[13] Hermann Röchling was tried in the French war crimes trials that were held under Control Council Law No. 10. A summary of the trial and appellate court decisions was published as France v. Roechling, 14 T.W.C., *supra* note 8, at 1075 (Gen. Tribunal of the Military. Gov't 1948); *see also* France v. Roechling, 14 T.W.C., *supra* note 8, at 1097 (Superior Military Gov't Ct. 1949).

[14] United States v. Friedrich Flick, 6 T.W.C., *supra* note 8 (1952) [hereinafter *The Flick Case*].

[15] The Farben case was published in two volumes of T.W.C: United States v. Krauch, 7 T.W.C., *supra* note 8 (1953) [hereinafter *The Farben Case*, vol. 7]; 8 T.W.C., *supra* note 8 (1952) [hereinafter *The Farben Case*, vol. 8].

[16] United States v. Krupp, 9 T.W.C., *supra* note 8 (1950) [hereinafter *The Krupp Case*].

[17] In the first few months of the Office of the Chief of Counsel for War Crimes (OCCWC), which began functioning prior to its official creation on October 24, 1946, the trial work was divided among different divisions: the Military, Ministries, SS, and Economics Divisions. In addition, two special 'trial teams' were set up to prepare the I.G. Farben and Flick cases for trial. After final decisions were made with respect to the choice of cases, the Economic Division, headed by Drexel A. Sprecher, was

invested in preparing for the Industrialist Trials and other evidence convey their relative importance.[18] Data and analysis produced in different corners of the U.S. Administration and legislature proved essential for building the case against the Industrialists.[19] The size of the companies involved and the scope of their activities resulted in the amassing of an enormous collection of documents, scattered evidence, and witnesses who were hard to trace. The Prosecution teams were confronted with a labyrinth of details, and time was of the essence.

The disarray of these early days proved especially detrimental to the first Industrialist case, that of Friedrich Flick and five other officials from the Flick Concern.[20] The case ran from 8 February to 22 December 1947.[21] '[I]n one of the smaller tribunal rooms in the Nuremberg courthouse, Friedrich Flick, the munitions maker, and five of his accessories have been busy since April of this year trying to defend themselves against charges that they used and abused slave labor, exploited the resources of occupied countries, and helped finance the criminal activities of the SS', reported Andy Logan for the New Yorker.[22] The six defendants were charged with the commission of war crimes and crimes against humanity. The specific counts cited criminal conduct relating to slave labour, the spoliation of property in occupied France and the Soviet Union, and the Aryanization of Jewish industrial and mining properties.

Meanwhile, the I.G. Farben case was the first Nuremberg Trial following the IMT case that included charges of *crimes against peace*. It was the largest of all three Industrialist cases. Since 1916, eight of the German chemical firms (BASF, Bayer,

---

eliminated and its personnel were reassigned to divisions established for the trials of these particular cases. TAYLOR, *supra* note 5, at 39–40.

[18] *See* Letter from D.A. Sprecher, Director, Econ. Div., OCCWC, to George Wheeler, Manpower Div., OCCWC (Feb. 8, 1946), OCCWC 1933–1949, Group 238, No. 159, 190/12/13/01-02, NARA (noting that OCCWC had positioned the trying of German industrialists as 'priority one').

[19] In February 1946, Alfred H. Booth requested that Taylor send him publications from any Senate committees, including the Kilgore Committee, which were investigating the actions of German industrialists. Booth wrote: 'It seem[ed] indispensable for the Prosecution of Nazi Industrialists to have ... certain documentary material which should be easily obtainable in Washington D.C.' Letter from Alfred H. Booth to Telford Taylor, Brigadier Gen., Chief of Counsel for War Crimes, US-OMGUS (Feb. 4, 1946), OCCWC 1933–1949, Group 238, No. 159, 190/12/13/01-02, NARA; *see also* Memorandum from Albert G.D. Levy to I.G. Farben Trial Team, 'Filing of Kilgore and Bernstein Exhibits' (Oct. 26, 1946), *Farben I* Trial Team, OCCWC, Group 238, No. 192, 190/12/32/07-12/33/01, NARA.

[20] In a letter to Walter Rapp, Sprecher conveyed his dissatisfaction with the preliminary briefs prepared by attorneys on the Flick, Roechling, and Poensgen cases. *See* Letter from D.A. Sprecher, Dir., Econ. Div., OCCWC, to Walter Rapp, 'Interrogations to Develop Materials in the Slave Labor Field' (July 16, 1946), 'Interrogation Committee File', OCCWC 1945–1949, Group 238, No. 159, 190/12/32/07-12/33/01, NARA (noting that the preliminary briefs were 'very scant').

[21] Judge Charles B. Sears, formerly an associate judge of the New York Court of Appeals, was the presiding judge. Judge William C. Christianson, formerly Associate Justice of the Minnesota Supreme Court, and Judge Frank J. Richman, formerly of the Indiana Supreme Court, were members of the Tribunal. Judge Richard D. Dixon, formerly of the North Carolina Supreme Court, was an alternative member of the Flick Tribunal. *The Flick Case, supra* note 14, at 8.

[22] Andy Logan, *Letter from Nuremberg*, NEW YORKER, Dec. 27, 1947, at 40. Logan was married to Charles S. Lyon, the Chief Prosecutor in the Flick case.

and Hoechst, along with five smaller manufacturers) collaborated in what was known in German as an *Interessengemeinschaft* (I.G.).[23] Unlike U.S. law, German law encouraged such collaborations and centralized control of business enterprises. Indeed, from 1925 to 1945, 'the I.G. Farbenindustrie AG was the largest non-state-owned corporation in Germany and ... the world's fourth largest such enterprise ... [T]he company produced an immense array of goods, from dyes and pharmaceuticals to aluminum, fuel, and rubber, and its well-funded research operations added constantly to the total, achieving such lastingly valuable discoveries as sulfa drugs, magnetic tape and a variety of synthetic fibers.'[24] Farben had pioneered the production of synthetic nitrates, which were crucial components of explosives, thus helping to free Germany from dependence on foreign imports.[25] The twenty-three defendants in the case were all individuals who served on the Farben Board of Directors (or *Vorstand*, in German). The case was conducted between 12 August 1947 and 12 May 1948.[26]

The third trial was that of the twelve officials of the Krupp company,[27] which began a few days after the I.G. Farben trial. The company was known for its production of metals and the processing of these metals into war materials, including ships and tanks. In 1903, Krupp changed into a corporation, known as Fried. Krupp A.G., and functioned as a private, limited liability enterprise. Expansion of the Krupp enterprises continued up until the outbreak of the First World War, during which it became one of Germany's principal arsenals. The First World War gun, 'Big Bertha', was named after the matriarch of the Krupp family. Alfried Krupp and eight of the defendants were members or deputy members of the company's *Vorstand* for varying periods of time, and the other three held other important positions in the firm.[28]

---

[23] For further analysis of I.G. Farben and its involvement in the Second World War, *see*JOSEPH BORKIN, THE CRIME AND PUNISHMENT OF I.G. FARBEN (1st ed., 1978); JOSIAH E. DuBOIS, GENERALS IN GREY SUITS: THE DIRECTORS OF THE INTERNATIONAL 'I.G. FARBEN' CARTEL, THEIR CONSPIRACY AND TRIAL AT NUREMBERG (1953); BENJAMIN B. FERENCZ, LESS THAN SLAVES: JEWISH FORCED LABOR AND THE QUEST FOR COMPENSATION 33–67 (2002) (1979) (discussing legal action taken by Auschwitz survivors against I.G. Farben); PETER HAYES, INDUSTRY AND IDEOLOGY: IG FARBEN IN THE NAZI ERA (1987); DIARMUID JEFFREYS, HELL'S CARTEL: IG FARBEN AND THE MAKING OF HITLER'S WAR MACHINE (2008); STEPHAN H. LINDNER, INSIDE IG FARBEN: HOECHST DURING THE THIRD REICH (Helen Schoop trans., 2008); RICHARD SASULY, IG FARBEN (1947).

[24] LINDNER, *supra* note 23, at xiii.

[25] *The Farben Case*, vol. 8, *supra* note 15, at 1086.

[26] The presiding judges were Judge Curtis Grover Shake, from the highest state court in Indiana; Judge James Morris, from the highest state court in North Dakota; and Paul M. Judge Hebert, the Dean of Louisiana State University Law School. *The Farben Case*, vol. 7, *supra* note 15, at 6.

[27] Krupp's operations were mainly concentrated in the Ruhr Valley, which lay within the British zone of occupation. Nonetheless, the British were not bound to the indictment of industrialists subsequent to the IMT trial. The British Foreign Office willingly transferred six industrialists, including Alfried Krupp, and three other suspects for trial in the American proceedings. Other British prisoners were transferred as well. Donald Bloxham, *British War Crimes Trial Policy in Germany, 1945–1957: Implementation and Collapse*, 42 J. BRIT. STUD. 91, 103 (2003).

[28] The case began on August 16, 1947, and the sentence was pronounced on July 31, 1948. The members of the Tribunal included the Presiding Judge Hu C. Anderson, Tennessee Court of Appeals, Judge

The indictments in these three cases contained four counts that were based closely on the Nuremberg Charter. The first count, crimes against peace, played a central role in both the case of Krupp and that of I.G. Farben. As Telford Taylor noted, 'I directed that the staff... concentrate a large share of its time and energy on the analysis of evidence and the preparation of charges relating to crimes against peace.'[29] As suggested in paragraph 2(f) of Article II of CCL10, a principal holding a high position in 'financial, industrial or economic life' was 'deemed, *ipso facto*, to have committed crimes against peace.'[30] Although this paragraph merely requires this fact to be taken into consideration, it repudiated the contention that private businessmen or industrialists could not be held responsible for 'crimes against peace.'[31] Although the U.S. Prosecutors considered the war as the main crime of the Industrialists, the charge of slave labour was significant in all three of the Industrialist cases. The defendants were also charged with looting or expropriation of property in violation of the laws of war. The category of 'crimes against humanity' also played a part in all three of the trials.

Let us now turn to analysing the influence of competing theories of the Nazi state on the Industrialist cases' jurisprudence of crimes against peace. First we will scrutinize key features of Neumann's description of the Nazi State as Behemoth, and his direct involvement in the Nuremberg proceedings. We will then examine how his ideas were reflected in the Prosecutors' arguments and the Tribunals' decisions on the Industrialists' responsibility for the war itself.

Intellectual Frameworks Shaping the Crime of Aggression

Should a private enterprise be held responsible for its involvement in the war effort of its country? Josiah DuBois Jr., Chief Prosecutor for the I.G. Farben case, echoed this question in his recollection of a conversation with Colonel Mickey Marcus, Chief of the War Crimes Division in the War Department, before he left for Nuremberg:

A lot of people in this Department are scared stiff of pinning a war plot on these men. There's no law by which we can force industrialists to make war equipment for us right now. A few U.S. manufacturers were Farben stooges. And those who weren't can say, 'Hell, if participating in a rearmament program is criminal, we want no part of it.'[32]

Edward J. Daly, Connecticut Superior Court, and Judge William J. Wilkins, Superior Court of Seattle, Washington. *The Krupp Case, supra* note 16, at 1.

[29] TAYLOR, *supra* note 5, at 66.
[30] *The Farben Case*, vol. 8, *supra* note 15, at 1299 (Herbert, J., concurring).
[31] *Id.* at 1299–1300.
[32] JOSIAH DUBOIS, THE DEVIL'S CHEMISTS 21 (1952).

The answer to Marcus's puzzle—how to make businesses liable for their involvement in a war and more broadly in violations of international standards—depended, *inter alia*, on the theory of the state and its relationship with business actors.[33] Such a theory could be found in the work of scholars employed by the U.S. Administration on Germany and the 'German Problem'. Several prominent scholars of the exiled Frankfurt School—especially Franz Neumann, Otto Kirchheimer, and Herbert Marcuse—were influential on policy-making at that time. In 1943, these three Jewish émigrés were employed in an intelligence organization that later became the Central Intelligence Agency, known then as the Research and Analysis Branch of the Office of Strategic Services [hereinafter the 'R&A' and the 'OSS', respectively]. Employed by the Central European Section of the R&A, they investigated and interpreted German intentions and capabilities. Of particular importance was Neumann's study of the German Nazi regime, entitled *Behemoth*.[34]

Beginning in the early 1940s, Franz Neumann utilized this study to present his understanding of the Nazi regime and the role industry played in it. Although *Behemoth* was undergirded by neo-Marxist ideology, it 'functioned as a major source and reference book for both the OSS and the Nuremberg prosecutors'.[35] Neumann's analysis of the Nazi regime and its relationship with industry posed a challenge to the prevalent model of the state. In the following section, I explore the features of this challenge.

Franz Neumann's 'Behemoth'

Neumann's analysis introduced a radical departure from the monolithic view of the totalitarian state and the premise of a concentrated monopoly over violence. His Behemoth concept conveyed the non-state essence of the Nazi regime. Under National Socialism, the political authority often identified with the state ceased to exist. Conversely, he described the Nazi regime as comprising

---

[33] One might suggest the antitrust sentiment as an additional explanation. For a discussion of the parallel route of the antitrust campaign and its implications for the Prosecution of the German Industrialists at Nuremberg, *see* Chapter 5. For an elaborate discussion *see* Doreen Lustig, Criminality of Nazi-Era German Cartels: The Rise and Decline of Anti-Trust in American Approaches to International Criminal Law at Nuremberg (unpublished manuscript, on file with author). On the epistemic communities that informed the debate on the German economy and shaped important aspects of the trials, including the antirust sentiment, *see* Kim Christian Priemel, 'A Story of Betrayal': Conceptualizing Variants of Capitalism in the Nuremberg War Crimes Trials, 85 J. Mod. Hist. 69 (2013).

[34] FRANZ NEUMANN, BEHEMOTH: THE STRUCTURE AND PRACTICE OF NATIONAL SOCIALISM 1933–1944 (Ivan R. Dee 2009) [1944].

[35] MICHAEL SALTER, U.S. INTELLIGENCE, THE HOLOCAUST AND THE NUREMBERG TRIALS: SEEKING ACCOUNTABILITY FOR GENOCIDE AND CULTURAL PLUNDER 573 (2009). Salter's book traces the influence of the American intelligence agency where Franz Neumann worked on U.S. postwar policy and particularly on the evidence of the Holocaust presented at the Nuremberg Trial.

four ruling classes that governed Germany: the Nazi party, the army, the bureaucracy, and the Industrialists. These four groups collaborated in a command-and-control authority structure that lacked coherence and rule of law. Neumann traced the origins of the Nazi regime back to the ills of the Weimar Republic. He attributed much of the Republic's failure to the imperialism of German monopoly capital:

> The more monopoly grew, the more incompatible it became with the political democracy ... Trusts, combines, and cartels covered the whole economy with a network of authoritarian organizations. Employers' organizations controlled the labor market, and big business lobbies aimed at placing the legislative, administrative, and judicial machinery at the service of monopoly capital.
>
> In Germany, there was never anything like the popular anti-monopoly movement of the U.S. under Theodore Roosevelt and Woodrow Wilson.[36]

Neumann explained how the Great Depression had led to the restoration of cartels and tariffs in a way that helped the economy in the short run, but at the same time intensified the threat posed by monopolistic power to democracy. However, monopolies were not the only factors that led to the collapse of the Weimar Republic. Neumann cited, first, the weakening of labor and trade unions, and second, the growing power of judges at the expense of the parliament, and the decline of the parliament and parliamentary supremacy. He wrote: 'Even before the beginning of the great depression ... the ideological, economic, social, and political systems were no longer functioning properly ... The depression uncovered and deepened petrifaction of the traditional, social and political structure. The social contracts on which that structure was founded broke down.'[37]

Neumann showed how the Weimar democracy sharpened antagonisms and led to the breakdown of voluntary collaboration, destruction of parliamentary institutions, suspension of political liberties, the growth of a ruling bureaucracy, and the renaissance of the army as a decisive political factor. This historical analysis of the Weimar Republic supported an argument implicit in Neumann's thesis: rather than see the tragic consequence of the Weimar years—the Nazi regime—as a manifestation of Prussian militarism or Junker aristocracy, Neumann argued that it was a result of a redistribution of social and political power. Additionally, he emphasized the productive power of German industry as one of the pillars of the Third Reich and challenged the identification of Germany's economic system as a form of *state capitalism*.[38] Conversely, 'the organization of the economic system is pragmatic.

---

[36] NEUMANN, *supra* note 34, at 14–15.
[37] *Id.* at 30.
[38] *Id.* at 222.

It is directed entirely by the need of the highest possible efficiency and productivity required for the conducting of war.'[39]

Neumann characterized the German economy under the Nazi rule as having two characteristics: 'It is a monopolistic economy and a command economy. It is a private capitalistic economy regimented by the totalitarian state.'[40] He also rejected any interpretation of National Socialism as a 'non-capitalistic economy' and, instead, described it as 'totalitarian monopoly capitalism'.[41] This form of capitalism is driven by profit and is competitive, yet competition is not for markets but for quotas, permits, shares, patents, and licenses. Indeed, Neumann described how National Socialism enabled, or at least facilitated, the rule of monopolies in Germany by creating the conditions that forced the whole economic activity of the country into the network of collaborations run by the industrial magnates. By enacting a statute for compulsory cartelization, the National Socialist government maintained and solidified existing organizational patterns. Initially, the objective in doing so was to secure the profits of the industrial combines even with the reduced production volumes. Economic policy shifted to refocus on achieving full employment and utilization of all resources in preparation for the enactment of the Four-Year Plan, a plan that was meant to make the German army and economy 'fit for war' by 1940.[42]

Neumann identified three types of economy in Nazi Germany: competitive, monopolistic, and command economies. Furthermore, he argued, monopolization of industry did not negate competition but, in many ways, asserted it. 'The struggle for production or sales quotas within the cartel—for raw materials, for capital, for consumers—determines the character, the stability, and the durability of the cartel.'[43] The command economy was embedded in state interference and regimentation but did not entail the nationalization of the private industry: 'Why should it? ... German industry was willing to cooperate to the fullest ... National Socialism utilized the daring, the knowledge, the aggressiveness of the industrial leadership, while the industrial leadership utilized the anti-democracy, anti-liberalism and anti-unionism of the National Socialist party.'[44]

Neumann's Behemoth theory challenged the traditional Leviathan theory of the state. The German regime dissolved the previous state apparatus and introduced an unfamiliar authority structure that lacked the essential elements of the modern state; most significantly, a unified apparatus controlling the exercise of coercion.

---

[39] *Id.* at 228.
[40] *Id.* at 261.
[41] *Id.*
[42] *Id.* at 267–68.
[43] *Id.* at 292.
[44] *Id.* at 361.

Behemoth at Nuremberg

How did ideas from Neumann's *Behemoth* find their way to the Prosecution of the Industrialist Trials? Barry M. Katz described three phases of the Frankfurt scholars' influence on American policy-makers. First, while engaged in defining their task in 1943, most of the Frankfurt scholars' research focused on analysis of the Nazi New Order and occupation regime. Second, the scholars shifted their attention to postwar-era preparations for occupation and peace in 1944. In the third phase, from 1945, they participated in preparations for the Prosecution of Nazi war criminals.[45] During this third phase, the already influential Behemoth thesis found its way into the drafts being prepared for the Nuremberg Trials.

While Neumann's intellectual prestige was an important factor in the thesis's impact, Behemoth's impact was also due to Neumann's government activities, as his work at the OSS 'strongly influenced the formulation of America's goals for postwar Germany'. In Neumann's conceptualization, these were expressed as the 'four Ds': 'the four key processes of de-Nazification, democratization (including recruitment of civil servants), demilitarization, and decartelization.[46] He became a member of the Prosecution team preparing for the Nuremberg Trials of major war criminals immediately after the war. The Central European Section of the OSS worked closely with Telford Taylor and others in the legal department of the Office of the Secretary of War.[47] 'In preparing this trial [the IMT]', noted one of the legal counsels, 'OSS has been delegated the major responsibility for collecting and integrating the proof on the charge that the major war criminals engaged in a common master plan to enslave and dominate first Germany, then Europe, and ultimately the world, using whatever means necessary.'[48] Neumann's emphasis on the ramifications of the breakdown of the trade unions and the empowerment of the Nazi regime, as well as the importance he attributed to the socialist movement for the future of Germany, and other themes in his work, found their way into the lawyers' preparations for

---

[45] BARRY M. KATZ, FOREIGN INTELLIGENCE: RESEARCH AND ANALYSIS IN THE OFFICE OF STRATEGIC SERVICES 1942–1945, at 34–61 (1989).

[46] Peter Hayes, *Introduction, in* FRANZ NEUMANN, BEHEMOTH, *supra* note 34, at vii.

[47] *See, e.g.*, Memorandum from James B. Donovan, Gen. Counsel, OCCWC Office of Strategic Serv. (April 12, 1945), OCCWC 1933–1949, Group 238, No. 159, 190/12/32/07-12/33/01, NARA (describing the lead-up to the formation of the war crimes programme); Memorandum from James B. Donovan, Gen. Counsel, OCCWC Office of Strategic Serv. to file (April 30, 1945), OCCWC 1933–1949, Group 238, No. 159, 190/12/32/07-12/33/01-02, NARA (listing categories of offenses in which OCCWC was interested in investigating); Memorandum from James B. Donovan, Gen. Counsel, OCCWC Office of Strategic Serv. to Sidney S. Alderman, 'Progress Report on Preparation of Prosecution' (May 30, 1945), OCCWC 1933–1949, Group 238, No. 159, 190/12/32/07-12/33/01-02 (describing work undertaken by the Research & Analysis branch).

[48] Letter from William H. Coogan, Office of the Gen. Counsel, to David S. Shaw, Labor Desk, S.I., Office of Gen. Counsel, and Dr. Franz Neumann (June 27, 1945), OCCWC, Group 238, No. 159, 190/12/13/01-02, NARA.

the trials.[49] During the summer of 1945, Neumann and his colleagues prepared briefs on German leaders such as Heinrich Himmler and Hermann Göring, on Nazi organizations involved in the commission of the war, and on Nazi plans to dominate Germany and Europe.[50] 'The structure of their case [the IMT indictment at Nuremberg] against the Nazi Behemoth grew out of Neumann's claim that it was a tightly integrated system ... managed by an interlocking directorate of political, military, and economic leaders.'[51]

By presidential order, the OSS ceased to function on 1 October 1945, a short while before the opening of the IMT at Nuremberg. However, the work of the émigrés echoed through the corridors of the Palace of Justice long after their return to academia. For example, Telford Taylor opened the first Industrialist case with a Neumannesque formula to describe industry under the Third Reich: 'The third Reich dictatorship was based on this unholy trinity of Nazism, militarism, and economic imperialism.'[52] Raul Hilberg, Neumann's student and later a Holocaust historian, reviewed the continuing influence of Neumann's thesis on the subsequent trials, and noted that documentary records were grouped into four series: Nazi government; party organizations, including the SS; the high command of the armed forces; and industrial documents. Hilberg muses, 'Does this scheme not sound familiar?' He then responds: 'Those are Neumann's four hierarchies.'[53]

Reports prepared by the OSS provided essential information on potential defendants in subsequent Industrialist Trials. In his instructions to establish a dossier collection on each individual on the OSS list as a basis for the Industrialist cases, D.A. Sprecher, Director of the Economic Division, wrote: 'The OSS biographies appear to me to be one of the best studies in our possession, particularly upon recalling that they were drawn up before the Nazi collapse.'[54] The acting chief of the War Crimes Branch concluded in a similar manner, in a letter attached to the transmittal of OSS R&A reports: 'It is felt that these reports may prove helpful as rebuttal testimony in the trials of the industrialists, if any of the listed individuals appear as witnesses for the defense.'[55] The influence of

---

[49] For example, while investigating the Industrialist cases, William H. Coogan of the OCCWC asked the head of the labour desk at the Office of General Counsel for any available evidence of the circumstances surrounding Nazi efforts to break up trade unions. *Id.*

[50] Interoffice Memorandum on Trial Preparations to the Exec. Counsel Trial Team in *Farben I* (May 16, 1945), Exec. Counsel of *Farben I* Trial Team, OCCWC, Group 239, No. 192, 190/12/32/07-12/33/01, NARA.

[51] KATZ, *supra* note 45, at 54.

[52] *The Flick Case, supra* note 14, at 32–33.

[53] Raul Hilberg, *The Relevance of Behemoth Today*, 10 CONSTELLATIONS 256, 262 (2003).

[54] Memorandum from D.A. Sprecher, Dir., Econ. Div., OCCWC, to Alfred Booth & Samuel Malo, 'Nazi Industrial Case: Some Initial Research Procedure' (February 4, 1946), OCCWC 1933–1949, Group 238, No. 159, 238/1/90/12/13/01-02, NARA.

[55] Memorandum from Cecil F. Hubbert, Acting Chief, War Crimes Branch, OSS, to OCCWC, Transmittal of OSS Research and Analysis Report (May 23, 1947), OCCWC 1933–1949, Group 238,

Neumann and his colleagues on the trial is also related to a debate among his-torians regarding some of the trial's more problematic implications. Following in the steps of their IMT predecessors, Prosecutors of the Industrialists emphasized *the war* as the latter's main crime, rather than crimes of slavery or concentration camp atrocities.[56]

In a memorandum from August 1946, one of the lawyers working on the trials[57] advised his colleagues to distinguish the subsequent trials from the IMT by reversing the storyline: 'The big German industrialists dreamed dreams of economic conquest of the world; that, to this end, military conquest was a pre-condition; and that Hitler was created by these same industrialists as their political arm and puppet to achieve this objective.'[58] He mentioned Farben of-ficials alongside Krupp and others. His views on the primacy of the industri-alist conspiracy were only partially adopted by the Prosecution. Eventually, the Prosecutors of Farben described it primarily as an instrument of the Nazi regime. The Krupp Prosecutors, however, followed this advice and described an inde-pendent plan that preceded Hitler. The argument of Farben's instrumentality and the focus of its directors' integration in the Four-Year Plan were reminiscent of an institutional position (*i.e.* close affiliation between industry and government).[59] Conversely, the argument for Krupp's *independent* conspiracy described a more autonomous operation conducted by the Krupp officials. When the Tribunals were called on to address these different approaches to relations between gov-ernment and business, they redefined the puzzle of these relations in terms of initiative and control. It is to these 'two conspiracies' and the Tribunals' response that we now turn.

No. 159, 238/190/12/13/01-02, NARA (regarding 'Sixty-five Leading German Businessmen'). The OSS report to the preparation of the Industrialist Trials is mentioned as a fruitful source of evidence in other correspondence. *See*, for example, Memorandum from D.A. Sprecher, Head Prosecutor, *Farben* Trial Team, OCCWC, to File (Jan. 21, 1946), OCCWC 1933–1949, Group 238, No. 159, 238/1/90/12/13/01-02, NARA (referencing 'the OSS study containing biographies of leading industrialists which may be useful in giving leads on this subject').

[56] This emphasis is more problematic when read in the context of Neumann's Spearhead Theory of Anti-Semitism. Shlomo Aronson's comprehensive study of the influence of Neumann's spearhead theory on the Nuremberg Trials represents a prominent example of this line of argument. Shlomo Aronson, *Preparations for the Nuremberg Trial: The O.S.S., Charles Dwork, and the Holocaust*, 12 HOLOCAUST & GENOCIDE STUD. 257 (1998). *But see* SALTER, *supra* note 35, at 589–699 (challenging some aspects of Aronson's analysis).

[57] Abraham Pomerantz, a New York commercial lawyer and deputy for the Nuremberg economic cases, was recruited to serve as a trial manager as well as a big-picture strategist.

[58] Memorandum from A.L. Pomerantz, Deputy Chief Counsel, OCCWC, to Telford Taylor, Brigadier General, Chief of Counsel for War Crimes, US-OMGUS, The Proposed Indictment of the Nazi Industrialists—A New Approach (Aug. 22, 1946), Berlin Branch, OCCWC, Group 238, No. 202, 190/12/35/01-02.

[59] Memorandum from L.M. Drachsler, Prosecutor, OCCWC, to J.E. Heath, 'Indictment of the Industrialists' 11 (Sept. 28, 1946), OCCWC 1933–1949, Group 238, No. 159, 238/1/90/12/13/01-02, NARA [hereinafter Memorandum from Drachsler to Heath].

Followers, Not Leaders: Two Companies, Two Conspiracies in the Crime of Aggression

This section explores how the two different theories of the Nazi state, together with antitrust sensibilities, informed the design of the Prosecution regarding the crime of aggression in the Industrialist Trials.

Followers? The I.G. Farben conspiracy

'The theory that German industrialists and financiers were the men who pulled the strings behind the Nazi regime, brought it to power, profited by it and were fundamentally responsible for its aggressions and other crimes will be put to judicial test', hailed the *New York Times* in February 1947.[60] Indeed, the Farben indictment accused the defendants (who were frequently referred to as 'the organization' and not individually) of becoming an indispensable part of the German war machine, for initiating cartel agreements, and for intensifying production for their own empowerment. The Prosecution's main challenge was to provide a convincing theory, backed by evidence, for such concerted efforts between government and industry. The Prosecutors' choice of narrative and strategy soon revealed their antitrust orientation and conflated the conspiracy to wage war with cartelization practice, to the judges' dismay.

The Prosecution's opening statement described the parallel routes of Farben's independent growth and Hitler's rise to power. The indictment began when the routes converged and related the following account: at 18:00 on 20 February 1933, a group of about twenty-five businessmen attended a private meeting with Hitler, the Reich Chancellor, in the Berlin villa of Hermann Göring, president of the Reichstag. Leaders of German industry in attendance included Georg von Schnitzler (chief of the *Vorstand* Commercial Committee of I.G. Farben and second-in-command to the Chairman of the Board of Directors) and Gustav Krupp von Bohlen und Halbach. Hitler spoke at length about the importance of fighting Communism and preserving the principle of private ownership: 'Private enterprise cannot be maintained in the age of democracy; it is conceivable only if people have a sound idea of authority and personality.'[61] Göring followed Hitler with a request for financial support. Von Schnitzler reported to the Farben officials on the meeting and they decided to contribute 400,000 marks to Hitler's campaign. This was 'the largest single contribution by a firm represented at the meeting.'[62]

---

[60] Dana Adams Schmidt, *Nazi Capitalists Face U.S. Charges*, N.Y. TIMES, Feb. 2, 1947, at E5.

[61] The prosecution quoted Hitler's speech as it was summarized by Gustav Krupp von Bohlen. The latter's notes were presented as evidence before the Tribunal. *The Farben Case*, vol. 7, *supra* note 15, at 122–23.

[62] *Id.* at 124.

'This meeting in Berlin', wrote one of the Prosecutors in his memo, 'must be shown as the connecting link or connective tissue that ties all the cases together into an intelligible unity ... Here is the perfect setting for a conspiracy. All major actors are present. All ingredients the law requires to establish "concert of action" are here.'[63]

Some sixty years later, the historian Adam Tooze offered a sober perspective on the meeting's importance:

[I]t was the donations in February and March 1933 that really made the difference. They provided a large cash injection at a moment when the party was severely short of funds and faced, as Goering had predicted, the last competitive election in its history... Nothing suggests that the leaders of German big business were filled with ideological ardour for National Socialism, before or after February 1933. Nor did Hitler ask Krupp & Co. to sign up to an agenda of violent anti-Semitism or a war of conquest... But what Hitler and his government did promise was an end to parliamentary democracy and the destruction of the German left and for this most of German big business was willing to make a substantial down-payment.[64]

This meeting served as the starting point from which the Prosecution began building its case of a sophisticated alliance between Farben, Adolf Hitler, and his Nazi Party. Following this critical election of March 1933, Farben made numerous financial contributions to Hitler and the Nazi party, up to 1944. However, this was hardly the sole link between the commercial giant and the Nazi regime. The Prosecution thoroughly described the spider's web of alliances through which 'Farben synchronized its industrial activities with the military planning of the German High Command' and participated in the rearmament of Germany and in the creation and equipping of the Nazi military for wars of aggression.[65] Further, the indictment alleged that Farben entered into cartel arrangements with U.S. companies (such as DuPont and Standard Oil) and used the information strategically in dealing with foreign countries, to weaken them. The indictment also included aspects of American suspicions of the cartel's involvement in espionage activities.[66]

---

[63] Memorandum from Drachsler to Heath, *supra* note 59.

[64] ADAM TOOZE, THE WAGES OF DESTRUCTION 101 (2006).

[65] *The Farben Case*, vol. 7, *supra* note 15, at 19–28. The Prosecution also charged Farben with participating in formation of transnational cartels to weaken Germany's enemies. Moreover, it accused Farben of engaging in 'propaganda, intelligence, and espionage activities'. *Id.* at 29–39. The Prosecution's allegations about Farben's extensive pre-war ties with U.S. companies attracted most of the attention in the United States. The indictment alleged that Farben entered into cartel arrangements with U.S. companies and used the strategic information on foreign countries to weaken them. The Court dismissed most of the evidence in this context. *Id.* at 29–31.

[66] *Id.* at 29–31. Though prominent, I.G. Farben was not the only German enterprise accused of espionage. The activities of German-owned enterprises in Latin America were also subject to investigation by the State Department. *See* Memorandum from Samuel Melo to Telford Taylor, Brigadier General,

These accusations were not incidentally reminiscent of the Justice Department's antitrust campaigns.[67]

The Prosecutors built the case of an ever-growing alliance between industry and the Nazi regime. What began on 20 February in Göring's villa was advanced by establishing a special organization in Farben (*Vermittlungsstelle Wehrmacht*), headed by Krauch, which had the declared objective of 'building up a tight organization for armament in the I.G., which could be inserted without difficulty into the existing organization of I.G. and the individual plants.'[68] Krauch was appointed Chief of the Department of Research and Development in the Office of the Four-Year Plan in 1936.[69] Some of the other defendants became members of different industrial organizations that exercised governmental powers in the planning of the German mobilization for war. The indictment quotes Albert Speer's remarks on Farben as an entity that was 'promoted to governmental status' and was frequently referred to as the 'state within the state.'[70]

The Prosecution considered additional aspects of Farben's operations as crimes against peace—not least, its contribution to making Germany's army self-sufficient with regard to three crucial raw materials essential to waging an aggressive war: nitrates, oil, and rubber. Further, when asked to order such materials, 'Farben put its entire organization at the disposal of the Wehrmacht'. In addition to direct involvement in facilitating the war, the firm was also engaged in economic warfare aimed at weakening Germany's potential enemies: 'Farben's international affiliations, associations, and contracts', claimed the indictment, were carefully destined to '[w]eaken the United States as an arsenal of democracy'[71] and led Great Britain to 'a desperate situation with respect to magnesium at the outbreak of the war'.[72] These are but a few of the key categories of evidence presented by the Prosecutors

---

Chief of Counsel for War Crimes, US-OMGUS, 'Report on Espionage Activities' (Feb. 6, 1946), OCCWC 1933–1949, Group 238, No. 159, 190/12/13/01-02, NARA.

[67] This argument is also developed by Mark E. Spicka, *The Devil's Chemists on Trial: The American Prosecution of I.G. Farben at Nuremberg*, 61 HISTORIAN 865, 871 (1999). *See also* interview by Richard D. McKinzie with Josaiah E. DuBois, Jr., Dep. Chief of Counsel for War Crimes in charge of I.G. Farben Case, Nuremberg, Ger., 1947–48, in Camden, N.J. (29 June 1973). Online: http://www.trumanlibrary. gov/library/oral-histories/duboisje#transcript(describing DuBois' work for the Treasury Department prior to his involvement in the Farben Prosecutor—he worked for the Treasury Department but the Justice department conducted the antitrust campaigns).

[68] *The Farben Case*, vol. 7, *supra* note 15, at 20.

[69] Carl Bosch, then president of the Farben, recommended to Goering that he retain the defendant Krauch to advise him in the planning and control of the chemical sector of the rearmament programme.

[70] *The Farben Case*, vol. 7, *supra* note 8, at 25. Peter Hayes provides a more nuanced account: 'Both Krauch and his subordinates rapidly identified with their new tasks, not their old employers, even when private corporations continued to pay their salaries.' HAYES, *supra* note 23, at 176–78. Furthermore, Hayes challenged the Prosecution's implicit claim—that the Four-Year Plan began as, or became, an I.G. Farben Plan. Conversely, he argued that '[t]here occurred in Germany after 1936, not a Farbenization of economic policy making, but a steady militarization of IG Farben'. *Id.* at 184–85.

[71] *The Farben Case*, vol. 7, *supra* note 15, at 29–30.

[72] *Id.* at 30.

to demonstrate Farben officials' support in strengthening Germany's war capabilities and potential.[73]

Despite its great zeal, the Prosecution sensed it was losing the case on crimes against peace. During the trial, Chief Prosecutor Josiah DuBois Jr. asked his colleagues in Washington for help:

> We are specifically interested in discussions relating to the meaning of aggressive war and the criminal liabilities of so-called private persons as distinguished from government officials. The motion filed by the defense ... was based on the argument that what we have proved does not fall within Control Council Law No. 10, which must be interpreted in the light of the London Charter and findings of the IMT.[74]

Joseph Borkin later remarked that the Prosecution began to develop the case as if it were an antitrust case, 'not ... a trial of war criminals charged with mass murder'.[75] The court's disapproving sentiment is well captured in DuBois' description of the trial's proceedings:

> From the very beginning the Prosecution had trouble convincing the court that our method of proof was appropriate. On a stand facing the court, we had set up panoramic charts of the Farben empire, showing banking houses from Bern to Bombay, production facilities on five continents... The Tribunal did not like this method... This was only the third day, and already the court was impatient.[76]

DuBois further recalled in his book the appeal of Emanuel Minskoff, one of the lawyers in the Prosecution team, to change the order and direction of the Prosecution case. He argued it would be more effective to open with the charge of slavery and mass murder, otherwise 'the court just can't believe these are the kind of men who could have been guilty of aggressive war'.[77] Sam Harris made a

---

[73] Historians such as Richard Overy and Peter Hayes contest the general view that economic circles supported and pressed the Nazi leadership into war. HAYES, *supra* note 23, at 213–18. Hayes argued that the war entailed weighty risks and costs for the concern. 'There is little support that IG Farben sought, encouraged, or directed the Nazi conquest of Europe.' *Id.* at 213. 'The combine reacted opportunistically and defensively to the regime's diplomatic and military triumphs, but IG did not foment them.' *Id.* at 218.

[74] Transcript of Washington to Nuremberg Teleconference (Dec. 17, 1947), War Crimes Branch, JAG, Group 153, No. 132, 270/1/4/03 at item D-23, NARA.

[75] BORKIN, *supra* note 23, at 141. For further discussion on the influence of the American antitrust policy vis-à-vis German industry on the Industrialist cases, *see* Chapter 5.

[76] DUBOIS, *supra* note 32, at 76–77. *See also The Farben Case*, vol. 7, *supra* note 15, at 583, for an exhibit illustrative of the Prosecution's approach.

[77] DuBois could not follow Minskoff's suggestion since he was obliged to proceed according to the sequence of the counts in the indictment. DUBOIS, *supra* note 32, at 99 (quoting Minskoff). Nonetheless, this troubling start forced the Prosecution to modify its approach. *Id.* at 77.

similar suggestion while preparing the Krupp case.[78] Minskoff's and DuBois' concerns were eventually substantiated. The Farben Tribunal dismissed the charges of crimes against peace, exonerating Farben's prewar contacts with U.S. companies and, implicitly, the conduct of the U.S. firms.[79]

The judges interpreted the IMT judgment as setting a high standard of proof for the analysis of the aggression charges, namely the need for conclusive evidence 'of both knowledge and active participation'.[80] Accordingly, the Farben Tribunal opened its discussion on crimes against peace by discussing how the IMT treated findings related to this charge 'with great caution'.[81] This analysis led the Tribunal to conclude that Carl Krauch, one of four men in charge of research and development in the Four-Year Plan managed by Göring, did not knowingly participate in the planning, preparation, or initiation of an aggressive war.[82]

It was especially difficult for the Tribunal to hold the Farben defendants responsible on the count of crimes against peace: first, due to the IMT precedent according to which rearmament, in and of itself, was not a crime unless carried out as part of a plan to wage aggressive war; and, second, in light of its acquittal of officials who held economic positions in the Nazi government.[83] The Tribunal answered the Prosecution's assertion that 'the magnitude of the rearmament efforts was such as to convey that knowledge [the personal knowledge needed to establish responsibility]', as follows: 'None of the defendants, however, were military experts... The field of their life work had been entirely within industry ... [t]he evidence does not show that any of them knew the extent to which general rearmament had been planned, or how far it had progressed at any given time.'[84] Further, the Tribunal dismissed the Prosecution's 'February 20th' conspiracy claim that donations made by Farben to the Nazi party in the early years of the regime indicated an alliance

---

[78] Transcript of Teleconference, Conway to Thayer (Sept. 24, 1947), Teleconference Copies, Jan. 29, 1947–Dec. 30, 1947, Correspondence and Reports, OCCWC, Group 238, No. 159, 190/12/13/01-02 at WD-29, NARA [hereinafter Teleconference, Conway to Thayer].

[79] While the defendants were exonerated on the counts of preparing and waging wars of aggression, some were convicted of Counts Two and Three: Plundering and Spoliation, and Slavery and Mass Murder.

[80] *The Farben Case*, vol. 8, *supra* note 15, at 1102.

[81] *Id.* Indeed, the IMT found parties guilty under Counts One and Two only when the evidence of both knowledge and participation was conclusive. No defendant was convicted unless he maintained, as did the defendant Hess, a very close relationship with Hitler or attended at least one of the four secret meetings at which Hitler disclosed his plans.

[82] *Id.* at 1227.

[83] The lawyers working on the Industrialist Trials had hoped that the indictment of Speer and Funk would provide some basis for trying the Industrialists. *See* Memorandum from Drachsler to Heath, *supra* note 59. However, with the acquittal of Speer, as noted by Judge Hebert in his dissenting opinion in *Farben*, 'it would not be logical in this case to convict any or all of the Farben defendants of the waging [of] aggressive war in the face of the positive pronouncement by the International Military Tribunal that war production activities of the character headed by Speer do not constitute the 'waging' of aggressive war'. *The Farben Case*, vol. 8, *supra* note 15, at 1306.

[84] *The Farben Case*, vol. 8, *supra* note 15, at 1113.

between the two.[85] Finally, the Tribunal concluded that the Prosecution's charges of propaganda, intelligence, and espionage on behalf of the German Government were not in reference to military or armament matters, but only to industrial and commercial matters.[86]

The Tribunal responded to the interpretation of waging aggressive war by making reference to the IMT decision and its limited definition, which confined it only to principals.[87] Indeed, it included industry in the concept of major war criminals as follows: 'Those persons in the political, military, [or] *industrial* fields ... who [were] responsible for the formulation and execution of policies' qualified as leaders of the Nazi regime.[88] But it added another aspect to the limitations derived from the concept of major war criminals, namely that crimes against peace are allegedly committed by sovereign states. Since international crimes are committed 'by men, not by abstract entities ... [t]he extension of the punishment for crimes against peace by the IMT to the leaders of the Nazi military and government, was therefore, a logical step'. In contrast: 'In this case we are faced with ... men of industry who were not makers of policy but who supported their government ... in the waging of war.'[89] Thus, men of industry could be held responsible for the crime of aggression only if they are policy-makers.[90] In its concluding remarks in reference to waging a war of Aggression, the Tribunal stated the need to avoid mass punishment:[91]

> The defendants now before us were neither high public officials in the civil government nor high military officers. Their participation was that of followers and not leaders. If we lower the standard of participation to include them, it is difficult to find a logical place to draw the line between the guilty and the innocent among the great mass of German people.[92]

---

[85]   *Id.* at 1117–19.

[86]   *Id.* at 1123.

[87]   'There is nothing [in the London agreement] or in the attached Charter to indicate that the words "waging a war of aggression," as used in Article II(a) of the latter, was intended to apply to any and all persons who aided, supported, or contributed to the carrying on of an aggressive war.' *Id.* at 1124.

[88]   *Id.* at 1124 (my emphasis). *See* Kevin Jon Heller, *Retreat from Nuremberg: The Leadership Requirement in the Crime of Aggression*, 18 EUR. J. INT'L L. 477, 483–84 (2007) (discussing the Tribunal's finding that Industrialists complicit in a state's act of aggression could be liable for the crime of aggression).

[89]   *The Farben Case*, vol. 8, *supra* note 15, at 1125.

[90]   For further discussion, *see* Heller, *supra* note 88, at 486–88 (suggesting the Prosecution lowered the threshold from the *leadership* requirement to *involvement at the policy level* in planning, preparing, or initiating the war). Heller advocated for the *shape and influence* requirement, rather than the *control or direct test. Id.* at 496. He analysed the *shape and influence* test as it appeared in the High Command Case, in which fourteen high-ranking officers in the German military were put to trial, and the *Ministries* case, in which twenty-one high-ranking officials in the Nazi Government and Nazi Party were charged with various crimes against peace. *Id.* at 486–87.

[91]   *The Farben Case*, vol. 8, *supra* note 15, at 1124–25.

[92]   *Id.* at 1126.

Leaders? The Krupp independent conspiracy

In the Krupp case, the Tribunal again considered policy-making essential to any finding of responsibility among private persons. When the allegations of crimes against peace came before the Krupp Tribunal, it acquitted the defendants on counts one and four—participating in wars of aggression and crimes against peace—and focused exclusively on slave labour and spoliation of property.

Krupp was a historic name in European war mythology. Throughout the nineteenth century, the firm grew to become 'the largest and most notorious armament enterprise of all time' and was considered 'Germany's principal arsenal' during the First World War.[93] During the Second World War, Krupp was the leading German manufacturer of artillery, armor, tanks, and other munitions, and a prominent producer of iron and coal.[94] But the evidence establishing responsibility for the first count was not only based on Krupp's involvement in the rearmament of Germany. As Thayer, the principal researcher for the Krupp case, wrote:

[It is] imperative that you secure release of Krupp Nirosta documents and send them here as rapidly as possible... Since the Krupp trial starts November 1st with the Aggressive War count. Allegations as to economic penetration rest exclusively on these documents as summarized in the Department of Justice report.[95]

We find early traces of these allegations in Henry Morgenthau's book, *Germany is Our Problem.*[96]

The Krupp ruling on the aggressive war count was published on 5 April 1948 and preceded the Farben decision.[97] Similar to the Farben Tribunal, the question posed was whether the Krupp defendant participated in (or knew of) the Nazi conspiracy to wage aggressive war. More specifically, it brought to the fore the question of the link between the *business* of arms manufacture and the *crime* of aggression. In his concurring opinion, Judge Anderson explained the Prosecution's distinction between the conspiracy charge in the indictment before the IMT and the Krupp case:

The contention is in substance that whereas in the indictment before the IMT the conspiracy charged was that originated by Hitler and his intimates, for convenience called the 'Nazi Conspiracy,' the conspiracy here is *a separate and*

---

[93] *The Krupp Case, supra* note 16, at 63.

[94] *Id.* at 11, 16, 404.

[95] Teleconference, Conway to Thayer, *supra* note 78.

[96] Morgenthau described how the Krupp firm used its organization of the Krupp-Nirosta company to maintain Germany's influence in Latin America. HENRY MORGENTHAU JR., GERMANY IS OUR PROBLEM (1945).

[97] *The Krupp Case, supra* note 16, at 390.

independent one originated in 1919 by Gustav Krupp and then officials of the Krupp concern, long before the Nazi seizure of power.[98]

Indeed, the Prosecution argued that Krupp's aggressive motivations 'antedated Nazism, and have their own independent and pernicious vitality that fused with Nazi ideas to produce the Third Reich'.[99] However, in rejecting the argument of an independent Krupp conspiracy, Judge Anderson wrote: 'Under the construction given ... by the IMT, the conspiracy to commit crimes against peace involving violations of a treaty is confined to a concrete plan to initiate and wage war and preparations in connection with such plan.'[100] He concluded:

> [T]he defendants were private citizens and noncombatants... None of them had any voice in the policies which led their nation into aggressive war; nor were any of them privy to that policy. None had any *control over the conduct of the war or over any of the armed forces;* nor were any of them parties to the plans pursuant to which the wars were waged and, so far as appears, none of them had any knowledge of such plans.[101]

Judge Wilkins wrote a concurring opinion that was more favourable to the Prosecution's case.[102] Wilkins noted that 'the Prosecution built up a strong *prima facie* case, as far as the implication of Gustav Krupp and the Krupp firm is concerned'.[103] It was the benefit of doubt that kept him from opposing dismissal.[104] As he later wrote in his memoirs, 'Had Gustav *or the Krupp firm as such* been before us, the ruling would have been quite different'.[105]

Despite the gravity attributed to this count by the U.S. Prosecution, neither the conspiracy element nor the notion of crimes against peace was a focal point of the IMT decision. Indeed, it had been almost completely diminished when it came before the U.S. Tribunals that tried the Industrialists.

Viewed through the lenses of crimes against peace and conspiracy, the prosecutorial strategies of the Farben and Krupp indictments put forth competing theories of conspiracy. In the Farben indictment, the defendants were depicted as part of the

---

[98] *Id.* at 407.

[99] *Id.* at 131.

[100] *Id.* at 419. Anderson argued that the acquittal of Speer on the charge of waging war was particularly relevant to the Krupp managers' responsibility. *Id.* at 447–48.

[101] *Id.* at 449 (my emphasis).

[102] *Id.* at 455–66.

[103] *Id.* at 456.

[104] Wilkins wrote, 'Giving the defendants the benefit of what may be called a very slight doubt, and although the evidence with respect to some of them was extraordinarily strong, I concurred that, in view of Gustav Krupp's overriding authority in the Krupp enterprises, the extent of the actual influence of the present defendants was not as substantial as to warrant finding them guilty of crimes against peace.' *Id.* at 457–58.

[105] WILLIAM J. WILKINS, THE SWORD AND THE GAVEL 209 (1981) (my emphasis).

war machine, complicit in the grand scheme of war initiated by the Nazi government. In the Krupp indictment, the defendants resembled a group of conspiring pirates. Thus, the framing of the Krupp Conspiracy was that of a gang of organized gangsters conspiring to achieve their aims by unlawful means. The Prosecution failed to prove its case in both instances.

In both the Farben and Krupp decisions, the Tribunals stressed the importance of the link to the policy realm. This reaffirmed the nature of the crime of aggression as a crime committed by the state and its organs. The underpinning rationale of crimes against peace relates to the violation of sovereign borders[106] or international treaties. Paradoxically, though clearly interfering within the sovereign's prerogative to wage war, it reaffirmed the state as the core subject of international law.[107]

The count of crimes against peace limited the perception of the international crime to traditional inter-state relations. The state's monopoly over violence was re-established through the insistence that only a close link to the policy-making realm could provide sufficient grounds for criminal responsibility. Thus, the decisions decried the limitations of the doctrine of crimes against peace and its constraints in a context of diffused responsibility. Despite the attempted shift towards individual criminal responsibility, the nature of the violence scrutinized by the Tribunals was only that which could be linked to the apparatus of the state. As elaborated in the following section, we can attribute these results to an impoverished conception of the Nazi state.

Behemoth vs. Leviathan: Business Responsibility and Competing Theories of the State

Neumann concluded *Behemoth* with the assertion that National Socialism had no political theory of its own:

> But if National Socialism has no political theory, is its political system a state? If a state is characterized by the rule of law, our answer to this question will be negative, since we deny that law exists in Germany. It may be argued that state and law are not identical, and that there can be states without law... A state is ideologically characterized by the unity of the political power that it wields. I doubt whether even a state in this restricted sense exits in Germany... It is doubtful whether National Socialism possesses a unified coercive machinery, unless we accept the leadership theory as a true doctrine. The party is independent of the state in matters pertaining to the police and youth, but everywhere else the state stands above

---

[106] *See* DAVID LUBAN, LEGAL MODERNISM 336–44 (1997) for a development of this argument.
[107] *See id.* at 337–39.

the party. The army is sovereign in many fields; the bureaucracy is uncontrolled; and industry has managed to conquer many positions.[108]

This incoherent structure, however, does not defy a shared objective. Neumann conveyed in *Behemoth* the emphasis on the war that the Prosecution picked up later. National Socialism had coordinated the diversified and contradictory state interferences into one system having but one aim: the preparation for imperialist war. This means that the automatism of free capitalism, precarious even under democratic monopoly capitalism, had been severely restricted. But capitalism remained.[109] Neumann's analysis suggested a reality full of contradictions. While industry often operated freely and out of self-interest, its operations were restricted by incorporation into a monopolistic structure and some aspects of the state bureaucracy. More generally, Neumann argued:

> [u]nder National Socialism ... the whole of the society is organized in four solid, centralized groups, each operating under the leadership principle, each with legislative, administrative, and judicial power of its own... The four totalitarian bodies will then enforce it with the machinery at their disposal. There is no need for a state standing above all groups; the state may even be a hindrance to the compromises among the four leaderships... It is thus impossible to detect in the framework of the National Socialist political system any one organ which monopolizes political power.[110]

Neumann thus regarded the four bodies of Nazi authority—the government, the party organizations, the army, and industry—as the 'non-state'. The Tribunals' opposition to the non-state structure of the Nazi regime was evident in their decisions on the crime of aggression. The judges' decisions were based on the premise of governmental control over the war. The Industrialists' culpability could be proven only if they were deemed to be policy-makers—principals of decision-making in the Nazi State. Neumann's theory was in clear tension with what he considered to be the familiar theory of the state: 'States, however, as they have arisen in Italy, are conceived of as rationally operating machineries disposing of [accessing] the monopoly of coercive power. A state is ideologically characterized by the unity of the

---

[108] NEUMANN, *supra* note 34, at 467–68. Hannah Arendt referred to Neumann, upon reaching similar conclusions a few years later: 'What strikes the observer of the totalitarian state is certainly not its monolithic structure. On the contrary, all serious students of the subject agree at least on the co-existence (or the conflict) of dual authority, the party and the state. Many, moreover, have stressed the peculiar 'shapelessness' of the totalitarian government.' HANNAH ARENDT, THE ORIGINS OF TOTALITARIANISM 395 (1994). Further, Arendt noted how '[a]bove the state and behind the façades of ostensible power, in a maze of multiplied offices, underlying all shifts of authority and in chaos of inefficiency, lies the power nucleus of the country'. ARENDT, *supra*, at 420.

[109] NEUMANN, *supra* note 34, at 360–61.

[110] *Id.* at 468–69.

political power that it wields. I doubt whether a state in this restricted sense exists in Germany.[111] The decisions of the Tribunals presupposed the Weberian imagery of the modern state as a default position. The notion of the Industrialists as equal partners in the crime of aggression was rejected, as they were assumed to be merely 'followers and not leaders.'[112]

Viewed from a normative perspective, Neumann's argument undermined the possibility of conceiving Germany as a state and therefore entailed a serious destabilizing risk for international lawyers of his time. Neumann asked his readers:

> But if the National Socialist structure is not a state, what is it? ... I venture to suggest that we are confronted with a form of society in which the ruling groups control the rest of the population directly, without the mediation of that rational though coercive apparatus hitherto known as the state. This new social form is not yet fully realized, but the trend exists which defines the very essence of the regime.[113]

Although the judicial verdict was clear, historians continued to deliberate on the nature of the relationship between businesses and government in the Third Reich. The imagery of an alliance between equals—industry and government— proved difficult to reconcile with the shift towards greater political direction and influence on the course of the war and economic policy from 1936. But, as Peter Hayes observed, '[i]f the primacy of politics reigned ... an amorphous and unpredictable Behemoth ruled.'[114] Government authorities responsible for the German war production were diffuse and somewhat in flux: 'Not even "total war" could cure Nazism's congenital inclination to multiply competencies, confuse lines of authority, and ordain competing objectives.'[115]

Does the fact that governmental decision-making over war and peace was diffuse and incoherent necessarily undermine the Tribunals' rationale that required a link to the policy-making realm to establish responsibility? Both the historical debate and the Tribunals' decisions share the assumption that political leaders initiate, manage, and control policies of war and peace. This premise assumes that wars always result from well-organized decision-making processes, orchestrated by a clearly defined circle of leaders. Put differently, the endorsement of the Hobbesian political *ideal* of war being solely conducted and decided upon by political leaders necessarily lead to the assumption that the crime of aggression is a 'crime of leadership'?

---

[111] *Id.* at 467.
[112] *The Farben Case*, vol. 8, *supra* note 15, at 1126.
[113] NEUMANN, *supra* note 34, at 470.
[114] HAYES, *supra* note 23, at 319.
[115] *Id.* at 320.

Historical Perspectives and the Behemoth Theory

One element contributing to the Tribunals' decision not to find the Industrialists responsible for crimes against peace was the coincidence between the change in the power balance between industry and government after 1936 (in favour of the latter) and the Tribunals' decision to limit their jurisdiction to post-1939 events. The allegations against the Industrialists' responsibility for the crime of aggression focused primarily on the early Nazi period, when the alleged conspiracy was established. Therefore, it is not surprising that the Krupp and Farben Tribunals' decision to limit their jurisdiction to post-1939 events pulled the rug from under this count. Yet, even beyond the restricted post-1939 perspective, while economic leaders enjoyed much greater influence on state economic policy during these early years of the Nazi regime than in future years, historians, too, have been reluctant to attribute responsibility for the rise of Nazism to power to German business leaders.[116] I will now expand on this post-1936 shift towards the primacy of politics.

The Prosecution tried to argue in both the Farben and the Krupp cases that economic actors' support of the initiation of the war (such as economic support and lobbying for the Nazi party) amounted to a concerted effort, a conspiracy, between business enterprises and the Nazi regime. This theory on the role of industry in the prospering of the Nazi state became a source of a heated debate among historians of the period. Influenced by the ideological clouds of the Cold War, the debate was polarized between those who argued for the supremacy of the capital interests in the Nazi regime (*i.e.* the primacy of economics) and others who argued for the clear supremacy of politics over industry.[117]

Initial historical accounts of the relationship between big business and National Socialism tended to focus on the extent to which the financial support of German corporations facilitated the rise of the Nazis to power during the Weimar years. During the period from 1933 to 1936, similar (albeit not identical) interests shared by the Nazi bloc, big businesses, and the army led to their mutual cooperation. Although big businesses were divided in their attitudes towards the rearmament plans, the work creation programme and the profits derived from armament sales drove them closer to the government.[118] The dictatorship's relative weakness in its

---

[116] RICHARD J. OVERY, WAR AND ECONOMY IN THE THIRD REICH 12 (1994).

[117] *See* Francis R. Nicosia & Jonathan Huener, *Introduction: Business and Industry in Nazi Germany in Historiographical Context, in* BUSINESS AND INDUSTRY IN NAZI GERMANY 1, 1–14 (Francis R. Nicosia & Jonathan Huener eds., 2004) (discussing scholarship on the relationship between German professionals and the Nazi regime); Volker R. Berghahn, *Writing the History of Business in the Third Reich: Past Achievements and Future Directions, in* BUSINESS AND INDUSTRY IN NAZI GERMANY, *supra*, at 129, 129–30 (describing the academic debate over the political responsibility and moral culpability of German businessmen under the Nazi regime).

[118] *See* DAN P. SILVERMAN, HITLER'S ECONOMY: NAZI WORK CREATION PROGRAMS, 1933–1936, at 6–8 (1998) (describing how German industrialists who initially opposed the Nazi work creation programme came to support it). Silverman's study suggests that partially effective work creation

early years placed businesses in a strong position. This was reflected in the extremely powerful position that Hjalmar Schacht—former President of the Reichsbank and, from 1934, Minister for Economics—held in the Nazi state.[119] Overy observed that 'under his careful guidance the position of the large German firms was strengthened. Cartelization was extended further at the expense of small businesses; output and profits rose under the stimulus of government-induced demand.'[120]

Historical investigations conducted after the Nuremberg Trials suggest that the closely interwoven aims and interests of Nazi leadership and of German capital mutually influenced and affected one another, thus 'making it difficult to separate a specifically "political" and specifically "economic" sphere and therefore to distinguish a clear "primacy".'[121] Some historians' view of the relationship between business enterprises and the Nazi regime is reminiscent of what the architects of the Nuremberg Trials envisioned. Ian Kershaw suggests we perceive the position and role of big businesses within the context of the complex and changing multidimensional (polycratic) power structures in the Third Reich.[122] Kershaw advises his readers to follow Franz Neumann in breaking away from the totalitarian model of a centralized command economy and monolithic state in the hands of Hitler and his clique of Nazi leaders. Kershaw also encourages his audience to eschew the alternative, almost equally monolithic, model of the Nazi state as the direct representative and most aggressive form of rule of finance capital. Conversely, 'despite the rationing and licensing activities of the state, [private firms in the Third Reich] still had ample scope to devise their own production and investment profile... There occurred hardly any nationalization of private firms under the Third Reich. In addition, there were few enterprises newly created as state-run firms.'[123]

Following Neumann's formulation, Kershaw describes the Nazi regime 'as an unwritten "pact" (or "alliance") between different but interdependent blocs in a "power-cartel".'[124] Despite some important differences, Kershaw's depiction is

---

programmes worked with a number of other factors to produce a rapid recovery of Germany's labor market under the Nazis. *Id.* at 245.

[119] Ian Kershaw, THE NAZI DICTATORSHIP: PROBLEMS AND PERSPECTIVES OF INTERPRETATION 59 (4th ed. 2000).

[120] OVERY, *supra* note 116, at 94–95.

[121] KERSHAW, *supra* note 119, at 56. The historical debate on the involvement of business enterprises in the Nazi regime grapples with two main issues: that of political responsibility of German business enterprises under the Nazi regime ('how far they had a hand in the rise and consolidation of Hitler's power') and that of moral and criminal culpability. Berghahn, *supra* note 117, at 129. Criminal responsibility is defined by international law and the Nuremberg Tribunals jurisprudence. Indeed, as the history of the scholarship in this context suggests, at the war's end, 'preoccupation with criminal culpability pushed the question of political responsibility into the background'. Berghahn, *supra* note 117, at 129–30.

[122] KERSHAW, *supra* note 119, at 47–68.

[123] Christoph Buchheim & Jonas Scherner, *The Role of Private Property in the Nazi Economy: The Case of Industry*, 66 J. ECON. HIST. 390, 390–91 (2006).

[124] KERSHAW, *supra* note 119, at 58.

surprisingly reminiscent of the Prosecutors' approach. His historical description of such an alliance 'focused on organized capitalism, namely "industrial organizations," cartels, and trusts such as the companies of heavy industry of I.G. Farben'.[125]

Although blocs in the power cartel remained intact until the end of the Third Reich, their interrelationship and relative weight within the cartel altered during the course of the dictatorship.[126] Internal conflicts among big businesses changed the balance of power between government and industry after the first phase of the Third Reich (until 1936) towards the relative dominance of the Nazi party. Economic policy shifted during the course of 1936 towards an accelerated rearmament and autarkic policy in preparation for war and imperial expansion. Schacht resisted the change, and was soon replaced by Göring as the dominant figure in the economy. This shift reduced constraints on industry for the Nazi leadership: 'however sympathetic to the business world and however dependent on it, the Nazi Government had its own interests which it was prepared to pursue'.[127] Following this shift, businesses 'could still profit from the system, [but] they were forced to do so on the party's terms. Profit and investment levels were determined by the state, on terms much more favorable to state projects'.[128] Thus, while some historians have concluded that politics took primacy over the economy after the first period,[129] German businesses were not entirely powerless at this time, and differed in their reaction and resilience to the shifting balance of power. Nevertheless, since the judgments of the subsequent trials followed the IMT's restrictive decision to exercise its jurisdiction only on post-1939 events, they could only consider the later post-1936 period that was much less compatible with the Prosecutors' claims for an alliance between industry and the Nazi regime that facilitated the latter's ascent to power (in the case of Farben) or the allegations of an independent conspiracy of Krupp to wage a war of aggression 'long before the Nazi seizure of power'. Indeed, Nazi policies after 1936 were aimed at 'recruiting' the economy for empire and conquest. Accordingly, the next section focuses on the Industrialists' activities in the age of empire.

---

[125] Buchheim & Scherner, *supra* note 123, at 391.

[126] KERSHAW, *supra* note 119, at 58. Other historical accounts go even further in challenging a coherent description of the industry–government relationship, revealing complex power structures within the Third Reich. *See, e.g.,* John R. Gillingham, INDUSTRY AND POLITICS IN THE THIRD REICH: RUHR COAL, HITLER AND EUROPE (1985); HAYES, *supra* note 23; OVERY, *supra* note 116.

[127] Alan Milward, *Fascism and the Economy, in* FASCISM: A READER'S GUIDE 409, 434 (Walter Laqueur ed., 1979).

[128] OVERY, *supra* note 116, at 106.

[129] This argument is most identified with Mason. Tim Mason, *The Primacy of Politics: Politics and Economics in National Socialist Germany, in* NAZISM AND THE THIRD REICH 175, 175–200 (Henry A. Turner ed., 1972).

The Normative State as the Private Sphere: Revisiting Ernst Fraenkel's Dual State Theory in the Crimes of Aryanization, Plunder, and Spoliation

The relationship between the responsibility of the Industrialists and the theory of the state was not only relevant for the crime of aggression. The crimes of Aryanization, plunder, and spoliation similarly highlighted the tension between crimes deemed, in essence, 'political', with private actors involved in their commission. The jurisprudence of the Industrialist cases concerning the crime of aggression raised the question of private actors' responsibility for the political crime of waging war. Interestingly, the discussion on spoliation penetrated a realm that is closer to private actors' conventional practices: that of business transactions. It turned the tables on the question of the 'political' crime, asking under what circumstances private transactions, even if conducted in the shadow of war and occupation, may be regarded as criminal. Such inquiry required further understanding of the Nazi state, including an analysis of the relationship between the public and private spheres in the Nazi regime.

Aryanization: The exclusion of plunder within state borders

The year 1936 marked a change in direction as the German economy moved towards autarky and armament. The Nazi policy was aimed at transforming the economy in the service of empire and conquest. Under these new conditions, the 'business community was characterized by defensive opportunism in the face of state power'.[130] The substance of German capitalism remained intact, but entrepreneurial independence was limited. The plan was to evict non-German capital from central-eastern Europe and to build up a new state-supervised German zone devoted to war production.[131] As noted by Mark Mazower, '[f]irms like chemicals giant I.G. Farben joined in. They had not been especially in favour of the war. But once it broke out, they too took full advantage of it.'[132] Farben's conduct brought to the fore the question of the German Industrialists' responsibility for the economic imperialism and military conquests of the Nazi regime.

Indeed, the crimes included in the count of Aryanization and spoliation were described by the Flick Prosecutors as 'intimately connected with the preparation by Germany for an aggressive war'.[133] This war, the Prosecutors argued, facilitated

---

[130] OVERY, *supra* note 116, at 17.
[131] MARK MAZOWER, HITLER'S EMPIRE 265 (2008).
[132] *Id.*
[133] *The Flick Case, supra* note 14, at 92. Correspondence between the Prosecutors and Raphael Lemkin conveys the importance they attributed to this link. Washington to Nuremberg Teleconference (March 25, 1947), Nuremberg Teleconferences, June 29, 1947–Feb. 26, 1947, War Crimes Branch, JAG, Group 153, No. 132, 240/1/4/06-7, NARA.

Flick officials' efforts to acquire Jewish property. Count Three of the Flick indictment charged three defendants in the Flick concern (including Flick himself) with the commission of crimes against humanity by criminal participation in the persecution of racial, religious, and political groups, including, in particular, 'Aryanization' of properties belonging in whole, or in part, to Jews.[134]

In a conversation between the Judge Advocate General (JAG) in Washington and the trials team at Nuremberg, one of the lawyers asked for the Aryanization count to be based on a similar rationale used in U.S. extortion cases: 'We vaguely remember a recent New York Civil Action (Flamm v. Noble we believe) where a private citizen threatened a radio station with government action unless this station was sold to him... This case might be good for us because of its factual similarity to our cases (Aryanization count).'[135] This brief communication succinctly captures the Prosecutors' understanding of Flick's strategy in gaining control over properties in Germany before the war by using the potential threat of government intervention.[136]

On 19 February 1947, one month before the Flick proceedings ended, Telford Taylor asked his colleagues in the JAG office in Washington for advice on how to proceed, given that the IMT restrictive decision took cognizance of crimes against

---

[134] The Aryanization process (*Arisierung*) comprised two stages: the so-called voluntary stage, from 1933–1938, during which Jews were gradually removed from German economic life, and the 'compulsory' stage that began immediately after the *Kristallnacht*. In this final stage, all Jewish-owned businesses that had not already been 'Aryanized' were forcibly confiscated. For a concise overview, *see* THE SHOAH RESEARCH CTR., INT'L SCH. FOR HOLOCAUST STUDIES, *Aryanization*. Online: https://www.yadvashem.org/odot_pdf/Microsoft%20Word%20-%205775.pdf (last accessed Oct. 10, 2019). For a more elaborate discussion, *see*MARTIN DEAN, ROBBING THE JEWS: THE CONFISCATION OF JEWISH PROPERTY IN THE HOLOCAUST, 1933–1945, at 17–171 (2008).

[135] Washington to Nuremberg Teleconference (June 25, 1947) Letters Received 1944–1951, War Crimes Branch, JAG, Group 153, No. 132, 270/1/4/03, NARA.

[136] In one such instance, Flick negotiated his control over the Ignaz Petschek brown-coal mines in central Germany by putting pressure on the German Government to allow no-one but him to negotiate its sale. Mr. Hans Petschek, who fled to London and then New York in 1938, provided the Prosecutors with valuable information on this transaction. For the correspondence between the Prosecutors, Petschek, and other officials involved, *see* Kempner's Materials (Jan. 22, 1947) WWII War Criminals Records, OCCWC 1933–1949, Group 238, No. 159, 190/12/13/01-02, NARA. L.M. Stallbaumer, who studied the Friedrich Flick concern's involvement in the Aryanization of Jewish property, stressed the opportunistic motivation of business leaders under Nazi rule. L.M. Stallbaumer, *Big Business and the Persecution of the Jews: The Flick Concern and the 'Aryanization' of Jewish Property Before the War*, 13 HOLOCAUST & GENOCIDE STUD. 1, 15–16 (1999). The lawyers preparing for the trial initially included Dresdner Bank as an additional firm to be indicted at Nuremberg. The Dresdner bankers' involvement in Aryanization practices was particularly notorious. *Cf.* Expropriation of the Property of the Nazi Opposition and the Aryanization of Jewish Property, Memorandum from Abraham L. Pomerantz, Deputy Chief Counsel, OCCWC, to Telford Taylor, Brigadier Gen., Chief of Counsel for War Crimes, US-OMGUS (Aug. 14, 1946) OCCWC Berlin Branch, OCCWC, Group 238, No. 202, 190/12/35/01-02 (explaining the origin of Dresdner Bank's involvement). Karl Rasche, a high-ranking official of the Dresdner Bank, was later tried in the Ministries Case at Nuremberg. Rasche was found guilty under Count Six for his participation in spoliation in Bohemia-Morava and Holland. *See* United States v. Ernst von Weizaecker, et al. (*The Ministries Case*), 14 T.W.C., *supra* note 8, at 772–84 (1949–1953). He was further charged with providing loans to firms, knowing that the money would be used to finance businesses utilizing slave labour. The Tribunal found him not guilty. *See* United States v. Ernst von Weizaecker, et al. (*The Ministries Case*), *supra*, at 621–22.

humanity only if they were committed after September 1939:[137] 'The further, more delicate question is, however, whether crimes against humanity committed within Germany against German nationals can be considered as international law, and therefore punishable on the footing of international law as announced in the London agreement and elsewhere.'[138]

Taylor's concerns were soon substantiated. The Flick Tribunal decided to follow the IMT's narrow interpretation and thus ruled that it lacked jurisdiction on crimes committed prior to the initiation of the Second World War. The Krupp and I.G. Farben Tribunals, as mentioned earlier, followed the same restrictive approach to their temporal jurisdiction. The Flick Tribunal further grappled with the question of whether the appropriation of property on racial or religious grounds, without compensation, by the use of pressure and duress, amounted to a crime against humanity. It concluded that a person does not become 'guilty of crimes against humanity merely by exerting anti-Semitic pressure to procure by purchase or through state expropriation of industrial property owned by Jews'.[139] It further held that crimes against humanity could not be properly interpreted to include '[c]ompulsory taking of industrial property, however reprehensible'.[140]

The puzzle of the reach of international legal scrutiny over coercion exercised by private businesses was further complicated by the discussion over practices of plunder and spoliation in the territories occupied by the Nazi regime. Under what circumstances would such transactions be regarded illegal under international law? What would the ramifications of war and occupation for these questions be? These queries lead our discussion in the next section.

Spoliation in occupied territories

The Flick Tribunal confined the doctrinal basis for the crime of plunder and spoliation to War Crimes as defined and embodied in the Hague Regulations.[141] The doctrine prevailing at the time of the war was far from clear in reference to

---

[137] Taylor noted, further, that the language upon which the IMT based its decision appeared in Article 6 of the Nuremberg Charter, but was not included in Article 2 of the CCL10. 1/4/03, Transcript of Teleconference (Feb. 19, 1947) Letters Received 1944–1951, War Crimes Branch, JAG, Group 153, No. 132, 270 NARA ('We have no doubt that we are in sound legal footing under [C]ontrol [C]ouncil [L]aw No. 10, inasmuch as it is certainly within the legitimate powers of the occupying countries to set up special courts for the punishment of acts which clearly were crimes under German Law prior to the Nazis and were under any civilized system of law. In view of the fact that there is no central government of Germany, the occupying powers are in many ways exercising *de facto* sovereignty in Germany').

[138] *Id.* Taylor repeated this line of reasoning in the opening statement of the Flick case, which began on April 19, 1947. Taylor clarified that Law No. 10 covered crimes against humanity committed prior to the attack on Poland in 1939. *The Flick Case, supra* note 14, at 82.

[139] *Id.* at 1215.

[140] *Id.*

[141] For further discussion, *see*Michael Bothe, *War Crimes, in* 1 THE ROME STATUTE OF THE INTERNATIONAL CRIMINAL COURT: A COMMENTARY 379, 383 (Antonio Cassese et al. eds., 2002).

practices involving private entities. Although directly engaging with these issues, the decisions of the Nuremberg Tribunals failed to provide further clarity. If anything, the Hague Regulations suffered a major setback due to the conduct of Second World War occupying forces. At the same time that the IMT in Nuremberg described these rules as being declaratory of customary international law, 'they effectively lost their normative value'.[142] Von Glahn notes, in 1957: '[i]n the absence of conventional law rules, both military manuals and the actual practices of modern occupants indicate clearly that the latter possess far-reaching powers as respects the control of nonbanking business enterprises'.[143] This ambiguity benefited the Industrialist defendants.

The IMT's deduction from Articles 48, 49, 52, 55, and 56 of the Hague Regulations of 1907 concluded that 'under the rules of war, the economy of the occupied country can only be required to bear the expense(s) of the occupation, and these should not be greater than the economy of the country can reasonably be expected to bear'.[144] Accordingly, the Flick Tribunal rejected the Prosecution's allegations of Flick's disproportionate use of resources in the occupied territories: 'If after seizure the German authorities had treated their possession as conservatory for the rightful owners' interests, little fault could be found with the subsequent conduct of those in possession'.[145]

However, in one instance, Flick alone was found guilty of exploiting a seized factory in an occupied territory.[146] The Tribunal stressed that, even though his involvement violated Hague Regulation 46, 'his acts within his knowledge did not intend to contribute to a program of "systematic plunder" conceived by Hitler regime'.[147] The Court found him guilty on this count, but indicated that his ignorance of the applicable law and the circumstances under which he acted might mitigate his punishment.

---

[142] EYAL BENVENISTI, THE INTERNATIONAL LAW OF OCCUPATION 98 (2004). As Benvenisti writes, 'Ultimately, this phase culminate[d] with the introduction of the 1949 Geneva Convention Relative to the Protection of Civilian Persons in Time of War, which reformulated several aspects of the law of occupation in response to the experience of the recent war.' *Id.* at 59.

[143] GERHARD VON GLAHN, THE OCCUPATION OF ENEMY TERRITORY: A COMMENTARY ON THE LAW AND PRACTICE OF BELLIGERENT OCCUPATION 207 (1957).

[144] '[U]nder the rules of war, the economy of the occupied country can only be required to bear the expense(s) of the occupation, and these should not be greater than the economy of the country can reasonably be expected to bear.' *The Flick Case*, 6 T.W.C., *supra* note 8, at 1204 (1952).

[145] *Id.* at 1206.

[146] This was the case of the Rombach Plant in Lorraine. This enterprise was administered by a special commissioner of the Reich and then immediately transferred by a contract to the Flick firm as its trustee. Goering's intention was to exploit it to the fullest extent for the German war effort. Flick had a different plan; he was interested in extending his organization through the acquisition of additional plants. *The Flick Case, supra* note 14, at 1205–08.

[147] *Id.* The *New York Times* reported that Hermann Röchling, another leading German industrialist, attempted to sabotage the transfer of the Rombach ore enterprises to Flick, asserting that it should be transferred to him instead. 'Röchling insisted that his own services to Germany constituted a better claim to the valuable property than those of Flick.' *Nazi Rivalry on Loot Shown in Flick Trial*, N.Y. TIMES, Apr. 22, 1947, at 23.

The Krupp Tribunal adopted a much stronger opposition to the practice of plunder and spoliation of private firms during the war. It opened its decision by quoting the following testimony:

> On May 18, 1940, the defendant, Alfried Krupp, and three other industrialists were gathered around a table intently studying a map while listening to a broadcast of German war news over the radio… At the conclusion of the broadcast the four men talked excitedly and with great intensity. They pointed their fingers to certain places on the map indicating villages and factories. One said, "this one is yours, this one is yours, that one we will have arrested, he has two factories." They resembled, as the witness Ruemann put it, "vultures gathered around their booty." … We are satisfied that this incident occurred as portrayed by the witness … and that it clearly indicates the attitude of the defendant Alfried Krupp during the period of Germany's aggressions.[148]

The court referred to several plants in which unlawful seizure of property was involved. All were declared to be violations of the Hague regulations. As stated by the Tribunal: 'The Krupp firm not only took over certain French industrial enterprises. It also considered occupied France as a hunting ground for additional equipment.'[149] Similar conclusions were drawn in reference to Krupp's involvement in other occupied territories.[150]

Farben, as noted by the IMT Tribunal, 'marched with the Wehrmacht and played a major role in Germany's program for acquisition by conquest.'[151] According to the Farben Tribunal, 'The Hague Regulations do not become inapplicable because the German Reich "annexed" or "incorporated" parts of the occupied territory into Germany'.[152] The Hague Regulations were broadly aimed at preserving the inviolability of property rights concerning both public and private property during military occupation. Nonetheless, private civilians of the nation of the military occupier, as the judgment suggests, could enter into agreements relating to the purchase of industrial enterprises or interests equivalent thereto, even during times of military occupation, if the owner's consent was voluntarily given.

The war presented the Tribunals with 'a relatively new development affecting the property rights of private individuals in German-occupied parts of Europe'.[153] The Tribunal indicated that Farben's administrators formed 'corporate transactions well calculated to create the illusion of legality' but their objective of pillage,

---

[148] *The Krupp Case, supra* note 16, at 1347–48.
[149] *Id.* at 1361.
[150] *Id.* at 1372. As concluded by the court, 'the acquisition of properties, machines, and materials in the occupied countries was that of Krupp firm and that it utilized the Reich Government and Reich agencies whenever necessary to accomplish its purpose'. *Id.*
[151] *The Farben Case,* vol. 8, *supra* note 15, at 1129 (quoting from the general findings of the IMT).
[152] *Id.* at 1137.
[153] VON GLAHN, *supra* note 143, at 189.

plunder, and spoliation clearly stands out.[154] In the case of Farben's activities in Poland, Norway, and France, the Tribunal found established proof that Farben undertook property transactions against the wishes of the owners, sometimes through 'negotiation' with private owners and sometimes following the confiscation of the Reich authorities. Further, these unlawful acquisitions were not meant to maintain either the German army population or that of the occupying forces. Instead, Farben was motivated purely by a desire to enhance and to enrich its enterprise.[155] As noted by the Tribunal, 'Where private individuals, including juristic persons, proceed to exploit the military occupancy by acquiring private property against the will and consent of the former owner, such action, not being expressly justified by any applicable provision of the Hague Regulations, is in violation of international law.'[156] Thus, business initiatives and governmental control were central considerations in the Tribunals' discussion of unlawful property transactions. In the following paragraphs, I explore these criteria of initiative and control.

The initiative criterion

The Farben Tribunal distinguished between spoliation practices initiated by the Reich (such as Nordisk-Lettmetall in Norway) and others initiated by Farben (as in the case of plants in Poland and France). In each conquered country, Farben's motto, according to the Prosecutors, was *combine and rule*: 'Farben endeavored to amalgamate the more valuable segments of its chemical industries into a single large combine, dominated by Farben, and to close down the rest altogether.'[157] Internal correspondence among the Nuremberg lawyers shows their concerns regarding the nature of proof required to demonstrate that such initiative was indeed taken by the Farben enterprise.[158] Early correspondence suggests they conceived businesses as complicit in governmental spoliation rather than as independent violators.[159] The division based on the initiative criterion

---

[154] *The Farben Case*, vol. 8, *supra* note 15, at 1140.

[155] *Id.*

[156] *Id.* at 1132–33. Five of the Farben directors were held criminally liable for the plunder. *Id.* at 1205–10.

[157] *The Farben Case*, vol. 7, *supra* note 15, at 181. The indictment includes the story of Mr. Szpilfogel who was a director of an important factory in Wola. All of Mr. Szpilfogel's property—business and personal—was confiscated by Farben soon after the capture of Warsaw. His plea from the Warsaw ghetto to the defendant von Schnitzler, whom he knew from previous business encounters, was never answered. *Id.*

[158] Expropriation of the Property of the Nazi Opposition and the Aryanization of Jewish Property, *supra* note 136.

[159] Sprecher instructed researchers in the OCCWC's spoliation department to 'complete a basic memorandum brief on the organizations, pseudo-government agencies, and party agencies which had connections to plunder and spoliation, showing how the spoliation activities of private individuals and concerns related thereto'. Memorandum from D.A. Sprecher, Dir., Econ. Div., OCCWC, to Sadi

corresponded, to some extent, with the distinction between eastern and western occupied territories.[160]

Later historical accounts distinguished between the early occupation of Austria and Czechoslovakia and the subsequent occupations under the New Order. Most firms did not derive much benefit from the early expansions, with the important exception of I.G. Farben. The giant chemical concern was deeply enmeshed in the industrial dimension of the Four-Year Plan and used its prominence to gain from the expanding empire. Thus, it reacted strategically to the conquests and sought to retain its power and control in both the eastern and western territories. In most cases of occupied territories in the *east*, the Reich organized the confiscated properties directly, and Farben's involvement was mainly derivative. One historian described its imperialism as the 'sort that *followed* the flag'.[161]

The Prosecutors argued that, when the *western approach* was applied in France, the German Government supported and encouraged the industry's plundering of property, but it was the industry's initiative and leadership that designed the course of action.[162] This distinction between the derivative form of spoliation and the direct one was later echoed in the Tribunal's decision,[163] which concluded that the defence of necessity is not available when the actions under scrutiny were the defendants' own initiative. Hence, the defence is not available because they cannot claim to be deprived of moral choice.[164] Later historical accounts offer a more nuanced reading of the *initiative* criterion, emphasizing the *responsive* mindset of businesses to the Nazi expansionism. Nevertheless, Peter Hayes concluded that '[t]he defensive pattern of the combine's behavior offered little consolation to those victimized by it in 1940–44 and would not have shielded their successors. But that pattern does clarify, at least, the problem of distinguishing between cause and effect in the Nazi conquest of Europe.'[165]

Mase, Chief, Spoliation Branch, OCCWC (Oct. 23, 1946), Admin. Records, Exec. Counsel, Econ. Div., OCCWC, Group 238, No. 165, 190/12/13/1, NARA.

[160] For a discussion of the two distinct patterns concerning spoliation—the Eastern and the Western pattern—*see* I.G. Farben, Spoliation, I.G. Farben Trial Team #1, OCCWC, Group 238, No. 192, 190/12/32/07-12/33/01, NARA.

[161] HAYES, *supra* note 23, at 264–65 (my emphasis).

[162] 'In subjugating the French chemical industry, Farben acted in closest cooperation with, but by no means under the leadership of, the Nazi government. The initiative was Farben's. Farben drafted the plan to eliminate French competition once and for all, to become master in the French house … The Nazi government had favorably received Farben's "New Order" plan, and from then on gave its support but no instructions.' *The Farben Case*, vol. 7, *supra* note 15, at 187; *see also* HAYES, *supra* note 23, at 281–82 (discussing the Farben's role in French dye companies).

[163] 'In these property acquisitions which followed confiscation by the Reich, the course of action of Farben clearly indicates a studied design to acquire such property. In most instances the initiative was Farben's.' *The Farben Case*, vol. 8, *supra* note 15, at 1140.

[164] *Id.* at 1178–79.

[165] HAYES, *supra* note 23, at 317.

The control criterion—and the presence
of governmental authority

The Tribunals were not only interested in the question of initiative:

> In those instances in which Farben dealt directly with the private owners, there
> was the ever present threat of forceful seizure of the property by the Reich or
> other similar measures; such, for example, as withholding licenses, raw materials,
> the threat of uncertain drastic treatment in peace treaty negotiations, or other ef-
> fective means of bending the will of the owners.[166]

The Farben Tribunal emphasized that an action of the owner would not be considered voluntary if it was obtained by threats, intimidations, and pressure from
exploiting the position of *power of the military*, although this could not serve as an exclusive indication of the assertion of pressure. Further, it held that commercial transactions in the context of a belligerent occupation should be closely scrutinized.[167] In
most of the cases reviewed by the Tribunal, 'the initiative was Farben's',[168] backed by
the threat of the state's use of violence: 'The power of the military occupant was the
ever-present threat in these transactions, and was clearly an important, if not a decisive, factor.'[169] This threat resulted in the enrichment of Farben.[170]

While the Krupp Tribunal followed a similar approach, emphasizing the firm's reliance on governmental officials to assist it in acquiring properties in the occupied
territories,[171] the Flick Tribunal set an even higher threshold, requiring that spoliation practices be *systematic*.[172] Thus, the Tribunals differed in the gravity they attributed to such crimes, from a lenient position regarding Flick to a harsher one in the
Krupp case. The issue of initiative—the extent to which the government was a *driving
force* in these transactions—remains unclear in the decisions. The two criteria of initiative and control embody a familiar tension in liberal theory. The requirement of
initiative assumes a realm of freedom within which businesses can freely pursue their

---

[166] *The Farben Case,* vol. 8, *supra* note 15, at 1140.

[167] *Id.* at 1135–36.

[168] *Id.* at 1140.

[169] *Id.*

[170] In reference to its transactions in occupied France, the Farben Tribunal held, as follows: 'Farben
was not in a position to enlist the Wehrmacht in seizure of the plants or to assert pressure upon the
French under threat of seizure of confiscation by the military … The pressure consisted of a possible
threat to strangle the enterprise by exercising control over necessary raw materials. It further appears
that Farben asserted a claim for indemnity for alleged infringements of Farben's patents, knowing well
that the products were not protected under the French patent law at the time of the infringement. This
conduct of Farben's seems to have been wholly unconnected with seizure or threats of seizures, expressed or implied, and while it may be subject to condemnation from a moral point of view, it falls far
short of being proof of plunder either in its ordinary concept or as set forth in the Hague regulations,
either directly or by implication.' *Id.* at 1151–52.

[171] *The Krupp Case, supra* note 16, at 1373.

[172] *The Flick Case, supra* note 14, at 1208.

commercial endeavours. But the state's existence is essential for such transactions to take place, while the involvement of *public* violence in the private transaction renders it illegal. The need for a public element to establish illegality elucidates the challenge presented by the case for international lawyers: can private coercion, regardless of the state coercive involvement, be regarded illegal in international law?

Initiative and control in the dual state

Historians in later decades struggled to determine the extent to which German industry preserved its autonomy under the Third Reich. Christoph Buchheim and Jonas Scherner argued that 'despite extensive regulatory activity by an interventionist public administration, firms preserved a good deal of their autonomy even under the Nazi regime. As a rule, freedom of contract, that important corollary of private property rights, was not abolished during the Third Reich, even in dealings with state agencies.'[173] The Third Reich employed various techniques to induce private industry to undertake war-related production and investments without violating private property rights and entrepreneurial autonomy. But the initiative generally remained with the enterprises:

> Even with respect to its own war and autarky-related investment projects, the state normally did not use power in order to secure the unconditional support of industry. Rather, freedom of contract was respected. However, the state tried to induce firms to act according to its aims by offering them a number of contract options to choose from.[174]

Furthermore, '[v]ery often that could be done only by shifting the financial risk connected to an investment at least partly to the Reich. For this purpose, the regime offered firms a number of contract options to choose from, implying different degrees of risk-taking by the state.'[175]

Ernst Fraenkel, one of Neumann's colleagues, famously described this feature— of a functioning private sphere—in his work on National Socialism, *The Dual State*. For Neumann, the jurisprudential ramifications of the rise of Behemoth were, *inter alia*, manifested in the deformalization of law.[176] His critical account of

---

[173] Buchheim & Scherner, *supra* note 123, at 394.

[174] *Id.* at 395.

[175] *Id.* at 403. For example, I.G. Farben concluded a contract with the Nazi government, which guaranteed its sales for a fixed minimum price (*Wirtschaftlichkeitsgarantievertrag*) for its first plant to produce Buna rubber in 1937. *Id.* at 409.

[176] For a brief overview of Neumann's theory on the proliferation of amorphous, deformalized standards, *see* WILLIAM E. SCHEUERMAN, BETWEEN THE NORM AND THE EXCEPTION: THE FRANKFURT SCHOOL AND THE RULE OF LAW 126–27 (1994). Neumann shared Weber's views on this legal development, but rather than pointing to the affinity between deformalized law and the rise of the welfare state,

the Nazi state began with the absence of the rule of law ('If a state is characterized by the rule of law, our answer to this question will be negative, since we deny that law exists in Germany').[177] But Neumann went even further, denying it any rationality or monopoly over the exercise of violence.[178] Fraenkel's thesis challenged this description of total arbitrariness and offered an alternative description of a system in which some legal mechanisms still functioned in the sphere of civil law.[179] The Nazis' deformalized legal practices of the 'prerogative state' were supreme, but nonetheless operated alongside the 'normative state':

> By the Prerogative State we mean that governmental system which exercises unlimited arbitrariness and violence unchecked by any legal guarantees and by the Normative State an administrative body endowed with elaborate powers for safeguarding the legal order as expressed in statutes, decisions of the courts and activities of the administrative agencies.[180]

Fraenkel further noted that the essence of the Prerogative State 'lies in its refusal to accept legal restraint, i.e. any "formal" bonds. The Prerogative State claims that it represents material justice and that it can therefore dispense with formal justice.'[181] He described how scholars such as Carl Schmitt, who supported the idea that the state is a pre-legal political entity that might act outside the limits of the rule of law, were inspired by the distinction between the international and domestic legal orders:[182] 'the concept which permitted an unlimited sovereignty to ignore international law is the source of the theory that political activity is not subject to legal regulation. This was the presupposition for the theory of the Prerogative State.'[183]

Fraenkel described the difference between the Prerogative State and the Normative State as a qualitative one. The Normative State was *not* identical to a state in which the Rule of Law prevailed (*i.e.* with the Rechtsstaat of the liberal period). The Normative State was a necessary complement to the Prerogative State and can be understood only in that light. Fraenkel's discussion of the Normative State was devoted to what we often consider to be the private sphere of the law:

---

he argued that such 'legal standards of conduct [blanket clauses] serve the monopolist' and emphasized the advantages of deformalized legal modes for the privileged and powerful. Quoted *Id.* at 127.

[177] NEUMANN, *supra* note 34, at 467–68.
[178] *Id.*
[179] *See generally* ERNST FRAENKEL, THE DUAL STATE: A CONTRIBUTION TO THE THEORY OF DICTATORSHIP (1941).
[180] *Id.* at xiii.
[181] *Id.* at 46.
[182] *Id.* at 65–66.
[183] *Id.*

[A]ccording to National Socialism, the freedom of the entrepreneur within the economic sphere should in principle be unconfined, questions of economic policy are usually regarded as falling within the domain of the Normative State ... In spite of existing legal possibilities for intervention by the Prerogative State where and whenever it desires, the legal foundations of the capitalistic economic order have been maintained.[184]

Following his survey of court decisions in key private law fields that demonstrated how courts had successfully maintained the legal system necessary for the functioning of private capitalism, Fraenkel concluded:

Although the German economic system has undergone many modifications it remains predominantly capitalistic... [It is a form of] organized private capitalism with many monopolistic features and much state intervention... a mere continuation, a somewhat more developed phase, of the 'organized capitalism' of the Weimar period.[185]

Fraenkel emphasized two main exceptions to the 'normative' function of the private sphere in Nazi Germany. First, in the field of labour, it sought the destruction of all genuine labour organizations and the persecution of labour leaders. Second, since Jews were regarded enemies of the Third Reich, 'all questions in which Jews are involved fall within the jurisdiction of the Prerogative State'.[186] Andrew Arato elaborated, further, how the dual structure offered by Fraenkel served as a condition for the institutionalization of the Nazi regime.[187]

In the complex reality of occupied Europe, it is probably more accurate to follow Arato's interpretation of Fraenkel's distinction as a tension or struggle between the Prerogative and Normative State.[188] The Industrialist decisions sought to retain the sovereignty of the occupied territories by applying the laws of war and criminalizing coerced private property transactions. Judge Wilkins (of the Krupp Tribunal) emphasized how the essence of the Hague Regulations was to keep intact the economy of the belligerently occupied territory. Their main objective was to prevent the state from forcing inhabitants of the occupied territory 'to help the enemy in waging the war against their own country or their own country's allies ... Beyond

---

[184] *Id.* at 71–72.

[185] *Id.* at 171–72; *see id.* at 184–85 (summarizing the Nazi economic system as one in which 'the Normative State functions as the legal frame-work for private property, market activities of the individual business units, all other kinds of contractual relations, and for the regulations of the control relations between government and business... [L]egal ways of defining and protecting individual rights against other members of the economy and against the encroachment of state authorities are still open and used').

[186] *Id.* at 89.

[187] Andrew Arato, *Dictatorship Before and Beyond Totalitarianism*, 69 Soc. Res. 473, 495–96 (2002).

[188] Arato revisited Hannah Arendt's analysis of totalitarianism through the prism of Fraenkel's Dual State framework. *Id.* at 496.

the strictly circumscribed exceptions, the invader must not utilize the economy of the invaded territory for his own needs within the territory occupied.'[189]

The Farben Tribunal distinguished between lawful and unlawful transactions under international law. The latter were considered to be plunder and spoliation, acquisitions of property incompatible with the laws of war; the former were business deals of purchase through agreement that may or may not be in violation of domestic private law. This distinction assumed Fraenkel's normative sphere, namely that a certain degree of legality prevailed in the 'private sphere' of occupied Europe. A few years after the trials, Hersch Lauterpacht challenged the logic of applying this rationale in the context of an illegal 'total war'.[190] He pointed to the problem of allowing any transfer of title, even if it was made in accordance with the laws of war, to become lawful in the context of an illegal war. He also highlighted the tension between adherence to the laws of war in this context 'for the sake of humanity and the dignity of man' and 'the principle that an unlawful act ought not to become a source of benefit and title to the wrongdoer'.[191] While Lauterpacht was concerned that legal scrutiny based on the laws of war would incidentally legitimize actions that were taken in a broken legal order,[192] he also stressed his reluctance 'to augment the evil by encouraging the abandonment of the normal consequences of the law of war in this or other spheres'.[193] If we were following Fraenkel's description—of conceiving the private sphere as a normative one—we could potentially avoid the Lauterpachtian dilemma. The illegality of the war, or the prerogative nature of the Nazi regime, stops at the gate of the private sphere. Such a conclusion, however, defines the prerogative in the same way coercion was often defined by the Tribunals: as related to the physical presence and influence of the government. But, for Fraenkel, the idea of the Prerogative State did not lie in the presence of the state apparatus or its direct influence.[194] Rather, Fraenkel focused on how power was exercised in the name of the law; that is, whether it was, or was not, constrained by it. The prerogative nature of spoliation practices derived from the lack of constraint on the Industrialists engaging in these transactions. This feature was often fostered, supported, and even materialized in cooperation with state officials or an organization, but this was not what made it part of the Prerogative State.

---

[189] *The Krupp Case, supra* note 16, at 1341–43.

[190] *See* Hersch Lauterpacht, *The Limits of the Operation of the Law of War*, 30 Brit. Y.B. Int'l L. 206, 224–33 (1953).

[191] *Id.* at 240.

[192] '[T]he various authorities of the Allies held on a number of occasions that booty and other property required by German forces validly transferred title to Germany—occasionally with the incidental result that such property subsequently recaptured by the Allies from Germany in turn transferred title to the Allies, so that the title of the original owners was deemed to be extinguished.' *Id.* at 230.

[193] *Id.* at 233.

[194] *See, e.g., The Krupp* Case, *supra* note 16, at 1372 (discussing spoliation and noting that the 'initiative for the acquisition of properties, machines, and materials in the occupied countries was that of the Krupp firm and that it utilized the Reich government and Reich agencies whenever necessary to accomplish its purpose, preferring in some instances . . . to remain in the background').

A different interpretation, inspired by Fraenkel's theory, would claim that, once rights could be infringed without legal constraint, the principles of the laws of war were infringed and undermined. Furthermore, the Tribunals' interpretation distinguished similar practices within and outside state borders. Aryanization practices—as mentioned by Fraenkel—manifest the clear involvement of the Prerogative State. The decision to exclude these practices from the Tribunal's jurisdiction implicitly situated the state beyond the rule of international law. Ultimately, the state not only manifests its influence through violence in supporting spoliation practices in occupied territories but exerts its power when persons residing in its jurisdiction are denied the potential for seeking remedy for their lost possessions. Such is the loss of the juridical person, the person as a subject of rights. That was the case of citizens stripped of their rights in the early 1930s in Nazi Germany and the fate of many who were governed by the Nazi occupation regime.[195]

Against the Tribunals' refusal to accept the Behemoth theory stands an implicit assumption of the Leviathan. Hobbes presented a liberal theory in *The Leviathan*. The liberal attributes of autonomy and freedom in the private sphere are echoed in the distinction the Tribunals made between the public and private in the Nazi regime. On the one hand, the Tribunals equated the Nazi regime with the Hobbesian ideal of a monolithic structure of concentrated authority. On the other hand, they reinstated a Hobbesian–liberal conception of the private sphere as both free and yet constrained by the rule of law.

Fraenkel would probably consider many of the private transactions reviewed by the Tribunals to be governed by a Prerogative State. Yet, the crucial question is: prerogative to whom? Without an assumption of the Industrialists' free will, there is no basis on which to establish their guilt. Since historians document how businesses enjoyed considerable freedom in their operations in the occupied zones, it is plausible to assume they experienced their practices as being governed by the Normative State. However, as Fraenkel emphasized, their freedom or the normative sphere of their operations was always in relation to (or in the shadow of) the Prerogative State, though not necessarily governed by it. The residents of the occupied territories experienced a different kind of relationship with the governing authorities, which is plausibly more compatible with the Prerogative State. This distinction between the relationship of the state vis-à-vis businesses and the residents of occupied Europe translated over to the power relations between the two sides of the transaction. Both the nature of these power relations and the presence of the Prerogative State, as Fraenkel defined it, are missing from the decisions.

---

[195] As Arendt explained: 'This was done, on the one hand, by putting certain categories of people outside the protection of the law and forcing at the same time, though the instrument of denationalization, the non-totalitarian world into recognition of lawlessness; it was done, on the other, by placing the concentration camp outside the normal penal system, and by selecting its inmates outside the normal judicial procedure in which a definite crime entails a predictable penalty.' ARENDT, *supra* note 108, at 447.

The Tribunals' decisions put a disproportionate emphasis on the violence of the Nazi state as the criterion for the illegality of certain business transactions. The focus on direct violence rather than the loss of a functioning legal system ignored the prerogative features of occupied Europe. And ignoring these features undermined the preservation of the private rights of the occupied population and ultimately the preservation of their sovereignty.

Indeed, a different understanding of the Industrialists' crimes would consider their profiting from the loss of the rule of law as a threat to sovereignty in an occupied territory. Hannah Arendt regarded such loss of the juridical person as a first step on the road to total domination: 'The destruction of a man's rights, the killing of the juridical person in him, is a prerequisite of dominating him entirely.'[196]

Conclusion

The competing theories of the totalitarian state—Neumann's Behemoth and the Hobbesian default position of the court—informed the understanding of the responsibility of the corporate officials standing trial at Nuremberg. The critical flaws of this position were twofold. First, the deliberations were not consciously informed by a rigorous theory of the Nazi state, and merely reduced complex aspects of Nazi operations to an assumed Hobbesian dictatorial regime. Second, the Hobbesian theory led the judges to require a link to the policymaking realm as a basis for responsibility. Businesses are always embedded in the political regime in which they operate. Understanding their conduct requires a sophisticated theory of their political environment. Yet, even such contextual understanding does not necessarily lead to the normative link between businesses and states. The former could function despite the latter's operations, in accordance with (or in relation to) other political constraints and considerations. The legal reasoning in the Industrialist decisions failed to develop a theory of business responsibility in cases where businesses are not fully governed or controlled by the state. Indeed, what could have been a remarkable moment of progressivism in international law was lost to a conservative understanding of the totalitarian state as a mega-Leviathan.

Arguably, this limited perception of the Nazi state influenced other jurisprudential developments. Hitler's Germany was the villain whose menace urged the promotion of an effective international human rights regime.[197] The lessons from the Nazi experience justifiably haunted legal theorists, who attempted to establish principles, institutions, theories, and rules that would stand in the way of similar future threats. Like the Nuremberg decisions, these debates often emphasized

---

[196] *Id.* at 451.
[197] For an early discussion, *see*HERSCH LAUTERPACHT, AN INTERNATIONAL BILL OF THE RIGHTS OF MAN 3–15 (1945).

governmental and public abuse of power and frequently assumed a monolithic state. This presumption of a functioning ideal type of 'modern state' failed to recognize the growing power of private enterprises. Applying a theory of responsibility to the structure of Behemoth, rather than of a state, required a radical departure from the statist logic and from the even more basic understanding of the international legal order as comprising autonomous, self-governing states.

Indeed, one of the most 'basic and highly provocative arguments' in *Behemoth* is that '[s]ome version of an identifiably modern state apparatus controlling the exercise of coercion remains a civilizational achievement worth defending'.[198] Recalling arguments made by Neumann, Duncan Kelly argued: 'The key point for Neumann was that, under National Socialism, the "state" *per se* has ceased to exist, and without the state there was simply a decisionistic, situation-specific, deformalized or dematerialized law that owed little, if anything, to the general rule of law he sought to defend.'[199]

What *were* the international responsibilities of businesses, then, when they were conducted 'as usual' before, despite, and because of the war or Nazi rule? Fraenkel and Neumann showed how the realm of 'business as usual'—the Normative State— was continuously tainted by the Nazi regime. Yet, both of them insisted on a certain degree of freedom and choice for those involved in commercial and industrial endeavours. One may go even further and conclude that the private sphere is never free, and thus shift the question away from the endless quest we find in such cases for a link to politics and policy. By insisting upon such a link, the Prosecution and the Tribunals failed to meet the normative challenge presented in the Industrialist Trials, namely to develop principles for establishing responsibilities among those enjoying 'private' power. The theory of responsibility for the business corporation in international law thus remained deficient and unclear.

---

[198] SCHEUERMAN, *supra* note 176, at 196.
[199] DUNCAN KELLY, THE STATE OF THE POLITICAL: CONCEPTIONS OF POLITICS AND THE STATE IN THE THOUGHT OF MAX WEBER, CARL SCHMITT AND FRANZ NEUMANN 296 (2003).

5

Without the Corporate Entity?

Theories of Corporate Authority and their Implications for Business Responsibility at Nuremberg

Introduction

The Prosecution cases in the Industrialist Trials tell the story of the extensive involvement of three companies and their officials in the commission of international crimes. Yet only some of the defendants were found guilty of only a limited number of crimes. This impunity gap is a familiar problem in the context of corporate criminal responsibility. A year after the Farben trial ended, Taylor addressed the challenges posed by personal responsibility in the context of private industry: 'Although the entire Farben directorate had approved the Auschwitz factory project ... the Nuremberg Tribunal held that only those few (four directors out of 20) who are personally and closely involved in its planning and execution were criminally responsible; the other directors were acquitted of the charge.'[1]

While the U.S. occupation regime focused on the industrialist's organizations as monopolies and dealt with them as such in the parallel anti-cartelization programme,[2] the corporate entity itself was not a subject of responsibility at

---

[1] Telford Taylor, Nuremberg Trials—Synthesis and Projection, *reprinted* from the Information Bulletin Issue No. 162 Magazine of U.S. Military Government in Germany, May 31, 1949 RG 238 OCCWC Berlin Branch Entry 196 ID # 89966 Correspondence, memoranda, etc.1948–1949 190/12/ 33/02-03, Box 1.

[2] In order No. 2 of July 1945, General Dwight D. Eisenhower directed the seizure of all I.G. Farben assets in the U.S. zone. Within days, a special agency of the office of the U.S. Military Governor was formed to take control of Farben. JOHN O. HALEY, ANTITRUST IN GERMANY AND JAPAN, THE FIRST FIFTY YEARS, 1947–1998, at 183 (2001). A cartel division was created, along with a separate I.G. Farben Control Office. The Division of Investigation of Cartels and External Assets was established on September 12, 1945. This division was 'to make investigations in Germany of the existence and scope of German cartels, syndicates, trusts and other concentrations of economic power, and to report the results of such investigations to the Legal Advisor together with recommendations to effect the elimination of such instrumentalities'. Headquarters, U.S. Group, Control Council (Germany), General Order No. 52, subject: Establishment of a Division of Investigation of Cartels and External Assets, September 12, 1945. Quoted by J.F.J. Gillen, Deconcentration and Decartelization in West Germany 1945–1953, 11 (Preliminary Draft, Historical Division, Office of the Executive Secretary, Office of the U.S. High Commissioner for Germany, 1953). Hearings before a Subcommittee of the Committee on Military Affairs United States Senate, 76th Congress, I.G. Farben Material submitted by the War Department (Washington, Part 7, December 1945) [hereinafter the I.G. Farben Study]. The purpose of the I.G. Farben Study was 'to uncover as much as information as possible concerning the nature and location of the far-flung and carefully concealed external assets of I.G. Farben' for the purpose of using such assets for 'the relief and rehabilitation of countries devastated by Germany'. However, because of the complexity of I.G., the report is limited in its attempts to present a picture of the labyrinthine financial

---

Veiled Power. Doreen Lustig, Oxford University Press (2020). © Doreen Lustig.
DOI: 10.1093/oso/9780198822097.001.0001

Nuremberg. The result was that the bureaucracy of the state and its division of labour with the company—and the structure of authority within the company itself—were not addressed under a clear theory of corporate responsibility in either of the decisions, resulting in impunity. As analysed in the previous section, in company–state relations, the Tribunals insisted on a link to public power as a basis for responsibility in international law. The company's culture, the problem that was 'greater than the sum of its parts', and the relevance of considering the corporate structure for all the parts of a disaggregated operation to hold its agents accountable are but a few facets of the impunity problem the Industrialist Cases exemplify.[3]

and industrial structure of the company: its 'world empire', its role in arming Germany for war, its role in economic and political warfare, its acquisitions by conquest and its military potential at the close of war. Allied Control Council No. 9 transferred the Title to I.G. Farben to the Allied Control Council on November 30, 1945. The Control Council's purpose was 'to insure that Germany will never again threaten her neighbors or the peace of the world'.

[3] The issue of collective and corporate responsibility in criminal law remains controversial in different jurisdictions, and has not been resolved in international law. For a general discussion on the question of corporate criminal responsibility and lack of consensus on this issue, *see*, for example, Thomas J. Bernard, *The Historical Development of Corporate Criminal Liability*, 22 CRIMINOLOGY 3 (1984); BRENT FISSE & JOHN BRAITHWAITE, CORPORATIONS, CRIME AND ACCOUNTABILITY (1993); JONATHAN CLOUGH & CARMEL MULHERN, THE PROSECUTION OF CORPORATIONS (2002); JAMES GOBERT & MAURICE PUNCH, RETHINKING CORPORATE CRIME (2003); Pamela H. Bucy, *Corporate Ethos: A Standard for Imposing Corporate Criminal Liability*, 75 MINN. L. REV. 1095 (1992); WILLIAM S. LAUFER, CORPORATE BODIES AND GUILTY MINDS: THE FAILURE OF CORPORATE CRIMINAL LIABILITY (2006). Corporate criminal responsibility has had a long history in common law jurisdictions but it is relatively new in states that follow the continental legal tradition. For a succinct comparative overview, *see* Thomas Weigend, *Societas, Delinquere non Potest? A German Perspective*, 6 J. INT'L CRIM. JUST. 927 (2008). On the question of international legal obligations of companies, see, for example, Anita Ramasastry, *Corporate Complicity: From Nuremberg to Rangoon: An Examination of Forced Labor Cases and Their Impact on the Liability of Multinational Corporations*, 20 BERKELEY J. INT'L L. 91 (2002); ANDREW CLAPHAM, HUMAN RIGHTS OBLIGATIONS OF NON-STATE ACTORS (2006); LIABILITY OF MULTINATIONAL CORPORATIONS UNDER INTERNATIONAL LAW (Menno T. Kamminga & Saman Zia-Zarifi eds., 2000); Beth Stephens, *The Amorality of Profit: Transnational Corporations and Human Rights*, 20 BERKELEY J. INT'L. L. 45 (2002); Carlos M. Vázquez, *Direct vs. Indirect Obligations of Corporations Under International Law*, 43 COLUM. J. TRANSNAT'L. L 927 (2005); Special Representative of the Secretary-General, *Promotion and Protection of All Human Rights, Civil, Political, Economic, Social and Cultural Rights, including the Right to Development: Protect, Respect and Remedy: A Framework for Business and Human Rights*, U.N. Doc A/HRC/8/5 (Apr. 7, 2008) (by John Ruggie); Wolfgang Kaleck & Miriam Saage Maaß, *Corporate Accountability for Human Rights Violations Amounting to International Crimes: The Status Quo and Its Challenges*, 8 J. INT'L CRIM. JUST. 699 (2010); INT'L COMM. OF THE RED CROSS, BUSINESS AND INTERNATIONAL HUMANITARIAN LAW: AN INTRODUCTION TO THE RIGHTS AND OBLIGATIONS OF BUSINESS ENTERPRISES UNDER INTERNATIONAL HUMANITARIAN LAW (2006); Erik Møse, *Corporate Criminal Liability and the Rwandan Genocide*, 6 J. INT'L CRIM. JUST. 973 (2008). David Scheffer, *Corporate Liability Under the Rome Statute*, 57 HARV. J. INT'L L. 35 (Spring 2016, Online Symposium). Michael J. Kelly, *Prosecuting Corporations for Genocide Under International Law*, 6 HARV. L. & POL'Y REV. 339 (2012); Harmen van der Wilt, *Corporate Criminal Responsibility for International Crimes: Exploring the Possibilities*, 12 CHINESE J. INT'L L. 43 (2013); Larissa van den Herik & Jernej Letnar Černič, *Regulating Corporations Under International Law: From Human Rights to International Criminal Law and Back Again*, 8 J. INT'L CRIM. JUST. 725 (2010); Mordechai Kremnitzer, *A Possible Case for Imposing Criminal Liability on Corporations in International Criminal Law*, 8 J. INT'L CRIM. JUST. 909 (2010); Joanna Kyriakakis, *Corporations Before International Criminal Courts: Implications for the International Criminal Justice Project*, 30 LEIDEN J. INT'L L. 221 (2017); Caroline Kaeb, *The Shifting Sands of Corporate Liability Under International Criminal Law*, 49 GEO. WASH. INT'L L. REV. 351 (2016).

The following analysis explores the conceptual and normative dimensions of the Nuremberg proceedings as a window to an array of attitudes towards the issue of business responsibility. I offer an interpretive framework that elaborates on the attitudes developed by different actors in the U.S. Administration, the Prosecution teams, and the judges' decisions towards corporate responsibility and the 'corporate entity'. The conceptual analysis, in turn, further complicates the narrative of 'sheer failure' by distinguishing between organizational features that were recognized and legally scrutinized by the American administration (monopolies) and others that were not (the corporate entity of the business corporation as a subject of criminal responsibility).

Breaking Cartels Rather than Targeting the Corporate Entity

The narratives regarding the Nuremberg Industrialist Trials and the Decartelization of the German industry are usually told separately from one another. However, the link between them is greater than is often assumed. The focus on cartelization practices and monopolies informed the Nuremberg doctrine, its interpretation, and the design of the Prosecutors' case. In addition, the emphasis on the monopolistic features of German businesses may *explain* the decision not to include the business entities as subjects of responsibility in the trials.

In 1941, the alleged memoirs of one of Germany's leading industrialists were published in the United States under the title *I Paid Hitler*. In this book, Emery Reves, a European journalist, described Thyssen's and other industrialists' close collaboration with the Nazi leadership in preparing for the Second World War.[4] Similarly, prominent economic studies published in the early 1940s addressed the correlation between cartelization and economic crisis, and connected

---

[4] Thyssen was one of Germany's leading industrialists who supported Hitler and his party. But the violent steps taken against the Jews and the Catholic Church in 1938 convinced him to oppose the Nazi regime. His opposition to the war led to his arrest and to the confiscation of his property by the Nazi government. 'I have the suspicion', wrote one of Thyssen's interrogators, 'that Thyssen considers himself some kind of martyr who tried his best to lead an opposition against Hitler.' Thyssen's interrogators described 'a rather frail looking man of 73 years [who] is somewhat hard of hearing. He also has a constant twitch or so-called nervous tick. He gives the impression of a healthy but weak and old individual ... Despite the above, he still makes a dignified appearance and wears clothing which, though shabby, shows that the wearer has seen better days.' Walter H. Rapp to General Taylor, Interrogation of Fritz Thyssen, November 26, 1946. Thyssen was initially jailed through the efforts of the Decartelization Branch. Josef Marcu to Telford Taylor, Fritz Thyssen, November 22, 1946. As early as November 26, Telford Taylor admitted to his colleague at Nuremberg that there was less than 'one chance in a hundred' that Fritz Thyssen would be prosecuted as a war criminal. Taylor further suggested considering him a potential witness and perhaps making his life more comfortable if he showed a sense of responsibility for his involvement with the Nazi regime during the early years of its rule. In July 1947, Sprecher advised Taylor to release Thyssen. D.A. Sprecher to Telford Taylor, Fritz Thyssen, Recommended Handling of the Case, July 1, 1947. RG 238, Collection of WWII War Criminals Records, Office of the Chief Counsel of War Crimes 1933–1949 Correspondence Reports Etc., Entry 159 190/12/13/01-02, Box 2, 'Thyssen' file, NARA, College Park.

fascism with monopolistic economic tendencies. These studies led many in the U.S. Administration to identify cartels and monopolies with the 'German problem'. Robert Brady investigated the role of industrialists in German politics in his book *Business as a System of Power*.[5] As discussed earlier, Neumann's *Behemoth* suggested that the expansionist spirit of German big business was the motivating force of the Nazi economic system. While not literally considering businesses the embodiment of the Nazi regime, he argued for their shared interest in imperialism.[6]

The groundswell of public interest soon reached the corridors of power. Legislative and executive branches studied the history and practices of German cartels and debated policies to address this issue.[7] Beginning in the autumn of 1943, a Subcommittee on War Mobilization of the Senate Committee on Military Affairs, chaired by Senator Harley M. Kilgore [hereinafter: the Kilgore Committee], studied the effects of cartels and monopolistic practices on war mobilization. It accumulated extensive evidence on the relationship between international cartels, mostly governed by the Germans, and the problem of national security. The debate reached its zenith in 1944. In the autumn of that year, Roosevelt was re-elected president for the third time. In his State of the Union Address, he enumerated the right to trade free from unfair competition and domination by monopolies at home or abroad as one of the eight rights in the Bill of Rights[8] and he officially announced the development of a joint international policy for curtailing cartel practices.

As the war progressed, those planning the occupation of Germany raised proposals for an international antitrust policy, specifically to eliminate German cartels such as Krupp and I.G. Farben, seen as causal agents of German aggression. Again in the autumn of 1944, the State Department's Committee on Private Monopolies and Cartels considered the view of *industry as agency* as somewhat exaggerated. Nonetheless, committee members argued for the importance of international

---

[5] ROBERT BRADY, BUSINESS AS A SYSTEM OF POWER (1943), followed two earlier publications by Brady, THE RATIONALIZATION MOVEMENT IN GERMAN INDUSTRY (1933) and THE SPIRIT AND STRUCTURE OF GERMAN FASCISM (1937).

[6] FRANZ NEUMANN, BEHEMOTH: THE STRUCTURE AND PRACTICE OF NATIONAL SOCIALISM 1933–1944 (Ivan R. Dee 2009) (1942). On the receptive response to these publications, *see* WYATT WELLS, ANTITRUST AND THE FORMATION OF THE POSTWAR WORLD 56 (2002)

[7] The Temporary National Economic Commission (TNEC) was a joint Congressional–Executive committee composed of members of both Houses of Congress and representatives of several Executive departments and commissions, created by joint resolution of Congress, 16 June 1938 (52 Stat. 705). The TNEC studied monopolies and the concentration of economic power, and made recommendations for legislation. *See,* for example, the TNEC, *Investigation of Concentration of Economic Power*, Monograph No. 40: Regulation of Economic Activities in Foreign Countries, Senate Committee Panel, 76th congress, 3rd session (1941) (Part II of this study is devoted to the history of control of the concentration of economic power in Germany and the regulatory experience in Germany under National Socialism).

[8] In his State of the Union address, Roosevelt included the 'right of every businessman, large or small, to trade in atmosphere of free trade from unfair competition and domination by monopolies at home or abroad' in his eight-point economic bill of rights. 13 FRANKLIN D. ROOSEVELT, THE PUBLIC PAPERS AND ADDRESSES OF FRANKLIN D. ROOSEVELT—VICTORY AND THE THRESHOLD TO PEACE 1944–1945, at 41 (1950).

antitrust policy in the postwar world order.[9] The State Department's position on the 'German question' supported a generous peace approach and advocated fostering democracy in Germany as the best way to prevent future aggression.[10] Parallel to the work of the State Department, the Kilgore Committee continued to conduct hearings and analyse studies. In December 1945, Colonel Bernard Bernstein, Director of the Division of Investigation of Cartels and External Assets at the U.S. Office of Military Government (OMGUS) (Germany), submitted an extensive report on I.G. Farben [hereinafter: the Bernstein Report].[11] The teams prosecuting in the Industrialist cases often discussed the work of the Kilgore Committee and the Bernstein Report as they prepared for the trials. [12] In a later interview, Colonel Bernstein recalled how '[t]he investigation at I.G. Farben, the huge—the largest I think of the German companies—resulted in evidence for a case to present to the international tribunal at Nuremberg for the Prosecution for war crimes.'[13] Indeed, information produced and collected by the Decartelization Branch was particularly influential in the early days of preparations for the trials.[14] Similarly,

---

[9] HARLEY A. NOTTER, POSTWAR FOREIGN POLICY PREPARATION, 1939–1945 (U.S. Dept. State., Office Pub. Affairs, 1949).

[10] The interdepartmental Executive Committee for Economic Foreign Policy (ECEFP) established by Roosevelt approved a State Department's plan for postwar Germany, endorsing the *moderate peace* approach. *See*, for example, 'Germany: General Objectives of United States Economic Policy with Respect to Germany', memorandum by the Executive Committee on Economic Foreign Policy, approved August 4, 1944 Foreign Relations, 1944, Volume I, 278–87.

[11] Hearings before a Subcommittee of the Committee on Military Affairs, United State Senate, 79th Congress, 1st session, pursuant to S. Res. 107 (78th Congress) and S. Res. 146 (79th Congress) Authorizing Study of War Mobilization Problems, Part 7, December 1945, I.G. Farben Material Submitted by the War Department p. 941 (Washington, 1945).

[12] In the winter of 1946, Alfred Booth, who worked as a researcher at Nuremberg, asked Taylor for a copy of the Kilgore Committee hearing records, regarding them 'indispensable for the Prosecution of Nazi industrialists'. Alfred H. Booth, senior researcher in the case against Nazi industrialists, to Colonel Telford Taylor, February 4, 1946, RG 238 Office of the Chief Counsel for War Crimes, 1933–1949 Correspondence, Reports and Other Records, Entry 159 190/12/13/01-02, Box 4. Booth, born Alfred Heilbuth in 1938, came from Hamburg. He was active in the trade union movement there as well as in the anti-Nazi movement. D.A. Sprecher to Walter Auerbach, International Transport Workers Federation, London England, February 13, 1946. RG 238 OCCWC 1933–1949 Correspondence, Reports etc. Entry 159 238/190/12/13/01-02 Correspondence (Incoming + Outgoing) 10/13/45–12/30/46 file.

[13] Bernstein further told his interviewer about his meeting in Frankfurt with Senator Kilgore, who recommended he meet President Truman. The President indeed showed interest in Bernstein's endeavour, and their meeting led to the involvement of other high-ranking officials and the recruitment of personnel from different departments in the American administration. 'I believe that the Senate committee [referring to the Kilgore Committee] felt that my reports and testimony made a contribution to the understanding of the role of German business in Germany's aggressions,' concluded Bernstein, 'German big business was deeply involved in the slave labor camps, and with the production of the chemicals that the Nazis used for the slaughter of—at the concentration camps, the Jews and others, and of the deliberate program of war and aggression. I think that German big businesses in that respect had a very bad record.' Ex. 141–152 of the Oral History Interview with Bernard Bernstein, by Richard D. McKinzie, July 23, 1975 Harry S. Truman Library, Independence, Missouri. Online: http://www.trumanlibrary.org/oralhist/bernsten.htm (last visited October 10, 2019).

[14] *See, e.g.*, Foster Adams to Decartelization Branch, Krupp, June 18, 1946 ('We are glad to have anything sent us which you think might be of interest'); D.A. Sprecher to Josif Marcu, acting Chief, Field Unit, Decartelization Branch, OMGUS, Profiles forwarded by you to this office, June 26, 1946. The Decartelization Branch was involved in arrests relevant to the trials. Josif Marcu reported to Taylor

the findings of the Kilgore Committee, which paid a lot of attention to cartelization practices, played a pivotal role in their design.[15] 'Decartelization Branch of Mil. Div. is our principal aid', wrote Sprecher to his staff in July 1946.[16]

The antitrust evidence, vocabulary, and rationale left their mark on three main aspects of the Industrialist Trials: the design and strategy of the Prosecution's case, the focus on the crime of aggression, and the evidence the Prosecutors chose to present. They were particularly influential in the Farben case. The Farben Prosecution's storyline oscillated from a theory of conspiracy among equals to the deliberate integration of the Farben industries into the Nazi war machine.[17]

on the arrest of German slave-labour camp directors, indicating: 'These arrests were made with a view to trial by the office of the chief of counsel. We based our arrests on the precedent established by your Division in the Krupp case, where directors were detained under similar circumstances.' Marcu further asked for Taylor's assistance to ensure the detainees were not released. 'We are at present subjected to a certain amount of pressure to release individuals held under arrest for some time ... We wish your office would send us a memorandum stating your interests in the continued detention of these prisoners.' Josif Marcu to Telford Taylor, Detention of Slave Labor Camp directors, July 2, 1946 (Confidential). RG 238 OCCWC 1933–1949 Correspondence, Reports etc. Entry 159 238/190/12/13/01-02, Box 1, Correspondence (Incoming + Outgoing) 10/13/45–12/30/46 file. The Counter Intelligence Section and other branches were also involved in providing information and documents on crimes in the industrial and financial fields. H.G. Sheen, Chief, Counter Intelligence Section to Telford Taylor, Investigation of War Crimes in the Industrial and Financial Fields, June 20, 1946. RG 238 OCCWC 1933–1949, Correspondence, Reports etc. Entry 159 238/190/12/13/01-02, Box 1, Correspondence (Incoming + Outgoing) 10/13/45–12/30/46 file.

[15] 'It seems indispensable for the prosecution of Nazi Industrialists to have at our disposal certain documentary material which should be easily obtainable in Washington D.C', wrote Alfred H. Booth to Telford Taylor. Booth further listed a series of publications of the Kilgore Committee hearings and Reports, indicating that 'the following publications are particularly urgent'. Alfred H. Booth to Colonel Telford Taylor, February 4, 1946 RG 238 OCCWC correspondence, Reports, etc., Entry 159 238/190/12/13/01-02, Box 3. For further evidence, see Sally F. Zeck (a member of the preparation team), Memorandum to all Research Analysts: The Farben and Krupp Cases, August 13, 1946, RG 238 OCCLWC Berlin Branch Economics, Entry 203, 190/12/35/02 Division correspondence, reports etc. 1946–8, Box 1; D.A. Sprecher to Greighton Coleman, Acting Chief, Decartelization Branch, Economic Division, OMGUS, April 15, 1946. RG 238 OCCWC 1933–1949 Correspondence, Reports etc. Entry 159 238/190/12/13/01-02 Correspondence (Incoming + Outgoing) 10/13/45–12/30/46 file; L.M. Drachsler, Intra-Office Memorandum, 23 July 1946. RG 238 Office of the Chief Counsel for War Crimes, 1933–1949 Correspondence, Reports and Other Records, Entry 159 190/12/13/01-02, Box 4; Benjamin Ferencz to Heath and Sprecher, Admissibility of Senate Hearings as Evidence, June 25, 1946, RG 238 Office of the Chief Counsel for War Crimes, 1933–1949 Correspondence, Reports and Other Records, Entry 159 190/12/13/01-02, Box 4. In this letter, Ferencz asked his colleagues whether it would be possible to include the Hearings of the Senate Committee from Part 7, December 1945, and part 10 of these Hearings, issued in February 1946.

[16] Sprecher's handwritten note to his staff appears in a letter from W.H. Draper to Telford Taylor, Investigations of War Crimes in the industrial and financial field, July 8, 1946, in which Draper notified Taylor that 'instructions have been issued to review the files of the Economic Division for evidence of an incriminating nature against the list of twenty six leading industrialist and financiers'. RG 238 OCCWC 1933–1949 Correspondence, Reports etc. Entry 159 238/190/12/13/01-02, Box 1, Correspondence (Incoming + Outgoing) 10/13/45–12/30/46 file. Similarly, Alfred H. Booth thanked his colleague in the Decartelization Branch for sending him materials on I.G. Farben: 'The material on I.G. Farben industry which you were kind enough to loan me is in the process of being exploited, and proves to be of great use to us.' Alfred H. Booth to Major C.A. Warner, Office of Military Government, Decartelization Branch, April 1, 1946. RG 238 OCCWC 1933–1949 Correspondence, reports, etc. Entry 159 238/190/12/13/01-02, Box 3.

[17] The list of particulars of the defendant's participation demonstrates this point quite vividly: 'a. The alliance of Farben with Hitler and the Nazi Party; b. Farben synchronized all of its activities with the

The monopolistic features of German industry were crucial to the Prosecutors' theory. The Industrialists were accused of using their influence and stature to establish relations with the Nazi Government that would promote their interests in waging an aggressive war. In addition, German Industrialists were accused of engaging in economic warfare. 'Farben's prewar activities', stated the indictment, 'were carefully designed to weaken the United States as an arsenal of democracy. Through its cartel arrangements, Farben retarded the production within the United States of certain strategic products....'[18] Joseph Borkin later described how '[t]he prosecution introduced organizational charts, cartel arrangements, patent licenses, correspondence, production schedules, and corporate reports, as is done in antitrust cases, not at a trial of war criminals charged with mass murder'.[19]

Early discussions between OMGUS and the Office of the Chief Counsel raised 'practical concerns' that justified *not* positioning the corporate entities as defendants. Such concerns included the fact that corporations cut across occupation zones.[20] But clear and sufficient evidence of the reasons that led the Nuremberg architects to exclude the corporate entity as a subject of responsibility in the Industrialist Trials is yet to be found.[21] However, even without a 'smoking gun', the centrality of antitrust sensibilities in the American attitude towards German industry sheds some light on this question. The lasting influence of the antitrust measures and policies explains the emphasis on the monopolistic features of the Industrialists' companies, and was compatible with the general U.S. focus on the war as the main crime addressed in the Nuremberg Trials. In addition, it, at least partially, explains the decision to concentrate on breaking up the German cartels rather than including the corporate entities themselves in the trial.

---

military planning of the German High Command; c. Farben participated in preparing the Four-Year Plan and in directing the economic mobilization of Germany for war; d. Farben participated in creating and equipping the Nazi military machine for aggressive war; e. Farben procured and stockpiled critical war materials for the Nazi offensive; f. Farben participated in weakening Germany's potential enemies; g. Farben carried on propaganda, intelligence, and espionage activities; h. With the approach of war and in connection with each new act of aggression, Farben intensified its preparation for, and participation in, the planning and execution of such aggressions and the reaping of spoils therefrom.'

[18] Farben indictment, United States v. Krauch, 7 TRIALS OF WAR CRIMINALS BEFORE THE NUREMBERG MILITARY TRIBUNALS UNDER CONTROL COUNCIL LAW NO. 10 (1949–53) [hereinafter T.W.C.], at 10, ¶ 53 (1953) [hereinafter *The Farben Case*, vol. 7. *See also id.* at 583 (1953) (illustrating the Prosecution's approach). The Farben case was published also in 8 T.W.C., *supra* (1952) [hereinafter *The Farben Case*, vol. 8].

[19] JOSEPH BORKIN, THE CRIME AND PUNISHMENT OF I.G. FARBEN 141 (1978).

[20] Memorandum to Telford Taylor, Brigadier Gen., OCCWC, Adams, Sprecher, OMGUS, Marcu, Economics Division, and Klepper, Finance Division, 'Summary of Pointes Covered in an OCC-OMGUS Meeting' (May 28, 1946), 'Secret' Collection of Second World War Criminals Records, 'Washington Correspondence,' OCCWC, 1933–1949, Group 238, no. 159, Box 1, 190/12/13/01-02.

[21] For a similar conclusion and further discussion on the Prosecution's deliberations on different theories of corporate responsibility to be used in the Industrialist Trials, *see* Jonathan A. Bush, *The Prehistory of Corporations and Conspiracy in International Criminal Law: What Nuremberg Really Said*, 109 COLUM. L. REV. 1094 (2009).

Furthermore, targeting the German businesses as cartels, not corporations, enabled the U.S. Prosecution to avoid the problem of establishing a general precedent that would preclude the cooperation of businesses with governments in times of war and taint the U.S. industries' essential contribution to the war effort.[22] The focus on the monopolistic features of German industry drew a useful distinction between German and U.S. businesses. German industry was described as either part and parcel of the Nazi regime or a cartelized enterprise in a market that was qualitatively different in both logic and structure from the Anglo-American economies. The emphasis on these features could justify the distinction between the limited accountability of U.S. businesses, which were also involved in the war effort in their country, and the fate of German industry. Nazi businesses were cartels, while the likes of the U.S. Fords and DuPonts were merely businesses. Thus, while the German businesses were recognized and targeted as monopolies, the criminal charges against them weren't based on a theory of corporate responsibility of the corporate entity. The following section is dedicated to the history of that absent theory and its ramifications.

In Search of a Theory of the Corporate Entity

In the months preceding the Industrialist Trials, the Nuremberg lawyers addressed the problem of personal responsibility of corporate agents by suggesting the corporate entity be added as a defendant in the trials. As early as July 1945, Bernard Glaser, who was assigned to a Treasury team that looked into the wartime activities of I.G. Farben, wrote a report in which he laid down the case against I.G. Farben *as a corporate entity* and its officials.[23] In the summer of 1946, Benjamin Ferencz, an investigator involved in the preparation of the trials, and the Chief Prosecutor in the Einsatzgruppan Trial, wrote to his colleague, Prosecutor James E. Heath: '[the] time has come when the bits of information we have are being pigeon-holed into specific briefs ... Most of our information, however, pertains not to individuals, but *to Farben as an entity*' (my emphasis). Ferencz proposed a brief that would show Farben's role in the Nazi economy in detail: 'The case against Farben industry, cannot, I feel, be severed from the case against the Directors.'[24] Hyman Richtin from the Justice Department shared Ferencz's assessment: 'We thought it would be a grave mistake to attack the individuals per se ... it would be impossible to point

[22] JOSIAH E. DuBOIS, THE DEVIL'S CHEMISTS 21 (1952).
[23] Bernard Glaser, The War-Guilt of I.G. Farben, July 30, 1945 (A report prepared for the Headquarters of the Finance Division, U.S. Group C.C., AFO 742, U.S. Army) Record Group 238 Office of the Chief Counsel of War Crimes, Executive Counsel Trial Team #1 (Farben) Correspondence, Reports and other Records, Entry 192 238/190/12/32/07-12/33/01.
[24] Benjamin Ferencz to James Heath, Memo: Brief on I.G. Farben, June 27, 1946 Records of the Office of the Judge Advocate General (Army) War Crimes Branch RG 238 190/12/13/01-02 Entry 159, Box 4 NACP, Washington D.C.

your finger at any one particular individual and say that he was mainly responsible for activities of the company. . . .'[25]

But neither Farben, Flick, nor Krupp was charged as a corporation under the indictments. As we have seen, the OMGUS and the Office of the Chief Counsel held concerns about the possible ramifications of not classifying the corporate entities as defendants.[26] Nevertheless, it was the theory of the Prosecution 'that the defendants individually and collectively used the Farben organization as an instrument by and through which they committed the crimes enumerated in the indictment'.[27] This premise led the Prosecutors to indict all the Board members of Farben (collectively, the *Vorstand*). This strategy seems to have dominated the preparation of the trials from an early stage. 'The briefs already outlined and those projected will encompass both the concept of individual responsibility for personal acts and individual responsibility for the acts (at least those of which he had knowledge) of an organization in which the individual served in a policy-making capacity', wrote Sally F. Zeck to her fellow researchers in August 1946. She continued:

> It cannot be too much emphasized that as desirable as documents might be signed by the four defendants showing them clearly guilty of black crimes, such documents will be found rarely, if ever, since these men were in positions of such importance that they rarely carried their plans into the realm of action themselves.[28]

The structure and magnitude of I.G. Farben required a thorough understanding of the corporate mode of operation, especially in light of the Prosecution's charges that the defendants were 'individually responsible for their own acts and for all

---

[25] In Leo M. Drachsler, Intra-Office Memorandum, 23 July 1946 Drachsler quoted this letter dated June 11, 1946 from Hyman B. Richtin, Department of Justice Washington D.C., Office of the Chief Counsel for War Crimes, 1933–1949 Correspondence, Reports and Other Records RG 238 190/12/13/01-02 Entry 159, Box 4 NACP, Washington D.C.

[26] As noted earlier, such concerns included the fact that corporations cut across occupation zones. In reference to the difficulties in indicting bank officials, '(a) it was stated that practical considerations would serve to prevent indictment and trial of financial or industrial enterprises as entities. (b) It was agreed that decisions made on the basis of practical considerations should be issued in such a manner as not to imply exoneration of corporations or individuals against whom there appeared a prima facie case... (d) It was agreed that the denazification program should be studied with a view to insuring the coverage of Nazis where, for practical considerations, U.S. or international tribunals would not be employed. This is particularly important where the individual offender is being charged with acts of a corporation of which he is a responsible official. Difficulty in this case arises out of the fact that the corporations may cut across Lander and zones, whereas the denazification program is decentralized on a Land level.' Summary of points covered in an OCC-OMGUS meeting, May 28, 1946 (For OCC, Gen. Taylor, Mr. Adams, Mr. Sprecher; for OMGUS Mr. Marcu (Economics Division); Mr. Klepper (Finance Division). 'Secret' Collection of Second World War Criminals Records, Office of the Chief Counsel of War Crimes 1933–1949 Correspondence Reports Etc.; RG 238 190/12/13/01-02 Entry 159, Box 1 'Washington Correspondence'.

[27] *The Farben Case*, vol. 8, *supra* note 18, at 1108–09.

[28] Sally F. Zeck (a member of the preparation team), Memorandum to all Research Analysts: The Farben and Krupp Cases, August 13, 1946, RG 238 OCCLWC Berlin Branch Economics, Entry 203, 190/12/35/02 Division correspondence, reports, etc. 1946–8, Box 1.

acts committed by any persons in the execution of such common plan or conspiracy'.[29] To address the question of responsibility under international criminal law, the Prosecution based its theory of *Vorstand*/management responsibility on German laws for determining what position the *Vorstand* occupied in the structure of the corporation and on 'principles common to civilized legal systems generally'.[30] The Prosecution's theory of managers' responsibility was crystallized in its closing statement: 'Farben was a cohesive organization with coherent policies, and well-disciplined organization for carrying out those policies ... But a ship is commanded from the bridge, *and Farben was commanded from the Vorstand*.[31] (my emphasis)

The judgment of the Tribunal followed the Prosecution by describing at length Farben's managerial organization, the principal positions held by the defendants, and their affiliations with political and governmental groups.[32] Its analysis began with the acts committed by Farben (the corporation).[33] However, despite a lengthy discussion of its violations of the Hague Regulations, the Tribunal concluded that it could not translate corporate criminal responsibility into personal and individual criminal acts. The Tribunal explained this anomaly in the following caveat, which I quote here in full because of its significance to our discussion:

> It is appropriate here to mention that the corporate defendant, Farben, is not before the bar of this Tribunal and cannot be subjected to criminal penalties in these proceedings. We have used the term 'Farben' as descriptive of the instrumentality of cohesion in the name of which the enumerated acts of spoliation were committed. But corporations work through individuals and, under the conception of personal individual guilt to which previous reference has been made ... [r]esponsibility does not automatically attach to an act proved to be criminal merely by virtue of a defendant's membership in the *Vorstand*. Conversely, one may not utilize the corporate structure to achieve immunity from criminal responsibility for illegal acts, which he directs, counsels, aids, orders, or abets. In

---

[29] *The Farben Case*, vol. 7, *supra* note 18, at 59.

[30] The Prosecution quoted German case law in which acts of corporate entities were attributed to their management ('the responsibility of *Vorstand* members for criminal acts committed under the authority of the *Vorstand* has been repeatedly recognized by German courts'. *The Farben Case*, vol. 8, *supra* note 18, at 1025.

[31] *Id.* at 1018–19. 'We are not imputing vicarious criminal responsibility, nor are we invoking any new principle of law ... Persons who assume and undertake to operate a machine or guide the destinies of an enterprise ... are under a duty to exercise their power of control and so to discharge their management responsibility that the enterprise under their guidance does not embark on a criminal course of conduct.' *Id.* at 1020–21.

[32] Before the trial began, the Prosecution submitted a manual entitled 'Basic Information on I.G. Farbenindustrie'. The first section of this manual was later reproduced in the case files. This was intended to avoid misunderstandings that might arise due to differences in corporate law and practices between the U.S. and Germany. For the extracts from 'Basic Information on I.G. Farbenindustrie', *see The Farben Case*, vol. 7, *supra* note 18, at 379–413.

[33] *The Farben Case*, vol. 8, *supra* note 18, at 1140.

some instances, individuals performing these acts are not before this Tribunal. In other instances, the record has large gaps as to where or when the policy was set... One cannot condone the activities of Farben in the field of spoliation. If not actually marching with the Wehrmacht, Farben at least was not far behind. But translating the criminal responsibility to personal and individual criminal acts is another matter.[34]

Despite the exclusion of the corporate entity as a subject of responsibility, the Prosecution and the judgments addressed different facets of the corporate entities and their relations with the Nazi state. But, as the following analysis demonstrates, in the absence of a comprehensive legal theory of the corporate entity and its relations with the political regime within which it operated, their analysis remained deficient and, as we have seen, led to a critical impunity gap.

Responsibility of Corporate Officials without the Inclusion of the Corporate Entity

Business enterprises' initiative, governmental control, and the division of labour between them

On 21 March 1942, Fritz Sauckel was appointed Plenipotentiary General for the Utilization (Allocation) of Labor; under his leadership, the Labor Mobilization Program became effective during the spring of that year. To meet the demands of the Reich in the occupied countries '[m]anhunts took place in the streets, at motion picture houses, even at churches, and at night in private houses'.[35] The International Military Tribunal (IMT) concluded that at least 5 million people were forcibly deported from the occupied territories and housed in concentration camps to support Germany's war efforts.

The Industrialist's judgments developed different legal requirements to establish responsibility of corporate officials without including the corporate entity as an independent subject of responsibility. Business enterprises' initiatives and governmental control were key criteria for determining responsibility for the atrocities committed against prisoners in the camps. In the Flick[36] and Farben[37] cases,

---

[34]   *Id.* at 1153 (my emphasis).

[35]   *Proceedings, 27 August 1946–1 October 1946*, 22 TRIAL OF THE MAJOR WAR CRIMINALS BEFORE THE INTERNATIONAL MILITARY TRIBUNAL 488 (1947) [hereinafter: I.M.T.].

[36]   'The defendants lived within the Reich. The Reich, through its hordes of enforcement officials and secret police, was always "present".' United States v. Friedrich Flick, 6 T.W.C., *supra* note 18, at 1201 (1952) [hereinafter *The Flick Case*]. Accordingly, this made the defense of necessity applicable to most of the defendants. There was one exception to this general conclusion, the Linke-Hofmann-Werke Plant owned by the Flick concern. *Id.* at 1198.

[37]   *The Farben Case*, vol. 8, *supra* note 18, at 1175 ('There can be but little doubt that the defiant refusal of a Farben executive to carry out the Reich production schedule or to use slave labor to achieve that

governmental influence and control over the slave-labour programme served as mitigating circumstances. Conversely, the Krupp Tribunal rejected the claims of necessity and provided ample evidence of Krupp officials' willingness to employ concentration camp inmates: 'The most that any of them had at stake was a job'.[38]

In addition to questions of initiative and control, the influence of corporate hierarchies on the scope of the Industrialists' responsibility was evident in various aspects of the decisions. It was, perhaps, most acute in the context of the discussion on the building and operation of the Auschwitz camp in the I.G. Farben case. The Tribunal described the division of labour between the Farben plant and the SS:

> They [the concentration camp inmates] were housed fed, guarded and otherwise supervised by the SS. In the summer of 1942, a fence was built around the plant site. SS guards were thereafter not permitted within the enclosure, but they still had charge of the prisoners at all times except when they were actually in the enclosed area. The plight of the camp workers in the winter of 1941–42 was that of extreme hardship and suffering. With inadequate food and clothing, large numbers of them were unable to stand the heavy labor incident to construction work. Many of those who became too ill or weak to work were transferred by the SS to Birkenau and exterminated in the gas chambers.[39]

The distinction between workers, and its significance for the Farben managers, is conveyed in an extract from a Farben-Auschwitz weekly report. On 9 August 1941, Dr. Ambros signed a report claiming that:

> in the last few weeks, the inmates are being severely flogged on the construction site by the Capos [guards] in increasing measure, and this always applies to the weakest inmates who really cannot work harder. The exceedingly unpleasant scenes that occur on the construction site because of this are beginning to have a demoralizing effect on the free workers (Poles), as well as on the Germans. We have therefore asked that they should refrain from carrying out this flogging on the construction site and transfer it to the inside of the concentration camp.[40]

The defence's main claim was that the concentration camp workers lived under the control of the SS and were hired and directed by the construction contractors. The Farben Tribunal indeed conceded that '[i]t is clear that Farben did not

---

end would have been treated as treasonous sabotage and would have resulted in prompt and drastic retaliation.')

[38] *Id.* at 1444. The Tribunal further established the view that the fear of the loss of property could not render the defense of duress available.

[39] *Id.* at 1184.

[40] *Id.* at 393.

deliberately pursue or encourage an inhumane policy with respect to the workers. In fact, some steps were taken by Farben to alleviate the situation.' However:

> it is evident that the defendants most closely connected with the Auschwitz construction project bear great responsibility with respect to the workers. They applied to the Reich Labor Office. They received and accepted concentration-camp workers, who were placed at the disposal of the construction contractors working for Farben ... Responsibility for taking the initiative in the unlawful employment was theirs and, to some extent at least, they must share the responsibility of mistreatment of the workers with the SS and the construction contractors.[41]

Nevertheless, the Farben Tribunal accepted in most cases the necessity claim, namely that the defendants were compelled to utilize involuntary labour to satisfy production quotas and therefore lacked criminal intent.[42] However, 'the defense of necessity is not available where the party seeking to invoke it was, himself, responsible for the existence or execution of such order or decree, or where his participation went beyond the requirements thereof, or was the result of his own initiative.'[43]

The Court established that Carl Krauch, as Plenipotentiary General for Special Questions of Chemical Production, dealt with the distribution of labour allocated to the chemical sector by Sauckel. The Tribunal concluded that Krauch knowingly participated in the allocation of forced labour to Auschwitz and other places where such labour was utilized in the chemical field. He was a 'willing participant in the crime of enslavement'.[44] However, the fact that Krauch supported the use of prisoners of war in the war industry was deemed 'not sufficient to warrant a finding of Guilty for the commission of war crimes under count three'.[45] The Tribunal concluded that it could not establish that the members of the TEA (technical committee) were informed of, or even knew of, the initiative being implemented by other defendants to obtain workers for Auschwitz.

The discussion of the TEA members' responsibility began with a quote from the testimony of the Director of the Office of the Technical Committee: 'The members of the TEA certainly knew that IG employed concentration-camp inmates and forced labourers. That was common knowledge in Germany but the TEA never discussed these things. TEA approved credits for barracks for 160,000 foreign workers for IG.'[46] The Tribunal's analysis of this testimony read:

---

[41] *Id.* at 1185.
[42] *Id.* at 1175.
[43] *Id.* at 1179.
[44] Carl Krauch himself, however, as Plenipotentiary General for Special Questions of Chemical Production, was involved in the allocation of involuntary foreign workers to various plants, including Auschwitz. The court held that 'in view of what he clearly must have known about the procurement of forced labor and the part he voluntarily played in its distribution and allocation, activities were such that they impel us to hold that he was a willing participant in the crime of enslavement'. *Id.* at 1189.
[45] *Id.*
[46] *Id.* at 1193.

The members of the TEA ... were plant leaders. Under the decentralized system of the Farben enterprise each leader was primarily responsible for his own plant and was generally uninformed as to the details of operations at other plants and projects. Membership in the TEA does not import knowledge of these details ... we are not prepared to find that members of the TEA, by voting appropriations for construction and housing in Auschwitz and other Farben plants, can be considered as knowingly authorizing and approving the course of criminal conduct.[47]

As for the *Vorstand*, the Tribunal concluded that its members 'all knew that slave labor was being employed on an extensive scale under the forced labor programme of the Reich'. However, 'this evidence does not establish that Farben was taking the initiative in the illegal employment of prisoners of war'.[48] Eventually, the Tribunal convicted the defendants Krauch, ter Meer, Ambros, Buetefisch, and Duerrfeld because of their proven *initiative* in procuring slave labour to build Farben's buna (synthetic rubber) plant at Auschwitz. They were given the longest sentences of any of the defendants in the Farben case, of between six and eight years' imprisonment each. [49] In all other respects, the slave labour charges were dismissed. The eighteen remaining defendants were all acquitted of the charges under this count. Included in the acquitted group were fifteen members of the *Vorstand*. The court found I.G. Auschwitz to be a wholly private project 'operated by Farben, with considerable freedom and opportunity for initiative on the part of Farben officials connected therewith'.[50]

One of the judges, Paul Hebert, Louisiana State University Law School Dean, issued a 'withering blast at his Midwestern colleagues, accusing them of bias in favor of the accused':[51]

I conclude from the record that Farben, as a matter of policy, with the approval of the TEA and the members of the Vorstand, willingly cooperated in the slave

---

[47] *Id.*

[48] The Tribunal further held that no sufficient evidence existed to prove that the availability of concentration camp inmates was a factor in the *Vorstand* officials' decision to choose Auschwitz as the location for their plant or that they were criminally responsible for the 'mistreatment of labor employed in the various Farben plants'. *Id.*

[49] 'It is untenable, in my opinion, to say that Schmitz, the Chairman of Farben's Vorstand, bears none of the responsibility for Farben's participation in the slave-labor program, including occurrences at Auschwitz, or that Schneider, Farben's Main Plant Leader in the labor field is not responsible. International law cannot possibly be considered as operating in a complete vacuum of legal responsibility—in which crime of such a broad scale can be actively participated in by a corporation exercising the power and influence of Farben without those who are responsible for participating in the policies being liable therefor'. *Id.* at 1323–24.

[50] *Id.* at 1186–87.

[51] ROBERT E. CONOT, JUSTICE AT NUREMBERG 517 (1983). For further analysis on Judge Hebert's involvement in the Farben case, *see* Albreto L. Zuppi, *Slave Labor in Nuremberg's I.G. Farben Case: The Lonely Voice of Paul M. Hebert*, 66 LA. L. REV. 495 (2005–2006).

labor program, including concentration-camp inmates ... It was generally known by the defendants that slave labor was being used on a large scale in the Farben plants, and the policy was tacitly approved ... Despite the existence of a reign of terror in the Reich, I am, nevertheless convinced that compulsion to the degree of depriving the defendants of moral choice did not in fact operate as the conclusive cause of the defendants' actions, because their will coincided with the governmental solution of the situation, and the labor was accepted out of desire for, and not only means of, maintaining war production.[52]

Judge Hebert refused to acknowledge the disappearance of free will in the co-operation between Farben and the Nazi regime in the slave-labour programme. Hebert emphasized the strangeness of the Tribunal's rationale that criminal responsibility could be established only in cases where *initiative* on the part of Farben—constituting willing cooperation with the slave-labour programme—was proved. No criminal responsibility resulted from *participation* in the utilization of slave labour. 'Under this construction Farben's complete integration into production planning, which virtually meant that it set its own production quotas, is not considered as "exercising initiative".'[53] Hebert rejected the necessity claim and asserted that 'Farben and these defendants wanted to meet production quotas in aid of the German war effort. In fact, the production quotas of Farben were largely fixed by Farben itself because Farben was completely integrated with the entire German programme of war production.'[54] Further, Hebert rejected the majority opinion's conclusion that the *Vorstand* members did not know of the plans to use concentration camp labour in their Auschwitz plant,[55] and rejected the majority's rationale holding Krauch responsible, unlike the other *Vorstand* members, because he was also a government official:[56]

---

[52] *The Farben Case*, vol. 8, *supra* note 18, at 1204.

[53] *Id.* at 1311.

[54] 'The defense of necessity as accepted by the majority would, in my opinion, lead logically to the conclusion that Hitler alone was responsible for the major war crimes and crimes against humanity committed during the Nazi regime. If the defense of superior orders or coercion, as directed in the Charter of the IMT, was not recognized in the case of the principal defendants tried by that Tribunal as applied to defendants who were subject to strict military discipline ... it becomes difficult to ascertain how any such defense can be admitted in the case of the present defendants.' Judge Hebert criticized the Flick decision, arguing that its recognition of the necessity defense constituted an 'unbridled license for the commission of war crimes and crimes against humanity on the broadest possible scale through the simple expediency of the issuance of compulsory governmental regulations combined with the terrorism of the totalitarian or police state'. *Id.* at 1309–10.

[55] 'Willing cooperation with the slave-labor utilization of the Third Reich was a matter of corporate policy that permeated the whole Farben organization. The Vorstand was responsible for the policy. For this reason, criminal responsibility goes beyond the actual immediate participants at Auschwitz.' *Id.* at 1312–13.

[56] '[T]he mere fact that Krauch was a governmental official operating at a high policy level is insufficient, in my opinion, to distinguish his willing participation exhibited by the other defendants according to their respective roles within Farben.' *Id.* at 1313.

The criminal intent required as a prerequisite to guilt under the charges of war crimes, and crimes against humanity alleged in count three, is present if the corporate officer knowingly authorizes the corporate participation in action of a criminal character ... From the outset of the project it was known that slave labor, including the use of concentration camp inmates would be a principal source of the labor supply for the project.[57]

The influence of Hebert's opinions was somewhat diluted by their late publication. But, 'late though these opinions are', wrote Sprecher in his weekly report to General Taylor, 'they both add much strength to the sum total of the purpose and results of the Nuremberg effort. We wonder how the German press will react?'[58]

The separation between ownership and control, an essential feature of the modern business enterprise, protected the Farben officials even further from the notion of culpability. Zygmunt Bauman defined such divisions as 'moral sleeping pills', 'made available by modern bureaucracy and modern technology'. For Bauman, this was an example of '[t]he natural invisibility of causal connections in a complex system of interaction, and the distancing of the unsightly or morally repelling outcomes of action to the point of rendering them invisible to the actor'.[59] While Bauman explained how bureaucracy may result in the 'sleeping morality' of the actor himself, the Industrialist Trials revealed how bureaucracy and complex organizations could render the most repellent outcomes invisible to the law.

---

[57] Id. at 1312–1313. Hebert rejected the majority opinion on the reason for Auschwitz's selection and concluded that it was selected with knowledge of the existence of the concentration camp and contemplated the use of concentration camp inmates in its construction. Hebert further established that the *Vorstand* and TEA members were aware of these reasons. Furthermore, 'the conditions at Auschwitz were so horrible that it is utterly incredible to conclude that they were unknown to the defendants, the principal corporate directors, who were responsible for Farben's connection with the project'. For example, the *Vorstand* and its subsidiary committees had to approve the allocation of funds for the housing of compulsory workers. This meant that members of the *Vorstand* had to know the extent of Farben's willing cooperation in participating in slave-labour programme and had to play an individual, personal part in furthering the programme. *Id.* at 1316. Hebert's dissenting opinion includes an element missing from the majority decision—testimonies of survivors. Frost, a British prisoner of war, offered the Tribunal the following insights: 'In addition to the IG foreman and other officials at Auschwitz, every once in a while big shots from the main firm would come down to the plant. In my opinion no one who worked at the plant or who came to the plant on business or inspections could avoid discovering the fact that inmates were literally worked to death ... Everyone who was there knew that the inmates were kept there as long as they turned out work and that when they were physically unable to continue, they were disposed of.' *Id.* at 1321–22.

[58] Drexler Sprecher to Telford Taylor, Weekly Report, 5 January 1949 RG 238 Collection of Second World War Criminals Records, Office of the Chief Counsel of War Crimes 1933–1949 Correspondence Reports Etc.; RG 238 190/12/13/01-02 Entry 159, Box 1 'Washington Correspondence'.

[59] Zygmunt Bauman, *Sociology After the Holocaust*, 39 BRIT. J. SOC. 469, 493 (1988).

Organizational hierarchy and the leadership principle

Beyond the ramifications of the division of labour between government and industry and within the organization of the different industries, the Trials' architects addressed the meaning of hierarchy in the Nazi regime for questions of responsibility. The Nuremberg doctrine sought to establish personal guilt by excluding the defence based on following superiors' commands. However, the Prosecutors' insistence on personal guilt, regardless of the duty to obey orders, ignored the important role hierarchical discipline plays in modern society. Franz Neumann and his colleagues at the Office of Strategic Services (OSS) were quite aware of these challenges. Neumann's strategy was to demonstrate how the Nazi concept of 'material justice' that was embedded in the leadership principle (the Nazi *Führerprinzip*) was the key to criminal responsibility in the totalitarian state. The leaders who controlled their respective pyramids would be held accountable for the programmes and practices in their realm of influence. An early secret memo of the OSS conveyed Neumann's strategy:

> Because of the peculiar structure of the Nazi State and because of the 'leadership principle' under which Hitler and his associates lay down broad fundamental principles but leave wide discretion in execution to their subordinates, such a departure is appropriate. For these reasons, lack of specific knowledge of a criminal act or its execution, or of an order authorizing it, should not be accepted as a defense to a charge involving a war crime.[60]

The teams working on the Industrialist Trials addressed the leadership principle as well.[61] The discussion is not an entirely coherent one, but can be roughly divided into two facets. First were the positions of leadership held by economic leaders in quasi-governmental agencies of the Reich. A central concept mentioned in this

[60] Office of Strategic Services, Research and Analysis Branch, Problems Concerning The Treatment of War Criminals, R&A # 2577 (Secret), 28 September 1944, RG 238 OCCWC 1933–1949 Correspondence, Reports, etc. Entry 159 238/190/12/13/01-02, Box 1, 'D.A. Sprecher, Planning, Preparation International Agreement War Crimes' File.

[61] 'We expect to show that the Nazi Industrialists organizations were self administrative, and through their use of the leadership principle participated:(a) In the preparation for aggressive war; (b) In the use of forced labor; and (c) In the economic spoliation of the occupied territories', wrote James M. Fitzpatrick to Benjamin Ferencz a few days before the IMT judgment was published. 'Any material which tends to indicate such participation is of value.' At this early stage 'the economic case' included both public and private organizations. 'The organizations principally concerned were the so-called Reich Groups, the Economic Groups, and the Chambers of Industry and Commerce, as well as other various sub-divisions. Evidence on all of such organizations is of value. We are, however, at present particularly interested in evidence concerning the organization in the iron and steel industry and the chemical industry.' James M. Fitzpatrick to B. Ferencz, Inter-Office Memorandum: Research on Nazi Industrial Organizations, September 25, 1946. RG 238 OCCWC Berlin Branch Entry 202 ID # 89986 Correspondence, memoranda, etc. 190/12/35/01-02, Box 2.

context was that of the *Wehrwirtschaftsführer*, the Wartime Economy Leader.[62] The second aspect concerns the source of authority in the corporate governance of private firms. The National Socialist Company Act of 1937 was designed to, *inter alia*, introduce the leadership principle to the corporate governance of firms operating in the Third Reich. Neumann's analysis of this reform suggests the decree did not go very far, but nevertheless strengthened the position of the board against its shareholders. Neumann described how this reform and other changes led to a radicalization of Berle and Means' theory of separation of ownership and control in Nazi Germany: "The right of the individual shareholder became a mere nuisance and in consequence the theory became one of identifying the enterprise with its board, which was thus freed from any control by the shareholders."[63] Despite Neumann's clear interpretation of the reform, Charles Lyon, Chief Prosecutor in the Flick case, was worried the decree would be viewed as empowering governmental leadership rather than that of the board of directors.[64]

Intriguingly, the *political* leadership principle ended up serving the very objective Lyon was concerned about. Article 8 of the London Charter does not allow the fact of obedience to orders to be taken into account in any manner for the purpose of relieving the defendant of responsibility.[65] Article II (4)(b) of *Control Council Law No. 10* (CCL10) is essentially equivalent to its Charter predecessor.[66] In *The Defence of 'Obedience to Superior Orders' in International Law*, Yoram Dinstein described how defense counsels in the IMT and subsequent proceedings tried to surmount the obstacle by proposing to benefit from the *Führerprinzip* prevalent in Nazi Germany.[67] The construction proposed by the defense was that the Charter and the CCL10 only related to ordinary orders and not to the exceptional orders of the *Führer*. Defence counsel in the subsequent trials often revived the defense refuted by Art. II (4)(b) by linking it to other arguments, such as compulsion:

> These defendants ... were no government officials, no political functionaries ... These defendants were private persons, employees of an industrial enterprise, like many thousands of their colleagues ... I shall prove that the State

[62] A. Sprecher, Inter-Office Memorandum: Work Assignments, Economics Division, October 22, 1946, RG 238 OCCLWC Berlin Branch Economics. Entry 203, 190/12/35/02 Division correspondence, reports, etc. 1946–8, Box 1.

[63] NEUMANN, *supra* note 6, at 286–88.

[64] Charles S. Lyon to Professor Arthur Nussbaum, Columbia Law School, August 1, 1946. RG 238 OCCWC 1933–1949 Correspondence, Reports etc. Entry 159 238/190/12/13/01-02, Box 1, Correspondence (Incoming + Outgoing) 10/13/45-12/30/46 file.

[65] Article 8 reads as follows: 'The fact that the Defendant acted pursuant to order of his Government or of a superior shall not free him from responsibility, but may be considered in mitigation of punishment if the Tribunal determines that justice so requires.'

[66] Indeed, the Flick Prosecutors indicated that one corresponds with the other. *The Flick Case, supra* note 36, at 1038.

[67] Dinstein's comprehensive study of the defense of obedience to superior orders in International law was based on his doctoral dissertation. *See* YORAM DINSTEIN, THE DEFENCE OF 'OBEDIENCE TO SUPERIOR ORDERS' IN INTERNATIONAL LAW 160–89 (1965).

took upon itself to encroach upon the entire industry by showing in evidence a countless chain of laws and regulations ... until during the second half of the war the term 'private enterprise' was the catchword of past liberal ages. Evidence will prove the serving part the industries had to play. It will also prove that the private persons here indicted were squashed by the events and were driven the same as the last of their apprentices, but not that they were responsible for the events.[68]

In her historical survey of the origins of the defense of superior orders, Hilaire McCoubrey argued that the application of the defence in the Nuremberg context has long been misunderstood. Given that the defendants were not 'simple' officers or soldiers but rather leaders of the Third Reich, the application of the defence of 'superior orders' in their case 'simply stated the natural application of the estab- lished "ought to know" doctrine in the very particular context of the cases with which they were called upon to deal'.[69] But whether or not the *Industrialists* 'ought to have known' was a central source of controversy in their trials.

As noted earlier, in the context of the crime of aggression, the Industrialists were described as 'followers' and not leaders. A person could be held responsible for such crimes only if extremely close to the decision-making realm of the policy- makers. Hence, the defence of obedience to superior orders found its 'back door' in the definition of the crime of aggression as a leadership crime. The Prosecutors' notions of co-conspirators or 'economic leaders', which were designed to overcome these problems, were rejected. This combination of inviting the defence of 'obedi- ence to orders' through notions of compulsion and necessity and the definition of the crime as a crime of followers paved the way for impunity of 'second-tier' de- fendants for the crime of aggression.

The influence of the hierarchical structure of authority in the different cases was similarly pivotal in the context of crimes of slavery and the atrocities of the camps. In this context, it was the hierarchical structure of the corporation and the know- ledge of high-ranking officials in the firm (especially the members of the *Vorstand*) that could be used as a basis for responsibility. Indeed, the notion that one should presume knowledge based on the hierarchical structure of the organization—the core of the OSS argument in favour of using the leadership principle—seems to

---

[68] United States v. Krupp, 9 T.W.C., *supra* note 18, at 185–87 (1950) [hereinafter *The Krupp Case*]. In the closing statement for all defendants on fundamental issues of law, Professor Wahl (special counsel for all defendants) argued that 'according to the rules of traditional international law the punishment of enemy war crimes is not admissible if the deed was not self-motivated, but committed in execution of superior orders; that is, if the deed can be imputed not to the individual perpetrator but to the gov- ernment of the state'. *The Farben Case*, 8 T.W.C., *supra* note 18, at 902. Yoram Dinstein refuted this line of argument: 'the Article is applicable whenever the plea of obedience to orders is raised, no matter whether such plea is a pure one or is interlinked with another plea; the Article is inapplicable only in the case where a pure plea of mistake or compulsion is involved'. DINSTEIN, *supra* note 67, at 169.

[69] Hilaire McCoubrey, *From Nuremberg to Rome: Restoring the Defence of Superior Orders*, 50 INT'L & COMP. L.Q. 386, 390–93 (2001).

have guided the architects of the Industrialist Trials in their choice of the *Vorstand* members as their main defendants. However, in many other contexts, the hierarchical structure of authority of each of the companies served to *reduce* the responsibility of the defendants. As the following analysis suggests, the importance of hierarchical structure for the question of responsibility in a bureaucratized corporation was disregarded in the Industrialist Trials. At times, that disregard prevented the officers of such hierarchical organizations from being held accountable.

The institutional position, which emphasized the extent to which these businesses were either state-like or linked to the state, limited responsibility only to cases where a clear influence, control, or link could be found between the corporation and the state. Alternatively, the organizational bureaucratized structure of authority and decision-making of these companies resulted in holding responsible only those who were directly linked to the crime scene or most obviously involved.

The combination of these features created a troubling paradox in the Nuremberg legacy. In Article 8 of the London Charter, the Allies sought to prevent the defense of superior orders from shielding those who had followed such orders from being held accountable for international crimes. The Article therefore assumed that leaders would be held accountable more easily than followers. But in the Industrialist cases it was easier to establish responsibility among lower-ranking officials; indeed it was almost impossible to do so for those at the top of the pyramid. Understanding the corporate structure as a chain of command proved essential to establishing responsibility among leaders (high-ranking managers) and followers (lower-tier officials). Without such understanding, those who gave orders were left untouched, leaving responsibility with the few who directly 'pulled the trigger' in mass atrocities such as the mass production of Zyklon B poison gas for use in the extermination camps.

The open question that remained long after the Trials concerns the gap between the criminal acts attributed to Farben as a corporation and those for which no specific individuals were found responsible. As noted earlier, Judge Hebert's dissent held that all the members of Farben's *Vorstand* should be held guilty under Count Three (slave labour) of the indictment.[70] Hebert further noted that the corporation was actively engaged in continuing criminal offences that constituted participation in war crimes and crimes against humanity on a broad scale, and under circumstances

> such as to make it impossible for the corporate officers not to know the character of the activities being carried on by Farben at Auschwitz ... [T]o permit the corporate instrumentality to be used as a cloak to insulate the principal corporate officers who approved and authorized this course of action from any criminal

[70] *The Farben Case*, vol. 8, *supra* note 18, at 1308.

responsibility therefore is a leniency in the application of principles of criminal responsibility.[71]

Indeed, in the Tribunal's decision, the division of authority among Farben's corporate officials was translated into a distribution of responsibility. Each member was made exclusively responsible only for the limited area within his designated authority, in a fragmented conception of the corporate function that ignores the integration of its disparate parts. With a cohesive notion of the corporate actor notably absent, responsibility was attributed either to individuals affiliated with the state (such as Krauch)[72] or to those who were directly involved in the commission of crimes. In his final statement, defendant Duerrfeld stated:

> The concentration camp and IG have been two entirely different spiritual worlds, outwardly and manifestly they are joined by the same name, but there is a deep abyss between the two. Over there you have the concentration camp; here you have reconstruction by IG. There orders of lunacy; here you have creative achievement. Over there you find hopelessness; here you find the boldest hopes. Over there you find degradation and humiliation; over here you find concern for the individual man. Over there you find death; here you encounter life.[73]

The reality of fragmented responsibility provides a plausible explanation for the impunity of the Farben defendants. It resonates with an established failure of the First Nuremberg decision: the failure to pinpoint bureaucratic crime (which has now been established in the literature, albeit not yet fully reconstituted in juridical terms).[74] The Farben Tribunal portrayed the reality of the camp as divided between two spheres of formal rationality. Avoiding the bureaucratic aspect of the crime in non-economic cases (such as the Eichmann trial) did not preclude the recognition of the criminal behaviour. In the Farben (and to some extent the Flick) case, however, the complex bureaucracy led to a more acute result. Accepting these structures of hierarchy allowed 'the corporate instrumentality to be used as a cloak to insulate the principle corporate officers who approved and authorized this course of action from any criminal responsibility'.[75] Judge Hebert emphasized that it did

---

[71] *Id.* at 1313–14.

[72] 'If we emphasize the defendant Krauch in the discussion which follows', argued the Farben Tribunal, 'it is because the Prosecution has done so throughout the trial and has apparently regarded him as the connecting link between Farben and the Reich on account of his official connections with both.' *Id.* at 1109.

[73] *Id.* at 1076.

[74] For further discussion, *see* Martti Koskenniemi, *Between Impunity and Show Trials*, 6 Max Planck Y.B. U.N. L. 1, 19–20 (2002). One important doctrinal attempt to address the systematic nature of the crime except from crimes against humanity is the development of the concept of genocide. *See* Raphael Lemkin, *Genocide as a Crime Under International Law*, 41 Am. J. Int'l L. 145 (1947) (discussing origins of the concept of genocide).

[75] *The Farben Case*, vol. 8, *supra* note 18, at 1313–14.

not matter whether, 'under the division of labor employed by I.G. Farben, supervision of the Auschwitz project fell in the sphere of immediate activity of certain of the defendants.'[76] 'Essentially', he wrote, 'we have action by a corporate board, participated in by its members, authorizing the violation of international law by other subordinate agents of the corporation.'[77] Hebert concluded:

> International law cannot possibly be considered as operating in a complete vacuum of legal irresponsibility—in which crime on such a broad scale can be actively participated in by a corporation exercising the power and influence of Farben without those who are responsible for participating in the policies being liable therefore.[78]

The impunity gap Judge Hebert described resulted, *inter alia*, from the absence of the corporate entity as a subject of responsibility at Nuremberg. The issue of collective and corporate responsibility is yet to be resolved in international law.[79] Indeed, the Tribunals may have had additional considerations in limiting responsibility so severely, such as the Cold War and the growing concern over the reconstruction of Germany that required the cooperation of the German industry.[80] Yet, in the absence of a principled approach to the corporate structure, their position left the door open for future epistemological biases to navigate the theory of responsibility of the firm in international law. Intriguingly, one form in which we encounter legal recognition of legitimate power in the Industrialists' cases is when the Judges steer clear of recognizing responsibility of certain actors, facilitating their operation in a sphere of impunity. [81] The specific symbolic effect of this non-recognition is to reaffirm the established order, proclaiming its orthodoxy.

---

[76] *Id.* at 1314.

[77] *Id.* at 1315.

[78] *Id.* at 1324.

[79] For general discussion on the question of corporate criminal responsibility and lack of consensus on this issue, *see supra* note 3. *See also* Bernard, *supra* note 3; FISSE & BRAITHWAITE, *supra* note 3; CLOUGH & MULHERN, *supra* note 3; GOBERT & PUNCH, *supra* note 3; Bucy, *supra* note 3; LAUFER, *supra* note 3.

[80] Alongside the stated wish to avoid mass punishment, circumstances significantly changed in the months during which the Industrialist Trials were underway. The Cold War had become a menacing reality. In addition, the announcement of the Marshall Plan and the turn away from retribution to rehabilitation probably played a role in the choice of rather lenient decisions and sentences. One may add the chilling effect a harsh decision on German industry could have had on American businesses as well as its symbolic force in the ideological war against the Soviet Union. For further discussion, *see* FRANK M. BUSCHER, THE U.S. WAR CRIMES TRIAL PROGRAM IN GERMANY, 1946-1955, at 29-31, 115-64 (1989); JOHN LEWIS GADDIS, THE COLD WAR: A NEW HISTORY (2006); MICHAEL HOGAN, THE MARSHAL PLAN: AMERICA, BRITAIN AND THE RECONSTRUCTION OF WESTERN EUROPE 1947-1952 (1987); TONY JUDT, POSTWAR: A HISTORY OF EUROPE SINCE 1945, at 13-128 (2005); PETER MAGUIRE, LAW AND WAR 159-718 (2000); MARK MAZOWER, DARK CONTINENT: EUROPE'S TWENTIETH CENTURY 212-49 (1998).

[81] 'What is at stake in this struggle is monopoly of the power to impose a universally recognized principle of knowledge of the social world—a principle of legitimized *distribution*.' Pierre Bourdieu, *The Force of Law: Toward a Sociology of the Juridical Field*, 38 HASTINGS L.J. 805, 837 (1987). The judgments of the Tribunals were acts of naming or of instituting. *Id.* ('The judgment represents the quintessential

All three decisions resulted in limited responsibility, yet they pose an additional puzzle: what could explain the difference in their scope of responsibility and sentences? In the following section, I discuss the three models of authority employed by each of the three corporations tried at Nuremberg—Flick, Krupp, and Farben—and how they may have affected the extent to which the Tribunal was willing to recognize these legal entities as criminally culpable actors under international law. I demonstrate how the difficulty of challenging Farben's innocence was not only due to the firm's bureaucratic, and thus disaggregated, form of operations, but also derived from a sense of affinity with its officials' quest for progress, innovation, and science. Conversely, the traditional Krupp imagery drew on the pernicious myth of the 'original sin' of German imperialism, subjecting its officials to the harshest verdict of all three. The charismatic persona of Friedrich Flick, the head of the Flick concern, led him to carry most of the responsibility for his company's criminal acts.

Structures of Authority, Sources of Legitimacy, and the Uneven Impunity Gap

One of Max Weber's greatest contributions to legal and political theory is his insight that systems of domination depend on effective *claims* of legitimacy. Weber distinguished between action that is motivated by self-interest and action that is guided by a belief in a 'legitimate order'.[82] In the latter case, individuals perform actions not merely because such actions are expedient but because they feel a sense of duty to perform them.[83] As noted by Craig Matheson, 'legitimations constitute types of explanations or understanding of power relationships, for they are "reasons why" one should obey someone'.[84] Weber characterized three types of legitimate authority—traditional domination, charismatic domination, and rational-legal domination[85]—to define three ways in which actors may 'ascribe' legitimacy to a social order.[86] Weber's point in this typology was to show how actors' belief in the

form of authorized, public, official speech which is spoken in the name of and to everyone ... [l]aw is the quintessential form of the symbolic power of naming that creates the things named, and creates social groups in particular.')

[82] 'Action, especially social action which involves a social relationship, may be guided by the belief in the existence of a legitimate order. The probability that action will actually be so governed may be called the "validity" (Geltung) of the order in question.' MAX WEBER, ECONOMY AND SOCIETY: AN OUTLINE OF INTERPRETIVE SOCIOLOGY 31 (Guenther Roth & Claus Wittich eds., 1978).

[83] Craig Matheson, *Weber and the Classification of Forms of Legitimacy*, 38 BRIT. J. SOC. 199, 206 (1987).

[84] *Id.* at 200.

[85] WEBER, *supra* note 82, at 212–307.

[86] For further discussion, *see* Susan J. Hekman, *Weber's Ideal Types: A Contemporary Reassessment*, 16 POLITY 119, 132 (1983).

legitimacy of domination is the most effective motive for obedience, as it ensures a stable structure of domination.[87]

I will now attempt to unravel how the different Industrialists resemble the three Weberian *ideal types* of authority and explain how such resemblance is related to questions of legitimacy and responsibility.[88] Informed by Weber's typology, in this section I consider how the differing corporate structures and forms of authority embodied by each of the industrialist firms tried at Nuremberg influenced the Tribunal's findings against the defendants. This explanation seeks to suggest that the models of authority employed respectively by the three corporations tried at Nuremberg—Flick, Krupp, and Farben—affected the extent to which the Tribunal was willing to recognize these legal entities as criminally culpable actors under international law.

Despite the relative leniency often attributed to the Tribunals' decisions overall, there are important differences between the Industrialist cases. The harshest sentences were reserved for the Krupp defendants,[89] and the Krupp Tribunal was the only one to order confiscation of a defendant's (Alfried Krupp) property, setting in motion a 'battle for property worth millions of dollars'.[90] By contrast, the Flick and Farben defendants were granted greater leniency. I suggest that the distinction between Krupp and Farben reflects a more deep-seated consciousness among U.S. officials regarding the corporate actors they addressed in these proceedings.

More than the other two cases, the case of Flick hinged on the man himself rather than his firm.[91] The *New York Times'* announcement of the trial captured the

---

[87] *Id.* at 133.

[88] *See* Terence Ball, *Review of Steven Lukes, Power: A Radical View and Nagel 1975*, 4 POL. THEORY 246, 249 (1976) ('When we say that someone has power or is powerful we are ... *assigning responsibility* to a human agent or agency for bringing (or failing to bring) about certain outcomes that impinge upon the interests of other human beings.').

[89] 'In the stiffest decisions handed down by a Nuremberg war crimes tribunal thus far, eleven of the twelve defendants in the trial of Krupp were found guilty today and received sentences, that with one exception, ranged from six to twelve years.' Kathleen McLaughlin, *Krupp and 10 Aides Guilty in War Case*, N.Y. TIMES, Aug. 1, 1948.

[90] *Krupp Trial Brings Fight for Property*, N.Y. TIMES, Aug. 2, 1948. On August 20, 1947, the German newspaper CHRIST UND WELT criticized the Krupp Tribunal decision: 'ultimately it is not a piece of private property but the fate of tens of thousands of German workers and employees, and the prosperity or ruin of the major German city of Essen that is at stake'. The paper continued to challenge the seizure by arguing it would benefit the Russians (who controlled a quarter of Krupp's property) and would confirm Hitler's Lex-Krupp in which Alfried Krupp was granted sole ownership of the firm. Such confirmation would be inconsistent with the Control Council's decision to abrogate all Hitler's laws. From CHRIST UND WELT (Stuttgart), *Nuremberg Before the Last Act*, 20 August 1949; the translation of the article appears in Collection of Second World War Criminals Records, Office of the Chief Counsel of War Crimes 1933–1949 Correspondence Reports Etc.; RG 238 190/12/13/01-02 Entry 159, Box 2. While the Tribunal had ordered the confiscation of all Krupp's Ruhr property in the name of the Allied Control Council, General Clay later changed the wording to provide confiscation by the Allied commanders of the zones concerned. Joseph W. Kaufman, the former Chief Prosecutor in the Krupp trial, harshly criticized this decision. In a telegram to General Clay, he asserted that the authority to confiscate lied with the Tribunal and would be challenged if transferred to the zone commanders. *Clay Challenged on Krupp Changes*, N.Y. TIMES, Apr. 10, 1949.

[91] This motif is clearly evident in the presentation of the case and its organization by the Prosecution. As noted by N.G. Barr in the course of preparing the Flick manuscript for publication: 'I believe the

personification of the case in Mr. Flick: 'Brig. Gen. Telford Taylor, chief of counsel, is expected to open late in March the trial of the 63-year-old, pro-Nazi industrialist who built a $400,000,000 empire that eventually extended throughout Germany and the occupied territories. Flick was probably the richest man in Germany at the end of the war.'[92] He was portrayed as a talented, hard-working entrepreneur, a man who '[had] always been an advocate of individual enterprise'.[93] The press release covering the Flick indictment stated that, even though he 'never became widely known to the general public or outside of Germany, largely because of [his] own shunning of publicity … his iron, steel and coal empire became larger than that of Krupp and [he] was probably the most important iron and steel magnate in Germany'.[94] Despite the obstacle of the Great Depression, the resilient entrepreneur had continued to acquire shares and companies, and in 1932, as Hitler loomed, he gained significant control of the steel industry in central Germany.[95]

The six defendants in the Flick trial were leading officials in the parent company or its subsidiaries. Flick's involvement in confiscation of property before and during the war occupied much of the Prosecutors' attention and was probably more central to this case than to the other two. These aspects brought to the fore the question of the German industrialists' responsibility for the economic imperialism and military conquests of the Nazi regime.

The story of the Krupps was radically different. In 1851, Victorian England hosted the Great Exhibition, displaying the most recent industrial innovations. One exhibit caught the attention of the British audience: 'a solid, flawless ingot of cast steel weighing two tons, presented by Krupp of Essen'.[96] These triumphant days of the early industrial age marked the dawn of prominence for the Krupp enterprise. The Krupp family's known roots go back to 1587,[97] and the family was established in Essen in the heart of the Ruhr industrial area. In the late-sixteenth century, Arndt Krupp developed a general store into a major real estate holding.

whole complex of the trial which was centered on defendant No 1 is not very well understandable if this information [regarding Flick's political and economic activities, his attitude towards Nazism, Hitler, Himmler etc.] is withheld from the reader.' N.G. Barr to J.H. Fried, Flick case—Selection Slave Labor, July 12, 1950. RG 238, Office of Chief Counsel of War Crimes, Executive Counsel, Correspondence, Reports and Other records, 1948–1949 Entry 196 238/190/12/33/02-3, Box 5.

[92] Dana Adams Schmidt, *German Steel Men Indicted for Crimes 'on a Vast Scale'*, N.Y. TIMES, Feb. 9, 1947.

[93] *The Flick Case, supra* note 36, at 1192.

[94] Office of Chief of Counsel for War Crimes, Special Release No. 106, 8 February 1947, Record Group 466, High Commissioner for Germany, 250/84/14/3-4 HighCog, Entry 55, Box 3.

[95] *The Flick Case,, supra* note 36, at 34–40. For a historical analysis that connects Hitler's rise to power with the Great Depression and, more specifically, discusses Flick's contacts with the Nazi regime as deriving from the former's attempts to 'save their sinking ship from disaster', *see* George W.F. Hallgarten, *Adolf Hitler and German Heavy Industry*, 1931–1933, 12 J. ECON. HIST. 222, 232–39 (1952).

[96] Drew Middleton, *The Fabulous Krupps: A New Chapter*, N.Y. TIMES, Feb. 18, 1951.

[97] For a historical overview, *see, e.g.*, NORBERT MUHLEN, THE INCREDIBLE KRUPPS: THE RISE, FALL, AND COMEBACK OF GERMANY'S INDUSTRIAL FAMILY (1959); WILLIAM MANCHESTER, THE ARMS OF KRUPP, 1587–1968 (1964).

The firm of Fried. Krupp was founded in 1811 as a small steel foundry in Essen. It retained its family character throughout the early part of the nineteenth century:

> For the rest of Europe Alfried Krupp … is Krupp's incarnate, head of the greatest armament producing combine of imperial and Nazi Germany, a complex of iron, steel and coal that pushed the long German columns across Western Europe from the Rhine to the English Channel and from Berlin to Oslo, Athens and Belgrade … In the decades between 1870 and 1914, as German armies marched and countermarched there became discernible behind the clank and rumble of the Kaiser's forces, a greater, less perishable institution—the house of Krupp.[98]

The Krupp firm's main business centred on producing metals and processing them into war materials, including ships and tanks. The Treaty of Versailles forced the Krupp management to choose whether to convert the firm's enterprises into a steel combine or fight to preserve its position in the armaments field.[99] Gustav Krupp (Alfried Krupp's father), who was mentioned as a possible defendant in the first Nuremberg Trial, and the other Krupp managers decided to maintain Krupp's potential as an armament factory. Gustav Krupp wrote that he 'wanted and had to maintain Krupp, in spite of all opposition, as an armament plant … Without arousing any commotion, the necessary measures and preparations were undertaken … Even the Allied snooping commissions were duped.'[100] The Nuremberg Prosecution described in its opening statements how 'the Krupp firm secretly flouted and violated the Treaty of Versailles during the era of the Weimar Republic'.[101]

In 1943, Gustav suffered a heart attack and retired as the head of the firm. Bertha Krupp, defendant Alfried Krupp's mother, owned a very small share of the company. With express governmental approval, Alfried Krupp was permitted to take over the properties signed over to him by his mother. In December 1943, Fried. Krupp A.G. was dissolved and, in accordance with provisions of the 'Lex Krupp', a special decree enforced by Hitler, Alfried Krupp became the proprietor of an unincorporated, privately owned concern that owned and controlled—directly and through subsidiary holding companies—mines and steel and armament plants.[102]

Taylor concluded the opening statement in the Krupp case by quoting Gustav Krupp's speech upon receiving the National Socialist Model Plant award, the Golden Banner. ' "It is in honor of a social-political attitude which, while having its roots in a 128-year-old tradition, has developed organically so as to fit into the new

---

[98] Middleton, *supra* note 96.
[99] *The Krupp Case, supra* note 68, at 64.
[100] Extract from article by Gustav Krupp in *Krupp Magazine*, March 1, 1942, concerning the maintenance of Krupp 'as an armament plant' after 1919; *The Krupp Case, supra* note 68, at 263–64.
[101] *Id.* at 72.
[102] *Id.* at 1332.

times, into the National Socialist Germany." These words accurately epitomize the defendants', concluded Taylor. He went on:

> The tradition of the Krupp firm, and the 'social-political' attitude for which it stood, was exactly suited to the moral climate of the Third Reich. There was no crime such a state could commit—whether it was war, plunder, or slavery—in which these men would not participate. Long before the Nazis came to power, Krupp was a 'National Socialist model plant'[103]

The Krupp indictment accused the defendants of a conspiracy that preceded the Nazi regime and made a mockery of the Allied victory in the First World War. The argument of an independent Krupp conspiracy portrayed Hitler as 'merely a convenient tool chosen by his predecessors as the vehicle for their plans of aggression'[104] The *Washington Post* reported: 'American prosecutors opening the war crimes trial of the House of Krupp charged today [that] the armament combine and German militarists are the indestructible common denominator of Germany's murderous and obstinately repeated lunges at the world's throat'[105]

I.G. Farben's history differed significantly from both Flick's and Krupp's. As noted in Judge Hebert's opinion, '[t]he history of Farben is virtually the developmental record of the chemical industry in Europe'[106] By the late 1930s, Farben controlled 98 per cent of Germany's dyestuffs, 60–70 per cent of its photographic film, and 50 per cent of its pharmaceuticals[107] I.G. Farben was an A.G. (*Aktiengesellschaft*), a corporation or a juristic person, most similar to a U.S. stock corporation. The stockholders of Farben numbered approximately half a million[108] As an A.G., Farben had two governing boards, one charged with general supervision (*Aufsichtsrat*) and the other, as we have seen, functioning as a board of directors or *Vorstand*. The *Vorstand* met, on average, every six weeks, and was presided over by a chairman who was regarded as its executive in some respects and in others merely as a *primus inter pares*. In addition to their joint responsibilities, the members of the *Vorstand* were assigned to positions of leadership in specific fields of activity[109] The twenty-three Farben defendants included all but one of the living members of the *Vorstand*, plus four subordinates. As the *New Yorker* reported:

---

[103] *Id.* at 131.

[104] Kathleen McLaughlin, *Trial Documents Krupp Conspiracy*, N.Y. TIMES, Dec. 11, 1947.

[105] *Prosecutors Lay German Wars to Krupp Militarists*, WASH. POST, Dec. 9, 1947.

[106] *The Farben Case*, vol. 8, *supra* note 18, at 1238.

[107] JOHN MICKLETHWAIT & ADRIAN WOOLDRIDGE, THE COMPANY: A SHORT HISTORY OF A REVOLUTIONARY IDEA 92 (2003).

[108] There was an annual meeting, usually attended by financial representatives of groups of shareholders. *The Farben Case*, vol. 8, *supra* note 18, at 1086.

[109] The numerous Farben plants were managed according to the so-called leadership principles, namely under the personal supervision of an individual *Vorstand* member, though in some instances one member was responsible for more than one unit and, in others, split responsibility was established according to production.

While the sessions are in progress, the defendants sit with a pile of manila folders in front of them, briskly writing memos, thumbing through the folders, passing slips of papers to one or another of the defense lawyers assembled in front of the dock, and generally acting as if the trial were a protracted business conference.[110]

Indeed, the Farben defendants were professionals, who did not in any sense own the 'means of administration' or their jobs or the sources of their funds, but rather lived off a salary. Thus, though the goal of the administration of the company for which they worked included the pursuit of money, other values such as professionalism and the advancement of science and technology were motivating their practices and legitimizing their affairs.[111]

According to the Weberian model of legal authority, Farben would be considered 'a continuous organization of official functions bound by rules'; obedience was owed to the legally established, impersonal hierarchical order. This obedience extended to the persons exercising the authority of office only by virtue of the formal legality of their commands and only within the scope of authority of the office in question.[112] Most notably, the legal authority at Farben was exercised through administrative coordination—or, in clear Weberian terms, 'bureaucracy'. As the Weberian rational-legal type of authority prescribes, the administrative staff at Farben were completely separated from *ownership* of the means of production and administration. Weber emphasized the importance of knowledge, professionalism, and expertise to bureaucratic organizations:

> Bureaucratic administration means fundamentally domination through knowledge. This is the feature, which makes it specifically rational. This consists on the one hand in technical knowledge, which, by itself, is sufficient to ensure it a position of extraordinary power. But in addition to this, bureaucratic organizations, or holders of power who make use of them, have the tendency to increase their power still further by the knowledge growing out of experience in the service.[113]

---

[110] Andy Logan, *Letter from Nuremberg*, NEW YORKER, Dec. 27, 1947 (Andy Logan was the wife of Charles S. Lyon, the chief Prosecutor on the Flick case). The trial of Friedrich Flick and five other officials of the Flick concern was the first of the so-called Industrialist Cases tried in Nuremberg.

[111] Heinrich Hoerlein, one of the I.G. Farben defendants, was a Nobel prizewinner in the field of medicine. He was Chief of Farben's Chemical Planning of vaccines, pharmaceuticals, and poison gases.

[112] These aspects of the Farben administration are reiterated in Peter Hayes's historical account: 'Ambition, achievement, and the avoidance of punishment were guiding elements in the behavior of the men who ran I.G. Farben, but so was professionalism. It insulated them from their actions; more than that, it transmogrified in their eyes the ethics of their deeds. Faced with political and economic conditions they had little role in creating, Farben's leaders acted as they thought their calling required. Their sense of professional duty encouraged them to regard every issue principally in terms of their special competences and responsibilities, in this case to their fields and stockholders. In obeying this mandate, they relieved themselves of the obligation to make moral or social judgments or to examine the overall consequences of their decisions.' Peter Hayes, INDUSTRY AND IDEOLOGY: IG FARBEN IN THE NAZI ERA 382 (1987).

[113] WEBER, *supra* note 82, at 225.

All three corporate entities introduced in the Industrialist cases were legal authorities; that is, legally established impersonal hierarchies. Each corporation—most notably Farben and Krupp—based its claim to power on a different source of legitimacy (in addition to the legal one). The distinction between Krupp and Farben reflects different attitudes of the officials working on the cases and most prominently the judges themselves. As noted by Josiah DuBois, the lenient position of the two majority judges in the Farben case derived from their acceptance of 'the fiction that Farben was the simple prototype of "Western capitalism." '[114] Farben represented a model of science, modernity, progress, and professionalism. Its structure was that of a sophisticated bureaucracy with global reach and an ambitious vision of the future. Conversely, Krupp was portrayed more as a traditional family business enterprise, with origins that embodied the historic German militarism that had led to two World Wars.

This distinction is reflected, *inter alia*, in the harsh treatment of the Krupp family, compared to the relative reluctance of the court to attach culpability to the Farben officials. One aspect of this reluctance is embedded in a perception of the Nazi crimes as irrational and primitive. But, from a normative perspective, this division (between 'modern' and 'traditional') operates as a basis of legitimacy. The modernized corporate actor echoed the U.S. self-image and was therefore granted greater legitimacy and less responsibility. The Krupps belonged to a former generation of German imperialists, the kind U.S. officials in occupied Germany tried to reform.

Flick's strong and charismatic presence overshadowed his accomplices and led to the identification of the company with the man who ran it. His dominant presence led the judges in the Flick case to assign him most of the responsibility. Yet the same features that led him to carry most of the blame provided his actions with a certain legitimacy. His fight to maintain his company in times of economic difficulty, war, and political turmoil was fuelled by a spirit of capitalist resilience and entrepreneurship. Viewed in this light, the Flick Tribunal's lenient attitude to his spoliation of resources in the occupied territories may not be so surprising.[115]

Despite these important differences, they should not lead us to a reductionist understanding of U.S. attitudes towards I.G. Farben. The U.S. anti-imperialist sensitivity that probably informed some aspects of the Krupp decision did lead to close scrutiny of the Farben enterprise, albeit beyond the Palace of Justice. Unlike the criminal trial, U.S. officials were partially successful in decartelizing Farben and other mega-trusts.[116]

---

[114] DuBois, *supra* note 22, at 355.

[115] *The Flick Case, supra* note 14, at 1206.

[116] *See also* Leora Bilsky's sophisticated analysis of the restitution class action suits brought against Swiss banks and German corporations before American federal courts in the 1990s in LEORA BILSKY, THE HOLOCAUST, CORPORATIONS AND THE LAW (2017).

Conclusion

In 1953, Tilo Freiherr von Wilmowsky, a relative of Krupp's and one-time executive in the Krupp industries, published a book on the 'Krupp affair', entitled *Warum Wurde Krupp Verurteilt?* (which translates as *Why Was Krupp Convicted?*). Professor Heinrich Kronstein of the Georgetown Law School concluded his review of the book with these telling remarks:

> But, hope on the side, can we allege that an 'international' or even western principle exists which imposes mandatory social responsibilities on those enjoying 'private' power positions? ... Admittedly we are only at the beginning of a full study of these relationships in modern society ... I do not believe that the Military Tribunal established such principles, either post factum or in future ... A much deeper problem is involved: the responsibility of the men who exercises factual power in society, even though they be subject to political power. Until this problem is clarified, even outspoken critics of private power, like the reviewer, will feel very badly about certain hypocritical attitude disclosed by the Tribunal.[117]

The main puzzle presented in von Wilmowsky's book regarding the Industrialist Trials was the stark discrepancy between the great evils in which the Industrialists were involved and their limited personal accountability. In this chapter, we have seen how the corporate structures of the different businesses contributed to the disaggregation of responsibility that facilitated, in turn, impunity. Despite various attempts to produce a coherent theory of responsibility of corporate actors at Nuremberg, the decisions do not convey any such compelling theory. The reality of the camps provides what is perhaps the most acute example of the Tribunals' insistence on the presence of, and link to, public power as a basis for responsibility in international law. The division of labour between government and industry in the administration of the camps was translated to a division of responsibility ('Over there you find hopelessness; here you find the boldest hopes').[118] Furthermore, Farben's corporate structure, which was the most sophisticated and bureaucratized of the three, diffused the responsibility of its agents. Hence, both the division of labour inside the firm and the division of labour between Farben and the government split the responsibility, leaving only the managers who were directly involved in the daily management of the camps to be held accountable.

Indeed, corporate entities were not formally included in the Industrialist proceedings. But their structures of authority, with the ethos of their officials and the public perceptions of their operations, did influence the apparent legitimacy of

---

[117] Heinrich Kronstein, Book Review, *Warum Wurde Krupp Verurteilt?*, 53 COLUM. L. REV. 139, 144–45 (1953) (my emphasis).

[118] *The Farben Case*, vol. 8, *supra* note 18, at 1076.

their actions and ultimately the scope of their responsibility. As noted earlier, the Farben officials presented compelling features of the modern enterprise: they were professionals and scientists who operated within a structure of formal rationality for the pursuit of profit. The Krupps, on the other hand, embodied the great ills of German militarism. Their legacy was responsible for two of the century's most terrible wars. Flick's imposing persona identified his company with him as an individual (in the spirit of *L'État, c'est moi*). And yet, his affinity with his U.S. counterparts (the Fords, the DuPonts) made it difficult to delegitimize his quest for power and profit, especially in the shadow of the Cold War's ideological battles over capitalism.

The corporate structure of the monopoly was another factor in the struggle over the legitimacy of German industry. Conceiving the German companies as primarily monopolies or cartels was an additional means of delegitimizing them and thus a source of justification for harsh legal measures against them. Furthermore, the antitrust campaign against Farben, Krupp, and (to some extent) Flick provides an additional explanation for their absence as corporate entities from the Nuremberg proceedings. The shifting attitudes from retribution to the rehabilitation of the economy translated into a milder antitrust policy against the German cartels. These shifts, alongside the Marshall Plan and other factors in the changing sentiments towards the German economy, found their way to Nuremberg and into the three Tribunals' decisions. These historical developments probably paved the way to an alternative vision of antitrust, one that endorsed decartelization because it facilitated further competition and the free operation of the market, rather than as a punitive measure against imperialistic forces in German society.

The aspiration of the Nuremberg architects was to hold men, rather than abstract entities, accountable under international law.[119] Yet, the call to pierce the corporate veil of the state assumed this could be achieved with no theory of the structures of authority—be it that of the state or that of the private corporation—at stake, and led to a limited and incomplete allocation of responsibility. Although Nuremberg is celebrated for putting individuals in the dock and holding them accountable for international crimes, it ended up equating the notion of the individual with political leadership. Personal responsibility, as such, was not seriously addressed. In the context of crimes against peace, it led the Tribunals to allocate responsibility only to those they identified as part of the *political* leadership. In the context of the atrocities committed in the camps, responsibility was allocated only to those with a direct physical link to the crimes. The Nuremberg jurisprudence did not quite accept the analogy between the corporate structure and the individual person; nor was it willing to fully consider its similarities with states' structures of authority ('a state within a state'). The business enterprise per se was overshadowed

---

[119]   United States v. Göring, 1 I.M.T., *supra* note 35, at 223 (1947).

by the structure of the trusts through which it was conceived, according to which the German industry was primarily held responsible for the crime of monopolization. As the Tribunals broke the link between monopolization and the crime of aggression, they failed to apply an alternative coherent theory of corporate responsibility. Without such a theory, businesses as such were not conceived as subjects of responsibility. This conceptual shortcoming reconstituted business enterprises within the archetype of individuality in international law, as an embodiment of the autonomous realm of non-interference. Indeed, the Industrialist Trials were part of the greater Nuremberg legacy that recognized natural persons as duty-holders under international law. However, the exclusion of business enterprises in the Industrialist cases legitimized the private exercise of violence, thus limiting the scope of protected human dignity to the public sphere. But the exclusion was not merely that of the business enterprise; it was also that of the individual. By piercing the sovereign veil to the level of individuals without sufficient attention to the structures of authority of the polity and the corporation, the jurisprudence in the Industrialist Trials failed to recognize the full concept of the human being.

The analysis of the Industrialist Trials here and in Chapter 4 exposed the consequences of the cases' impoverished legal theory on complex organizational structures such as 'the state' or the 'private business corporation' vis-à-vis questions of criminal responsibility in international law. Chapter 6 shifts our focus on business accountability from the question of direct individual and corporate criminal responsibility to the question of self-determination during the postwar era of decolonization. In Chapter 6 I concentrate on the legal dispute between the Iranian state, a British company, and the British Government over the ownership of oil in Iran, demonstrating how that reluctance of international lawyers to pierce the sovereign veil of the state and the corporation served, at least initially, as a source of empowerment for the weaker party, the Iranian state. At the same time, this very reluctance resulted in the exclusion of the corporation and the state from the scope of international legal scrutiny.

6

Back to Informal Empire?

The Anglo-Iranian Struggle over Oil, 1932–1954

Introduction

The Anglo-Persian Oil Company (APOC)—in 1935, renamed the Anglo-Iranian
Oil Company (AIOC) and in 1954 renamed again British Petroleum (BP)—is a
peculiar species in business history. It was founded by a British émigré to Australia,
William D'Arcy, who decided to invest his fortune in the quest for oil in Persia.
Unlike Harvey Firestone, who needed the investment for the survival of his business, or Cecil Rhodes, who was personally and politically invested in South Africa,
D'Arcy remained far removed from his black fortune. But he was to scarcely enjoy
any of it before the complexities of the search for oil left him with little choice but
to seek outside investment. Coming to the rescue, the British Government became
the private business corporation's primary shareholder. This was a strategic move
for Britain, whose leaders, like those of the United States and other powers, came
to realize the importance of oil in twentieth-century warfare and political survival.
The AIOC soon became a central source of Britain's income and a strategic asset in
its losing fight to maintain imperial status. The British control over the company
reinforced what was already a sore point to many Iranians: their land and natural
resources were being exploited by foreigners with little or no regard for their right
to a fair share. During the years of its operations in Iran, the AIOC came to symbolize the great ills of colonialism and imperial rule.[1] The events surrounding the
dispute between the weakening British Empire and the Iranian Government between 1951 and 1954 constitute the Abadan Crisis.

The eruption of the Abadan Crisis marked an important milestone in the history
of decolonization. The Iranians' argument for their sovereign right to oil was part
of a broader claim over the meaning of sovereignty as *permanent* and an attempt
to pursue an equitable international economic order that would undermine the
colonial hierarchies of the past. Initially, the Iranians seemed to have won their
cause. Their nationalization decree was not challenged by the Security Council,

---

[1] Sundhya Pahuja and Cait Storr argue that the Anglo-Iranian Oil Case is an important key to
understanding the relationship between Iran and international law. *See* Sundhya Pahuja & Cait
Storr, *Rethinking Iran and International Law: The Anglo-Iranian Oil Company Case Revisited*, *in* THE
INTERNATIONAL LEGAL ORDER: CURRENT NEEDS AND POSSIBLE RESPONSES, ESSAYS IN HONOUR OF
DJAMCHID MOMTAZ 53 (James Crawford et al. eds., 2017).

Veiled Power. Doreen Lustig, Oxford University Press (2020). © Doreen Lustig.
DOI: 10.1093/oso/9780198822097.001.0001

nor was it held to be illegal by the International Court of Justice (ICJ). Quite the opposite: the ICJ sided with the Iranian Government and accepted its argument for lack of jurisdiction. But what seemed at first glance to be a clear endorsement of the Iranian position by the ICJ did not result in long-term Iranian control over its natural resources. The AIOC, in coalition with other oil companies and Britain's alliance with the United States, eventually regained control over oil while significantly undermining Iran's political and economic stability.

A common explanation for the endurance of inequality and the favoured position of private companies and imperial powers in this case would point to the reign of hegemonic interests in international relations, in disregard of international law and its juridical concepts and institutions. Such a realist perspective would dismiss the ICJ's support of the Iranian position as too marginal, or immaterial to the long-term developments of this case. But if international law is nothing but a mirror to what Hobbes would regard as our nasty, brutish, and short life in the anarchical society, why would the World Court bother to side with the Iranians in the first place? The troubling ramifications of this case are not easily found in a hidden alliance between international jurists and powerful interests, but elsewhere. Moreover, the conceptual framings of this case would have lasting consequences for the international economic order and the relationship between business corporations and the postcolonial state. To unravel their influence, the following analysis identifies three possible interpretations to frame the relationship between nations and companies in the AIOC case: the *inter-state*, the *imperial*, and the *transnational* approaches.

The inter-state interpretation

The inter-state modality considers the empowerment of nation states and their prerogative to regulate their affairs and relations vis-à-vis strong economic actors as the main vehicle for promoting equality on a world scale. Over the course of the second half of the twentieth century, this was a central strategy of weaker states in their attempts to fulfil their right to self-determination and secure liberation from colonial rule. They based their argument on international principles of sovereign equality and rights. This was also the Iranian position: since the AIOC was a private actor, its concession agreement with the Iranian state fell short of being an inter-state treaty and could not be subject to the jurisdiction of the World Court. The Iranian position adhered to the corporate veil of the state—the formal marker for its sovereign prerogative to regulate as it saw fit, within its jurisdiction—as a justification for the expropriation of the company's assets. It also insisted on the corporate veil of the company to sustain the separation between ownership (the British Government) and control (the company's management) and thus prevent the British Government from litigating the case as a dispute between two states.

The imperial order interpretation

The British stood firm against the Iranian inter-state argument. They framed the conflict through the old imperial order modality and the entitlement to Iranian oil that it enshrined, arguing that it was consistent with, and representative of, the present state of affairs. What is more, they challenged the relevance of the separation between the corporation and its main shareholder (the British Government) and redefined the concession agreement as an inter-state contract between Iran and Britain. Under this interpretation, the corporation was mainly an instrument of the British Government and lacked any real meaning as a legal personality independent of its shareholders. This interpretation of government–company relations was reminiscent of the informal empire scenario I discussed in Chapter 2 to this book, in which the chartered company, though operating fairly independently, was legally considered the long arm of imperial rule.

As this chapter will describe in some detail, the ICJ eventually sided with the Iranian Government and accepted its argument for lack of jurisdiction. By upholding the Iranian claim that it lacked jurisdiction, the Court reinstated Iran's sovereign prerogative to nationalize AIOC assets in its territory, boosting its spirit of self-determination, nationalism, and anti-imperialism. But the ICJ decision also resulted in the exclusion of the corporation and the state, as well as placing the concession agreement beyond the reach of international legal scrutiny.

The transnational interpretation

Phillip Jessup, whose writings on transnational law were developed as the AIOC case was unfolding, challenged both statist and imperialist interpretations in favour of the third option of a *transnational law* approach. This vision called for international regulation of the relationships between states, companies, international organizations, and other actors: 'It will be the function of transnational law to reshuffle the cases and to deal out jurisdiction in the manner most conductive to the needs and convenience of all members of the international community.'[2]

Methodologically, his theoretical perspective was reminiscent of the British realism that challenged the relevance of legal fictions to solving problems in world governance. His *normative* position, however, sided with the weak, hoping for their empowerment vis-à-vis the powerful.

These three conceptual frameworks proved highly consequential for this case and for future relationships between companies and postcolonial governments. While the Industrialist Trials at Nuremberg showed how the corporate veils of

---

[2] PHILIP JESSUP, TRANSNATIONAL LAW 70–71 (1956).

the state and the company served as a shield against responsibility, they were sustained in the Anglo-Iranian case to support the cause of the weaker (Iranian) party and the broader principles of self-determination, sovereignty, and perhaps even equality. But the congruence between the formalist tendencies of the Court (in favour of sovereignty, the public/private distinction between the company and the state, and the separation between ownership and control) and Iran's interests were not eventually translated into an equal and just international economic order. In the short run, the Iranians may have won the legal battle, but, targeted by economic boycotting and a coup d'état, they lost in the war over oil to the British Government and its allies.

We, the New Sovereigns: Nationalization at the League of Nations

The 1920s marked an era of transition in Iranian politics. The nationalist movement in Iran, as well as other forms of political organization, had gained prominence after the example set by the Russian Revolution of 1917. Opposition to the central government in Tehran reached a new peak with the publication of the 1919 Anglo-Iranian Agreement. Ervand Abrahamian described how, for the opposition and for 'most foreign observers, the agreement was a typical imperialist scheme designed to transform Iran into a vassal state of the British Empire'.[3] As such, it was deeply unpopular and a source of considerable unrest. In the midst of the crisis, Colonel Reza Khan, a relatively obscure officer, led his force of some three thousand men to Teheran. Reza Khan won the support of the gendarmerie officers and the British military advisors before marching into Teheran and seizing the city on 21 February 1921. In the years following the coup, Reza Kahn transformed into Rezah Shah (King of Iran). He gained the crown in 1926 and moved to consolidate his power by building and strengthening the army, the governmental bureaucracy, and the court patronage system. The reforms he introduced enabled him to wield control over the political system and pursue his vision of rebuilding a central government and creating a unified, authoritarian Iranian state.[4]

Rezah Shah launched a comprehensive campaign against foreign influence. Among other achievements, he annulled the nineteenth-century capitulations that had granted extraterritorial jurisdiction to Europeans. This campaign would prove crucial to the ICJ decision in the AIOC case. The Shah further transferred the right to print money from the British-owned Imperial Bank to his recently established National Bank of Iran. He also took over the administration of the telegraph system from the Indo-European Telegraph Company and the collection of

---

[3] Ervand Abrahamian, Iran Between Two Revolutions 114 (1982).
[4] *Id.* at 118–49.

customs from the remaining Belgian officials. And he narrowed the rights of aliens, particularly missionaries. He failed, however, 'in one major area—that of reducing the formidable influence of the Anglo-Iranian Oil Company'.[5] This failure was not for want of trying.

The British initially welcomed Reza Shah's rule as an antidote to chaos but, as favourable public sentiment toward him gradually waned,[6] the economic conditions in Iran (as in other parts of the world) deteriorated, leading to social and political unrest.[7] In November 1932, the Shah paid a visit to the oil field at Khuzistan, 'and something must have happened there to make him decide on drastic action'.[8] On 27 November 1932, the company's representative in Tehran, B.R. Jackson, received a letter from the Minister of Finance informing him that the D'Arcy concession had been annulled. 'The government's decision was greeted with rejoicing throughout Persia. A two-day national holiday was declared, and festivals were held throughout the provinces.'[9] Meanwhile, officials in different British Government departments held conflicting views on the right strategy toward the crisis in Persia.[10]

The British Cabinet sent a note emphasizing that the cancellation was in breach of the 1901 agreement, which provided for arbitration. This note, typical of 'pre-League diplomacy',[11] demanded the immediate withdrawal of the notification and warned Persia that the British Government would take all legitimate measures to protect its lawful interests.[12] The Persian Government refused to withdraw the cancellation order, but, softening its reply, stated its wish to resolve the matter peacefully.[13] On 8 December the British warned that if the Persian Government did not withdraw its annulment within seven days, the matter would be referred to the Permanent Court of International Justice. The Persian representative on the

---

[5] *Id.* at 144.

[6] MOHAMMAD MOSADDEQ AND THE 1953 COUP IN IRAN 3 (Mark J. Gasiorowski & Malcolm Byrne eds., 2004).

[7] Another source of tension with Britain was the refusal of the Persian Government to recognize a British treaty with the Sheikh of Bahrein, arguing it was contrary to the territorial integrity of Persia. The British concession to exploit Bahraini oil augmented that controversy and aggravated the notion of British misuse of Persian resources. The discontent was conveyed in a letter signed by Foroughi, the Persian Minister for Foreign Affairs: 'My Government (the Persian Government) protests energetically against the concession in question and against any other concession not granted directly to the Persian Government in the Bahrein Islands, and declares such concessions null and void ... my Government considers itself at liberty to claim and demand the restitution of any profits that may accrue from the concession in question, without prejudice to the damages relating thereto.' Letter From the Persian Government to the Secretary-General of the League of Nations, July 23, 1930. 11 LEAGUE OF NATIONS O.J. 1083 (1930).

[8] LAURENCE P. ELWELL-SUTTON, PERSIAN OIL: A STUDY IN POWER POLITICS 75 (1955).

[9] *Id.*

[10] For an elaborate discussion, *see* Peter J. Beck, *The Anglo-Persian Oil Dispute 1932–33*, 9 J. CONTEMP. HIST. 123 (1974).

[11] 2 FRANCIS P. WALTERS, A HISTORY OF THE LEAGUE OF NATIONS 572 (1952).

[12] *Id.*

[13] Dispute Between His Majesty's Government in the United Kingdom and the Imperial Government of Persia in regard to the Concession held by the Anglo-Persian Oil Company, Memorandum from Imperial Government of Persia, Annex 1422b C.851.M.395.1932.VII, 14 LEAGUE OF NATIONS O. J. 289 (1933).

Council of the League denied the jurisdiction of the Court and proposed laying a formal complaint before the Council. The diplomatic crisis was further exacerbated by increasing acts of violence against the company.

The Persian response threatening recourse to the League reached the British Minister in Teheran in Geneva. In *A History of the League of Nations*, F.P. Walters described him running to the League offices in order to get there first with Britain's formal demand that a special meeting be called to discuss the matter.[14] His submission was made under Article 15, which refers to 'a dispute likely to lead to a rupture, which is not submitted to arbitration or judicial settlement'. The Persian Government protested the implicit threat embedded in this choice.[15] These developments coincided with the return of Cadman (the company's Chief Executive Officer (CEO)) from the United States. Cadman learned only after the fact that the company was not to play a part in the proceedings before the League and that his presence in Geneva was considered unadvisable in view of the adverse publicity it would attract. He did eventually arrive in Geneva in January 1933 for the Council meeting.[16] The question of the legality of the Iranian decision to annul the concession was placed on the agenda for the next regular session of the League in January 1933.[17] The debate opened with a speech from British Foreign Secretary Simon, who described the dispute as a story of diplomatic protection. He explained that the company, a British national, had endeavoured to do business in Persia but had fallen victim to Persia's misuse of its sovereign power.[18] Davar, the Persian Minister of Justice, contested this line of reasoning, arguing that if this had been regarded as a diplomatic protection case, the company should have turned to Persian courts and exhausted its local remedies. The dispute was not an intergovernmental one, he argued, but between Persia and the company. It would take another two decades before the two countries appeared before the Court, in its post Second World War form, to address this question.

On 30 January 1933, following a series of private talks, Edvard Beneš, the foreign minister of Czechoslovakia who was appointed to act as a Rapporteur for this matter,[19] managed to bring members of the company and the Iranian delegation

---

[14] WALTERS, *supra* note 11, at 572.

[15] In an early discussion on this matter, M. Sepahbodi, the Persian Representative, quoted a telegram from his government criticizing the British attitude: 'The Persian Government had already decided to notify the Council of the intimidating—it might almost be said, threatening—attitude which His Britannic Majesty's Government has thought fit to adopt toward Persia. We have therefore no objection to the matter being laid before the Council ... I wonder whether the present situation really necessitated an appeal to Article 15.' M. Sepahbodi, Sixteenth Meeting (Public), December 19, 1932 at 6 pm, 13 LEAGUE OF NATIONS O.J. 1987 (1932).

[16] JAMES H. BAMBERG, THE HISTORY OF THE BRITISH PETROLEUM COMPANY: THE ANGLO-IRANIAN YEARS, 1928–1954 (1994).

[17] Item no. 3206, First Meeting (Private, then Public) January 24, 1933, 14 LEAGUE OF NATIONS O.J. 180, 192 (1933).

[18] Third Meeting (Public), Dispute Between the United Kingdom and Persia in regard to the Concession held by the Anglo-Persian Oil Company 14 LEAGUE OF NATIONS O.J. 197, 198–200 (1933).

[19] Item no. 3206, *supra* note 17.

together at an unofficial luncheon.[20] This meeting in Geneva eventually led to the renewal of negotiations in Tehran in 1933 under the auspices of the League. This time, the negotiations were between the company representatives and Iranian government officials, including the occasional involvement of the Shah.[21] On 29 April 1933, a new contract was signed by the Persian Government and the company [hereinafter: the 1933 Concession].[22] On 29 June 1933, the Persian Government notified the Secretary-General that the Persian Parliament had ratified the new agreement.[23]

The 1933 Concession included a system of enhanced tonnage payments; a reduction of the concessionary area; a lengthening of the concession's duration; a guaranteed gold convertibility clause; a 20 per cent Iranian share of the company's dividend payments; and a firm commitment to the increasing Iranianization of staff. However, it did not bring about any significant changes in the unequal shares; nor did it create a substantial increase in the absolute value of the government's oil income.[24] At the 12 October 1933 meeting of the League Council, the special Rapporteur announced that, since the Persian Government had notified the Council of its ratification of the new concession agreement, the dispute between the two countries was 'now finally settled'.[25] While the agreement itself quickly proved to be highly problematic, the episode had an empowering effect on the small nation in international circles.[26] The initial dispute under the auspices of the League embodies the controversy that would later erupt again after 1945. The Iranians' wish to assert their sovereign rights over oil required the company to remain private, a distinct legal entity separate from the British Empire. Conversely, the British Government's wish was to approach this matter as if the company were a governmental enterprise and to use its sovereign authority to dictate the terms of the concession. This time, the negotiations were between the company representatives and Iranian governmental officials, including the occasional involvement of the Shah.[27] The 1933 Agreement was hardly a story of success for the Persian Government, and it would continue to haunt Anglo-Iranian relations for a further two decades. Historians also debate whether this was a success for the League[28]

---

[20] BAMBERG, *supra* note 16, at 41.

[21] *Id.* at 41–62.

[22] Annex 1467, Agreement between the Imperial Government of Persia and the Anglo-Persian Oil Company Limited, made at Teheran on April 29, 1933, 14 LEAGUE OF NATIONS O.J. 1653 (1933).

[23] Dispute between the United Kingdom and Persia in Regard to the Concession held by the Anglo-Persian Oil Company, C. 371.M.182.1933.VII, 14 LEAGUE OF NATIONS O.J. 996 (1933).

[24] For a detailed analysis, *see* MASSOUD KARSHENAS, OIL, STATE AND INDUSTRIALIZATION IN IRAN 82 (1990).

[25] Item no. 3336, Second Meeting (Public, then Private) October 12, 1933, Dispute between his Majesty's Government in the United Kingdom and the Imperial Government of Persia in Regard to the Concession held by the Anglo-Persian Oil Company, 14 LEAGUE OF NATIONS O.J. 1606 (1933).

[26] ELWELL-SUTTON, *supra* note 8, at 79.

[27] BAMBERG, *supra* note 16, at 41–62.

[28] '[T]he past history of such incidents, and the first reaction of the British government in this case, showed the dangers that might have arisen but for the existence of a higher authority which both countries were bound to respect … The dispute over the Anglo-Persian oil concession, after rash actions

or just another example of its manipulability by powerful states.[29] Given the historical climate in which these negotiations were held—1933, a time of growing instability for the League—it deserves credit for managing the dispute by peaceful means. I return to this query toward the end of this chapter and compare the institutional performance of the League in comparison to its heir: the United Nations.

The Road to Nationalization in the Aftermath of the Second World War

Three economic and political contexts are necessary to understand the Iranian turn to nationalization in the aftermath of the Second World War: the growing economic and political importance of oil; the emphasis on sovereign control over natural resources in the postwar wave of decolonization; and the attempts of other states to use nationalization as an act of resistance in the preceding decades.

The growing importance of oil

In the aftermath of the Second World War it became clear that oil had replaced coal as the principal source of energy in industrialized countries. Oil was cleaner, more efficient, and less expensive than coal, whose costs rose because of labour demands for higher wages and better working conditions. Safety and environmental standards contributed to this shift as well. In addition, technological developments and the availability of cheap oil on the global markets made it a primary fuel for industries.[30] Unprecedented rates of consumption by the Allies during the war, along with a reduction in world supplies as a result of enemy victories, brought the United States face-to-face with the possibility of dependence on others for its oil after the war.[31] 'Toward the end of the recent war', wrote Herbert Feis, a State Department advisor, in *Foreign Affairs*, 'the American government and people became greatly alarmed over the inadequacy of their future oil supply.'[32]

The early recognition of the growing importance of oil is evident from its being one of the key commodities in the Marshall Plan. More than 10 per cent of the total

on each side in its early stages, was carried to settlement in conditions that were creditable to both.' WALTERS, *supra* note 11, at 573.

[29] Beck, *supra* note 10.

[30] For further analysis, *see* Euclid A. Rose, *OPEC's Dominance of the Global Market: The Rise of the World's Dependency on Oil*, 58 MIDDLE EAST J. 424, 429 (2004).

[31] For further analysis, *see* Michael B. Stoff, *The Anglo-American Oil Agreement and the Wartime Search for Foreign Oil Policy*, 55 BUS. HIST. REV. 59 (1981).

[32] Herbert Feis, *Oil for Peace or War*, 32 FOREIGN AFF. 416 (1954).

aid granted under the Plan was spent on oil—more than on any other single commodity. This aid provided Europe with the energy it needed and served to maintain markets for U.S. oil companies.[33] In the wake of the Second World War, practically all the oil discovered in the Middle East was under concession to companies owned by the major British and American companies, such as the AIOC and Standard Oil.[34] The U.S. companies and their affiliates supplied most of the oil financed by the Marshall Plan.[35] As the demand for oil and the proportion supplied by the Middle Eastern countries continued to grow, this heightened the strategic importance of Middle Eastern oil to Western economies.

In her classic work, *Britain's Moment in the Middle East, 1914–1971*, Elizabeth Monroe argued that Britain suffered a decline of confidence about empire during the Second World War.[36] Yet, the Cold War worked to the advantage of the British Empire. The United States, despite its tradition of anti-colonialism, collaborated with the British colonial system for Cold War purposes until the mid-1960s.[37] During the postwar era, the two main multinational firms based in Britain—the AIOC and Royal Dutch Shell—produced enormous income flows for Britain, particularly the AIOC, whose production facilities were located almost entirely in the Middle East. The AIOC not only controlled 100 per cent of oil production in Iran (and a considerable percentage in Kuwait and Iraq) but also benefitted from the British Government's dominant shareholding position from 1914 to 1979. This feature, combined with the British nationality of the company's managers, led many to regard the AIOC and the British Government as one.

From the First World War to the 1950s, eight oil firms, the first seven of which were referred to as the Seven Sisters,[38] gained control over two-thirds of total global oil production.[39] Their concessionary contracts worked to the advantage of the companies, primarily because they granted them exclusive rights to explore for oil in agreed-upon areas in each country. The Seven Sisters further used their privileged position to control the price of oil and prevent small competitors from entering their markets.[40] This imbalanced relationship and the growing importance of oil to economic and political interests form the background to Iran's second attempt to nationalize its oil.

---

[33] David S. Painter, *Oil and the Marshal Plan*, 58 BUS. HIST. REV. 359, 362 (1984).

[34] For an elaborate analysis, *see* Thomas C. Berger, *Middle Eastern Oil Since the Second World War*, 401 ANNALS AM. ACAD. POL. & SOC. SCI., AM. & MIDDLE EAST 31 (1972).

[35] Painter, *supra* note 33, at 363.

[36] ELIZABETH MONROE, BRITAIN'S MOMENT IN THE MIDDLE EAST, 1914–1971 (rev. ed., 1981).

[37] William Roger Louis, *Introduction, in* 4 THE OXFORD HISTORY OF THE BRITISH EMPIRE 29 (Judith M. Brown & William Roger Louis eds., 1999).

[38] Esso; Mobil; Standard Oil of California; Gulf; Texaco of the U.S.; the Anglo-Iranian Oil Company (later British Petroleum); Shell, the Anglo-Dutch firm; and the *Compagnie Française des Pétroles* of France.

[39] Rose, *supra* note 30, at 429.

[40] For a concise overview of this history, *see id.* at 429–31.

Asserting economic sovereignty in a decolonized world

Mohammad Mossadegh, Iran's thirty-fifth Prime Minister, was born in 1879 to a royal princess of the Kajar dynasty then ruling Persia; his father served as the country's finance minister for thirty years. At the age of eighteen, he was appointed to a government post in the province of Khorasan. After serving there for ten years he went to study economics in Paris and later completed his doctorate in law in Switzerland. He returned to Tehran an active and vocal advocate for judicial and financial reform. He fell in and out of favour with the political leadership and was exiled from the political stage a few times. 'In 1919 he hardened his policy into a simple Persia-for-the-Persians. While the rest of the world went through Versailles, Manchuria, the Reichstag fire, Spain, Ethiopia and a World War', chronicled *Time* magazine, 'Mossaddegh kept hammering away at his single note. Nobody in the West heard him.'[41] In 1944, he was elected to the fourteenth Majlis (Persian Parliament). In the autumn of 1944, he proposed his famous bill prohibiting oil concessions. He formed the National Front and led this group vigorously in a campaign against foreign influence. 'It was perhaps this last strain that earned him his extraordinary sway over the masses', noted L.P. Elwell-Sutton. 'Not a notably religious man himself ... he won over the religious-minded through his recognition of the destructive influence unchecked foreign penetration was having on the life of people.'[42]

'The Second World War changed the map of the world', stated Prime Minister Mossadegh in his address to the Security Council on 15 October 1951. He continued:

> In the neighborhood of my country, hundreds of millions of Asian people, after centuries of colonial exploitation, have now regained their independence and freedom ... It is encouraging to know that the United Nations has spared no pains to help to bring such aspirations to fruition. Iran ... expects this exalted international tribunal and the Great Powers to help it too, to recover economic independence, to achieve the social prosperity of its people, and thus to affirm its political independence.[43]

The Iranians were not conveying these sentiments in a vacuum. In December 1952, only six months after the ICJ decision in the Iranian case, the UN General Assembly adopted a resolution according to which 'the right of peoples freely to use and exploit their natural wealth and resources is inherent in their sovereignty'.[44]

---

[41] Mohammed Mossadegh, *Persons of the Year*, TIME MAG., Jan. 7, 1952.
[42] ELWELL-SUTTON, *supra* note 8, at 193.
[43] UN Security Council Official Records, 560th meeting (October 15, 1951), 3–4. S/PV. 560.
[44] G.A. Res. 626 (VII) (Dec. 21, 1952).

This principle came to be known also as *economic self-determination*[45] enshrined in the doctrine of *permanent sovereignty over natural resources*.[46] These early years of decolonization were marked by a struggle over the meaning of sovereignty in the decolonized world. Rights over natural resources would become part of the struggle for, and meaning of, self-determination.

The Iranian claim for control over its oil was an early step in this struggle against economic colonization.[47] In his argument before the Security Council, the Iranian representative described his country's history under imperial rule and exploitation, and positioned the concession agreement with the AIOC as a prominent chapter in this history of British imperialism. Iran had been coerced into concluding the 1933 Concession, to its 'glaring disadvantage'. As the Iranian representative told the Security Council: 'The former Company is commonly spoken of in Iran as the "Colonial Exploitation Company".[48] The Iranian struggle was an early, though not the earliest, attempt at conveying the sensibilities and spirit of a developing emphasis on decolonization and collective rights at the United Nations. The struggle over racial discrimination in South Africa and the deliberations of the General Assembly's Social, Humanitarian, and Cultural Affairs Committee (the Third Committee) on the inclusion of the right of self-determination were in the background, filling the postwar setting of the United Nations with echoes of the interwar Wilsonian moment.[49] Indeed, in the *Observations Préliminaires* the Iranian Government issued to the Court, it cited the importance of the sovereign rights of all nations and the constitutive nature of natural resources to the collective identity of the state: 'mineral resources, watercourses, etc. are an integral part of the identity of the framework of a country and are attributes to which no provision of the Charter gives authority of intervention to the United Nations'.[50]

The British, perhaps in denial of the fragile status of their sinking empire, showed no signs of remorse. 'It is not for me to excuse any excess of so-called imperialism

---

[45] For an early account of such discussions, *see* James N. Hyde, *Permanent Sovereignty over Natural Wealth and Resources*, 50 AM. J. INT'L L. 854 (1956).

[46] For an elaborate discussion, see, generally, James Crawford, *The Right for Self Determination in International Law: Its Development and Future*, in PEOPLE'S RIGHTS 7 (Philip Alston ed., 2001); PERMANENT SOVEREIGNTY OVER NATURAL RESOURCES IN INTERNATIONAL LAW (Kamal Hossain & Subrata Roy Chowdhury eds., 1984); MANNARASWAMIGHALA SREERANGA RAJAN, SOVEREIGNTY OVER NATURAL RESOURCES 14–38, 117–34 (1978); NICO SCHRIJVER, SOVEREIGNTY OVER NATURAL RESOURCES: BALANCING RIGHTS AND DUTIES (1997).

[47] As noted earlier, during the Second World War, Iran was occupied by British and Russian forces but their formal control over the country ended at the end of the war.

[48] UN Security Council Official Records, 560th meeting (Oct. 15, 1951), 8. S/PV. 560.

[49] For a detailed analysis of the influence of Wilson and the principle of self-determination, *see* EREZ MANELA, THE WILSONIAN MOMENT: SELF DETERMINATION AND THE INTERNATIONAL ORIGINS OF ANTICOLONIAL NATIONALISM (2007). Evan Luard marked 1955 as a turning point in his historical study of the United Nations. The second volume of the book, devoted to the history of the United Nations 1955–1965, is entitled THE AGE OF DECOLONIZATION. EVAN LUARD, THE HISTORY OF THE UNITED NATIONS (1982). Others mark its nascence earlier.

[50] *Observations Préliminaires: Refus du Gouvernement imperial de reconnaître la competence de la Cour*, Anglo-Iranian Oil Co. (U.K. v. Iran), 1951 I.C.J Rep. 281, 288, 294.

that happened in the past.'[51] '[W]hatever may be thought of what was called imperialism in the past', concluded the British delegate, 'it is useless to think that the new emergent nationalities, in Asia, for instance, can lay the foundations for their own prosperity, or even for their own continued existence, on nationalism alone.'[52]

International legal scholar Ian Brownlie wrote: 'In classical international law natural resources had no place. The operation of the principle of consent and the doctrines of alienability and the "open door" could, and often did, result in the transference of ownership and control of major resources into the hands of foreign interests.'[53] But nationalization of assets protected by concession gradually emerged as an act of resistance against colonialism. In addition to the growing economic and political importance of oil and the emphasis on sovereign control over natural resources in the postwar wave of decolonization, the nationalization was an act of resistance. Its history and its consequences in international law is important for understanding the AIOC case.

Nationalization as an act of resistance

Nationalization was a central strategy in postcolonial and weaker states' attempts to resist colonial presence and assert sovereign identity and control. The Iranians were not the first to choose nationalization as a form of resistance. The jurisprudence of the nineteenth century protected alien property by referring to the domestic law of the host state, with the implicit assumption that each state would protect private property within its jurisdiction.[54] In 1868, the Argentine jurist Carlos Calvo published a study in which he challenged the imbalanced ramifications in the exercise of diplomatic protection.[55] In 1833, Latin American bonds were in default, leading to the collapse of many businesses and investors operating in the area. The limited capacity of local authorities to protect foreigners' property led foreign investors to seek relief from their home governments. These attempts resulted in several notorious European interventions in Latin American states.[56] In response, the Calvo Doctrine proposed equal treatment for aliens and

---

[51] UN Security Council Official Records, 559th meeting (Oct. 1, 1951), 23–24. S/PV. 559.

[52] *Id.* at 24. S/PV. 559.

[53] Ian Brownlie, *Legal Status of Natural Resources in International Law (Some Aspects)*, 162 RECUEIL DES COURS 253 (1979).

[54] For a succinct historical overview that covers some aspects of this period, *see* RUDOLF DOLZER & CHRISTOPH SCHREUER, PRINCIPLES OF INTERNATIONAL INVESTMENT LAW 1–30 (2008).

[55] For an elaborate discussion of Carlos Calvo and other semi-peripheral jurists, *see* ARNULF BECKER LORCA, MESTIZO INTERNATIONAL LAW: A GLOBAL INTELLECTUAL HISTORY 1842–1933, at 58–69, 103–07 (2014).

[56] One example was the 'Jecker Claim', which led to the invasion of Mexico by France's Napoleon II. For further discussion, *see* DANIEL SHEA, THE CALVO CLAUSE 12–14 (1955); Christopher K. Dalrymple, *Politics and Foreign Direct Investment: The Multilateral Investment Guarantee Agency and the Calvo Clause*, 29 CORNELL INT'L L.J. 161, 164–65 (1996).

nationals: since nationals were entitled to seek redress for their grievances only before the local courts and authorities, aliens should be subject to the same rules and not entitled to seek redress through foreign authorities. The Calvo Clause in concession agreements required that aliens commit themselves, by the contract with the state, not to seek diplomatic protection against the contracting state from the state of which they were nationals.[57]

In 1910, U.S. Senator and former Secretary of State Elihu Root sought to refute the rationale of the Calvo Doctrine by stating what was, for many, the prevalent position: that host states were bound by rules of international law. These rules encompassed the standard of justice as accepted by

> all civilized countries as forming a part of the international law of the world ... If any country's system of law and administration does not conform to that standard, although the people of the country may be content or compelled to live under it, no other country can be compelled to accept it as furnishing a satisfactory measure of treatment to its citizens.[58]

The Soviet Union's expropriations of national enterprises without compensation after the 1917 Revolution revived the debate over the international law of expropriation. One of the disputes resulting from this process was brought before the Lena Goldfields Arbitration Tribunal of 1930. Lena Goldfields, Ltd. was a British company operating in Siberia. In 1929, the Soviet Government brought the company's operations to a halt. Arthur Nussbaum vividly described the 'class war against the Lena employees, the disorganization of the company and the seizure and arrest of its managers and engineers'.[59] The Arbitration Tribunal required the Soviet Union to pay compensation to the alien claimant. Its decision provides an early example of a private arbitration tribunal applying a general principle of law recognized by civilized nations, by reference to Article 38(1) of the Statute of the Permanent Court of International Justice, namely compensation for unjust enrichment.[60]

---

[57] For a concise overview, *see* PATRICK JULLIARD, CALVO DOCTRINE/CALVO CLAUSE MAX PLANCK ENCYCLOPEDIA OF PUBLIC INTERNATIONAL LAW (2011). The commentary on Article 14 in the Draft Articles on Diplomatic Protection defines the Calvo Clause as follows: 'a device employed mainly by Latin American States in the late nineteenth century and early twentieth century, to confine an alien to local remedies by compelling him to waive recourse to international remedies in respect to disputes arising out of a contract entered into with the host State'. International Law Commission, Draft Articles on Diplomatic Protection with commentaries 73 (2006) A/61/10.

[58] Elihu Root, *The Basis of Protection to Citizens Residing Abroad*, 4 AM. J. INT'L L. 517, 528 (1910).

[59] Arthur Nussbaum, *The Arbitration Between Lena Godlfields, LTD. and the Soviet Government*, 36 CORNELL L.Q. 31, 32 (1950).

[60] For an analysis of the Lena Goldfields Arbitration (1930), see, for example, V.V. Veeder, *The Lena Goldfields Arbitration: The Historical Roots of Three Ideas*, 47 INT'L COMP. L.Q. 747 (1998). The decision was summarized by 5 HERSCH LAUTERPACHT, ANNUAL DIGEST CASES NOS. 1 AND 258 (1929–1930), at 3, 426 (1935).

Vladimir Robertovich Idelson presented the case on behalf of Lena Goldfields before the tribunal. Idelson was a Russian jurist who had escaped the Revolution for eventual exile in France and England. Arriving in London in 1920, he soon became extensively involved in disputes resulting from Russian nationalization decrees. After the Lena arbitration, he was hired by the AIOC to draft what became the 1933 Concession Agreement. Idelson would return to the scene in 1951, towards the end of his life, to advise the British Government with regard to its arbitration proceedings against Iran and the complaint before the ICJ.[61] The Lena Award was cited in the U.K.'s memorial.

The Permanent Court of International Justice recognized the right of a state to nationalize property within its territory in the 1928 Chorzow Factory case. The decision provided a basis for the principle of just compensation in international law ('reparation must, as far as possible, wipe out all the consequences of the illegal act and re-establish the situation which would have existed if that act had not been committed').[62] But this decision, like previous holdings of international tribunals, was not able to withstand the attacks against its potentially disempowering implications. The dispute over the Mexican nationalization of American oil and agricultural businesses in 1938 led to a famous exchange between the U.S. Secretary of State, Cordell Hull, and his Mexican counterpart. In this correspondence, Secretary Hull laid out the rules of international law of expropriation that became known as the Hull Formula.[63] According to the Hull Formula, the rules of international law allowed

---

[61] Veeder, *supra* note 60, at 769–70.

[62] The Case concerning the Factory at Chorzow, 1928 P.C.I.J., Ser. A, No. 17, at 46–47. Herz, in an early analysis of the issue, stated that, '[a]part from the case where a special treaty stipulation expressly forbids expropriation, such a measure is a lawful faculty or right of the state which leads to an international obligation to pay compensation for the value taken'. John H. Herz, *Expropriation of Foreign Property*, 35 AM. J. INT'L L. 243, 253 (1941). This case was preceded by a jurisprudence influenced by the Russian and Mexican revolutions, which undermined the importance of private property and the right to compensation. But, as noted by Andreas Lowenfeld, the Chorzow factory case was '[b]y far the best known and most often quoted case on state responsibility to private investors'. ANDREAS F. LOWENFELD, INTERNATIONAL ECONOMIC LAW 474 (2008). The Chorzow factory case arose out of the changing border between Germany and the newly-established Poland at the end of the First World War. The Polish Government's taking of a nitrogen factory that was initially established when the territory belonged to the German Reich was the source of this controversy. The Geneva Convention, in implementing the Treaty of Versailles, authorized the Polish Government to take property in Silesia previously owned by the German government; such property would be credited against Germany's obligation to pay reparations. The Polish Government's position was that the factory was owned by the German Government or that the transfer of ownership to private parties had been fraudulent. The PCIJ decided in favour of Germany. The principles laid out in the decision were subject to scholarly controversy, but eventually the case became a common source in asserting the obligation of just compensation in international law.

[63] The correspondence was later published in 3 GREEN H. HACKWORTH, DIGEST OF INTERNATIONAL LAW (1942) and 5 GREEN H. HACKWORTH, DIGEST OF INTERNATIONAL LAW (1943). For further discussion on Cordell Hull's foreign economic agenda, *see* MICHAEL BUTLER, CAUTIOUS VISIONARY: CORDELL HULL AND TRADE REFORM (1933-1937) (1998); Susan Aaronson, *How Cordell Hull and the Postwar Planners Designed a New Trade Policy*, 20 BUS. & ECON. HIST. 171 (1991).

expropriation of foreign property, but required 'prompt, adequate and effective compensation'.[64]

The AIOC case was part of a subsequent wave of expropriation cases between 1945 and 1970. Andreas Lowenfeld described the jurisprudence of these cases as incoherent and thus hardly a basis for a specific rule in customary international law. The different agreements reached between firms and states 'were driven by political and economic considerations, generally without even an attempt to fit them into international legal doctrine'.[65] Advocates of the Calvo Doctrine and later objections to the application of international legal standards conceived them as standards of the powerful—a vehicle of imperial intervention, strengthening the unbalanced relations between investors and the governments of weaker states.

Nationalization and the Struggle over the Meaning of the Concession Agreement

By 1949, the British had grown increasingly concerned over the Shah's lack of control over his country and the Iranian economy's degeneration into a state of paralysis.[66] The oil issue became a rallying point, a focus of national frustration. For many Iranians, the AIOC came to symbolize all the evils of imperialist control and, in particular, British imperialism.[67] In 1949, the representatives of the AIOC and the Iranian Government signed a revised agreement known as the Supplemental Oil Agreement, and held high hopes for a breakthrough in the economic development of Iran. The government, however, fearful of parliamentary opposition, held back and did not submit the agreement to the Majlis for almost a year, until June 1950.[68] When it did, the new concession was fiercely rejected by the Parliament's Oil Committee, which also called for the cancellation of the concession and the nationalization of the AIOC assets in Iran. The ensuing fury over this move led to the assassination of a pro-British politician and to the Prime Minister's resignation. The Shah then nominated Ali Razmara, the Army's Chief of Staff, as the new Prime Minister.[69] In late March 1950, the young Shah,

---

[64] For further discussion, see ANDREAS H. ROTH, THE MINIMUM STANDARD OF INTERNATIONAL LAW APPLIED TO ALIENS (1949); DOLZER & SCHREUER, supra note 54, at 13–14, 124.

[65] LOWENFELD, supra note 62, at 484–85.

[66] WILLIAM ROGER LOUIS, THE BRITISH EMPIRE IN THE MIDDLE EAST 1945–1951: ARAB NATIONALIZATION, THE UNITED STATES, AND POSTWAR IMPERIALISM 632–36 (1984).

[67] Between 1945 and 1950, the AIOC registered a £250 million profit, compared to Iran's £90 million royalties—that is, the British Government received more in taxes from the AIOC than Iran did in royalties. To aggravate matters still further, a substantial part of the company's dividends went to its majority owner, the British Government, and it was rumoured that the AIOC sold oil to the British navy at a substantial discount. DANIEL YERGIN, THE PRIZE: THE EPIC QUEST FOR OIL, MONEY & POWER 433–34 (1991).

[68] BAMBERG, supra note 16, at 383–409.

[69] YERGIN, supra note 67, at 433–34.

sporting an admiral's uniform, received a *New York Times* reporter for an interview in his private palace. Speaking in English and smoking an American cigarette, he declared '[t]here is no use writing treaties until economic conditions are bettered'.[70]

The situation continued to deteriorate and, by August 1950, Foreign Office officials were expressing concern that the Razmara government might not survive. Despite the British Government's holding of 51 per cent of the AIOC shares, the Foreign Office was unable to force the company to fund (or subsidize) economic development beyond what was provided by the agreed-upon royalties. William Fraser, the Chairman of the AIOC, was not willing to concede to the pressures of the British government. 'It was for Governments to lend money to Governments', stated Fraser, 'not oil companies'.[71] The British Foreign Office continued to put pressure on the company to no avail,[72] until the autumn of 1950, when the company's management became more responsive to these pressures. William Roger Louis attributed this shift to the ARAMCO agreement with the Saudis that split the profits on a fifty-fifty basis. The Iranians were offered a revised AIOC concession with 50 per cent in royalties, but since this was not equivalent to half the profits, it was not enough to save the situation for the British.[73]

On 15 and 20 March 1951, the Iranian Majlis and Senate, respectively, passed a law enunciating the principle of nationalization of the oil industry in Iran. In the last days of April, the British sent gunboats to convey their position in the worsening crisis. Nationalization was implemented by the Iranian Oil Nationalization Law of 1 May 1951.[74] According to this legislation, 'the entire revenue derived from oil and its products [was] indisputably due to the Persian nation' as of 20 May 1951. The establishment of the National Iranian Oil Company [hereinafter: NIOC] followed.

Henri Rolin, who argued the case before the ICJ on behalf of Iran, described the meaning of these events to British interests:

> The British were abruptly cut off from one of the principal supplies of petroleum upon which the free nations of Europe, and particularly the British fleet and merchant marine were depending, in a moment when the world political situation was exceedingly ominous ... the ultimate outcome of this dispute could easily affect the future of foreign oil concessions in other oil producing lands.[75]

---

[70] C.L. Sulzberger, *Iran Not to Allow New Concessions*, N.Y. TIMES, Apr. 1, 1950, at 2.

[71] Minutes of a meeting held at the F.O. 2 Aug. 1950, FO 371/82375/EP1531/40, quoted by LOUIS, *supra* note 66, at 644.

[72] BAMBERG, *supra* note 16.

[73] LOUIS, *supra* note 66, at 647.

[74] English translation in Application Instituting Proceedings, Anglo-Iranian Oil Company Case, 58 (Annex C).

[75] Henri Rolin, *The International Court of Justice and Domestic Jurisdiction: Notes on the Anglo-Iranian Case*, 8 INT'L ORG. 36 (1954).

And the *New York Times* concluded:

> Socialist Britain is in the position of defending a company that has pursued policies of the old imperialism in an age when imperialism is all but outlawed and at a time when she lacks the power to enforce her will even on such a small and backward country as Iran. All that is left is a waiting game.[76]

The AIOC applied to the President of the ICJ, according to the terms of the 1933 Concession Agreement, to appoint a sole arbitrator between itself and the Iranian Government. On 21 June, 'nationalist youth battered down the Anglo-Iranian Oil Co. signs and parliament gave Premier Mohammed Mossadegh a unanimous vote of confidence to strengthen his hand in taking over the company's operations'.[77] On 22 June 1951, the United Kingdom submitted a request that the ICJ should indicate provisional measures to preserve its rights. The Court, by order of 5 July 1951, granted the request for interim protection measures. The company sought to retain its British experts as long as it could. But they too would soon be forced to move out.

Rolin wrote in a later essay: 'The Iranian move reflected in the first instance the surge of nationalism sweeping the Middle East in the wake of World War II, and the resolution of many of these peoples to free themselves of former restraints.'[78] As Rolin further noted, '[t]he unusual interest of the Anglo-Iranian dispute brought before the Court lay ... in the passionate revolt of the Iranian people against the attempt of Great Britain to control what they considered to be a matter within the exercise of their sovereign domestic rights'.[79] The Iranian Prime Minister conveyed this point quite clearly in his speech before the Security Council: 'The movement which is manifesting itself in Iran is supported by a people fully conscious of its rights.'[80]

The Iranian representative described the liberating force of nationalization, an act of Iranian resistance against imperialist control. 'The general feeling that nationalization of the oil industry would provide an answer to the country's problems certainly derived momentum from the suffering and privations of the Iranian people over the previous half century.'[81] This was not merely an argument before the Security Council. It was the motivation for a massive social movement, headed by Mossadegh and his supporters. But the case also raised the issue of expropriation in the highly complex circumstances of weaker states. It therefore put the question of nationalization as an act of resistance squarely on the table of the Security Council and the ICJ.

---

[76] Raymond Daniel, *Britain Sees More Than Oil at Stake in Iran*, N.Y. TIMES, Jun. 24, 1951, at 127.
[77] *Iran Youths Raid Tehran Offices of Oil Company*, WASH. POST, Jun. 22, 1951, at 1.
[78] Rolin, *supra* note 75, at 36.
[79] *Id.*
[80] UN Security Council Official Records, 560th meeting (Oct. 15, 1951), 4–5. S/PV. 560
[81] *Id.* at 21. S/PV. 560

The Controversy Over the Concession Agreement Reaches the United Nations: Between the Statist and the Imperial Positions

Interim measures and the Security Council

Only six years into the United Nation's existence (it began operations in October 1945), the Iranian episode marked the first instance in which the ICJ implemented interim protection measures, the first case in which such measures were disregarded, and the first time a legal dispute was brought before the Security Council.[82] The oral hearing on the interim measures was held on the morning of 30 June 1951. The Iranian Government chose not to send a representative to argue its case, and thus it was only the British statement by Sir Frank Soskice that was heard before the Court.[83] The incapacity of the Iranian Government to take over the company's assets was a major theme in his argument. As for the measures themselves, the request was to allow the company to carry on the enterprise in broadly the same manner as it was entitled to do under the 1933 Concession and without greater interference from the authorities of the Imperial Iranian Government.[84] As noted earlier, the Court duly granted the request for interim measures. It also indicated, pending its final decision, that the Iranian and U.K. Governments

> should each ensure that no action is taken which might prejudice the rights of the other Party in respect of the carrying out of any decision on the merits which the Court may subsequently render... Ensure that no action of any kind is taken which might aggravate or extend the dispute submitted to the Court ... to hinder the carrying on of the industrial and commercial operations of the Anglo-Iranian Oil Company, Limited as they were carried on prior to May 1951 and that the Company's operations in Iran should continue under the direction of its management as it was constituted prior to May 1st, 1951.[85]

---

[82] For further analysis on the case in the context of compliance with provisional measures, *see* CONSTANZE SCHULTE, COMPLIANCE WITH DECISIONS OF THE INTERNATIONAL COURT OF JUSTICE 275–320 (2004).

[83] The British team also included Sir Eric Beckett, the British Attorney General, Professor Hersch Lauterpacht of the University of Cambridge, Mr. A.K. Rothnie of the Eastern Department of the Foreign Office, H.A.P Fisher, Member of the English Bar, and D.H.N Johnson, Assistant Legal Adviser of the British Foreign Office.

[84] Oral Proceedings concerning Interim Measures of Protection, held at the Peace Palace, The Hague, on June 30 and July 5, 1951, Statement by Sir Frank Soskice (U.K.), Anglo-Iranian Oil Co. Case (U.K. v. Iran),—1951 I.C.J. Pleadings 398, 434 (June 30, 1951).

[85] Two Judges, B. Winiarski and Badawi Pacha, dissented, arguing that the question of interim measures was closely linked with that of jurisdiction and that if the Court found it had no jurisdiction on the merits, there could be no jurisdiction to establish interim measures of protection. Anglo-Iranian Oil Co. Case (U.K. v. Iran), Order, 1951 I.C.J Rep. 89, 97 (July 5).

Iran refused to accept the order, on the grounds that the Court was competent neither to deal with the case nor to indicate interim protection measures.[86] The Iranian Government further stated that it 'hopes that the Court will declare that the case is not within its jurisdiction ... Under these circumstances the request for interim measures of protection would naturally be rejected.'[87] Once the Iranian refusal to adhere to the Court's decision became evident, the British and U.S. governments initiated diplomatic attempts (the Stokes Mission) to negotiate with the Iranians, but failed to reach any agreement.[88] The Iranian Government ordered the evacuation of the remaining British staff at the Abadan refinery,[89] and Iranian troops seized the refinery on 27 September 1951, bringing its operations to a halt.[90]

Neither the company nor the British Government was going to give up the Abadan oil without a fight. In a last resort against the expulsion order, the British turned to the Security Council. 'The Security Council is to convene in special session tomorrow morning', reported the *New York Times*. 'The session will certainly be dramatic ... Whether the Council can take any important action before the deadline in Abadan, Thursday, is highly uncertain.'[91] It was further reported that 'diplomatic quarters said the Royal Navy may impose a virtual "oil blockade" while it waits for a United Nations ruling.'[92]

On 28 September 1951, the U.K. delegation to the UN Security Council requested that the following item be placed on the provisional agenda of the Council: 'Complaint of failure by the Iranian Government to comply with provisional measures indicated by the International Court of Justice in the Anglo-Iranian Oil Company Case.' The British argued that the Council should enforce the Court's decision, as an 'executive' branch of the United Nations, so to speak. The British representative, Sir Gladwyn Jebb, argued that it was the duty of the Security Council to uphold the international obligation to comply with the Court's interim measures. Jebb referred to Article 94 of the Charter, according to which a party may have recourse to the Council in case the other party fails to perform the obligations incumbent upon it under a judgment rendered by the Court. He further argued that the situation in Iran posed a threat to peace ('No one can doubt ... the essentially inflammatory nature of a situation of the kind which now exists in those parts of Iran which are affected') and thus provided the United Kingdom with the right, under Articles 34 and 35 of the Charter, to appeal to the Security Council.[93]

---

[86] In a telegram dated July 9, 1951 Iran Informed the U.N Secretary General of its decision to withdraw its declaration of October 2, 1930, concerning the acceptance of the compulsory jurisdiction of the ICJ. *See* U.N. Doc. Press Release PM/2219.

[87] 1951 I.C.J. Rep. 93.

[88] The Memorial of the United Kingdom, 1951 I.C.J. Rep. 67–69.

[89] *Middle East Munich*, ECONOMIST, Oct. 6, 1951, at 779–80.

[90] For a description of the events during this period leading to the Security Council discussions, *see* ALAN W. FORD, THE ANGLO-IRANIAN OIL DISPUTE 85–126 (1954).

[91] *The World*, N.Y. TIMES, Sept. 30, 1951.

[92] *Britain Asks U.N. to Act in Oil Fight*, WASH. POST, Sept. 29, 1951.

[93] UN Security Council Official Records, 559th meeting (Oct. 1, 1951), 4. S/PV. 559.

The Iranian representative, Mr. Selah, argued that the Security Council lacked jurisdiction to lend its authority to the provisional measures indicated by the World Court. He based his argument on Article 2(7) of the UN Charter and claimed the Security Council should not intervene in Iranian internal affairs. Iranian sovereignty was grounded in its rights over its natural resources and decolonization, namely its resistance to the imperialistic exploitation of the British and Russian Empires and the AIOC. The Iranian delegate asked for ten more days to enable Iran's representatives to reach New York from Tehran.[94] The U.S. delegate, reflecting his government's differences with the British position, presented a proposal siding with the Iranian suggestion for postponement. The Security Council duly suspended the discussion for ten days, frustrating the objective of the urgent meeting in light of the immediate expulsion of the British personnel. '[T]he majority of the British personnel at Abadan embarked on the HMS Mauritius on 3 October [1951], to be followed by the last of the senior staff the following day. For the moment, the Company was out of Iran.'[95] The *Los Angeles Times* reported: 'Humiliated British Oilmen Leave Iran ... Less than a day before they faced ouster by Iran, the cruiser Mauritius and a British airliner took out the 330 remaining technicians from the world's biggest oil refinery at Abadan.'[96] Under the headline 'Middle East Munich', the *Economist* reported:

> The evacuation of Abadan is a deeply humiliating episode and a grave defeat for British policy. What might weeks ago have been a deliberate act of strength, forcing Dr. Mossadegh to recognize that Persians had neither the skill nor the resources to run the oil industry alone, became through delay and hesitation a last-moment rout ... The strength of the nationalist movement in Persia was misjudged both by the oil company and the British Embassy in Tehran.[97]

The next meeting of the Security Council took place on 15 October 1951. The deep controversy between member states and the threat of a Russian veto ultimately led the Council to adjourn discussions until the World Court ruled on the question of *its* jurisdiction. The British representative conceded, since any type of resolution was clearly out of reach. At the conclusion of the Security Council's discussion, the Iranian Prime Minister travelled to Washington to meet with President Truman and initiate further negotiations. Like other attempts, this initiative proved fruitless. The next phase of the struggle was the legal dispute before the Court and its judgment on this matter.

---

[94] *Id.* at 25. S/PV. 559.
[95] BAMBERG, *supra* note 16, at 458.
[96] *Humiliated British Oilmen Leave Iran*, LOS ANGELES TIMES, Oct. 4, 1951.
[97] *Middle East Munich*, ECONOMIST, October 6, 1951, 779–80.

Statism and Imperialism before the ICJ

The ICJ dispute between the Iranian revolved on three axes that I will discuss next: (i) the applicability of capitulation-related treaties to establish the ICJ jurisdiction; (ii) the legality of the Iranian Nationalization Act; and (iii) the definition of the Concession treaty as either a public (inter-state) or a private (company–state) agreement. Each axis epitomizes a different angle on the struggle between the British Government's attempt to reassert its position as the sovereign behind AIOC and the Iranian claim for sovereignty and self-determination.

Colonial or postcolonial interpretation? The capitulations-era treaties and the jurisdiction of the Court

The ICJ delivered its judgment on the preliminary objection on 22 July 1952.[98] The majority opinion framed the conflict as a diplomatic protection dispute, in which the United Kingdom adopted the cause of action of the British company and submitted, 'in virtue of the right of diplomatic protection', an application to the Court instituting proceedings in its name against the Imperial Government of Iran. The discussion revolved entirely around the issue of jurisdiction. In this case, the Court observed, its jurisdiction depended on the declaration made by the parties under Article 36, paragraph 2, on condition of reciprocity. Since the Iranian declaration was more limited in scope than that of the United Kingdom, it was the former on which the Court had to base its considerations. The dispute over the interpretation of Iran's declaration was twofold. The Court had to conclude first whether the declaration was limited to the application of treaties or conventions accepted by Iran *after the ratification of the declaration,* or whether it applied to treaties or conventions *accepted by Iran at any time.* Based on the answer to this first question, it would need to interpret which treaties, if any, might be regarded as a basis for its jurisdiction.

The Court found historical evidence of the Iranian government's intention to limit the jurisdiction of the ICJ. In 1927, the Iranian Government had denounced all treaties with other states relating to the regime of capitulations and commenced negotiations with these states to replace the denounced treaties with a new regime based on equality. When Iran's declaration was signed in 1930, it was still unclear whether all capitulatory treaties had ceased to be binding. It was therefore unlikely, concluded the Court, that Iran would have been willing to submit disputes based on such treaties to the ICJ. The Iranian law by which the Majlis approved the

---

[98]   1952 I.C.J. Rep. 93.

declaration provided a decisive confirmation of Iran's intention. The Court therefore concluded that the Iranian declaration was limited to disputes relating to the application of treaties or conventions accepted by Iran *after* the ratification of the declaration.

The United Kingdom argued that, even with this finding, the Court had jurisdiction in the present case. It relied on a series of treaties of friendship, establishment, and commerce concluded between Iran and Denmark (1934), Switzerland (1934), and Turkey (1937), respectively, which required Iran to treat nationals of these powers in accordance with the principles and practice of ordinary international law. Since the AIOC was not treated in accordance with these principles, the Most Favoured Nation (MFN) clause in two earlier treaties between Iran and the United Kingdom (from 1857 and 1903) could be invoked to provide a basis for the Court's jurisdiction. MFN clauses, as referenced in the British argument, sought to diminish differential treatment and promote the equality of states, and thus were considered essential elements in the governance of free trade. They aimed 'to establish and to maintain at all times fundamental equality without discrimination among all of the countries concerned'.[99]

The Iranians' rejection of the applicability of capitulation-related treaties via the MFN clause conveyed their rejection of the imperial economic order in favour of a new order, crafted in the spirit of free trade and the general principles of international law. While capitulations formed a network of interconnected charters and privileges,[100] such regimes were not simply mechanisms for direct imposition of European laws on foreign populations. Rather, they facilitated the creation of 'legal islands' that would satisfy their needs.[101] The Iranian denunciation of the capitulation regime conveyed a broader and deeper transition in sensibilities over the regulation of world trade and commerce.

An intriguing articulation of this shift in sensibilities appears in the opinion of Judge Arnold Duncan McNair, who had to step down from presiding over the AIOC case because of his British nationality, and joined the majority opinion against his country. His stance emphasized the importance of regarding the capitulation regime as a thing of the past. 'Iran's treaty system was in a state of suspense and transition' when it issued its declaration on the jurisdiction of the Court, he noted. The MFN clauses, McNair held, played a significant role in creating a network of capitulatory systems in Iran and elsewhere:

---

[99] Rights of Nationals of the United States of America in Morocco (France v. United States of America) in 1952 I.C.J. Rep. 192.

[100] Maurits H. van den Boogert, The Capitulations and the Ottoman Legal System: Quadis, Consuls and *beratlis* in the 18th Century 304 (2005). *See also* Lorca, *supra* note 55, at 79–85.

[101] Gad G. Gilbar, *Resistance to Economic Penetration: The Kāraguzār and Foreign Firms in Qajar Iran,* 43 Int'l J. Middle East Stud. 5, 8 (2011).

[F]rom the point of view of a State which has been subject to a system of Capitulations for at least a century and had only recently denounced them and emerged *into a new status*, it would be surprising if the most-favoured-nation principle was not regarded as an obnoxious concomitant of the system. Such a state ... would naturally be shy of accepting any compulsory jurisdiction in terms wide enough to expose itself to the invocation of any part of its old treaty system that might still survive.[102]

McNair, supportive of the Iranian case, offered the Iranian denunciation of the capitulation regime as a vantage point to appreciate and interpret the Iranian position. Unconventionally, two often-contradictory paths merged in his argument: Iranian national resistance walked hand-in-hand with the liberalization of markets and the turn to a more equitable commercial legal order. McNair, and the majority opinion, prevented the MFN clause from being used, as it had been in the past, to constitute or maintain a discriminatory commercial system. Indeed, it is not at all clear that an application of the MFN mechanism in this case would have resulted in preferential treatment. And yet McNair considered the very imposition of the Court's jurisdiction (regardless of the content of its decision) problematic, because of its symbolic meaning. By rejecting the application of the principles of international law to the capitulations-era treaties, McNair facilitated an interpretive break from the problematic role of MFN clauses in the past. That is to say, by endorsing Iran's rejection of the old capitulation regime, the proponents of international economic law were able to liberate themselves, just like the Iranians, from a tainted legal past. Eventually, the Court's interpretation of the Iranian declaration took seriously its narrative of resistance to the British imperial rule. 'It is reasonable to assume', concluded the Court, 'that when the Government of Iran was about to accept the compulsory jurisdiction of the Court, it desired to exclude from that jurisdiction all disputes which might relate to the application of the capitulatory treaties, and the Declaration was drafted on the basis of that desire.'[103]

The legality of the Nationalization Act

During the crucial year of 1951, and until he retired from the Bar, Professor Hersch Lauterpacht was involved in the British case against Iran.[104] Lauterpacht was asked to prepare the first draft of the legal argument in the memorial on the merits of the case. An amended version of his draft formed the central part of the memorial filed

---

[102] 1952 I.C.J. Rep. 119.
[103] 1952 I.C.J. Rep. 105.
[104] 4 INTERNATIONAL LAW: BEING THE COLLECTED PAPERS OF HERSCH LAUTERPACHT (E. Lauterpacht ed., 1978).

by the British Government on 10 October 1951.[105] The British argument sought to define the dispute as an inter-state dispute and therefore a public one, hence subject to the Court's jurisdiction. The Iranians argued for the mirror position; this was a private controversy between a company and a state and thus should remain a private matter for the Iranians to handle, subject only to the authority of the Iranian state.

The British argument for the public nature of the dispute focused on three issues: the concession agreement; sovereignty and nationalization; and remedies (compensation, restitution, and arbitration). The British Government argued that the *concession agreement* had a dual character, as both a concessionary convention operating between the AIOC and the Iranian Government and an implied agreement between the governments of the United Kingdom and Iran. The combination of the implied agreement and the description of the private concession through the prism of the doctrine of diplomatic protection enabled the British to redefine the agreement as an inter-state contract. The United Kingdom further maintained that, in light of the proceedings between the two governments in the League of Nations, the concessionary agreement was 'a contract between two parties, one of which is a State and the other of which is not a State but a national of the United Kingdom' and 'an agreement (*possibly of private law character*) between the Government and the Company'.[106] The AIOC was mentioned mostly in the passages describing the great benefits of the concession agreement for Iranian welfare.[107]

The discussion on the Iranian right to nationalize the AIOC's assets revolved around the question of *Iranian sovereignty*. Here, the British argument, probably influenced by Lauterpacht's careful drafting, conveyed a recognition of a certain right to nationalize. 'While a State possesses the right to nationalize', concluded the argument, 'it is entitled to do so only subject to conditions laid down by international law'.[108] It should be noted that, subsequent to producing this statement, in the eighth edition of Oppenheim's *International Law* Lauterpacht qualified his position further by pointing to those cases where:

> fundamental changes in the political and economic structure of the state or far-reaching social reforms entitle interference, on a large scale, with private property. In such cases neither the principle of absolute respect for alien private property nor rigid equality with the dispossessed nationals offers a satisfactory solution of the difficulty. It is probably that, consistently with legal principle, such solution must be sought in the granting of partial compensation.[109]

---

[105] The final Memorial thus differs on a few points from Lauterpacht's position.
[106] Memorial of the United Kingdom, 1951 I.C.J. Rep. 74–75 (my emphasis).
[107] *Id.* at 72.
[108] *Id.* at 81.
[109] OPPENHEIM'S INTERNATIONAL LAW 352 (Hersch Lauterpacht ed., 8th ed. 1955).

This later position was far removed from the British final memorial. While conceding that the general principles of international law may allow nationalization under certain conditions, the British argument asserted that the express obligation under the concession agreement not to cancel it unilaterally rendered nationalization unlawful in this case. The unlawfulness was further grounded in the fact that the nationalization was directed exclusively against foreigners as such, and not toward a public interest.

The Iranian Government filed a document entitled 'Preliminary Observations: Refusal of the Imperial Government to recognize the jurisdiction of the Court'. The Iranian objection relied, *inter alia*, on Article 2(7) of the UN Charter, which precludes the United Nations from intervening in matters that are essentially within the domestic jurisdiction of a state. The Court's decision on interim measures was, to the Iranians, an intervention in their private affairs within their territory.[110]

Defining the agreement: A concession or an inter-state treaty?

The Iranians rebutted the British description of the dual character of the concession agreement. Any such implied agreement, they claimed, '[did] not possess the character of a treaty or convention, because it was not concluded between states, was not put in writing, and was not registered in conformity with Article 18 of the covenant of the League of Nations'.[111] Last, the Iranians stressed that the company's failure to exhaust remedies in Iran prevented it from seeking remedy in this proceeding.

By claiming sovereignty over their natural resources, the Iranians were protesting against the unequal terms of the concession and against their disempowered status in an unequal world. They were not rejecting international law—quite the contrary. The Iranians' argument—that they should be free as sovereigns in their own territory to resolve the dispute in their own manner—would, despite being anti-colonial in nature, come to be regarded as conservative and was based on the inter-state interpretation introduced at the beginning of this chapter. The British argument, which followed an imperial order logic of interpretation, sought to convince the judges that this was an *international* dispute that needed to be addressed by using international concepts and doctrines and should therefore be resolved in an international setting. The source of coherence in the British arguments derived from their consistent use of a functionalist methodology, one that rejected history and opted for a pragmatic and realist understanding of the world. They

---

[110] *Observations Préliminaires: Refus du Gouvernement imperial de reconnaître la competence de la Cour*, Anglo-Iranian Oil Co. (U.K. v. Iran), 1951 I.C.J. Rep. 281, 286.

[111] This translation of the Iranian claims appeared in the analysis of William W. Bishop Jr., *Judicial Decisions*, 46 Am. J. Int'l L. 733, 738 (1952).

argued against the relevance of historical circumstances to interpret the Iranian declaration on the Court's jurisdiction. The changes made by the MFN clauses to previous agreements between the United Kingdom and Iran *de facto* constituted a new legal order between them. The formal aspects of its source (a new contract or not) were less important.

The British also asked the Court to recognize the concession agreement as an inter-state agreement. Holding the negotiations for the 1933 Concession under the auspices of the League changed its identity from a private to an inter-state agreement, they contended. Accepting the British argument holds further meanings. The formal separation between ownership and control of the company was diminished, and the British Government's ownership became equivalent to control. As noted earlier, this view seems reminiscent of an informal empire scenario in which the chartered company, though operating fairly independently, was legally considered part and parcel of imperial rule.

The Court eventually held that the U.K. Government was not a party to the agreement, and it established no obligations between the Iranian and British Governments. The concession had only one purpose: to regulate the relationship between the Iranian Government and the company. The Court further refuted the proposition that the fact that the agreement was negotiated under the auspices of the League might alter its conclusion. Rather, it asserted that 'in submitting the dispute with the Iranian Government to the League Council, [the U.K. government] was only exercising its right of diplomatic protection'.[112] The Court thus arrived at the conclusion that it had no jurisdiction to deal with the case submitted to it by the U.K. Government.[113] This interpretation coloured the Iranian resistance as internationally legitimate. Nine judges concurred with this finding and five dissented (the judges of the United States, Canada, France, Chile, and Brazil). As noted earlier, the British Judge, Sir Arnold McNair, voted against Britain.

Among the dissenting opinions vis-à-vis the Court's ruling, the Brazilian Judge, M. Levi Carneiro, was particularly harsh. He expressed his frustration with the limited jurisdiction of the Court that was required to 'shut its eyes to the situation [of the dispossession of the Company's concession and of all its property] so arising … Does international law permit this?'[114] A similar critique of the Court's formalist interpretive approach would appear a few years later. In the 1956 Storrs lectures at Yale University, Philip C. Jessup (1897–1986) developed and popularized the concept of *Transnational Law* as an alternative conceptual framework to the rigid distinction between public and private conveyed in the ICJ's ruling.[115]

---

[112] 1952 I.C.J. Rep. 112.

[113] 1952 I.C.J. Rep. 114.

[114] U.K. v. Iran, Judgment, 1952 I.C.J. Rep. 166 (July 22).

[115] Philip Caryl Jessup was born in New York City in 1897 to a family of prominent American lawyersJessup studied international law at Columbia and transferred to the Yale Law School where he received his law degree in 1924. He began his career at the Columbia Law School but soon began to

His functionalist approach was reminiscent of the British interpretation but with opposite, progressive, objectives of greater equality between postcolonial nations and former imperial governments. This interpretive transnational perspective laid the intellectual foundations for the later inclusion of private corporations as recognized subjects and litigants in international investment disputes (which I discuss in Chapter 7). However, its later endorsement would lack Jessup's progressive sensibilities. Furthermore, the endorsement of the transnational perspective ultimately failed to materialize within the UN institutions and instead took hold in other, new institutions, devoted to investor–state dispute settlement under international law.

In the following section, I describe Jessup's transnational law vision and then turn to address the limitations of the UN institutions—the ICJ or the Security Council—in comparison with the flexible institutional disposition of the League. These conceptual and institutional shortcomings were to have lingering effects: not least, they informed the shortcomings of the New International Economic Order's (NIEO) attempt to regulate the conduct of Transnational Companies, which we will examine in Chapter 7.

Progressive Pragmatism: Jessup's Transnational Law Critique of the AIOC Case

Philip C. Jessup's Storrs lectures presented the Anglo-Iranian controversy as a prominent example of a transnational case. For Jessup, there was nothing in the *character of the parties* (be they corporations, individuals, or organizations) that precluded the application of one or the other bodies of law into which the legal field is traditionally divided ('the liability of a corporation or of an individual may be determined by national law, foreign law, conflict of laws, or public international law'). Similarly, he noted: 'there is nothing in *the character of the forum* which precludes it from applying one or these other bodies of law ... [and] ... no distinction between *civil and criminal law* in terms of its applicability to individuals, corporations, or states.'[116]

Jessup challenged the traditional bases of jurisdiction (territoriality, nationality, and so on) as historically contingent rather than premised upon normative

---

serve as the legal advisor to the American ambassador in Cuba (1930) and the chief of training and personnel in the Office for Foreign Relief and Rehabilitation, a State Department agency later absorbed into UNRRA, and the held key positions at the United Nations between 1947 and 1953. During those years, he was involved in the work on trusteeship. In the early 1950s, Jessup returned to the Columbia Law School. He was elected as the President of the American Society of International Law in 1955 and became the Vice President of the Institut de Droit International and received a unique appointment from the Rockefeller Foundation in 1959. In 1960, he was appointed to the ICJ at The Hague. *See* Oscar Schachter, *Philip Jessup's Life and Ideas*, 80 AM. J. INT'L L. 878 (1986).

[116] JESSUP, *supra* note 2, at 104–05.

justifications. He argued against a compartmentalized and rigid view of the national legal system that is not equipped to cope with an economic order of international dimensions. 'The use of transnational law,' he contended, 'would supply a larger storehouse of rules on which to draw, and it would be unnecessary to worry whether public or private law applies in certain cases.'[117]

Jessup's definition of transnational law paid homage to the French functionalist tradition in international law and its leading figure Georges Scelle (1878–1961). 'The concept [of transnational law] is similar to but not identical with Scelle's monistic theory of *un Droit intersocial unifié*. One is dealing, as he says, with "human relationships transcending the limits of the various states." '[118] Yet, Jessup rejected what he considered to be Scelle's emphasis on individuals as the sole subjects of international law and insisted on the inclusion of the reality of corporate bodies. For Jessup, the corporate body of the state, the business enterprise, and international organizations were all analogous to one another. 'Corporate bodies, whether political or nonpolitical, have certainly been treated in orthodox theory as fictions, but their essential reality as entities is now well accepted and law deals with them as such....Transnational situations, then may involve individuals, corporations, states, organizations of states, or other groups.'[119]

For Jessup, the analogy between the state and other corporate actors was not only a basis for a different epistemological view of the relevant actors and subjects of international law, but also a basis for a normative theory. In his view, corporate governance considerations (which he termed 'corporate democracy') were analogous to democratization processes in other arenas such as the United Nations or the domestic realm of the national state, as well as to the growing concern for minorities, human rights, and the administration of colonial or non-self-governing peoples.[120] Yet:

> [t]o be sure, the United Nations is not a corporation and the states members are not shareholders and the analogy is very far from perfect. But the modern state, like the big corporation, has developed, for different reasons, a new sensitivity to public pressures; and the law (United Nations Charter or United States statute) has taken account of the new social consciousness.[121]

Indeed, democratization and growing concern for minority rights and the interests of weaker parties are not merely features of corporate governance. Jessup situated his vision of the international legal field as transnational law in a new social

---

[117] *Id.* at 15.
[118] *Id.* at 3.
[119] *Id.*
[120] *Id.* at 27–28.
[121] *Id.* at 30.

consciousness that shaped the politics and law of the state and the corporation during his time:

> The fact remains that, from Woodrow Wilson and the League mandate system on through Franklin Roosevelt and the United Nations trusteeship and allied systems, the manifestations of the awakening social conscience have appeared simultaneously in the domestic and the international fields. The New Freedom and the New Deal were not sold only in the domestic market.[122]

Jessup regarded the Calvo Doctrine, as well as the establishment of the UN Committee on Restrictive Business Practices, as translations of the turn to the regulatory state in the international context.[123] Indeed, he conceded that:

> ... in the international arena there is to date no power that is likely to be able to compel well-to-do nations to share their substance with the less well-to-do ... but perhaps just as much power in the form of the pressures generated by Communist–non-Communist rivalries, the consciousness of need for security, and perhaps economic or humanitarian pressures.[124]

Throughout his text, Jessup returned to the AIOC case to exemplify what he meant by transnational law. The mélange of different bodies of law, as well as the diversity of fora and procedures involved in the Anglo-Iranian case, rendered it an important example of transnational law:

> ... One notes that the problem of extracting and refining oil in Iran may involve – as it has – Iranian oil, English law, and public international law. Procedurally it may involve – as it has – diplomatic negotiations, proceedings in the International Court of Justice and in the Security Council, *business negotiations with and among oil companies, and action in the Iranian Majlis* [my emphasis].[125]

Jessup's work presents a changing sensibility in the relationship between international law and economic actors that gained prominence in the decades following the Second World War. The puzzle, however, is the following: Jessup considered his theory of transnational law compatible with the progressive movement in American law. Yet despite what seems to be his moral affiliation (with greater accountability for stronger powers vis-à-vis weaker actors and states), he sided with the British position and the jurisdiction of the Court.

---

[122] *Id.* at 31.
[123] *Id.* at 33.
[124] *Id.* at 34.
[125] *Id.* at 6.

Revisiting the controversy before the ICJ through Jessup's framing of old/international/formal/statist law vs. new/transnational/functionalist/beyond-the-state law exposes intriguing affiliations. The Iranians' hermeneutical position followed a familiar conceptual framework of doctrinal distinctions and boundaries (public–private; sovereignty; treaty–concession) to make the postcolonial case against the British. They used an old toolbox to promote their vision of the new: a postcolonial world order, transnational equality, and distributive justice. The British suggested an opposite conclusion, conceiving the agreement as an implied inter-state agreement. In his analysis of the case, Jessup sided with the British (for the jurisdiction of the Court) but insisted that it was the concession's transnational feature—being a contract between a company and a state in need of cross-border regulation—that constituted a sufficient basis for the jurisdiction of the court.

How do we reconcile, if at all, Jessup's progressive agenda (for decolonization) with his endorsement of the internationalization of the case? His views seem especially perplexing in light of the history of previous attempts to introduce international standards to the regulation of economic relations. As shown earlier, these were used to favour the powerful against the weak. Iran was not subject to formal colonial rule, but its arguments against economic influence certainly echoed the cry of other newly-constituted nations against a repressive colonial past. Furthermore, the layers of informal imperialism were not merely constituted by the chartered companies. Informal imperial relations were often facilitated by international legal doctrines surrounding the nature and function of concessions, the regulation of trade relations (such as MFN clauses), and the diplomatic protection of investors. At the same time, this history of economic colonial relations is populated with important attempts at resistance and renegotiation of terms, as exemplified by the case of Iran.

The Iranian strategy of pushing back against colonialism and toward distributive justice through the redistribution of formal control—through self-determination—became the prevalent position of postcolonial states. Yet, as Benedict Kingsbury wrote:

> ... the concept of state sovereignty allows questions of social and economic inequality among people to be treated in international law as a responsibility of territorial states. International law and legal institutions are able to promote market activity ... while in theory leaving largely to states the responsibility of mitigating social and economic inequalities associated with markets.[126]

By arguing against the intervention of the ICJ, the Iranians were asking the Court to uphold this very strategy of 'live and let live.' But their strategy, though perhaps

---

[126] Benedict Kingsbury, *Sovereignty and Inequality*, 9 Eur. J. Int'l L. 599, 602–03 (1998).

bearing important *symbolic* fruits, had rather devastating results in the immediate term, for it failed to immunize the Iranians against further colonial economic influence and control. This is probably why Jessup insisted on transnational law. His appreciation of the power of markets and the need to intervene in their regulation makes him a man of his time. He endorsed not only the political agenda of many New Dealers, but also their dominant methodological claim against formalism in law. Adopting the hermeneutics of legal realism, he criticized the formal distinctions in international law between public and private, and between states and other actors. He argued for a functionalist, pragmatic approach that considered the different fictions of the corporation, the state, and the international organization as potential subjects of international scrutiny.

Back to the Anarchical Society? UN Institutions' Endorsement of the Iranian Position Diminishes the Scope for Peaceful Renegotiations

On 22 July 1952, the ICJ concluded that it lacked jurisdiction to decide the case. The decision reinforced Mossadegh's power and was a moment of catharsis for the Iranian national movement. By upholding the Iranian claim that it lacked jurisdiction, the Court reinstated Iran's sovereign prerogative to nationalize AIOC assets in its territory, boosting its spirit of self-determination, nationalism, and anti-imperialism. The celebrations, however, were to be short-lived. The following months were marked by a steep decline in economic and political stability, while the closure of the Abadan refinery and dwindling revenues crippled the Iranian economy to the verge of collapse.

The Iranian Government barely held its ground. Internal political instability, a looming British military presence, and the AIOC boycott all contributed to undermine and destabilize Mossadegh's rule.[127] By August 1953, the British and American schemes to remove Mossadegh from power by a coup bore fruit, even if not exactly according to their original plan. The British- and U.S.-inspired overthrow of Mossadegh's government resulted in a sharp increase in the Shah's power in Iran—a development that had fateful consequences for the entire region.[128]

---

[127] For a general analysis, *see* William Roger Louis, *Musaddiq, Oil, and the Dilemmas of British Imperialism*, in WM ROGER LOUIS, ENDS OF BRITISH IMPERIALISM: THE SCRAMBLE FOR EMPIRE, SUEZ AND DECOLONIZATION, COLLECTED ESSAYS 728 (2004). On the boycott, *see* Mary Ann Heiss, *The International Boycott of Iranian Oil and the Anti-Mosaddeq Coup of 1953*, in MOHAMMAD MOSADDEQ AND THE 1953 COUP IN IRAN, *supra* note 6, at 178. On the American decision to undertake the Coup, *see* Malcolm Byrne, *The Road to Intervention: Factors Influencing US Policy Toward Iran, 1945–1953*, in MOHAMMAD MOSADDEQ AND THE 1953 COUP IN IRAN, *supra* note 6, at 201.

[128] The Abadan Crisis is discussed in many works. *See, e.g.,* LOUIS, *supra* note 66, at 632–89; MOSADDIQ, IRANIAN NATIONALISM AND OIL (James A. Bill & William Roger Louis eds., 1988); JAMES CABLE, INTERVENTION AT ABADAN: PLAN BUCCANEER (1991); MOSTAFA ELM OIL, POWER, AND PRINCIPLE: IRAN'S OIL NATIONALIZATION AND ITS AFTERMATH (1992).

In November 1953, Mossadegh was tried for treason and eventually retired to his family estate, where he spent the rest of his life. Iran lost its full control over oil to a consortium agreement that provided it with more control than it had prior to the nationalization act but clearly not to the extent for which Mossadegh had fought. International institutions such as the ICJ, the Security Council, and the World Bank were involved in the dispute, but their roles are considered marginal and un-fruitful.[129] Even if Iran's position under the oil agreement had improved, the events that made it possible were hardly peaceful. Both Iran and later the British used last-resort measures, such as nationalization and deportation of the AIOC's workers (by Iran) and sending warships and instituting covert operations to overthrow the Iranian Government (by the British) to meet their objectives. Despite recurring interventions by the newly-founded international institutions, the adherence of the parties to their last-resort measures could not be curtailed.

The UN institutions—the Court and the Security Council—played a central role in manufacturing these structural effects. Deliberating over whether or not the Security Council should intervene, the Ecuadorian delegate emphasized the im-portance of distinguishing between the Council and the Court: 'where the question is purely legal, it is inadvisable for the Security Council to go against that ruling by the judicial organ of the United Nations.' His framing led to a lively discussion over the nature of the dispute: Was it political? Did it pose a threat to peace? Or was it purely legal? What did the phrase 'domestic jurisdiction' in Article 2(7) mean, and what should the relationship between the Council and the ICJ be?

The Ecuadorian delegate concluded that the Council did not have competence under Chapter VII, since the dispute was not 'an international dispute or situation between two States or nations ….'[130] He nonetheless concluded that this did not mean that the Council should refrain from any action. 'On the contrary, we think that it ought to endeavor to facilitate agreement between the parties.'[131]

The U.S. representative, Warren R. Austin, had a different interpretation. He quoted different statements made by the Iranian delegate to demonstrate that 'this dispute was of a dangerous nature.'[132] It was 'the high function of the Security Council to assist in achieving pacific solutions of difficult international problems, the continued existence of which might endanger peace.'[133] Since the negotiations

---

[129] The World Bank intervened as a mediator in the disputes after the Anglo-Iranian negotiations reached a deadlock in November 1951. The Bank offered funds and to act as a trustee of oil fields and the huge Abadan refinery. Amy L.S. Staples described how World Bank officials believed that their exclusive managerial control was essential, that Iranians should (and would) accept the reintroduction of British workers, and that the bulk of oil exports would be sold through British channels. The Bank's attitude led the U.S. Ambassador to Iran, Loy Henderson, to conclude 'rather incredulously' that the bankers seemed to be 'enveloped' by an 'unrealistic atmosphere'. Amy L.S. Staples, *Seeing Diplomacy Through Banker's Eyes: The World Bank, the Anglo-Iranian Oil Crisis, and the Aswan High Dam*, 26 DIPLOMATIC HIST. 397, 405 (2002).

[130] UN Security Council Official Records, 560th meeting (Oct. 17, 1951), 6–7 S/PV. 562.

[131] *Id.* at 9. S/PV. 562.

[132] *Id.* at 7. S/PV. 563.

[133] *Id.* at 8. S/PV. 563.

between the two governments failed to produce a settlement and the British were engaging in violent measures ('it was not a private corporation that sent warships'), Austin reached the conclusion that 'a dispute exists between the two governments,' and that the Council therefore had jurisdiction. Other delegates similarly emphasized the importance of reaching a settlement by peaceful means.[134]

The members of the relatively new Security Council struggled to define their role—whether they should leave the issue to the ICJ or consider themselves the executive body in charge. They eventually chose the former option and reduced the dispute to its juridical meaning, leaving it for the Court to decide.[135] The Court, in turn, concluded it had no jurisdiction over the dispute and defined it in a way that left too little leeway and political space for the parties to reach a peaceful settlement. The gladiators in this story were left with little choice other than to use their old tricks of gunboat diplomacy, covert operations, and economic boycotts. The rest of the story is now quite familiar. As Jessup noted:

> The fundamental question [in the issue of jurisdiction] is to determine which national authorities may deal effectively with which transnational situations— effectively in the sense that authorities of other states will recognize that the exercise of authority is reasonable and will therefore give effect to judgments rendered or refrain from protests through the diplomatic channel .... It will be the function of transnational law to reshuffle the cases and to deal out jurisdiction in the manner most conductive to the needs and convenience of all members of the international community.[136]

At this point in history, the flexibility exercised by the League in facilitating a peaceful renegotiation of the concession was lost to a rigid interpretation of the distinction between law and politics (it was not a matter for the Court to decide) and between public and private (the sovereign demarcated the private sphere of non-intervention in international law). The League, operating in an earlier period, had not merely been empowering for the weaker party, but had also been crucial in promoting peace and stability. In later decades, as the dispute came before the new institutions of the United Nations, the political space gave way to legal formalism and political prudence. The turbulence of economic sanctions and the Anglo-American sponsored coup d'état seem far-removed from the envisioned role, enshrined in the UN Charter, of maintaining international peace and security.

---

[134] See, for example, the statements made by the Chinese delegate. UN Security Council Official Records, 560th meeting (October 17, 1951), 36. S/PV. 563.

[135] The Iranian representatives were hardly innocent victims of greater powers. They both missed opportunities for 'better deals' than the one they ended up with, and insisted on symbolic political assets at the cost of the survival of their economy. I am not to judge these decisions; I do not think there can be a clear judgment. Perhaps symbolic politics and the mere fight for it are superior to other interests, or at least that was the view of the Iranian public at the time.

[136] JESSUP, *supra* note 2, at 70–71.

Transnational Law and the Return of International Legal Institutions

How much really changed for businesses operating overseas and their relationships with local communities and states of origin in the early years after the Second World War? In some ways, very little. The British were still seeking to sustain their imperial power, and decolonization had not yet gained its full momentum. More broadly, the understanding of the international economic world as one of transnational commerce, foreign investments, and exploitation of weaker states' natural resources had long been part of international politics. Yet some aspects of this interplay did change. The company, no longer legally dependent on the charter system, became increasingly significant to the world of commerce and politics across the globe. The political project of international law required rethinking after the Second World War. International lawyers had to differentiate their field from the failed League of Nations and remove its haunting presence from their operations. Despite the transition from imperial governance through chartered companies to state–company relations, business corporations were still protected by the backing of strong governments such as the United States, in the context of Liberia, and Britain, in the context of the AIOC.

The AIOC case exposed how the deep legal rationales of privately-incorporated companies—the meaning of the corporate veil in constituting the corporation as a private entity, and its separating function between ownership and control—served to insulate such enterprises from international legal scrutiny. The ICJ decision regarding the AIOC clarified that corporations, even if significantly owned by states, could not themselves be conceived as states under international law and were therefore excluded from the (formal and direct) interference of international legal institutions. The British attempt to conflate its ownership with the identity of the corporation was an attempt to radicalize the meaning of diplomatic protection beyond its previous rationale of government endorsement of its national interests into a view that government-owned shares in a company were equivalent to a clear identity between the company and the state. This view was rejected by the Court.

As Chapter 7 elaborates, this issue would come before the ICJ less than two decades later with the Case Concerning the Barcelona Traction, Light and Power Company, Ltd.[137] The Barcelona Traction case addressed Belgium's right to exercise diplomatic protection of Belgian shareholders in a company that was constituted as a juristic entity incorporated in Canada. Following its previous line of reasoning in the AIOC case, the ICJ ruled that the right of diplomatic protection in respect of an injury to a corporation belonged to the state under the laws of

---

[137] Barcelona Traction, Light & Power Company, Limited (Belgium v. Spain) Judgment, 1970 I.C.J Rep. 3 (Feb. 5). This judgment stemmed from a new application made to the Court in 1962. The case was originally initiated in 1958 but removed from the Court's General List in 1962.

which the corporation was incorporated and in whose territory it had its registered office—*not* to the national state(s) of the shareholders of the corporation.

The limitations of the doctrine of Diplomatic Protection in the age of privately-incorporated companies would crystalize in the ICJ jurisprudence of the early decades following the Second World War. According to the ICJ interpretation of this doctrine, companies could not rely on the governments of their shareholders to protect their interests beyond state borders. The lack of support of the international legal framework for their cause, as exemplified in the AIOC case, posed significant political and economic challenges to governments and companies in the Global North and initially empowered self-determination sensibilities. The Abadan Crisis involved costly strategies for the protection of foreign investment worldwide and lacked the stability and security a global economic market required. It is therefore not surprising that the growing need to protect the interests of private business corporations would give rise to a new institutional framework in international law for that particular purpose: the international investment law regime. This regime would recognize and include corporate entities as litigants in international law and protect them in disputes with host states. It would replace the rigid separation between the public (treaties) and the private (concessions) with a functionalist attempt to settle disputes between companies and governments. International investment law marked a new phase in the history of diplomatic protection that would overcome the difficulties that the corporate veil of private business corporations posed to the international legal protection of corporate interests. This transition echoed central elements of Jessup's transnational law framework without his concern for equality and self-determination.

While the corporate veil would no longer hamper the international legal participation of private investors in proceedings under the auspices of the emerging international investment law, it would remain intact in the context of international criminal law and human rights law violations. These two facets of corporate regulation—protection of private interests and lack of accountability—were not always conceived as separate and distinct. In the next chapter, we look at the early attempt of NIEO advocates to combine the two, and the history of the divergence between them.

7

From the NIEO to the International Investment Law Regime

The Rise of the Multinational Corporation as a Subject of Regulatory Concern in International Law

Introduction

This chapter tells the story of how multinational corporations (MNCs) came to be a subject of international legal concern after the Second World War; how MNC debates fared with decolonization; and how discussion of the MNC and the challenges it posed was channelled through a fragmented international legal architecture, into fora generally favourable to the interests of capital-exporting countries. Here we excavate the history of the formation of the global regulatory architecture for private business corporations since the 1970s and the factors that facilitated the right of corporations to sue governments for damages and to choose the forum in which to do so.[1]

In the wake of the Second World War, the United States and other capital-exporting countries, such as Britain and Germany, sought new regulatory means of securing foreign investment. Their experiments included a multilateral arrangement that covered both trade and investment (the International Trade Organization, ITO), and bilateral arrangements with different approaches to dispute settlement. In 1957, the foreign assets of the 500 largest U.S. industrial corporations represented only 5 per cent of their domestic assets. By 1966, this

---

[1] It is widely recognized that states have granted private business corporations significant capacities to act on the international stage. *See*, for example, Julian Arato, *Corporations as Lawmakers*, 56 Harv. Int'l. L.J 229 (2015); Anthea Roberts, *Triangular Treaties*, 56 Harv. Int'l L.J. 353 (2015'); José Alvarez, *Are Corporations Subjects of International Law?*, 9 Santa Clara J. Int'l L. 1 (2011); Roland Portmann, Legal Personality in International Law (2010). For other discussions on the history of international investment law, *see* Kate Miles, Origins of International Investment Law 17–122 (2013); Stephan Schill, he Multilateralization of International Investment Law 23–64 (2009); International Investment Law and History (Stephan W. Schill et al. eds., 2018); Kenneth J. Vandevelde, Bilateral Investment Treaties: History, Policy, and Interpretation (2010); Antonio R. Parra, The History of ICSID (2d ed. 2017); Taylor St. John, The Rise of Investor-State Arbitration: Politics, Law, and Unintended Consequences (2018); Antony Anghie, Imperialism, Sovereignty and the Making of International Law (2005); Sandhuya Pahuja, Decolonizing International Law: Development, Economic Growth and the Politics of Universality (2011).

Veiled Power. Doreen Lustig, Oxford University Press (2020). © Doreen Lustig.
DOI: 10.1093/oso/9780198822097.001.0001

proportion had increased to 7.6 per cent, and by 1977 to 16.95 per cent,[2] giving rise to an extensive body of literature on the phenomenon. The growing influence of corporations and their operations in postcolonial settings also sparked conceptual and normative debates: how should international legal doctrines and institutions approach the corporate entity or its shareholders—as subjects of international law, as participants, or as nationals of their state?

Some of these debates drew inspiration from the policy-oriented theories of Myres McDougal and the New Haven School and from Hersch Lauterpacht's ideas on the access of individuals to international courts.[3] In McDougal's 1953 Hague Lectures on International Law, Power and Policy, he conveyed an early unease with international lawyers' overemphasis on states and natural persons. McDougal famously regarded the individual human being as the 'ultimate actor in all arenas and on the world scene'.[4] Nevertheless, he argued that the rise of a 'host of new and powerful functional organizations', including the 'transnational private association', required further attention. 'International law can, in its prescriptive formulations, continue to blind itself to these facts only at the cost of becoming increasingly inconsequential', he concluded.[5] Almost a decade later, Wolfgang Friedman offered a conceptual framework for corporate entities as participants in international law. He pointed to three meanings of their participation: first, as participants in mixed international transactions to which governments or public international organizations could be parties; second, as participants with equal standing before supranational judicial bodies and as active participants in, and subject to, the activities of international organizations; and third, as requiring public executive and judicial control.[6] In his Hague Lectures of 1969, Friedman drew a line that directly linked the ideas of Myres McDougal and Philip C. Jessup to his argument in favour of allowing corporations to participate in proceedings before the International Court of Justice (ICJ): 'It is of course inevitable that entities that lack territory, population, and other attributes of State organization can only have limited subjectivity. But one quite unnecessary and outdated limitation is their lack of standing before the International Court of Justice.'[7]

---

[2] United Nations Centre on Transnational Corporations, *Transnational Corporations in World Development: Trends and Prospects*, U.N. Doc. ST/CTC/89 (1988).

[3] I hope to further examine this possible link between McDougal and the international investment law regime in future work.

[4] Myres McDougal, *International Law, Power and Policy: A Contemporary Conception*, 82 COLLECTED COURSES OF THE HAGUE ACADEMY OF INTERNATIONAL LAW 11 (1953).

[5] *Id.* at 161–62. McDougal's policy-oriented jurisprudence drew inspiration from legal realism but sought to develop a scientific method that would allow an evaluation of policy decisions against the background of a set of values. For a fascinating analysis of the New Haven School, *see* ANDREA BIANCHI, INTERNATIONAL LAW THEORIES 91 (2017).

[6] WOLFGANG FRIEDMAN, THE CHANGING STRUCTURE OF INTERNATIONAL LAW 127 (1964).

[7] Wolfgang Friedman, *General Course in Public International Law*, 127 RECUEIL DE COURS 39, 122 (1969).

This statement encapsulated the meaning of the corporate entity for international lawyers for the foreseeable future: corporations would henceforth have a limited subjectivity and thus would not be recognized as subjects of responsibilities or duties, but they would be recognized as right-bearers with direct and full access to judicial bodies equipped to discuss disputes concerning the violation of their rights. Friedman supported his claim with the new World Bank Convention on the Settlement of Investment Disputes that came into being during those years and the early European Bilateral Investment Treaties (BITs) that granted private enterprises and associations procedural standing equal to that of governments.

In 1977, Rosalyn Higgins, a former student of Myres McDougal who would go on to serve as President of the ICJ in 2006,[8] similarly proposed breaking away from the dichotomy of the subject–object and instead thinking of international law as a decision-making process. Within that process, there were 'no "subjects" and "objects" but only participants. Individuals are participants, along with governments, international institutions ... and private groups.'[9] This sentence would appear again in her 1994 book, *Problems and Process*, but with two distinctive changes: the words 'private groups' were replaced with 'multinational corporations' and the term 'private non-governmental groups' was added.[10] In the earlier 1977 article, Higgins focused on the access of individuals to courts as central to her concept of participation. Access meant the extent to which individuals could make claims about areas of international law that affected their interests. By 1994, the question of access to courts was clearly related to corporate entities. 'It is now commonplace for a foreign private corporation and states who have entered into contractual relations to agree to international arbitration in the event of a dispute', she noted. 'Arbitral clauses which refer to international law as the applicable law', she continued, 'effectively remove the alleged inability of individuals to be the bearer rights in international law.'[11] The possibility of conceiving of corporations as participants with full access to courts to secure their internationally recognized rights probably became accessible to international law because of a shift in jurisprudential sensibilities, from a more formalist approach to law towards the New Haven/Manhattan School visions. Traces of these anti-formalist sensibilities can be found in the British position in the AIOC case and Philip Jessup's transnational law perspective discussed in Chapter 6 and the Barcelona Traction case.

---

[8] Rosalyn Higgins, *McDougal as Teacher, Mentor, and Friend*, 108 YALE L.J. 957 (1998–1999).

[9] Rosalyn Higgins, *Conceptual Thinking About the Individual in International Law*, 4 BRIT. J. INT'L STUD. 1 (1978) *reprinted in* ROSALYN HIGGINS, THEMES AND THEORIES: SELECTED ESSAYS, SPEECHES AND WRITINGS IN INTERNATIONAL LAW (2009).

[10] Rosalyn Higgins, PROBLEMS AND PROCESS 50 (1994).

[11] Higgins drew attention to the Iran-United States Claim Tribunal as a case in point. *Id.* at 54–55. For comparable views, *see* ANDREW CLAPHAM, HUMAN RIGHTS OBLIGATIONS OF NON-STATE ACTORS 80 (2006); Robert McCorquodale, *The Individual and the International Legal System*, in INTERNATIONAL LAW 307–32 (Malcolm Evans ed., 2d ed. 2006); Alvarez, *supra* note 1, at 7–9. For further discussion, *see* Peter T. Muchlinski, *Corporations in International Law*, in MAX PLANCK ENCYCLOPEDIA OF PUBLIC INTERNATIONAL LAW (Rüdiger Wolfrum ed., 2014).

Ironically, the normative question of how to secure foreign investment in international law derived from the swift expansion of the UN membership of postcolonial states after 1955. Postcolonial nations challenged the legitimacy of an international legal order that enhanced the power of investors without taking the interests of the new states into account. The coalition of postcolonial states under the auspices of the New International Economic Order (NIEO) launched a series of initiatives against the growing influence of foreign companies and brought to the fore a distributive justice approach to international investment regulation. The prominent objective of the NIEO coalition was to secure their governments' regulatory supremacy in their relations with corporate investors, and to undermine the existing hierarchies of the international legal order. Contrary to the anti-formalist, policy-oriented approach of capital-exporting countries to the question of investment regulation, the NIEO arguments were often cast in formalist terms and were based on a positivist understanding of the international legal order as an inter-state regime.

An unexpected ally joined the critical voices from the Global South against MNCs in the 1960s and 1970s: civil society and academics in the United States and Europe. The polemic surrounding the involvement of the U.S. ITT Corporation in the coup d'état in Chile, the Watergate scandal, and the turmoil around the Lockheed bribery cases turned the regulation of MNCs into a major public concern for stakeholders in these regions. During the late 1960s and throughout the 1970s, the MNC was a subject of inquiry in diverse disciplines such as economics, political science, international relations, business management, and history. In addition to the support of civil society for capital-exporting countries, NIEO-affiliated countries were able to promote their cause in UN institutions and found support for their claims in proceedings related to foreign investment before the ICJ.

Indeed, the ICJ limited the protection international law granted to foreign corporations in the watershed decisions of the AIOC case and the Barcelona Traction case. In both, it refused to grant jurisdiction and protect a (British) company or (Belgian) shareholders whose rights and interests were mitigated by another state. In both cases, it based its decisions on the corporate law principle of the separation between ownership and control. By addressing the corporate personality as a separate entity from its public (British state) or private (Belgian citizens) shareholders, it empowered the position of the host state vis-à-vis the corporate entity. As described in Chapter 6, the decision in the AIOC case prompted many Iranians to rally and celebrate their victory in the streets. The 1970 Barcelona Traction decision convinced scholars that the South would no longer be ignored in future negotiations over the economic international legal order. These ICJ decisions, the opposition from the South, and the critical voices of the civil society in the North, eventually ushered the leaders of both sides to negotiate a first-of-its-kind Code of Conduct for Multinational Corporations, under the auspices of the United Nations.

However, the ICJ decisions did not only send an empowering signal to the NIEO states. They also clarified to the United States and European countries that they could not entrust the interests of their investors to proceedings before the ICJ. The Barcelona Traction decision of 1970 thus marked a turning point in the relationship between powerful nations and the United Nations in the context of investment. Capital-exporting countries would henceforth seek alternative institutional and legal means to protect their investors.[12] They would marginalize the United Nations as a regulatory arena for investment issues, in favour of institutions under their control, such as the Organisation for Economic Co-operation and Development (OECD) or the World Bank. The recourse to such institutions would turn the tide in favour of bilateral instruments (*e.g.* BITs), and countries and investor–state disputes would move away from the ICJ towards alternative investor–state dispute settlement (ISDS) mechanisms, in which private corporations could argue their case independently, as equal litigants to states. This regulatory architecture was designed to redress the mistreatment of foreign investors, *not* foreign investor wrongdoing. It conferred a set of rights and privileges on private corporations (and other kinds of investors) with no corresponding responsibilities. Together, these divide-and-rule measures, for bilateralism and arbitration, constituted the regulatory infrastructure for corporations operating transnationally after the 1970s.

This chapter tells the story of the road not taken in the history of international investment law. The contemporary international investment law regime was not the only possible path to take after the Second World War. Between the mid-1950s and the late 1970s, postcolonial countries positioned themselves as the harbingers of a new global order. Their vision included the regulation of corporations in international law. Why did their vision not prevail? What could explain the rise of the alternative regulatory regime for corporations in the 1980s? This chapter is devoted to addressing these puzzles.

The Emergence of the New International Economic Order and the Early Regulatory Experiments in the Protection of Foreign Investment

The Bandung Moment

The ICJ's endorsement of the Iranian position in the AIOC case in the early 1950s, as we discussed in Chapter 6, marked a high point for postcolonial countries' struggle against imperial concessionary arrangements.[13] Its devastating aftermath,

---

[12] Barcelona Traction, Light and Power Company, Limited (Belg. v. Spain), Judgement, 1970 I.C.J. 3, 43 (February 5) [hereinafter Barcelona Traction Case].

[13] For a discussion on the history of the Anglo-Iranian Oil Co. Case, *see* Chapter 6.

however, left the United Nations with limited influence to restrain the Cold War battles over natural resources. International arbitration awards of the early 1950s struck additional blows as they replaced the law of the host state (previously the law of imperial governments and now the law of the postcolonial state) with rules recognized under 'the modern law of nature'.[14] As Lord Asquith wryly observed, in the Abu Dhabi case: 'It would be fanciful to suggest that in this very primitive region there is any settled body of legal principles applicable to the construction of modern commercial contracts.'[15]

The trajectory may have been rather grim for postcolonial states, but swift expansion of the UN membership of such states after 1955 reshuffled the cards. With sixteen new members joining the General Assembly, the Bandung Conference,[16] and the Assembly's vote in favour of the right to national self-determination in a future human rights covenant, 1955 marked a major turning point for third world nations. Following in the footsteps of Iran in 1951, the Libyan Arab Republic expropriated the Libyan American Oil Company's (LIAMCO) concessions in 1955, and Egypt nationalized the Suez Canal in the following year.[17] These events, together with the nationalization of sugar interests in Cuba in the 1960s, posed new challenges to international investment regulation.[18] International lawyer Georg Schwarzenberger surveyed British practice in the Anglo-Iranian, Suez, and related postwar British cases, and concluded that seeking violent measures to secure investments in the postwar era required the approval of the United States ('one's hegemonial Power'). The British were also reluctant to forge new bilateral arrangements because these seemed too closely related to imperial practices. In such circumstances, '[t]he United Kingdom was ready for new experiments' to protect its foreign investments, such as concluding a treaty on a multilateral basis.[19]

While powerful nations such as Britain struggled to design a legal regime that would protect their investors, postcolonial nations introduced the concept of

---

[14] Petroleum Development (Trucial Coast) Ltd. v. The Sheikh of Abu Dhabi (1951) 18 I.L.R. 147 [hereinafter Abu Dhabi Award]; Ruler of Qatar v. International Marine Oil Co. (1953) 20 I.L.R. 534. For further analysis, see ANGHIE, supra note 1, at 225–35. For an elaborate analysis on the history of the NIEO and its ideological vision of global distributive justice, see Samuel Moyn, NOT ENOUGH 91–117 (2018).

[15] Abu Dhabi Award, supra note 14, at 149.

[16] Twenty-nine Asian and African states were invited by the Indian Prime Minister, Jawaharlal Nehru, and Indonesian President Sukarno to reject colonialism and call for the UN membership of additional newly independent states. On Bandung, see MEANINGS OF BANDUNG: POSTCOLONIAL ORDERS AND DECOLONIAL VISIONS (Quynh N. Pham & Robbie Shilliam eds., 2016); INDONESIAN NOTEBOOK: A SOURCEBOOK ON RICHARD WRIGHT AND THE BANDUNG CONFERENCE (Brian R. Roberts & Keith Foulcher eds., 2016); BANDUNG, GLOBAL HISTORY AND INTERNATIONAL LAW (Luis Eslava et al. eds., 2017).

[17] For further discussion on the AIOC case and the related events in the history of investment law, see Chapter 6.

[18] On the expropriations trend, see ERIC N. BALKANOFF, EXPROPRIATION OF U.S. INVESTMENTS IN CUBA, MEXICO AND CHILE (1975).

[19] GEORG SCHWARZENBERGER, FOREIGN INVESTMENT AND INTERNATIONAL LAW 105 (1969).

permanent sovereignty to establish their normative rights over natural resources within their respective jurisdictions. South American lawyers' experience proved pivotal to this surging struggle of postcolonial states over natural resources.[20] In the UN Human Rights Commission, the Chilean representative advocated the inclusion of permanent sovereignty as part of self-determination, leading to the establishment of the UN Commission on Permanent Sovereignty over Natural Resources, in 1958.[21] In November 1960, the UN General Assembly voted on the Declaration on the Granting of Independence to Colonial Countries and Peoples.[22] Two years later, the Assembly then adopted a resolution on 'the right of peoples and nations to permanent sovereignty over their natural wealth and re-sources'. The Declaration on Permanent Sovereignty asserted the supremacy of the public interest of the sovereign state over domestic and foreign individual or pri-vate interests. The rising number of cases in which countries expropriated foreign assets reinforced the growing importance of the right to permanent sovereignty as it was promulgated in the Declaration. Together, these initiatives were designed to harness the power of the state to fend off unrestrained private investors and related market forces. Governmental and commercial leaders in industrialist economies could not remain indifferent to these processes and sought new, experimental regulatory forms to protect their investments.

Four distinct models for investment protection emerged in the aftermath of the Second World War until the 1970s: the ITO; the new U.S. Friendship, Commerce and Navigation (FCN) treaties (the FCN model); the Abs–Shawcross Convention (and the first BIT); and the World Bank's Convention on the Settlement of Investment Disputes. As the following analysis suggests, none of these approaches succeeded in becoming the new model for investment regulation right away. However, some elements in these models would become the building blocks of the international investment regime that would gradually gain momentum in the 1980s, and together form the essential backdrop against which to evaluate the competing NIEO vision for investment as it emerged in the 1960s and early 1970s.

The rise and fall of the ITO

The postwar reconstruction phase positioned the United States as the world's undisputed economic leader.[23] In the two decades between 1949 and 1971,

---

[20] ANGHIE, *supra* note 1, at 209.

[21] For further discussion, *see* MATTHEW CRAVEN, THE DECOLONIZATION OF INTERNATIONAL LAW: STATE SUCCESSION AND THE LAW OF TREATIES (2007).

[22] Adopted by G.A. Res. 1514(XV) (Dec. 14, 1960).

[23] MICHAEL J. HOGAN, THE MARSHALL PLAN: AMERICA, BRITAIN, AND THE RECONSTRUCTION OF WESTERN EUROPE 1947–1952, at 415 (1987); EDWARD S. MASON & ROBERT E. ASHER, THE WORLD BANK SINCE BRETTON WOODS: THE ORIGINS, POLICIES, OPERATIONS, AND IMPACT OF THE INTERNATIONAL BANK FOR RECONSTRUCTION AND DEVELOPMENT AND OTHER MEMBERS OF THE WORLD BANK GROUP (1973). For an elaborate discussion on the influence of the United States in the design of the ITO, *see* Mona Pinchis-Paulsen, *Trade Multilateralism and U.S. National Security: The Making of the GATT Security Exception*, 41 MICH. J. INT'L L. 109 (2020).

the economies of postcolonial nations grew rapidly, and while European multinationals rebuilt their global presence, the vast majority of new foreign direct investments (FDIs) came out of the United States.[24] The stock of outward FDI by U.S. MNCs rose sharply between 1946 and 1967.[25] Reconstruction, which had the primary objective of rehabilitating Europe, was ushered through the Bretton Woods institutions, the International Bank of Reconstruction and Development (IBRD, later the World Bank), and the International Monetary Fund (IMF).

Another important pillar of international economic reconstruction was supposed to be the creation of an ITO. One aspect of this plan was materialized in 1947, with the conclusion of the General Agreement on Tariffs and Trade (the GATT). It took a further two years before the final version of the ITO Charter was signed on 24 March 1948, by fifty-three countries. It was a formidable agreement in its scope and ambition. It included fair labour standards, economic development, and reconstruction, and intended, together with the GATT, to form a comprehensive investment and trade regime. Most notably for our purposes, Article 12 of the Charter (entitled 'International Investment for Economic Development and Reconstruction') recognized the value of investment in promoting development, and encouraged countries to afford investors from other countries opportunities and security for their investment. It further codified the right of any member state 'to take appropriate safeguards necessary' to ensure that foreign investment did not interfere in its internal affairs; 'to determine whether and, to what extent and upon what terms, it [would] allow future foreign investment', 'to prescribe and give effect on just terms to requirements as to the ownership of existing and future investments', and 'to prescribe and give effect to other reasonable requirements with respect to existing and future investments'.[26]

The very comprehensive spirit of the ITO may be the reason for its failure to materialize. The supremacy of economic development over the protection of foreign investors led U.S. industry—which initially supported the ITO and even spearheaded the agreement—to turn against it.[27] Amid the opposition of the U.S. business community and its influence in Congress, President Truman decided not to

---

[24] According to John Dunning, 99 per cent of the stock of FDI originated in Western countries, primarily the U.S., which retained its previous dominant position and expanded with others to Canada, Europe, and increasing number of developing countries. JOHN DUNNING & SARIANNA M. LUNDAN, MULTINATIONAL ENTERPRISES AND THE GLOBAL ECONOMY 117–26 (2d ed. 2008).

[25] Yair Aharoni & David M. Brock, *International Business Research: Looking Back and Looking Forward*, 16 J. INT'L MGMT. 5 (2010).

[26] Article 12 1(c) without prejudice to existing international agreements to which Members are parties, a Member has the right: (i) to take any appropriate safeguards necessary to ensure that foreign investment is not used as a basis for interference in its internal affairs or national policies; (ii) to determine whether and, to what extent and upon what terms it will allow future foreign investment; (iii) to prescribe and give effect on just terms to requirements as to the ownership of existing and future investments; (iv) to prescribe and give effect to other reasonable requirements with respect to existing and future investments.

[27] WILLIAM DIEBOLD JR., THE END OF THE I.T.O 9 (1952).

submit the charter to ratification.[28] Postcolonial countries raised their own doubts about the ITO approach.[29] Other initiatives of the U.S. business community and the Ninth International Conference of American States to reach a multilateral arrangement were similarly unsuccessful.[30]

The inclusion of the corporate entity in the new generation of U.S. FCN Treaties, 1946–1966

When the GATT entered into force, it created a multilateral agreement over trade but left investment outside its framework. In previous years, the international legal rules governing investment relations had drawn on customary international law[31] and on treaty law, primarily FCN treaties.[32] In 1946 the United States, which sought the lead role in the architecture of the global economy after the Second World War, presented the FCN treaties with a new generation of U.S. bilateral agreements.[33]

The early (pre-1946) FCNs were concerned primarily with the trade and shipping rights of individuals; property protection provisions were not a central concern of these agreements and, if inserted, were designed to protect the property of individual, not corporate, investors. The post-1946 series of FCNs shifted the regulatory focus of these agreements to the protection of individual investors. In *The First Bilateral Investment Treaties: U.S. Postwar Friendship, Commerce and Navigation Treaties*, Kenneth J. Vandevelde described how this generation of FCN treaties was reconceptualized in the late 1940s as providing investment protection on a bilateral basis.[34]

For our purposes, I would like to highlight another important innovation of the post-1946 FCN treaties: they extended their protection to corporate entities.[35] This new model of treaties demonstrates how, after 1946, U.S. policy-makers recognized

---

[28] For further discussion, *see* Todd S. Shenkin, *Trade-Related Investment Measures in Bilateral Investment Treaties and the GATT: Moving Toward a Multilateral Investment Treaty*, 55 U. Pitt. L. Rev. 541, 554–58 (1994).

[29] Riyaz Dattu, *A Journey from Havana to Paris*, 24 Fordham Int'l L.J. 275, 286–88 (2000); Clair Wilcox, A Charter for World Trade (1949).

[30] On the International Chamber of Commerce's International Code of Fair Treatment of Foreign Investment (1949), *see* Arthur Miller, *Protection of Foreign Investment by Multilateral Convention*, 53 Am. J. Int'l L. 371, 371–72 (1959). On the International Conference of American States in Bogota, *see* Charles G. Fenwick, *The Ninth International Conference of American States*, 42 Am. J. Int'l L. 561 (1948).

[31] *See* Chapter 6.

[32] A central precedent for the modern rules on foreign investment is the 1778 treaty between the United States and France, which was followed by a series of treaties between the United States and European states and later the new Latin American States. Robert R. Wilson, United States Commercial Treaties and International Law 2 (1960).

[33] The United States. entered into twenty-one new FCN agreements starting in 1946 for a period of twenty years. Wilson, *supra* note 32; Herman Walker Jr., *Modern Treaties of Friendship, Commerce and Navigation*, 42 Minn. L. Rev. 805 (1958).

[34] Kenneth J. Vandevelde, The First Bilateral Investment Treaties: U.S. Postwar Friendship, Commerce and Navigation Treaties (2017).

[35] Herman Walker Jr., *Provisions on Companies in United States Commercial Treaties*, 50 Am. J. Int'l L. 373 (1956).

corporations as the main vehicle for investment and sought to grant them an equivalent protection to natural persons. Corporations under this new model gained the right to conduct business in other countries on a non-discriminatory, national treatment basis. Herman Walker attributed the previous hesitance towards extensive treaty commitments in favour of corporations to the fear that third countries, not party to the agreement, would free-ride the rights conferred on corporations by using the corporate entity to pursue their interests.[36] Accordingly, the post-1946 treaties facilitated the piercing of the corporate veil under such circumstances. These past suspicions may have stemmed from an understanding of corporations as mere tools in the hands of states (or empires). One can cautiously argue that the inclusion of the corporate entity in the FCN treaties after 1946 signifies a shift in the conception of the corporate entity in international law and international relations, towards an autonomous, private—rather than public—actor.

Another important innovation of the new FCN treaties was a dispute resolution provision consenting to the jurisdiction of the ICJ over disputes involving the interpretation or application of the agreement.[37] The subjection of the treaty to the jurisdiction of the ICJ still required local remedies to first be exhausted and the will of the home state to espouse the investor's claim. Thus, the internationalization of investment disputes under this framework was dependent on state consent and was still conceived as an inter-state dispute. Corporate entities and individual investors remained dependent on the goodwill of their respective governments to protect their interests. Even twenty years after this new generation of FCNs first saw the light of day, postcolonial countries remained sceptical about its benefits and were reluctant to join such treaties.[38] By the late 1960s, it had become apparent that the new model of U.S. FCN was failing to deliver a viable solution to the regulation of international investor–state relations, although the United States continued its efforts to negotiate FCN treaties for another decade, until Jimmy Carter's administration abandoned the FCN form altogether in 1977.[39]

From the Abs–Shawcross Draft Convention to the first BIT

While FCN arrangements faltered, European governments under German leadership negotiated an alternative model that was eventually to shape international investment law in the decades to come.[40] Perhaps the most important figure in

---

[36] *Id.* at 380.

[37] For the innovations in the FCN 1946–1966 generation, *see* Kenneth J. Vandevelde, *A Brief History of International Investment Agreements*, 12 U.C. Davis J. Int'l L. & Pol'y 157, 163–66 (2005).

[38] Jeswald W. Salacuse, *BIT by BIT: The Growth of Bilateral Investment Treaties and Their Impact on Foreign Investments in Developing Countries*, 24 Int'l Law. 655, 656–57 (1990); Scott Gudgeon, *United States Bilateral Investment Treaties: Comment on Their Origin, Purposes, and General Treatment Standards*, 4 Int'l Tax & Bus. L. 105, 107–08 (1986).

[39] For an elaborate history of the limited success of the FCN treaties and their rationale under different administrations, *see* Vandevelde, *supra* note 34.

[40] This section is slightly longer than the others, because it includes aspects of this transition that were not studied as comprehensively as other processes addressed in this chapter.

German policy in this context, and certainly the most visible one, was Hermann Joseph Abs. Abs was a former senior manager at Deutsche Bank before and during the Second World War.[41] He was a central player in Deutsche Bank's expropriation of Jewish property during the war[42] and a key protagonist in many restitution proceedings in German courts throughout the 1950s.[43]

In 1957, the Society to Advance the Protection of Foreign Investment, an organization of German businesspeople, with headquarters in Cologne, published a draft instrument entitled 'International Convention for Mutual Protection of Private Property Rights in Foreign Countries'. As the leader of this initiative, Abs called for a 'Magna Carta for the Protection of Foreign Property' in the form of a global treaty, which was to establish 'global standards to protect investors' and a 'permanent arbitral tribunal' with far-reaching enforcement powers.[44] Unlike previous treaties, this new model sought to create a basic legal framework to govern foreign investment exclusively. His vision took two parallel tracks: first, a multilateral treaty that was later entitled the Abs–Shawcross Convention,[45] and later the BIT.

Almost simultaneously with the German initiative, Hartley Shawcross and Elihu Lauterpacht's heavy involvement in the negotiations relating to the AIOC dispute led them to advocate for alternatives to the existing international legal doctrines and mechanisms available for investment protection. Hartley Shawcross was a well-known figure in international law. In 1945, at the age of forty-three, he had travelled to Nuremberg to lead the British Prosecution at the International Military Tribunal and deliver the opening and closing speeches for the British case. As later reported by the British newspaper the *Guardian*, his oral presentations were 'the finest and deadliest presentations of a very long trial'.[46] He continued to engage with international legal matters after the trial, representing the United Kingdom in the Corfu Channel case before the ICJ, while serving as Attorney General, and acting as Principal Delegate for the United Kingdom to the General Assembly of the United Nations. Controversies with the Labour Party led to his eventual resignation from parliament in 1958. As noted in Chapter 6, Iran lost its full control over oil to a consortium agreement involving U.S. and European companies.[47]

---

[41] His involvement is described in HAROLD JAMES, THE DEUTSCHE BANK AND THE NAZI ECONOMIC WAR AGAINST THE JEWS: THE EXPROPRIATION OF JEWISH OWNED PROPERTY (2001).

[42] *Id.*

[43] For an elaborate discussion, *see* ST. JOHN, *supra* note 1, at 73–88. *See also* Lothar Gall, *Hermann Josef Abs and the Third Reich: 'A Man for All Seasons'?*, 6 FIN. HIST. REV. 147 (1999).

[44] Quoted in RUDOLF DOLZER & CHRISTOPH SCHREUER, PRINCIPLES OF INTERNATIONAL INVESTMENT LAW 18 (2008).

[45] *Draft Convention on Investments Abroad*, in Hermann Abs & Hartley Shawcross, *The Proposed Convention to Protect Private Foreign Investment: A Round Table Journal of Public Law*, 9 EMORY L.J. 115, 115–18 (1960).

[46] Dan van der Vat, *Lord Shawcross of Friston*, GUARDIAN, July 11, 2003. Online. http://www.theguardian.com/news/2003/jul/11/guardianobituaries.obituaries.

[47] Mary Ann Heiss, *The United States, Great Britain, and the Creation of the Iranian Oil Consortium, 1953-1954*, 16 INT'L HIST. REV. 511 (1994).

However, the ICJ decision prompted Shawcross to propose an umbrella treaty that would turn violations of the agreement between the consortium and Iran into violations of international law that could be litigated before the ICJ.[48]

Inspired by his work as a counsel for the AIOC (later British Petroleum), in 1958 he initiated the Shawcross Draft, in which Article 6 was devoted to the settlement of disputes between investors and states, and referred to the ICJ as its dispute settlement mechanism. Nevertheless, despite his great zeal and the possible lobbying of his clients, the British Government 'found arbitration to be a non-starter' and refused to commit to compulsory arbitration at this point.[49]

Regardless of the lack of enthusiasm of the British and German Governments, Elihu Lauterpacht and Hartley Shawcross joined forces with Herman Abs in 1959 and, together with lawyers, businessmen, and diplomats, drafted the Abs–Shawcross Draft Convention. Article VII of this Convention focused on the dispute resolution mechanism. It described the establishment of an Arbitral Tribunal to which states parties could submit disputes regarding the interpretation or application of the Convention, and stipulated that only if they failed to reach an agreement on the settlement could they submit the case to the ICJ. The greatest novelty of the convention was contained in Article VII(2):

> a national of one of the state parties claiming that he has been injured by measures in breach of this Convention may institute proceedings against the Party responsible for such measures before the Arbitral Tribunal referred to in paragraph 1 of this Article, provided that the Party against which the claim is made has declared that it accepts the jurisdiction of the said Arbitral Tribunal in respect of claims by nationals of one or more Parties, including the Party concerned.[50]

In short, the Convention granted private investors the right to pursue an international remedy. Indeed, that right was subject to the consent of the state, but once the state accepted the possibility of such arbitration when it joined the Abs–Shawcross Convention (or at a later stage), the Convention granted the arbitral tribunal jurisdiction to hear a case between a private investor and a state. While the substantive clauses in the Convention were influenced by the U.S. 1946 FCN treaties, its novelty lay in its procedural provisions that enabled companies to arbitrate directly with a state without applying for diplomatic protection.

---

[48]   For a historical analysis of Elihu Lauterpacht's involvement in the Anglo-Iranian Consortium negotiations, *see* Yuliya Chernykh, *The Gust of Wind: The Unknown Role of Sir Elihu Lauterpacht in the Drafting of the Abs–Shawcross Draft Convention*, *in* INTERNATIONAL INVESTMENT LAW AND HISTORY, *supra* note 1, at 241.

[49]   ST. JOHN, *supra* note 1, at 86.

[50]   Abs & Shawcross, *supra* note 45, at 115–18.

In 1961, Shawcross delivered a lecture at The Hague Academy of International Law entitled 'The Problems of Foreign Investment in International Law'. In his opening remarks, he noted the different paths that had led him to the subject: as a delegate to the United Nations, impressed by the pressing need to raise living standards in vast areas of the world; as Attorney General, concerned with the problems arising out of the nationalization of the AIOC;[51] as the President of the British Board of Trade; and, more recently, as Director of the Shell Petroleum Company. Throughout his lecture, Shawcross described the revolutionary meaning of the newly acquired sovereignty of postcolonial states for international investment law.[52] Rather than insisting on sustaining the same international legal rules and principles that had governed similar relations in the past, Shawcross considered the acquired sovereignty of postcolonial states to be a game-changer that transformed investment protection, from being based on property law (the sovereignty of the imperial government and the property of the colonized community) to contract law (between investors and decolonized nations).[53] He also emphasized the importance of an independent third-party review for the protection of foreign investment.[54]

In this 1961 lecture, Shawcross further commented on the disadvantages of the ICJ jurisdiction, which was dependent on the will of state to espouse the cause of their national interest in a process that was 'elaborate, expensive and lengthy'. He further argued that '[w]hat is really needed in this field is some International Arbitral Tribunal accepted by State parties to the Convention and to which private nationals might have recourse in direct proceedings against the State concerned'.[55] The greatest advantage of such direct proceedings lay in keeping 'this kind of dispute out of the arena of international politics and prestige', he observed.[56] Schwarzenberger, who was quite critical of the Abs–Shawcross Draft, similarly argued for 'an impartial authority and the enforcement of these rules through legally controlled processes' as the desired legal development for the protection of foreign investments.[57]

---

[51] In the 1951 British elections, Churchill criticized the Attlee government's handling of the Abadan Crisis. In return, the Labour party repeatedly accused the Tories of being warmongers. The campaign reached its zenith in the *Daily Mirror*'s election-day headline: 'Whose finger on the trigger?' Winston Churchill sued the paper for libel and Shawcross was chosen to represent the paper. Eventually, the case was settled out of court. DAVID BUTLER, THE BRITISH GENERAL ELECTIONS OF 1951 (1952).

[52] Lord Shawcross, *The Problems of Foreign Investment in International Law*, 102 COLLECTED COURSES OF THE HAGUE ACADEMY OF INTERNATIONAL LAW 339, 348–50 (1961).

[53] Accordingly, he suggested that investment contracts be governed by an analogous doctrine to *rebus sic stantibus* to secure the continuity of rights under such agreements. 'The principle may be expressed thus—that an alteration in contractual rights between a State and an alien can only take place (apart from agreement) when, in the first place, the event which occurs is of an entirely unforeseen kind and, secondly, it renders the obligations of one party so onerous that it may be assumed that if he had had them in contemplation at the time, he would not have made the contract.' *Id.* at 355.

[54] *Id.* at 362.

[55] *Id.*

[56] *Id.*

[57] SCHWARZENBERGER, *supra* note 19.

The question of whether or not the ICJ was the most suitable arena for investor-state dispute settlement would reach its focal point towards the end of the decade, with the 1970 Barcelona Traction decision. In the aftermath of that decision, the Abs–Shawcross formula for dispute resolution would eventually revolutionize international investment law. However, in the early 1960s, it was still conceived as being beyond reasonable reach. Parallel attempts to either formulate particular substantive standards in the 1961 Harvard Draft on International Responsibility of States for Injuries to Aliens,[58] or to synthesize the law of the treatment of aliens, law of human rights, and the law of state responsibility (as envisioned by the First Special Rapporteur on State Responsibility, García Amador)[59] also failed to materialize.[60]

The Abs–Shawcross Draft Convention was presented to the Organisation for European Economic Co-operation (OEEC) in 1959 for consideration.[61] Eventually, after the reorganization of the OEEC into the OECD, it succeeded in re-commending a Draft as a model for the conclusion of BITs by its member states.[62] The OECD Draft included a dispute resolution mechanism that followed the Abs–Shawcross Model and was subject to state consent.[63] As noted by Shawcross, '[t]he idea of concluding such a treaty between OEEC nations, which in practice observe this principle anyway, was to show them [postcolonial nations] what industrialized countries have done to promote progress and invite them: 'Come in and join the club.'"[64] The OECD Draft was deliberated on for nearly ten years, including con-sultations with developing countries. Initially, it received little or no support from key capital-exporting countries, most prominently the United States and Britain, before the tide gradually shifted towards the two pillars of the future investment regime: an independent dispute settlement mechanism devoted to arbitrating in-vestment, and BITs.

---

[58] Draft Convention on the International Responsibility of States for Injuries to Aliens, reprinted in Louis B. Sohn & R.R. Baxter, *Responsibility of States for Injuries to the Economic Interests of Aliens*, 55 Am. J. Int'l L. 548 (1961) [hereinafter 1961 Draft Convention].

[59] 'Revised Draft on International Responsibility of the State for Injuries Caused in Its Territory to the Person or Property of Aliens', in F.V. García-Amador, *Sixth Report on State Responsibility*, in 1961(II) Y.B. Int'l L. Comm'n 1, 46 , U.N. Doc. A/CN.4/SER.A/1961/Add.1 (1961); Daniel Müller, *The Work of García Amador on State Responsibility for Injury Caused to Aliens*, in The Law of International Responsibility 69 (James Crawford et al. eds., 2010).

[60] After that, the International Law Commission, under the initial guidance of Roberto Ago, shifted its attention away from drafting primary rules on the treatment of aliens and focused on secondary rules regarding state responsibility.

[61] It intersected with other initiatives in the Council of Europe and other organizations. *See* Michael Brandon, *Recent Measures to Improve the International Investment Climate*, 9 J. Pub. L. 125 (1960).

[62] On October 12, 1967 the OECD Council adopted a Resolution [C(67)102] reaffirming the adher-ence of Member States to the principles of international law embodied in the Convention, and this gave it a legal status similar to an OECD Recommendation.

[63] Article IX of the OECD Draft Convention was slightly broader than the Abs–Shawcross Convention and included natural persons and not just companies.

[64] Shawcross, *supra* note 52, at 362.

The World Bank International Centre for Settlement of Investment Disputes (ICSID)

The growing number of expropriation disputes in the 1950s and the 1960s was a source of great concern and thorough deliberation for the World Bank management. Taylor St. John described how certain developments brought the project of designing an investment protection regime to the doorstep of the institution.[65] In 1965, the International Centre for Settlement of Investment Disputes (ICSID) was born.[66] But by1974, only one case had come to arbitration. As noted by one of the contemporary commentators, this was testament 'to the lack of enthusiasm of the less developed countries for this approach to private investment problems'.[67]

As the 1960s came to a close, it became clear that the time was not yet ripe for a multilateral treaty. Parallel to the previous attempts to pursue such a treaty, Germany launched the first BIT with Pakistan in 1957. In the initial BIT model, investments were protected according to the law of the host state. For the time being, it referred to the ICJ or ad hoc state-to-state arbitration.[68] Other European countries very slowly followed suit.[69] By the late 1960s, the tide began to shift towards BITs, with the OECD Draft Convention as a possible model for their content.[70]

The hesitance of industrialized states to endorse new regulatory investment schemes may seem puzzling when viewed against the backdrop of expropriations by postcolonial states. One plausible answer to this puzzle is that the stakes were not high enough before the late 1960s. The successful advocacy of postcolonial nations for the recognition of permanent sovereignty at the United Nations and the related expropriations did not challenge foreign investors with any great impact before that time.[71] The limited effect of these earlier expropriations was related to their association with Communism, which, in turn, triggered severe U.S. economic sanctions that had proved quite effective until the mid-1960s. In addition, MNCs' collective

---

[65] First, the Bank's involvement with proposals to create an investment insurance agency exposed some of the difficulties involved and the deep-seated disagreements between capital-exporting and importing countries. The second development was Herman Ab's Deutsche Bank purchase of over 66 per cent of the World Bank's first European bond issue in 1959. That purchase sustained large losses for Deutsche Bank but earned Abs a lot of support from the World Bank's management. Finally, the Bank's managers had experience of success in the mediation of the Suez Canal Company and City of Tokyo Bonds cases. These factors probably led Bank officials, and most prominently Aron Broches, to set aside the substantive aspects of an investment law regime and focus their efforts on establishing a Centre for Arbitration. Taylor St. John described how the idea of using the proposed center to enforce BITs was present from the start. Taylor St. John, *Enriching Law with Political History: A Case Study on the Creation of the ICSID Convention, in* INTERNATIONAL INVESTMENT LAW AND HISTORY, *supra* note 1, at 286, 305–10.

[66] For further discussion, *see* PARRA, *supra* note 1; ST. JOHN, *supra* note 1.

[67] Stanley D. Metzger, *American Foreign Trade and Investment Policy for the 1970s: The Williams Commission Report*, 66 AM. J. INT'L L. 548 (1972).

[68] *See, e.g.*, Article 11 of the Bilateral Investment Treaty Concluded Between Germany and Pakistan, Nov. 25, 1959, 457 U.N.T.S. 24.

[69] Switzerland and Tunisia (1961), France and Tunisia (1972).

[70] See archival materials on this shift in ST. JOHN, *supra* note 1, at 93.

[71] For a thorough analysis of this trend, *see* CHARLES LIPSON, STANDING GUARD: PROTECTING FOREIGN CAPITAL IN THE NINETEENTH AND TWENTIETH CENTURY 97–139 (1985).

action, as exemplified by the coalition of the seven oil companies against Iran, re-inforced the U.S.'s bargaining position.[72] As noted by Charles Lipson, '[e]xcept for communist countries, very few foreign investments were seized without adequate compensation during this period [1945–late 1960s]'.[73] An important exception was Africa, which was dominated by investment from foreign colonial powers and experienced a higher rate of expropriations without compensation.[74]

The status quo began to change dramatically after the mid-1960s. The growth of German and Japanese foreign investment spurred on the participation of multi-national firms from all advanced countries.[75] Even though U.S. investments were still greater than those of other countries, their relative importance declined, not least because the rise in international competition gave host countries more le-verage over the terms on which foreign capital could be invested.[76] The numbers of expropriations also grew markedly; they were largely directed at single indus-tries of particular foreign firms and implemented with greater sophistication. Corporate adaptation measures (such as changes in ownership structure and fi-nancing models) were not sufficiently effective at limiting the negative effects of expropriation. Customary international law, economic warfare, and military inter-ventions all fell short of providing solutions. Unlike the case of international fi-nance, which was secured through the coordinating role of the IMF, investors had no coordinated and institutionalized system to protect their assets. Charles Lipson concluded his 1985 analysis as follows: 'The spread of expropriations and the de-cline in compensation standards clearly indicates that the United States can no longer protect foreign investment by itself. The next step is obvious: seek help.'[77]

In the interim period—between the failure of the ITO and the postwar FCN treaties and the rise of BITs and related ISDS mechanisms—a unique window of opportunity opened for postcolonial countries to introduce their own vision for an economic order and the regulation of global investor–state relations. That window also ushered in the corporate entity as a subject of inquiry, concern, and regulation in international law in the 1970s. Key factors in this process were: first, the naming of the MNC as an issue of academic and public debate; second, the ICJ's attitude to international investment disputes; and third, the discrepancy be-tween the disagreements between Europe and the United States over the regu-lation of foreign investment and a markedly different political reality that now

[72] For further discussion, see Chapter 6.
[73] LIPSON, supra note 71, at 103.
[74] Id. at 109–11.
[75] As documented by a report by the Department of Economic and Social Affairs of the UN Secretariat, between 1960 and 1971, the most dramatic increase in investment flow was registered in Japan—a fifteenfold rise and an almost equally impressive performance of the Federal Republic of Germany, which exhibited an almost tenfold increase in investment stock to $7.3 billion by 1971. Department of Economic and Social Affairs of the United Nations, MNCs in World Development, ST/ECA/190 (1973) at 8.
[76] LIPSON, supra note 71, at 105–06.
[77] Id. at 137.

characterized postcolonial states. Countries affiliated with the NIEO joined forces in a series of initiatives against the growing influence of foreign companies. Their struggle reached its zenith with the 1973 Organization of the Petroleum Exporting Countries (OPEC) Oil Crisis. These factors paved the way for a first-of-its-kind Code of Conduct on Transnational Corporations, under the auspices of the United Nations.

The Naming of the Multinational Corporation as a Subject of Inquiry and Source of Concern

Economists coin the term 'multinational corporations'

Even though MNCs were an important feature of foreign investment from its earlier stages, they rarely attracted attention as a subject for extensive research and inquiry. This was about to change dramatically in the 1960s. 'Suddenly, it seems, the sovereign states are feeling naked', wrote Raymond Vernon in his influential book on multinationals, *Sovereignty at Bay.* 'In only a few years', he observed, 'there have been scores of books and hundreds of articles about corporations that are "global" or "transnational" or "international" or "multinational" ... governments have begun to ask how these entities were affecting their national interests and what polices were needed to deal with them.'[78]

In 1960, Stephen H. Hymer completed his PhD thesis at MIT, entitled 'The International Operations of National Firms: A Study of Direct Investment (1960)'. He concluded, as did others before him, that there was substantial growth in the foreign activities of U.S. firms. The innovation of his thesis lay in the explanation he sought for this trend. Hymer was, by various accounts, the first economist to point to certain inadequacies of neoclassical theory to explain direct investment.[79] His dissertation drew attention to the theory of expansion of the firm, and he examined how firms created competitive advantage by organizing themselves in such a way as to overcome entry barriers. A few years later, he used Coasian analysis to explain the rationale behind the cross-border vertical and horizontal integration of firms.[80] His teacher and supervisor, Charles Kindleberger, described how firms,

---

[78] RAYMOND VERNON, SOVEREIGNTY AT BAY 13 (1971).

[79] For an analysis of this literature, *see* John H. Dunning, *The Key Literature on IB Activities 1960–2006, in* THE HANDBOOK ON INTERNATIONAL BUSINESS 39, 40, 42–43 (Alan Rugman ed., 2d ed. 2009).

[80] Stephen Hymer, The International Operations of National Firms: A Study of Direct Investment (1970) (unpublished Phd Thesis, MIT, on file with author); *La Grande Firme Multinationale,* REVUE ECONOMIQUE, 14/b 949 (1968); STEPHEN H. HYMER, THE INTERNATIONAL OPERATIONS OF NATIONAL FIRMS (1976). In a 1956 article in the Economic Journal, appeared prior to Hymer's PhD thesis, Edith Penrose dealt extensively with MNCs. However, she did not address the question 'why MNCs' or the 'nature of the MNC' and thus Hymer remains the acclaimed father figure of the theory of the MNC. For further discussion, *see* Christos Pitelis, *Edith Penrose and a Learning-Based Perspective on the MNE and OLI,* 21 DEV. & LEARNING ORG. 207 (2007).

in their quest for profits, increased world efficiency by reducing competition and acting as 'protectors of markets', mobilizing and organizing a complex bundle of productive factors in combinations, at scales, and in locations that minimized real costs of production.[81]

Another key figure in the academic impulse of the time was Raymond Vernon. In the twenty-four years Vernon spent in the Securities and Exchange Commission and the Department of State, he was involved in various aspects of the architecture behind U.S. economic foreign relations. In 1956, he received an offer from the Dean of the Harvard Graduate School of Public Administration to head its New York Metropolitan Region Study. He later joined the Harvard Faculty and stayed there for the rest of his career. In 1965, Vernon set up the Multinational Enterprise Project at the Harvard Business School to study the operations of U.S. and foreign multinational enterprises. His team of researchers looked at these enterprises in terms of finance, organization, production, marketing, and business–government relations. In 1966, he published what would later be known as the Product Cycle Theory to explain the international spread of U.S. firms, emphasizing country-specific factors and the location of business activities to explain why these firms were able to penetrate foreign markets and create barriers to potential competitors.[82]

Thanks, in great part, to the pioneering work of Vernon and Hymer, the impact of multinational activity on the economic welfare of host states became a central topic of research for economists throughout most of the 1960s.[83] Vernon's Product Cycle Theory would lose some of its relevance in later years,[84] but his remarkable talent for popularizing economists' concerns about companies penetrated various disciplines in the United States and around the world. His book *Sovereignty at Bay* and the later monograph *Storm over the Multinationals* (1977) marked the spirit of their time and engendered an academic storm of their own.

In 1967, Jean Servan-Schreiber published *Le Défi Américain* to warn against the negative influence of the rapid growth of U.S. multinational corporate investment on European markets.[85] Similar accounts were soon to appear in

---

[81]   Charles P. Kindleberger, AMERICAN BUSINESS ABROAD: SIX LECTURES ON DIRECT INVESTMENT 187–92 (1969). Other influential studies on the role of MNCs were published in 1969: JACK N. BEHRMAN, SOME PATTERNS IN THE RISE OF THE MULTINATIONAL ENTERPRISE (1969); SIDNEY E. ROLFE, THE INTERNATIONAL CORPORATION (1969). For a survey of ideas and studies on development economics in this strand, *see* SANJAYA LALL & PAUL STREETEN, FOREIGN INVESTMENT, TRANSNATIONALS AND DEVELOPING COUNTRIES (1977).

[82]   David Fieldhouse, *The Multinational: A Critique of a Concept*, *in* MULTINATIONAL ENTERPRISE IN HISTORICAL PERSPECTIVE 9, 23 (Alice Teichova et al. eds., 1986).

[83]   For an analysis of this literature, *see* Dunning, *supra* note 79, at 39.

[84]   Fieldhouse, *supra* note 82.

[85]   According to the findings of one survey of European public opinion carried out during the 1970s, multinationals were often assumed to be either American or based on American organizational models, *see* G. PENINOU ET AL., WHO'S AFRAID OF THE MULTINATIONALS: A SURVEY OF EUROPEAN OPINION OF MULTINATIONAL CORPORATIONS (1979), quoted by JENNIFER A. ZERK, MULTINATIONALS AND CORPORATE SOCIAL RESPONSIBILITY 9 (2006).

Canada.[86] In *Global Reach* (1974), R.J. Barnet and R.E. Miller brought the news to U.S. audiences. They combined a critique condemning the Vietnam War (as a war promoted by the military–industrial complex) with the threat that MNCs could pose for the future of U.S. labour.[87] U.S. labour unionists, for example, accused MNCs of harming the country by transferring jobs, capital, and technology abroad.[88] Over time, the very notion of 'the multinational corporation' became a concept in its own right, and was identified as being to blame for all economic and political ills. Some attribute the first appearance of the term 'multinational corporation' to David Lilienthal, who defined such entities as 'corporations—which have their home in one country but which operate and live under the laws of other countries as well'.[89] Mira Wilkins, one of the leading historians in the field, asserts that

> [f]oreign direct investment is one of a multinational enterprise's many activities, albeit an essential one for without the investment (however small) there is no extension of the firm and no internalization that is fundamental to an analysis of the international business. The modifying nationality ... defines the multinational enterprise. A multinational enterprise provides intra-firm connections, a tissue that unifies on a regular basis; it is not merely a channel for one-time transactions but a basis for different sorts of internal and external organizational relationships.[90]

The meaning of the term remained contested. The multinational was redefined by some as the transnational,[91] while by others the corporation was reconceived as the enterprise.[92] But the shared impetus was to convey the distinctiveness of the phenomenon and even use its very naming as a vehicle for critique and political struggle.

Once the concept of the MNC was in vogue, economists specializing in the theory of the firm joined in. 'As trade follows the flag, so does applied economics

[86] Kari Levitt argued that the high volume of American foreign investment in Canada was turning her country into a new colony of its Southern neighbour. KARI LEVITT, SILENT SURRENDER: THE MULTINATIONALS AND CANADA (1970).

[87] RICHARD J. BARNET & RONALD E. MÜLLER, GLOBAL REACH: THE POWER OF THE MULTINATIONAL CORPORATIONS (1974).

[88] Vernie Oliveiro, *The United States, Multinational Enterprises, and the Politics of Globalization*, *in* THE SHOCK OF THE GLOBAL: THE 1970S IN PERSPECTIVE 143, 143–44 (Nial Ferguson et al. eds., 2010). Their opposition would later lead, *inter alia*, to the Burke–Hartke Bill (The Foreign Trade and Investment Act of 1972), which would have restricted trade and put penalties on foreign direct investment, if enacted.

[89] David Lilienthal, *The Multinational Corporation (1960)*, *in* MANAGEMENT AND CORPORATIONS (Melvin Anshen & G.L. Bach eds., 1985).

[90] Mira Wilkins, *The History of the Multinational Enterprise*, *in* THE HANDBOOK ON INTERNATIONAL BUSINESS 5 (Alan Rugman ed., 2d ed. 2009).

[91] See discussion of the Group of Eminent Persons, *infra* text accompanying notes 162–64.

[92] See ILO and the opposing views of socialist countries which wanted to exclude public corporations and thus objected the broadening of the term to enterprises.

follow the newspapers', wrote Richard Caves in 1971.[93] A group of economists at Reading University in the United Kingdom developed new theoretical approaches to the analysis of the multinational firm. One of their leading figures was John Dunning who founded what became known as the Reading School of international business and developed an eclectic paradigm to consider ownership, location, and the advantages of internalization, where asset-rich and entrepreneurial firms could make use of locational benefits to centralize control over subsidiaries abroad. In the forthcoming years, Dunning would be involved in the various endeavours to design an international policy to address these concerns.

Back in the United States, the influence of Hymer on Latin American dependency theorists 'was striking'.[94] In a series of essays published between 1970 and 1974, Hymer described how MNCs' pursuit of monopoly profit and their capacity to internalize their global activities created a hierarchical world order and an international division of labour. Hymer's concept of an international hierarchy also inspired Osvaldo Sunkel to write an article in *Foreign Affairs* in 1972 in which he asserted:

> The recent burst of nationalism is in fact a reaction to long-term and increasingly intolerable dependence on foreigners. The development strategy of industrialization as a substitute for imports was supposed to free the economy from its heavy reliance on primary exports, foreign capital and technology. It has not only failed to achieve these aims, but has in fact aggravated the situation and nature of 'dependencia'.[95]

Sunkel argued that MNCs had moved from exporting commodities to controlling key sectors in the domestic economy and tended to monopolize rather than diffuse their skills and technology.[96] For him, the era of favourable conditions for direct foreign investment was coming to an end: 'possible cooperation with foreign firms is not totally excluded ... What is opening up is a new era of hard bargaining and negotiations, of pragmatic and detailed considerations of specific cases, of weighing the conditions offered by Japan, Europe, the socialist countries and the U.S., of building up alliances with countries with similar interests'.[97] The representatives of the Inter-American Development Bank (IDB), meeting in 1968 in Bogotá, similarly discussed the need for collective self-sufficiency assisted by foreign investment in the spirit of the Japanese model of encouraging inflow of

---

[93] Richard Caves, *International Corporations: The Industrial Economics of Foreign Investment*, 38 ECONOMICA 1 (1971).

[94] Fieldhouse, *supra* note 82, at 23; Stephen Hymer, *Life and the Political Economy of Multinational Corporate Capital*, 21 CONTRIBUTIONS TO POL. ECON. 9 (2002).

[95] Osvaldo Sunkel, *Big Business and 'Dependencia'*, 50 FOREIGN AFF. 517, 517–18 (1972).

[96] *Id.*

[97] *Id.*

well-screened foreign investment. They talked about enhancing local adaptive capabilities, the need for coordinated effort, and the dream of developing a regional
home-grown multinational of their own.[98] Albert O. Hirschman, who had recently
returned from South America and experienced first-hand the climate of unrest
there, conveyed similar concerns about the displacement of local firms by foreign
investment: 'Private investment is a mixed blessing, and the mixture is likely to become more noxious at the intermediate stage of development which characterizes
much of present-day Latin America.'[99]

The critique against multinationals was often defined in distributional terms.
Growing unemployment, accompanied by increasing maldistribution of income
in many countries (especially in Latin America), were central concerns. It was not
labour conditions, as such, that were on the agenda, but rather the influence of the
interference of MNCs on the question of labour distribution. The concern was that
'[t]he rich of the world would be integrated transnationally, while the poor remain
marginal'.[100] Stephen Hymer defined the structural concern as the

> hierarchical division of labor between geographical regions corresponding to the
> vertical division of labor within the firm. It would tend to centralize high-level de-
> cision-making occupations in the advanced countries, surrounded by a number
> of regional sub-capitals, and confine the rest of the world to lower levels of activity
> and income.[101]

The emergence of the multinational enterprise as a subject of historical inquiry

In the 1970s, historians came to challenge the concept of the MNC and the motivation for its rising influence.[102] In 1970 and 1974, respectively, Mira Wilkins
published *The Emergence of Multinational Enterprise: The Emergence of American
Business Abroad from the Colonial Era to 1914* and *The Maturing of the Multinational
Enterprise: American Business Abroad from 1914 to 1970*. As noted by Wilkins,
'[t]hese studies were prepared during the 1960s when US-headquartered multinational corporations were expanding globally and capturing the headlines'. In
1974, *Business History Review* (the journal of U.S. business historians, published

---

[98] Tagi Sagafi-Nejad, The UN and Transnational Corporations: From Code of Conduct
to Global Compact 35–36 (2008).

[99] Albert O. Hirschman, *How to Divest in Latin America and Why*, 76 Princeton Essays Int'l Fin.
320 (1969).

[100] Robert W. Cox, *Labor and Transnational Relations, in* Transnational Relations and World
Politics 233 (Robert Keohane & Joseph S. Nye eds., 1973).

[101] Stephen Hymer, The Multinational Corporation and the Law of Uneven Development
125 (1975).

[102] Fieldhouse, *supra* note 82, at 24–26.

by the Harvard Business School) devoted an entire issue to the history of European multinational enterprises.[103] These studies showed that the expansion of MNCs was not a post-Second World War phenomenon but actually had a long history.

International relations scholars: A political economy critique of the problem of the MNC

By the early 1970s, international relations scholars had also joined the discussion. Some of them challenged the prevailing distributional critique of the multinational corporation. They further criticized the idea of 'sovereignty at bay'—the notion that corporations posed a threat to states and could render them redundant. Conversely, they pointed to the various ways in which corporate actors forged alliances with governments to defend their positions[104] or used the internal tensions within host and home states to promote their interests, and the similar use of multinationals by elites to pursue political aims. Stephen Krasner differentiated between the influences of different types of company and demonstrated how oligopolistic companies posed the greatest risk of constraining public policy but were also the least likely to oppose the state.[105] Joseph Nye led a series of studies on the influence of multinationals during the 1970s. For him, 'the radical critique of multinationals, focusing on their penetration of weak states ... ignores the fact that these enterprises can also affect the coherence of home governments and societies'.[106] Direct investment, according to Nye, created transnational interdependence that groups or governments (host and home) could attempt to manipulate for their own political purposes. He provided examples of the corporate influence on foreign political decision-making in home and host states as well as examples in which both weaker and stronger states used corporations as instruments of influence.[107] Robert Keohane and Van Doorn Ooms showed how resistance to multinationals was not a general sentiment in host countries but rather the agenda of elites in postcolonial countries.[108] David Jodice also showed how, since the 1960s, expropriation had become an element of political-economic strategy: '[R]ulers who are unwilling or unable to coerce dissidents will use expropriation of foreign firms as a

---

[103] Wilkins, *supra* note 90. *See also* CHARLES WILSON, MULTINATIONALS, MANAGEMENT AND WORLD MARKETS: A HISTORICAL VIEW (1975).

[104] T.H. Moran, *Transnational Strategies of Protection and Defense by Multinational Corporations: Spreading the Risk and Raising the Cost for Nationalization in Natural Resources*, 27 INT'L ORG. 273 (1973).

[105] Stephen D. Krasner, *Business Government Relations: The Case of the International Coffee Agreement*, 27 INT'L ORG. 465 (1973).

[106] Joseph S. Nye, *Multinational Corporations in World Politics*, 53 FOREIGN AFF. 153, 157 (1974).

[107] *Id.*

[108] Robert Keohane & Van Doorn Ooms, *The Multinational Firm and International Regulation*, 29 INT'L ORG. 169, 170 (1975).

means of distracting attention from their own shortcomings and for building domestic support.'[109]

MNCs in international law: The Barcelona Traction
case as a turning point

While their colleagues in related disciplines filled their library shelves with mono-
graphs and essays on the MNC or enterprise, the debate among international
lawyers was rarely directly concerned with the concept of the MNC itself. A few
lectures at The Hague Academy were devoted to the issue of the business enterprise,
signalling its growing prominence in different circles.[110] Some scholars reflected
on the corporate entity in the context of international economic law, natural resources, conflict of law rules,[111] and the protection of foreign investment,[112] while
others referred to its menacing presence in the debates over self-determination and
the rise of the NIEO. It was during this period that Charles Henry Alexandrowicz
published his influential studies on the history of international law in Africa and
Asia, and drew attention to the history of the late-nineteenth-century involvement
of chartered companies in the colonization of Africa and the use of treaties of cession (African treaties) for that purpose.[113] While the international legal journals
and treatises of this period tell the intriguing story of a nascent discipline of international economic law,[114] the MNC or multinational entity itself was much less
visible in international legal writings.[115]

---

[109] David A. Jodice, *Sources of Change in Third World Regimes for Foreign Direct Investment 1968–
1976*, 34 INT'L ORG. 177, 205 (1980).

[110] In 1964, Professor Paul de Visscher lectured on the diplomatic protection of artificial persons,
De Visscher, *La Protection Diplomatique des Personnes Morales*, 102 RECUEIL DES COURS 399 (1961).
Charles M. Spofford discussed litigation concerns for companies in cross boundary transactions in
Third Party Judgment and International Economic Transactions, 113 RECUEIL DES COURS 121 (1964).
In 1966, Florentino P. Feliciano lectured on *The Legal Problems of Private International Business
Enterprises: An Introduction to the Law of Private Business Associations and Economic Development* (118
RECUEIL DES COURS 213 (1966)). The lecture described the different legal systems in which foreign in-
vestors operate and its related jurisprudence. Two years later, Homer G. Angelo, gave another lecture
at The Hague Academy, this time carrying the explicit title: *Multinational Corporate Enterprises*, 125
RECUEIL DES COURS 447 (1968).

[111] Ignaz Seidl-Hohenveldern, *The Impact of Public International Law Conflict of Law Rules on
Corporations*, 123 RECUEIL DES COURS 7 (1968).

[112] *See, e.g.*, David N. Smith & Louis T. Wells, *Mineral Agreements in Developing Countries: Structures
and Substance*, 69 AM. J. INT'L L. 560 (1975); David Gantz, *The Marcona Settlement: New Forms of
Negotiation and Compensation for Nationalized Property*, 71 AM. J. INT'L L. 474 (1977).

[113] Charles H. Alexandrowicz, *The Afro-Asian World and the Law of Nations (Historical Aspects)*, 123
RECUEIL DES COURS 117, 172–210 (1968).

[114] *See, e.g.*, SCHWARZENBERGER, *supra* note 19; GEORG SCHWARZENBERGER, ECONOMIC WORLD
ORDER? A BASIC PROBLEM OF INTERNATIONAL ECONOMIC LAW (1970).

[115] A few notable exceptions are Florentino P. Feliciano lecture, *supra* note 110, and Homer G. Angelo,
who gave another lecture at The Hague Academy in 1968, *supra* note 110.

The publication of the 1970 ICJ decision in the Case Concerning the Barcelona Traction, Light and Power Company, Ltd. broke this relative silence.[116] The case addressed the right of Belgium to exercise diplomatic protection on behalf of Belgian shareholders of a company that was incorporated in Canada and maintained its operations in Spain. The majority opinion acknowledged that the case addressed the problem of the MNC:

> Considering the important developments of the last half-century, the growth of foreign investments and the expansion of the international activities of corporations, in particular of holding companies, which are often multinational, and considering the way in which the economic interests of states have proliferated, it may at first sight appear surprising that the evolution of law has not gone further and that no generally accepted rules in the matter have crystallized on the international plane.[117]

The main issue put before the Court was whether Belgium, a home state of the majority of shareholders, had, under customary international law, a right of diplomatic protection in favour of the shareholders of the bankrupt company, namely: whether Belgium had a *ius standi* and, thus, whether its claims were admissible before the court. The ICJ ruled that the right of diplomatic protection in respect of an injury to a corporation belonged to the state under the laws of which the corporation was incorporated and in whose territory it had its registered office, and not to the national state(s) of the shareholders of the corporation.[118] Furthermore, only the national state of the investing company could make a claim under diplomatic protection if an unlawful act had been committed against the company. Beyond some exceptions, the protection of shareholders, the Court concluded, had not yet developed into a recognized rule under customary international law. [119]

There was no shortage of critics to the reasoning of the Court.[120] In fact, the judges themselves harshly criticized the majority decision. Eight judges wrote

---

[116] Barcelona Traction Case, *supra* note 12. This judgment from a new application made to the Court in 1962. The case was initiated in 1958 but removed from the Court's General List in 1962.

[117] *Id.* ¶ 89.

[118] *Id.* at 43.

[119] The ICJ mentioned three exceptions to this rule: (i) where the corporation has been incorporated in the state that inflicts the injury; (ii) where the state of incorporation has liquidated or wound up the corporation after the injury was inflicted by some third state; (iii) where the injury is inflicted directly on the shareholders and not indirectly through the damage to the company. *Id.*

[120] *See, e.g.,* Richard B. Lillich, *The Rigidity of Barcelona,* 65 AM. J. INT'L L. 522 (1971). Lillich lamented the narrow scope of the Court's analysis that failed to include the lump-sum settlement agreements that were concluded in former decades to provide compensation for the nationalization of foreign property and which uniformly authorized or were construed to authorize shareholder claims. In the same AJIL volume, Stanley Metzger criticized Barcelona for suggesting 'an unworkable standard' and offered instead the standard of investment guarantee schemes. *See* Stanley D. Metzger, *Nationality of Corporate Investment Under Investment Guarantee Schemes—The Relevance of Barcelona,* 65 AM. J. INT'L L. 532

separate opinions, and one judge, ad hoc Riphagen, dissented. One possible reading of the decision is that the Court may have reacted to the ramifications of a complex and fragmented identity of shareholders in the context of MNCs, that would extend the right to diplomatic protection to shareholders' whose holdings are scattered across different jurisdictions around the globe. Such an interpretation draws on the following paragraph from the majority opinion:

> opening the door to competing diplomatic claims, could create an atmosphere of confusion and insecurity in international economic relations. The danger would be all the greater in as much as the shares of companies whose activity is international are widely scattered and frequently change hands.[121]

Another possible reading highlights the compatibility between the opinions of the different judges and the interests of their respective nations. The British Judge Fitzmaurice wrote in his separate opinion that international law had failed to provide the resources necessary for protecting, on the international plane, not only the interests of the shareholders but the company itself.[122] Elsewhere, Judge Rosalyn Higgins bitterly criticized the Court's reluctance to move beyond the *lex lata* on this point.[123]

The opinion of the U.S. Judge, Philip C. Jessup, whose theory of transnational law we discussed in Chapter 6, is particularly relevant for such a reading. Jessup stated that his opinion relied on the U.S. perspective and legal practice on this matter, and addressed the need to expand the scope of diplomatic protection over corporations in light of the 'increase in the permissible limits of the exercise of State authority over foreign corporate enterprises'.[124] Jessup further explained that diplomatic protection should not be about the interests of the injured national, but about protecting the national interest of the state—not the private interest of the shareholder, but 'the realization of the national economic importance of foreign investments as State interests'.[125]

Loyal to his pragmatist approach, Jessup further challenged the formalistic approach of the court. Quoting and paraphrasing a recent decision of the Supreme Court of the United States in an antitrust case, he stated: 'the International Court of Justice in the instant case is "not bound by formal conceptions of" corporation law … "[w]e must look at the economic reality of the relevant transactions" and

---

(1971); F.A. Mann, *The Protection of Shareholders' Interests in Light of the Barcelona Traction Case*, 67 Am. J. Int'l L. 259 (1973).

[121] Barcelona Traction Case, *supra* note 12, ¶ 96.
[122] *Id.* at 64, 72–78 (separate opinion of Judge Fitzmaurice).
[123] Rosalyn Higgins, *Aspects of the Case Concerning the Barcelona Traction, Light and Power Company Ltd.*, 11 Va J. Int'l L. 341 (1970–1971).
[124] Barcelona Traction Case, *supra* note 12161, 168, ¶ 14 (separate opinion of Judge Jessup).
[125] *Id.* at 196, ¶ 59.

identify "the overwhelmingly dominant feature".[126] He also demonstrated how such protection was compatible with U.S. practice: 'the government maintains that it is entitled under international law to protect substantial American share-holders' interests in foreign corporations and that it declines to protect American companies in which the substantial interest is alien-owned'.[127] Jessup's opinion re-flected the perspective adopted by the Restatement (Second) of Foreign Relations of the United States from 1965, which clearly anticipates the situation where the shareholder's state espouses the claim of the shareholders.[128]

Given the surge in Japanese foreign investments during this period, it may not be surprising that the Japanese Judge, Kōtarō Tanaka, similarly argued in favour of shareholder protection: 'A vacuum with respect to protection should not be toler-ated: otherwise shareholders would be left in an entirely helpless condition and the result would be injustice and inequity which would be harmful for the healthy de-velopment of international investment'.[129] Indeed, even though the majority of the ICJ judges may have agreed on the outcome, they presented competing rationales for their decisions.

While Judge Philip Jessup denied the relevance of the case to colonial and postcolonial tensions,[130] academic leaders who were committed to decolonized nations, such as Georges Abi-Saab, thought otherwise. In 1971, Abi-Saab pub-lished an article entitled 'The International Law of Multinational Corporations: A Critique of American Legal Doctrines', in which he criticized the U.S.'s pragmatic approach as an attempt to secure advantages vis-à-vis the capital importing coun-tries for powerful nations and the MNCs.[131] His critique was nonetheless opti-mistic. He considered the decisions of the Court in the AIOC and the Barcelona Traction cases as signifiers of the end of the era in which the major powers dic-tated international law. For Abi-Saab, these cases showed how the court realized the need to take third world countries into account. He further noted that the ICJ's formalistic or even conservative approach in both cases was favourable to new states: 'the technical orthodoxy of the Court, reflects, on the legislative policy level, a forward looking and progressive attitude'.[132] Furthermore, in the aftermath of de-colonization, a 'wider consensus is needed which cannot be based on the interests of one categories of states alone'.[133] Abi Saab conveyed his conviction that future

---

[126] *Id.* at 169, ¶ 17.
[127] *Id.* at 199, ¶ 63.
[128] Restatement (Second), Foreign Relations of the United States, § 173 (1965).
[129] Barcelona Traction Case, *supra* note 12, at 114, 130 (separate opinion of Judge Tanaka).
[130] 'The Court is not involved here in any conflict between great capital exporting States and States in course of development. Belgium and Spain are States, which, in those terms, belong in the same grouping... Basically the conflict was between a powerful Spanish financial group and a compar-able non-Spanish group. This case cannot be said to evoke problems of "neo-colonialism". Barcelona Traction Case, *supra* note 12, at 165, ¶ 10 (separate opinion of Judge Jessup).
[131] Georges Abi-Saab, *The International Law of Multinational Corporations: A Critique of American Legal Doctrines*, 2 ANNALES D'ETUDES INTERNATIONALES 97 (1971).
[132] *Id.* at 122.
[133] *Id.* at 121.

reforms in international law would not be pursued without seeking consensus with the developing world and 'accommodating the interests of all groups of States concerned'.[134]

Abi-Saab's critique and optimism echoed the confidence of those governments behind the NIEO leadership that the future of international investment law was dependent on their cooperation. As the following section describes, their confidence relied on their ability to join forces amid the hostility and difficulties of capital-exporting countries to form a coalition of their own.

A Window of Opportunity Opens for the NIEO Vision for International Corporate Regulation

Divided in the North, united in the South

The 1970s were turbulent times for international economic relations. The waning optimism about development coincided with the devastating critique on the part of academics and civil society over MNCs. The United States was facing new challenges that were initially marked by the 1971 abandonment of the dollar-based fixed exchange rate and the growing economic stature of Japan, Germany, and Western Europe.[135] In March 1972, investigative journalist Jack Anderson reported that the International Telephone and Telegraph Company (ITT) had plotted with the Central Intelligence Agency (CIA) to block the election of Salvador Allende, who threatened to nationalize ITT's majority share in the Chilean national company. He further alleged that the president of ITT had offered the Nixon Administration considerable political support to keep Allende out of power.[136] The ITT scandal encompassed almost all the controversial features of the growing global influence of corporations: the postcolonial concern that foreign companies would intervene in local politics and undermine their sovereignty and the fear of powerful states that they lacked sufficient means to protect their national investors against postcolonial nationalization attempts. In the winter of 1972, Allende addressed the General Assembly to voice his own concerns:

> We are faced by a direct confrontation between the large transnational corporations and the [postcolonial] states. The corporations are interfering in the fundamental political, economic and military decisions of the states. The corporations

---

[134] *Id.* at 122.

[135] By the early 1960s, the U.S. dollar's fixed value against gold was seen as overvalued. In August 1971, U.S. President Richard Nixon announced the 'temporary' suspension of the dollar's convertibility into gold. This crisis marked the breakdown of the system.

[136] Jack Anderson & Daryl Gibson, Peace, War and Politics: An Eyewitness Account 194–200 (1999).

are global organizations that do not depend on any state and whose activities are not controlled by, nor are they accountable to, any parliament or any other institution representative of the collective interest.[137]

Following the publication of Anderson's reports, the Senate Foreign Relations Committee established a subcommittee to undertake the study of MNCs and their impact on U.S. foreign policy. Senator Frank Church chaired the hearings between 1973 and 1976 [hereinafter: the Church Committee].[138] Together with the ITT affair, the Church Committee discussed the influence of U.S. companies on foreign governments in the Middle East and also in Europe and Japan.[139]

Meanwhile, the public atmosphere generated by the later Watergate investigations and the Church Committee brought the issue of bribery and corruption in international business transactions into the spotlight. In July 1973, the Watergate Special Prosecutor, Archibald Cox, publicly called for companies to disclose their illegal contributions to the 1972 U.S. presidential campaign. Cox gathered information on those MNCs that had contributed illegally to U.S. political campaigns and to foreign governments and foreign political parties.[140] The Securities and Exchange Commission (SEC) launched its own investigations and found examples of corporate bribery, unaccountable distribution of money, and further violations of U.S. security laws (the so-called Lockheed bribery cases). These eventually resulted in the U.S. Congress passing the Foreign Corrupt Practices Act in 1977.[141] By September 1973, a coup d'état, sponsored by the United States, had overthrown the Chilean regime.[142] Together, the Chilean affair, the Watergate scandal, and the turmoil around the Lockheed bribery cases turned the regulation of MNCs into a major public concern in the United States.

Alongside U.S. citizens growing suspicious over the influence of their corporations overseas, Europeans became weary of U.S. influence. The Vietnam War and the Nixon Administration's plan to abandon the Bretton Woods system of fixed

---

[137]   UNGAOR, 27th Sess., 2096th Plen. Mtg., U.N. Doc. A/PV.2096 (Dec. 4, 1972). For an earlier speech, see *Salvador Allende Press Conference*, RADIO CLASSICS (Jan. 1, 1972), http://www.unmultimedia.org/classics/asset/C115/C1152/.

[138]   Subcommittee on Multinational Corporations, the International Telephone and Telegraph Company and Chile, 1970–1971 (for the Committee on Foreign Relations, U.S. Senate, 1973). LEORY ASHBY & ROY GRAMER, FIGHTING THE ODDS: THE LIFE OF SENATOR FRANCK CHURCH (1994).

[139]   For a brief overview of its proceedings, *see* SAGAFI-NEJAD, *supra* note 98, at 45–47.

[140]   Multinational Corporations and United States Foreign Policy, Hearings before the Subcomm. On Multinational Corporations of the Senate Comm. of Foreign Relations 94th Cong. 5 (1975) microforms on CIS No. 76-S381-6 (Congress. Infor Serv.) quoted by Alejandro Posadas, *Combating Corruption Under International Law*, 10 DUKE J. COMP. & INT'L L. 345, 348 (2000).

[141]   For further information, see the Criminal Division of the U.S. Department of Justice and the Enforcement Division of the U.S. Securities and Exchange Commission, A Resource Guide to the U.S. Foreign Corrupt Practices Act (2012). Online. http://www.sec.gov/spotlight/fcpa/fcpa-resource-guide.pdf.

[142]   E-16 Documents on Chile 1969–1973 III FRUS 2015.

exchange rates established at the end of the Second World War were two of the main causes of growing tensions between Europe and the United States. In 1973, Britain joined the European Economic Community (EEC), signalling the viability of a serious European coalition.[143] Amid these U.S.–Europe tensions, postcolonial countries were gaining momentum. Mossadegh (the Iranian Prime Minister whose failed expropriation attempt and resistance to the AIOC were elaborated in Chapter 6) was gradually becoming a 'beacon from the past, and much more, a martyr to an unmovable cause'.[144] In the 1960s, the quest for economic justice gradually transformed, as oil elites joined the resistance of postcolonial states and challenged the fairness of oil deals between governments and oil companies as imperial practices.[145] Expropriation rates surged to unprecedented levels,[146] and expropriations increased in frequency from ten or fewer per year in the early 1960s, to very high levels a decade later. Each year between 1971 and 1975, at least twenty countries nationalized foreign firms.[147] More importantly, leaders of oil-exporting countries learned that their strength lay in their concerted collective action.[148] In the 1960s, oil-exporting countries created OPEC. At the outbreak of the war between Arab States and Israel in October 1973, OPEC's Arab members imposed an embargo of oil shipments to the United States and its supporters, and cut oil production. In December 1973, the price of crude oil quadrupled in what industrialized countries called the 'oil shock' and oil-producing countries dubbed the 'oil revolution'.[149]

Oil-exporting countries were not the first to engage in collective action. Five, and later six Latin American countries had adopted the Andean Pact in 1969 in an effort to pool their economic powers in a joint policy against MNCs. This move denied foreign-owned enterprises the advantages of the incipient free trade area among the Andean Pact countries unless the enterprises committed to a divestiture

---

[143] *See* Giuliano Garavini, AFTER EMPIRES: EUROPEAN INTEGRATION, DECOLONIZATION, AND THE CHALLENGE FROM THE GLOBAL SOUTH, 1957–1986 (2012); Vanessa Ogle, *State Rights Against Private Capital: The 'New International Economic Order' and the Struggle over Aid, Trade and Foreign Investment, 1962–1981*, 5 HUMANITY 211, 222–23 (2014).

[144] Christopher R. W. Dietrich, *Mossadegh Madness: Oil and Sovereignty in the Anticolonial Community*, 6 HUMANITY 63, 68 (2015).

[145] For the numerous meetings and initiatives regarding such economic cooperation, see, for example, ODETTE JANKOWITSCH & KARL P. SAUVANT, THE THIRD WORLD WITHOUT SUPERPOWERS: THE COLLECTED PAPERS OF THE NON-ALIGNED COUNTRIES (1978–1993); THE THIRD WORLD WITHOUT SUPERPOWERS, SECOND SERIES: THE GROUP OF 77 (Karl P. Sauvant & Joachim W. Mueller eds., 1981–1995).

[146] Stephen J. Kobrin, *Expropriation as an Attempt to Control Foreign Firms in LDCs: Trends from 1960 to 1979*, 28 INT'L STUD. Q. 329, 329–34 (1984).

[147] Jodice, *supra* note 109, at 181.

[148] For a contemporary (1974) political economic analysis of their strategy, *see* Zuhayr Mikdashi, *Cooperation Among Oil Exporting Countries with Special Reference to Arab Countries: A Political Economy Analysis*, 28 INT'L ORG. 1 (1974).

[149] Giuliano Garavini, *From Boumedienomic to Reaganomics, Algeria, OPEC and the International Struggle for Economic Equality*, 6 HUMANITY 79 (2015).

program that would place majority ownership and control in local hands. Further, it sought to alter licencing agreements and loans. Nevertheless, the actual application of these provisions was quite limited.[150] The clear turning point in the post-colonial resistance to MNCs and the existing investment regime was therefore the 1973 oil shock triggered by OPEC. For the OECD countries, the oil crisis of 1973–74 was a key factor in the transition from the long era of postwar prosperity to a phase of stagnation.[151]

The oil crisis ushered in the NIEO's finest hour. Houari Boumedienne, leader of Algeria and one of the prominent drivers of this OPEC strategy, called on UN Secretary General Kurt Waldheim to convene a special General Assembly session, which was held in 1974.[152] At this General Assembly, two NIEO resolutions were adopted and presented a clear vision of the superiority of the sovereignty of the host state over the MNC. The Declaration on the Establishment of a NIEO referred to '[r]egulation and supervision of the activities of transnational corporations by taking measures in the interest of the national economies of the countries where such transnational corporations operate on the basis of the full sovereignty of those countries'.[153] The Charter of Economic Rights and Duties of States stated in Article 2 that

[e]very State has and shall freely exercise full permanent sovereignty, including possession, use and disposal, over all its wealth, natural resources and economic activities ... To regulate and supervise the activities of transnational corporations within its national jurisdiction and take measures to ensure that such activities comply with its laws, rules and regulations and conform with its economic and social policies. Transnational corporations shall not intervene in the internal affairs of a host State. Every State should, with full regard for its sovereign rights, cooperate with other States in the exercise of the right set forth in this subparagraph.[154]

While postcolonial countries were conveying solidarity,[155] and Americans were losing faith in their government and their corporations' overseas endeavours, confrontation between European countries and the United States over this

---

[150] See Covey T. Oliver, *The Andean Foreign Investment Code: A New Phase in the Quest for Normative Order as to Direct Foreign Investment*, 66 AM. J. INT'L L. 784 (1972); RAYMOND VERNON, STORM OVER MULTINATIONALS 196 (1977).

[151] See DANIEL J. SARGENT, A SUPERPOWER TRANSFORMED: THE REMAKING OF AMERICAN FOREIGN RELATIONS IN THE LATE 1970S, at 149–61 (2015).

[152] For further discussion on the Algerian leadership, see Garavini, *supra* note 149.

[153] G.A. Res. 3201 (S-V1), Declaration on the Establishment of a New International Economic Order (May 1, 1974).

[154] G.A. Res. 3281(XXIX), Charter of Economic Rights and Duties of States (Dec. 12, 1974).

[155] This was not a perfect coalition. Concerns over TNCs were not shared by all postcolonial or European states. For examples, *see* SAGAFI-NEJAD, *supra* note 98, at 53–54.

issue intensified.[156] This pressure from inside civil society in the Global North, the rising power of the NIEO, and the tensions between capital-exporting countries opened a window of opportunity for a new international policy regime on MNCs.

The UN and transnational corporations

Concerns over the implications of MNCs were expressed in the United Nations as early as 1965.[157] In 1972, Chile filed a complaint before the UN's Economic and Social Council concerning ITT.[158] The Council tabled a resolution to conduct a research project on the role of the 'multinational corporations and their impact on the process of development and to submit recommendations for further action'.[159] The resolution further asserted '[t]he International community has yet to formulate a positive policy and establish effective machinery for dealing with the issues raised by the activities of these corporations'.[160] The resolution also ordered the appointment of a Group of Eminent Persons (GEP) to study the matter, formulate conclusions, and submit recommendations for international action.[161] The GEP comprised twenty experts from nineteen countries,[162] and the prime architect of the resolution was Philippe de Seynes, the Under-Secretary-General for Economic and Social Affairs,

As background to the GEP work, de Seynes' staff prepared a study reviewing the many terminologies for companies engaged in profit-seeking activities outside their home countries, leading to the later consensus of the GEP on 'transnational corporations' as the principal term [hereinafter: TNCs]. The report drew on datasets from around the world but flagged the scarcity of knowledge and need for further information and study. It described the immense growth in the economic activities of TNCs and their positive potential. The scholarly work of many of the academics we met in earlier chapters appeared in the study and in later hearings

---

[156] Ogle, *supra* note 143, at 222–23; STEPHEN D. KRASNER, DEFENDING THE NATIONAL INTERESTS: RAW MATERIALS INVESTMENTS AND U.S. FOREIGN POLICY 52 (1978).

[157] UN General Assembly passed resolution 2087 (XX) in 1965, UNCTAD resolutions in 1964 and 1968, and ECOSOC resolution 1286 (XLIII) in 1967. G.A Res. 2087(XX) (Dec. 30, 1965); Economic and Social Council Res. 1286 (XLIII) (Nov. 14, 1967).

[158] 53 U.N. ESCOR (1822nd Mtg.) 19, 22, U.N. Doc. E/SR.1822 (1972).

[159] ECOSOC Res. 1721, 53 U.N. ESCOR Supp. (No. 1) 3, U.N. Doc. E/5209 (1972).

[160] 53 U.N. ESCOR, *supra* note 158. Their report was submitted in 1974. Report of the Group of Eminent Persons, The Impact of Multinational Corporations on Development and on International Relations. U.N. Doc. E/5500/Rev. 1, ST/ESA/6 (1974).

[161] 53 U.N. ESCOR, *supra* note 158.

[162] On the composition of the group, *see* SAGAFI-NEJAD, *supra* note 98, at 57–59; KHALIL HAMDANI & PORRAINE RUFFING, UNITED NATIONS CENTRE ON TRANSNATIONAL CORPORATIONS: CORPORATE CONDUCT AND THE PUBLIC INTEREST 9–11, 27–28 (2015).

before the GEP.[163] 'Multinational corporations', the study asserted, 'have tended to concentrate in a few developing countries… Sporadic data suggest that despite their visibility and presence in key sectors, the contribution of foreign affiliates to the total gross domestic product of developing countries remains relatively small in most host countries.'[164]

While the GEP was holding its hearings, news of the Chilean coup d'état of 11 September 1973 emerged, followed by the Yom Kippur War and the OPEC oil embargo in the following month. In 1974, the GEP submitted its report, entitled 'The Impact of Multinational Corporations on Development and in International Relations'. It recommended creating a better framework for the TNC–host state relationship. And, perhaps inadvertently, given the diversity of voices and participants, the tenor of the report voiced NIEO central themes such as distributive justice and the importance of sovereignty.

For de Seynes, who had been involved in the preparation of the Havana Charter, the time was ripe for a second chance—but what form might it take? The GEP considered 'an appropriate long-term objective to be the conclusion of a general agreement on multinational corporations having the force of an international treaty and containing provisions for machinery and sanctions', but at the same time recognized that 'it is premature to propose serious negotiations on such an agreement and the machinery necessary for its enforcement'.[165] In 1975, the United Nations established the Commission on Transnational Corporations, and an Information and Research Center on Transnational Corporations.[166] The Commission, in turn, recommended the establishment of an Intergovernmental Working Group to formulate a code of conduct.[167] In 1978, the Working Group issued a draft code of conduct.[168]

The general atmosphere seemed supportive of greater control over TNCs, but the rationale and desired format of such control differed between countries. At the time that the negotiations on the Code of Conduct on Transnational Corporations commenced, all postcolonial countries were recipients of FDIs, with almost no outward FDIs. Postcolonial countries did not want to restrict

---

[163] SAGAFI-NEJAD, *supra* note 98, at 64–78.

[164] Department of Economic and Social Affairs of the United Nations, Multinational Corporations in World Development, ST/ECA/190 (1973) 18–20.

[165] UN Secretary-General, *The Impact of Multinational Corporations on Development and on International Relations*, U.N. Doc. E/5500/Rev.1 ST/ESA/6 (1974), 54. It is hard to conclude why the Code was chosen for this purpose, but earlier precedents and the fact that it was preferred by the business community probably influenced the decision. In 1972, the International Chamber of Commerce, representing major TNCs, launched its Guidelines for International Investment, and a number of large U.S. companies also adopted codes of conduct during the 1970s, with a particular emphasis on curtailing questionable payments.

[166] Economic and Social Council Res. 1913 (Dec. 5, 1974).

[167] 61 U.N. ESCOR, Supp. (No. 5) 3, U.N. Doc. E/C.I0/16 (1976).

[168] U.N. Commission on Transnational Corporations, Transnational Corporations: Code of Conduct; Formulations by the Chairman, U.N. Doc. E/C.10 2/8 (1978).

their governments' treatment of foreign investors and maintain their national policy space; their main focus was on establishing rules constraining the behaviour of transnational corporations. Socialist countries primarily used the deliberations over the Code as a platform to advocate their anti-capitalist critique. Countries in the Global North, though both home and host to investors, were less concerned about corporate abuse (thanks to the domestic machinery they had developed to constrain monopolies and regulate labour relations, utilities, and natural resources) and instead channelled their efforts into the protection of their firms abroad.[169] Nevertheless, the unrest within U.S. civil society following the Chilean crisis may have prompted Henry Kissinger, Secretary of State, to acknowledge publicly in 1975 that his government 'was prepared to make a major effort' to arrive at 'an agreed statement of basic principles'. In his speech to the UN General Assembly he stated:

> The United States therefore believes that the time has come for the international community to articulate standards of conduct for both enterprises and government ... we must reach agreement on balanced principles. These should apply to transnational enterprises in their relations with governments, and to governments in their relations with enterprises and with other governments. They must be fair principles, for failure to reflect the interests of all parties concerned would exacerbate rather than moderate the frictions which have damaged the environment for international investment.[170]

It was nonetheless far from obvious that a single multilateral international agreement was, indeed, possible. Negotiations on the Code lingered in the following decades until the whole project was eventually abandoned in 1992. But this does not mean that the regulation of international investment remained untouched—quite the contrary. The history of the failure to reach an agreed-upon Code of Conduct is also the history of the emergence of the regulatory components that came to the fore in its place. The following section addresses the processes that changed the tide, pushing against the NIEO-inspired code and moving in favour of an international investment law comprising inter-state bilateral agreements and investor–state dispute settlement mechanisms.

---

[169] Karl P. Sauvant, *The Negotiations of the United Nations Code of Conduct on Transnational Corporations: Experience and Lessons Learned*, 16 J. WORLD INV. & TRADE 11, 21–27 (2015).
[170] Henry Kissinger, Global Consensus and Economic Development Address by U.S. Secretary of State to the Seventh Special Session of the United Nations General Assembly, Delivered on September 1, 1975 by Daniel P. Moynihan, U.S. Representative to the United Nations 432–33 (Department of State Bulletin, Vol. 73 No. 1891, September 22, 1975).

Toward a New Architecture for Corporate Regulation in International Law

The late 1970s: U.S. policy-makers turn to bilateralism

Writing in 1974, and with all options still on the table, Joseph Nye, who was then a young professor at Harvard University's School of Government, appeared at the hearings of the GEPs working on the future of MNC regulation at the United Nations. Nye would soon come to be known as one of the leading figures (together with Robert Keohane) of the liberal or institutionalist strand in international relations, a theory that favoured, *inter alia*, multilateral cooperation as a means to enhance global welfare.[171] Intriguingly, Nye dampened the enthusiasm for a multilateral code on corporate regulation under the auspices of the GEP. Conversely, he argued that '[a] process of realistic discussions and bargaining with individual host countries is what is needed, and what a UN commission charged with developing international codes of conduct should attempt to promote—rather than rigid rules that cannot hope to cover the great variety of cases and political attitudes involved'.[172] Nye was arguing for bilateral arrangements and flexible rules.

> Given deep-seated differences among countries, moreover, it is unrealistic at this stage to expect, for example, a strong supranational organization to oversee the activities of multinationals. It also stems from the basic political reality that underlies corporation–state bargaining, particularly between rich and poor.

He raised further doubts over poorer countries' motivation to secure their position while they were relatively weak and poor,[173] and noted the importance of information sharing and gathering under the auspices of the United Nations, a function the United Nations would come to fulfil in future decades.[174]

His colleagues, the aforementioned Robert Keohane and Van Doorn Ooms, raised similar doubts. 'International facilitation of foreign investment is not where the action is', they wrote in 1975. 'Governments see little incentive in the present environment to commit themselves further to protection of multinational firms, particularly when this could mean sacrificing powers to outside authority'.[175] They pointed to significant efforts among European countries and the United States to collaborate on various policies affecting multinational firms, in areas such as antitrust policy, export controls, and securities regulation, and the lack of similar enthusiasm

---

[171] ROBERT O. KEOHANE & JOSEPH S. NYE, POWER AND INTERDEPENDENCE: WORLD POLITICS IN TRANSITION was first published in 1977 and almost immediately became a classic.
[172] Nye, *supra* note 106, at 172.
[173] *Id.*
[174] *Id.* at 175.
[175] Keohane & Ooms, *supra* note 108, at 190–91.

in the context of investment.[176] Their scepticism echoed the early warnings of Professor Wolfgang Friedman from the 1960s. Friedman conducted a country-by-country study on problems of foreign investment in joint ventures and expressed the view 'that it would be one hundred and fifty years before I would expect any formal agreement between developing countries and capital exporting countries on the principles of international law ... The alternative to waiting one hundred and fifty years was to proceed with ad hoc investment and the ad hoc agreement.'[177] That is exactly the direction investment regulation was to take in the coming years.

One immediate factor that curbed enthusiasm towards the multilateral code was the commencement of negotiations between OECD countries on a similar code.[178] The OECD guidelines were prepared in eighteen months and adopted six months before the United Nations began work on its Code of Conduct in January 1977.[179] Once completed, the OECD guidelines took considerable pressure off OECD countries and enabled them to signal what they were willing to accept in accordance with a narrower, more like-minded, bargaining table.[180] Similarly, the International Labour Organization's (ILO) Tripartite Declaration was completed during the first year of the Code negotiations, while the United Nations Conference on Trade and Development (UNCTAD) Restrictive Business Practices Set was also negotiated during an active phase of the Code negotiations.[181] Together, the actions of the ILO and the UNCTAD mitigated the concerns of trade unions.[182]

---

[176] *Id.* at 197 quoting Seymour Rubin, *Report on the Conference, in* INTERNATIONAL CONTROL OF INVESTMENT: THE DÜSSELDORF CONFERENCE ON MULTINATIONAL CORPORATIONS 9 (Don Wallace Jr. ed., 1974). Koehane's and Ooms' conclusion was similar: 'the divergences of interests between relevant actors – enterprises, trade unions, governments—make it unfeasible to construct a single system with a new and powerful international organization at its center'. Keohane & Ooms, *supra* note 108, at 209. For a similar position, *see* Raymond Vernon: 'for the present, they [the different coalitions] are unable as a group to bargain realistically over a new regime that would reduce the tensions associated with the multinational form of enterprise ... at this juncture [1977] it is hard to detect among the leaders of government and business any disposition to begin serious work on building an acceptable international regime'. VERNON, *supra* note 150, at 260–62.

[177] Proceedings, Regional Meeting American Society of International Law, New York, March 2, 1961, 'Economic Development and Foreign Investment—Role of Law'. Quoted by James N. Hyde, *Remedy and Performance: Planning Future Development Agreements*, 105 COLLECTED COURSES OF THE HAGUE ACADEMY OF INTERNATIONAL LAW 356 (1962).

[178] In January 1975, when the negotiations on the Code were underway, the OECD established a Committee on International Investment and Multinational Enterprises. In the OECD June 21, 1976 ministerial meeting, it approved the Declaration on International Investment and Multinational Enterprise.

[179] Organization for Economic Cooperation and Development, Guidelines for Multinational Enterprises, June 21, 1976 15 ILM 696 (1976) [hereinafter OECD Guidelines 1976]. The OECD updated these guidelines in 2000 and again 2011. For the current version, see http://www.oecd.org/daf/inv/mne/48004323.pdf (last accessed October 10, 2019); for a comparison between the two latest versions, see http://www.oecd.org/daf/inv/mne/49744860.pdf (last accessed October 10, 2019).

[180] Sauvant, *supra* note 169, at 31. For further discussion, *see* PETER T. MUCHLINSKI, MULTINATIONAL ENTERPRISES AND THE LAW 658–60 (2d ed. 2007).

[181] For participants in the drafting of the Code, it remains unclear '[h]ow far the OECD guidelines were intended to neutralize or render irrelevant the UN initiative on the code of conduct for TNCs'. SAGAFI-NEJAD, *supra* note 98, at 111.

[182] Sauvant, *supra* note 169, at 37.

Another crucial factor was the Barcelona Traction decision. The Court effect-ively left investors with little choice but to look elsewhere for protection and seek remedy in alternative forums to the ICJ.[183] The fact that initiatives in non-UN arenas proved more fruitful was not incidental. In such arenas, capital exporting nations were able to divert international decision-making processes away from the UN General Assembly, where they suffered from 'the tyranny of the majority'.[184] The issues that destabilized the 1970s—including bribery, investment protection, and development—were channelled towards regulatory frameworks where OECD governments could dictate the rules. As described earlier, in the case of bribery, the U.S. Congress took on a pioneering role and adopted the Foreign Corrupt Practices Act (FCPA) in 1977, the first law prohibiting transnational bribery. The scope of the FCPA was limited to corrupt practices related to business transactions. The U.S. Government, pressured by the business community, started to lobby for an international anticorruption treaty to level the international playing field. The gov-ernment, meanwhile, urged postcolonial countries to tie the anti-corruption nego-tiations to the negotiations on the Code, but to no avail. By 1981, negotiations had broken down.[185] In the case of development, the World Bank and the IMF recon-figured their development strategy and became much more influential in develop-ment policy for postcolonial countries henceforth.[186]

While progress on the Code had stalled, the BITs were moving up a gear—and the OECD was leading the way in this context as well. As noted earlier, the 1967 OECD Draft Convention on the Protection of Foreign Property was not open to signature but became a model for the conclusion of BITs. Postcolonial countries were initially resistant to the rules of this Draft Convention. By 1970, just sixty-four states had joined the World Bank's ICSID.[187] Most of the initial signatories of the ICSID Convention were either from the Global North or countries in Asia and Africa.[188] Hungary was the first Eastern Bloc country to join the ICSID, in 1986, and from the end of the Cold War the tide continued to grow.[189]

---

[183] In the following decades, BITs were to establish special mechanisms for investment protection that would challenge the distinction between company and shareholders that the Court sought to em-phasize. *See* Ian A. Laird, *A Community of Destiny: The Barcelona Traction Case and the Development of Shareholder Rights to Bring Investment Claims, in* INTERNATIONAL INVESTMENT LAW AND ARBITRATION: LEADING CASES FROM THE ICSID, NAFTA, BILATERAL TREATIES AND CUSTOMARY INTERNATIONAL LAW 77 (T. Weiler ed., 2005). For a discussion on the role of the ICJ in this case, *see* Christian J. Tams & Antonios Tzanakopoulos, *Barcelona Traction at 40: The ICJ as an Agent of Legal Development,* 23 LEIDEN J. INT'L L. 781 (2010).

[184] Quoted by MARK MAZOWER, GOVERNING THE WORLD: THE HISTORY OF AN IDEA 309 (2012).

[185] Kenneth W. Abbott & Duncan Snidal, *Values and Interests: International Legalization in the Fight Against Corruption,* 31 J. LEGAL STUD. S141 (2002).

[186] For further discussion, *see* PAHUJA, *supra* note 1.

[187] The ICSID Convention entered into force on October 14, 1966: Convention on the Settlement of Investment Disputes Between States and Nationals of Other States, Mar. 18, 1965, 575 U.N.T.S. 159.

[188] The World Bank Group, *ICSID: List of Contracting States and Other Signatories of the Convention.* Online: https://icsid.worldbank.org/en/Documents/icsiddocs/List%20of%20Contracting%20States% 20and%20Other%20Signatories%20of%20the%20Convention%20-%20Latest.pdf (last accessed October 10, 2019).

[189] *Id.*

U.S. FCN negotiations ceased in the late 1960s, and in 1977 the Office of the Legal Advisor at the U.S. Department of State began to formulate the U.S. BIT programme.[190] President Carter's administration formulated the basic policy for BITs but it would only fully materialize under the later administrations of Reagan, Bush, and Clinton.[191] In 1981, the United States finally produced a draft model BIT to use in negotiations with other countries. During the 1980s, the number of BITs was relatively small and their content relatively weak.[192] In the coming decades, key elements of these arrangements would bear fruit and by the end of the Cold War would revolutionize the regulation of investment worldwide.[193] The world was not yet ready for Abs' 1957 vision, but began to edge towards it in 1981 and more so after 1989. Ironically, NIEO-affiliated countries were the primary negotiating parties in this new regime.[194] By the end of the 1980s, 371 BITs had been negotiated, and by the end of the 1990s this figure had risen to 1,862.[195]

Human rights, free market ideology, and the collapse of the NIEO coalition
Ideological transformations and the diminishing collaboration between postcolonial states paved the way to the closure of the NIEO window of opportunity for a multilateral code, if indeed such a window ever existed. Among the key ideological transformations were the growing emphasis on human rights that began in the Carter years and the rising influence of free market ideology under Thatcher and Reagan. Despite an abrupt end to more than a decade of détente, with the Soviet invasion of Afghanistan, the Carter administration emphasized national policies as causes of instability in the Global South and attributed special importance to human rights. Whether this new vision could include the Code seems rather doubtful.[196] The very emphasis on human rights and transnational movements

---

[190] The preparation of a model treaty that could be used in negotiations took four years.

[191] KENNETH J. VANDEVELDE, UNITED STATES INVESTMENT TREATIES: POLICY AND PRACTICE 21–22 (1992).

[192] José Alvarez participated in some of the Code negotiation sessions as part of the U.S. delegation in his capacity as an attorney adviser in the U.S. Department of State. He stated, 'the typical [BIT] treaty ... combined relatively weak investment protections with an ineffectual investor–state dispute settlement clause'. *See* JOSÉ ALVAREZ, LOOKING TO THE FUTURE: ESSAYS ON INTERNATIONAL LAW IN HONOR OF W. MICHAEL RIESMAN 607, 615 (2010).

[193] The United States initiated another effort to regulate international investment in a multilateral treaty under the auspices of the OECD in 1995: the Multilateral Agreement on Investment (MAI). A coalition of Southern governments and NGOs managed to divide the Northern coalition, and the negotiations on MAI collapsed. DAVID HENDERSON, THE MAI AFFAIR: A STORY AND ITS LESSONS (1999). *See also* Eyal Benvenisti & George W. Downs, *The Empire's New Clothes: Political Economy and the Fragmentation of International Law*, 60 STAN. L. REV. 595, 616–17 (2007).

[194] José Alvarez, who was at the State Department during this period, described how the U.S. negotiated BITs with 'countries with which it [the US] did not have FCNs ... LDCs that had not long before generally supported the New International Economic Order (NIEO) at the UN—and had therefore suggested some sympathy with taking bad actions towards foreign investors'. José Alvarez, *The Evolving BIT*, 1 TDM (2010).

[195] UNCTAD, WORLD INVESTMENT REPORT 2015, at 106 (2015) (Figure III.4, trends in IIAs signed 1980–2014).

[196] But further archival research is needed on this point.

that would become Carter's foreign policy trademark[197] was not compatible with the spirit of the Code that emphasized the NIEO vision of permanent sovereignty over natural resources, distributive justice, and cooperation between governments. Nevertheless, the NIEO vision would soon be lost to human rights as the next normative rationale for corporate responsibility.[198]

With the election of President Ronald Reagan in 1980 and the election of Prime Minister Thatcher in the United Kingdom a year earlier, the political climate of Northern countries transformed. Reagan's economic policies championed free trade and the expansion of foreign investment, and he successfully meshed his foreign policy and Cold War strategy with global consciousness.[199] The new international vision included human rights, environmental concerns, and free market ideologies as its key components.[200]

The changing sentiment is captured in the *Economist*'s reporting on the international regulation of corporations over the years. The *Economist*'s Business Brief of 24 January 1976 bitterly described the greater scrutiny over corporate behaviour: '[s]o new efforts to draw up codes for the multinationals largely assume that they are a bunch of baddies.'[201] More than a decade later, the publication signalled a sigh of relief, using 'Come Back Multinationals' as the title of a 1988 edition. 'Multinational companies once seemed fated to succeed colonial powers as the bogeymen of UN agencies and their third-world acolytes', continued the subtitle. 'In the market-conscious 1980s, they look nicer than bank loans.'[202]

In addition to these ideological transformations, postcolonial countries were experiencing dramatic shifts on various fronts that destabilized their coalition. Perhaps most significantly, one should mention the Islamic revolution in Iran, leading to a second oil shock and the debt crisis, which started in Mexico in 1982 and heralded a 'lost decade' of growth for African and Latin American countries.[203] The creation of an alternative coalition for Northern countries, with the establishment of the G7 in 1975, gradually eclipsed the bargaining power of the NIEO-affiliated countries. As noted by one of the participants in the process, '[t]oward the middle of the 1980s, the criticism of TNCs and their foreign investments had died down, and the overlapping self-interests between developed and developing countries in a comprehensive instrument had waned.'[204]

---

[197] On the disparity between the anticolonial movement and human rights and the rising influence of the human rights movement in the 1970s, *see* SAMUEL MOYN, THE LAST UTOPIA 84–75 (2010).

[198] For an insightful historical and analytical comparison between the Code and the Draft Norms, *see* Jennifer Bair, *Corporations at the United Nations: Echoes of the New International Economic Order?*, 6 HUMANITY 159 (2015).

[199] Mark Atwood Lawrence, *Containing Globalism: The United States and the Developing World in the 1970s*, *in* THE SHOCK OF THE GLOBAL: THE 1970S IN PERSPECTIVE (Nial Ferguson et al. eds., 2010).

[200] For a discussion of these processes, *see* MAZOWER, *supra* note 184, at 313–42.

[201] ECONOMIST, January 24, 1976, at 68.

[202] ECONOMIST, November 26, 1988, at 103.

[203] For a discussion on these processes, *see* Ogle, *supra* note 143, at 223–26.

[204] Sauvant, *supra* note 169, at 61.

For postcolonial countries, the prominent objective of the Code of Conduct on Transnational Corporations was to secure their governments' regulatory supremacy in their relations with corporate investors. The rising influence of BITs reversed their hoped-for supremacy. Jose Alvarez described how '[i]t was the Grenadas and Bangladeshes of the world that had to reform their laws and practices to be sure that they could satisfy the U.S. BITs' treatment standards'.[205] A few fragmentation strategies were implemented in this context.[206] Different issues that were supposed to be governed by the Code were fragmented between different mechanisms devoted to specific issues; the United Nations was marginalized as a regulatory arena in favour of institutions governed by the United States or OECD countries (such as the World Bank); and new policies were implemented through bilateral (*e.g.* BITs) or unilateral (such as the FCPA) instruments. Together, these measures destabilized the already fragile and weakened the Southern coalition in favour of Northern countries and an alternative vision for the global economy. They further empowered the independent authority of corporate entities and private investors.

Corporations as shielded subjects: The regulatory regime that emerged in lieu of the code

The UN Code of Conduct on Transnational Corporations was never adopted. In its final drafts, it attempted to provide either mandatory or voluntary guidelines for corporations by encouraging contribution to the 'development goals and objectives of the countries in which they operated'. The Code further attempted to facilitate cooperation with, and among, states on issues relating to TNCs, and addressed contract negotiation and implementation, non-collaboration with racist regimes, non-interference with political affairs and intergovernmental relations, anti-corruption measures, and environmental protection.[207] The UN Commission on TNCs and the UN Centre on TNCs (UNCTC) became part of the New York-based Department of Economic and Social Affairs from 1974 to 1992. Together, they gathered data and information, published studies, and trained host countries' officials on investment-related issues.[208] In 1992, the UNCTC was reorganized and relocated to Geneva to become part of UNCTAD. It was renamed the Division of Investment Technology and Enterprise Development (DITE). Its new assignment would become UNCTAD's flagship publication, *The World Investment Report*.

---

[205] Alvarez, *supra* note 194.
[206] Eyal Benvenisti and George W. Downs coined the term 'fragmentation strategies' to describe their use by stronger political actors to promote their interests at the international arena. *See* Benvenisti & Downs, *supra* note 193.
[207] UN Code of Conduct on Transnational Corporations, 23 I.L.M. 626 (1984).
[208] For a survey of their work, *see* SAGAFI-NEJAD, *supra* note 98, at 89–110.

Key features from some of the embryonic regulatory experiments for corporate regulation that were developed during the period 1945–1980 found their way into the emerging international investment regime. The recognition of the corporate entity as an international actor, as already identified by the post-1946 FCN treaties and the academic storm over multinationals, brought the corporation to the fore as an equal participant in investment litigation disputes. In the aftermath of the Barcelona Traction case, the ICJ was no longer a preferred arena for settling investment disputes (as it had been, for example, in the 1946 FCN Treaties or the Shawcross Convention). Herman Abs' idea of permanent arbitration regimes for investors would become a reality, with the ICSID as a leading model. And the rules for these emerging investment regimes would be promulgated in a dense network of almost identical BITs.[209]

These measures clearly enhanced the legal protection of investors. So what happened to the concerns over the MNC? Indeed, these concerns did not die away, but their normative content and regulatory context changed significantly. The normative content of such mechanisms would no longer address distributive justice concerns or the sovereignty of the host state but would be redefined in human rights terms. Soft-law mechanisms and self-regulation were to become the dominant regulatory mechanisms in the context of transnational corporate regulation. In the course of this process, corporations became equal litigants and thus subjects of rights in international investment dispute mechanisms—regulators of the rules that governed their behaviour in the context of human rights or environmental concerns—without being recognized as subjects of international responsibility.

Furthermore, the battles over the Code of Conduct at the UN reinforced the use of voluntary rules as a suitable regulatory framework for the question of corporate responsibility in international law. While postcolonial countries objected to voluntary standards until quite late in the negotiations, parallel initiatives at the OECD and the ILO pursued non-obligatory frameworks to regulate the conduct of corporate businesses. Voluntary codes of conduct relied on corporate self-regulation for their enforcement, while corporations participated as parties to the international legal negotiating table. Corporate executives were key participants in the legislative processes of the Code of conduct from the hearings before the GEP throughout additional phases of negotiations.[210] Their participation moved corporations from the position of a behind-the-scenes interest group in international legal matters, to the front row.[211]

---

[209] See Laird, supra note 183.

[210] The GEP included Tore Browaldth (Chairman of Svenska Handelsbanken in Sweden), J. Irwin Miller (chairman of Cummins Engine Co., Inc., from the U.S.). The GEP invited nineteen business leaders to express their views including those from corporations such as IBM, Fiat, DuPont, Exxon, General Motors, Pfizer, Rio Tinto Zinc, General Tire, Unilever, Pechiney, Siemens, Massey-Ferguson, and Shell. Two business executives from India and Latin America testified as well. SAGAFI-NEJAD, supra note 98, at 64.

[211] For general discussion on the history of the CSR movement, see ZERK, supra note 85, at 15–44, 93–103, 243–98.

Conclusion

The 1970s marked an institutional shift in the regulation of corporations away from the United Nations as the ultimate regulatory arena that codified the rules applicable to corporations. The alternative was a dispersal of the question of corporate regulation under international law into different institutional sites and regimes. The terms of the emerging investment regime would be hitherto set in bilateral agreements that 'divided' the South and leveraged exporting nations to dictate rules that were compatible with their (investors') interests. Similarly, the ICJ's decisions in the AIOC and the Barcelona Traction cases probably led powerful nations to seek alternative forums to adjudicate international investment protection disputes.

These institutional transitions were accompanied by conceptual and doctrinal transformations. Conceptually, the political and economic theories developed in the 1960s and 1970s failed to transform the MNC into a meaningful signifier for a regulatory challenge or a clear market failure, as monopolies had become in the past. From a legal theory point of view, the growing recognition of individuals as subjects of international law coincided with non-formalist approaches to international legal theory, as demonstrated by the British functionalist approach to the AIOC case or Jessup's Transnational Law perspective in the Barcelona Traction case. Corporate responsibility in international law would hitherto be defined primarily in human rights terms and implemented through soft law mechanisms. These institutional, conceptual, and doctrinal transformations provided the basis for the new regulatory architecture of business corporations in international law, in which the corporation was constituted as a shielded subject.

8

The Long History of the Regulation of Private Business Corporations in International Law

The 1990s are frequently defined as *the* watershed period during which a new sensibility emerged towards the responsibility of private business corporations as subjects of international legal responsibility. Ecological crises stemming from the involvement of private business corporations in the control and management of natural resources (most famously, the complicity of Royal Dutch Shell in the execution of Ogoni indigenous leaders in Nigeria),[1] anti-sweatshop campaigns against prominent apparel companies,[2] intense civil society campaigns against large-scale development projects of the World Bank and powerful economic actors,[3] the 1999 riots against the World Trade Organization in Seattle, alongside the turn to ATS litigation as a vehicle to hold corporations accountable for the violations of human rights and environmental standards,[4] are all prominent markers of the prevailing 1990s narrative. The historical thrust of this account is that international law (and lawyers) had limited influence (or none at all) on the regulation of private business corporations until the very last decade of the twentieth century, and even then they did not pay corporations much attention. This book has questioned the very premises on which the historical narrative about the influence of international law on the private business corporation is based. The underlying premises of the prevailing account this book sought to problematize might be summarized as three-fold. First, the international legal influence over the conduct of private business corporations is associated with the late 1990s critique over their role in human

---

[1] In *Kiobel,* a class action was brought by the widow of one of the leaders of the protest movement of the Ogoni people against Shell's operations in the Niger delta. The plaintiffs claimed that Royal Dutch/ Shell, the Dutch and U.K. parent companies, and their Nigerian subsidiary had aided and abetted human rights abuses. *See* Kiobel v. Royal Dutch Petroleum Co., 569 U.S. 108 (2013).

[2] John Cavanagh, *The Global Resistance to Sweatshops, in* No Sweat: Fashion, Free Trade, and the Rights of Garment Workers 39 (Andrew Ross ed., 1997); David J. Doorey, *The Transparent Supply Chain: From Resistance to Implementation at Nike and Levi-Strauss,* 103 J. Bus. Ethics 587 (2011) (describes the events that led Nike and Levis to disclose their global supply chain).

[3] Doreen Lustig & Benedict Kingsbury, *Displacement and Relocation from Protected Areas: International Law Perspectives on Rights, Risks and Resistance,* 4 Conservation & Soc'y 404 (2006).

[4] Since the 1990s, Alien Tort Statute (ATS) jurisprudence has evolved into a central pillar in the regulation of private business corporations well, most famously in the controversy over the Kiobel decision. Doreen Lustig, *The Paradigms of Corporate Responsibility in International Law: The Kiobel Moment,* 12 J. Int'l Crim. Just. 593 (2014).

Veiled Power. Doreen Lustig, Oxford University Press (2020). © Doreen Lustig.
DOI: 10.1093/oso/9780198822097.001.0001

rights violations. Second, the history of international law and the private business corporations is a story of *exclusion* of the private business corporation as a subject of international legal scrutiny. And, third, the (relatively recent) international legal conceptual framework for the private business corporation is based on corporations as *subjects* of responsibility under international law.

These premises raise a few puzzles. The first puzzle is: how might we reconcile the growing significance and influence of business enterprises in the global arena over the course of the twentieth century with their marginality as subjects of interest, scrutiny, and jurisprudential concern until the 1990s? The second puzzle is: how can we reconcile the assumed exclusion of the private business corporation from international legal regulation with the influence and centrality of international legal doctrine, practices, institutions, and actors in the common regulatory contexts for global business operations such as trade and investment? Perhaps the exclusion of businesses *as subjects of international law* is not the only relevant conceptual framing for the issue of private business corporations in international law. The third puzzle is, therefore: could we trace alternative conceptual framings to the private business corporation in international law? Could we conceive of private business corporations as something other than subjects or non-subjects in international law?

The Prologue to this book sought to answer the first puzzle. When chartered companies appeared at the beginning of the modern era, public and private identities were in flux. We tend to narrate the late-nineteenth-century period as a transition to a world of nation-states imagined as self-contained units. Throughout this book, I have endeavoured to break away from the claim for a clear positivist shift, to arrive instead at a more nuanced understanding of the interdependent relationship between governments and private enterprise. The co-emergence of the international legal vocabulary (doctrines of sovereignty and treaty-making), developments in corporate law (the shift to free incorporation), and ideological sensibilities in favour of the public/private divide provided the legal vocabulary and tools for private business corporations to externalize to imperial governments the growing administrative challenges of the colonization of the African hinterland. At the same time, the coexistence of recognized sources of sovereignty alongside non-recognized ones enabled imperial governments to manoeuver away from bearing administrative responsibilities whenever possible and helped indigenous actors seize opportunities to further their interests and political agendas. This global regulatory space, more than the rigid distinctions between sovereigns (and other political organizations) or the public and the private, captures the meaning of international law for the regulation of businesses in imperial Africa at the dawn of the twentieth century. It also provides a lens through which to understand how global capitalism came into being.

Indeed, international legal concepts, institutions, practices, and doctrines were conceived as elements of public law and addressed states as their main subjects. But it was precisely this configuration of the public and private divide that facilitated the new alliance between governments and commercial corporations, in which governments bore the administrative and coordination costs of their global endeavours, based on international legal doctrines of sovereignty and treaty law, while businesses focused their attention on implementing commercial projects and sharing some of their profits with the states that facilitated their success.

Corporate historians long classified corporate governance and structure—fundamental components in the flourishing of the corporate entity—as the most influential organizational pillars of commercial relations in the twentieth century. But examining the additional facet of the relationship between governments and corporations, and how international law shaped this relationship, helps shed further light on the rising influence of the corporate entity. I believe the supposed marginality of the business enterprise in international law, ingrained as it is in the commonly accepted narrative, is *a conceptual bias* that facilitated (rather than prevented) the emergence and reach of the private business corporation and legitimized the elements in the international legal order that enabled it to thrive.

This leads directly to the second puzzle: how might we reconcile the apparent failure to regulate businesses by international law with the growing relevance of international law to global commercial (and other) arenas? Rather than thinking of the private business corporation as excluded from international law, I have emphasized in this book how international legal doctrines in the context of labour, natural resources, investment, and criminal responsibility directly informed the regulation of the private business corporations in global settings.

The positivist shift in the regulation of slavery, captured in Chapter 1, demonstrates this point quite clearly. While embracing the humanitarian commitment to abolish slavery, international lawyers of the League of Nations era framed the regulation of slavery as an inter-state regime that recognized the state as the *effective* regulatory and *legitimate* regulatory authority (because it was public) in the context of labour relations (which were, in turn, conceived as part of the private domain of the state). While states in the industrialized world became regulatory states in the first decades of the twentieth century, they remained an important buffer against regulation in colonial settings. The positivist framework that emphasized the responsibility of states over their communities in international law had a dialectic influence. The regulation of slavery under the Slavery Convention shifted the impulse behind the abolition of slavery: away from the relationship of ownership between the slaveholder and the slave, and towards the positivist obligation of the (Liberian) state. Shifting the regulatory attention to the state as the sole regulatory authority justified the lack of direct scrutiny of the private business corporation. In other words, while the state was recognizable to international law, it also constituted the private realm of non-interference.

The redefinition of the commitment to abolish slavery as an inter-state obligation did not do away with slavery altogether. The loss of the original humanitarian logic undermined the interpersonal responsibility and relational commitment of the business agents to affected stakeholders. The limited findings of responsibility in the Nuremberg decisions for atrocities committed vividly demonstrate this point. Their analysis further demonstrates how the possibility of holding individuals accountable as subjects of criminal responsibility in international law was severely hindered as it was not shaped by any informed theory of personal responsibility vis-à-vis those who operate behind the double veils of the state and the business corporation.

But, as I have demonstrated in this book, the statist or positivist emphasis on the centrality of states as the primary actors in international law had dialectical implications and was not always implemented *against* corporate responsibility. The growing influence of collective sensibilities of class, self-determination, and nationalist sentiments were often aligned with the positivist, statist position and transformed the fight to liberate slaves into the struggle of weaker states against empires, stronger states, and companies from the Global North. The statist position emphasized the imperial enslavement of Liberia as a state while diluting power relations within Liberian society. Liberia's efforts to liberate itself from economic enslavement paralleled Iran's attempt to gain control over its oil, explored in Chapter 4. The endorsement of these causes by the League of Nations in various contexts joins other accounts of the League as providing an important regulatory space in which postcolonial sensibilities and ideological concerns could be addressed during the interwar period.[5] Chapters 1, 4, and 5 have further chronicled how postcolonial communities endorsed the shift to positivism as an empowering device for their collective aspirations and sought to use it to constrain and challenge business corporations.

Exposing these features addresses the third puzzle: what were the conceptual framings of private business corporations if they were *not* conceived as subjects? The prevailing narrative is that the question of the corporate entity in international law, as it arose in the 1990s, is the question over the private business corporation as a subject of international legal responsibility. However, the pre-1990s cases chronicled in this book challenge the notion that the question of businesses as *direct subjects* of international legal responsibility was the only normative framing developed to engage with the influence of private business corporations in international law. During the negotiations on the 1970s Code of Conduct for Multinational Corporations, the main focus of postcolonial nations was on rules constraining the behaviour of transnational corporations as *investors* and on securing their governments' regulatory supremacy in their relations with corporate investors. The direct responsibility of private business corporations to uphold human rights would

---

[5] *See also* Susan G. Pedersen, *Back to the League of Nations: Review Essay*, 112 AM. HIST. REV. 1091 (2007); SUSAN PEDERSON, THE GUARDIANS: THE LEAGUE OF NATIONS AND THE CRISIS OF EMPIRE (2015); PATRICIA CLAVIN, SECURING THE WORLD ECONOMY: THE REINVENTION OF THE LEAGUE OF NATIONS, 1920–1946 (2013); Natasha Wheatley, *Mandatory Interpretation: Legal Hermeneutics and the New International Order in Arab and Jewish Petitions to the League of Nations*, 227 PAST & PRESENT 205 (2015).

appear later, when it became the rationale for the next (quite ineffective) regulatory scheme for corporate responsibility in the 2000s.

Thus, even when businesses were 'on the table' as a source of concern for international legal regulation in the 1970s, the focus was not on them as *subjects of direct responsibility*. Rather, the history of the failure to reach an agreed-upon Code of Conduct in the 1970s was, at the same time, the history of the emergence of the regulatory components that came to the fore in lieu of the Code.

Countries of the Global North used different regulatory schemes to fragment the regulation of corporations into specific instruments they could govern, and applied bilateral and unilateral measures to undermine the coalition of New International Economic Order-affiliated countries. Businesses became litigants on a par with states in international investment disputes and equal partners to states in a variety of corporate social responsibility initiatives. 'Soft law', 'self-regulation', and 'corporate governance mechanisms' became central to the cause of business responsibility in international relations.[6] While many corporations turned to develop self-regulation initiatives and self-imposed codes of conduct,[7] the turn to private regulation was not the initiative of corporate actors alone. Non-governmental organizations, international organizations, and government agencies played an important role in their rise to prominence.[8] The UN's 2011 Guiding Principles on Business and Human Rights, led by John Ruggie, the UN Special Representative for this area, epitomizes this vision of *businesses as participants* in the framing and enforcement of international legal standards, while rarely defining it in such terms.[9] The 1970s debate over business responsibility thus formed a turning point that took businesses from behind the scenes of international law to the forefront as active *participants* in international legal regulation, and thus marked an important shift and the end of the particular regulatory framework this book has sought to unravel (1886–1981).

'Businesses as participants' was not the only alternative for the conceptual framing of the private business corporation. Parallel to the conceptual neglect of the corporate entity as a subject of concern and dispute, the category of *monopoly*

---

[6] Ronen Shamir, *Legal Pluralism, Privatization of Law and Multiculturalism: Corporate Social Responsibility: Toward a New Market Embedded Morality?*, 9 THEORETICAL INQUIRIES L. 371 (2008); Tim Bartley, *Transnational Corporations and Global Governance*, 44 ANN. REV. SOC. 145 (2018).

[7] Prominent examples include the establishment of the Fair Labor Association in 1998, following Nike's sweatshop scandal in 1998; the Forest Stewardship Council in 1993; the Fairtrade Labeling Organizations International for coffee trades in 1998; the Extractive Industry Transparency Initiative in the energy and mining sector in 2002. For further discussion, *see* Tim Bartley, *Institutional Emergence in an Era of Globalization: The Rise of Transnational Private Regulation of Labor and Environmental Conditions*, 113 AM. J. SOC. 297 (2007).

[8] *See* John W. Maxwell et al., *Self-Regulation and Social Welfare: The Political Economy of Corporate Environmentalism*, 43 J.L. & ECON. 583 (2000); Magali Delmas & Ann Terlaak, *Regulatory Commitments to Negotiated Agreements: Evidence from the United States, Germany, the Netherlands and France*, 4 J. COMP. POL'Y ANALYSIS 5 (2002).

[9] U.N. Doc. HR/PUB/11/04.

remained a critical, negative signifier in debates for and against business practices in the international arena. Chartered companies of the late-nineteenth century were exercising *de facto* sovereign authority and were the beneficiaries of monopolistic arrangements. As the charter model dissolved, private business corporations gave up such monopolistic features (sovereign authority, monopoly over trade) as their defining characteristics. By divorcing itself from the charter, the private business corporation was not only able to allocate the governance and coordination costs to governments, but also to disassociate itself from the Gordian knots historically synonymous with the colonial corporation: its association with public violence, which was henceforth the prerogative of the sovereign state, and its association with commercial profitability based on the monopoly over trade.

In the forthcoming decades, both notions of monopoly—the sovereign monopoly over violence and monopolistic market practices—would continue to serve as useful negative signifiers in the context of business practices. The Nuremberg Tribunals at the Industrialist Trials equated the Nazi regime with the Hobbesian ideal of a monolithic structure of concentrated authority, and put a disproportionate emphasis on the violence of the Nazi state as the criterion for the illegality of certain business transactions. Even though antitrust regulation against monopoly, in favour of competition, did not amount to a fully blown international legal framework, the case studies in this book provide some evidence of its effectiveness as a justification for regulatory intervention. For example, accusations against British antitrust measures in the interwar rubber market played a significant role in Harvey Firestone's successful campaign to enlist the support of the U.S. Government for his Liberian endeavours. Similarly, antitrust sentiments were central to the criminal cases against the German Industrialists at Nuremberg and provided the regulatory basis for the dissolution of the Industrialists' corporate entities.

Indeed, the antitrust campaigns of the 1940s had provided an important catalyst for the inclusion of the Industrialists in the Nuremberg proceedings in the first place. Their lasting influence may similarly explain the Allies' choice to concentrate on the dissolution of the German cartels, rather than holding the corporate entities themselves accountable. The whole understanding of the economy as either part and parcel of the Nazi state or based on a unique set of practices and organizational forms (cartels, monopolies, the collective market)—coupled with the emphasis on the war—diminished the 'business-like' characteristics of the Industrialists' commercial entities. Indeed, U.S. economic policy towards German businesses was far from coherent, organized, or consistent in its treatment of different businesses. However, this patchwork of policies tells a story of a relative U.S. consensus against German cartels that was initially articulated in terms of retribution. The changing geopolitical circumstances then paved the way for the United States to shift its position, towards rehabilitating Europe. These changes, in turn, proved highly consequential for the Industrialist Trials and their troubling aftermath. In the chapter on the Anglo-Iranian dynamic, we once again encountered the relevance of monopoly and cartelization to the international legal regulation of private business corporations. This time, cartelization of businesses proved a useful resistance strategy and a source of pressure for British and U.S. companies against the Iranian Government and for Organization of Petroleum Exporting Countries against industrialized economies (in Chapter 4). Together, these cases present a rather surprising history of antitrust sensibilities influencing international regulation of businesses, even though an international legal antitrust framework failed to materialize at the global level.

One might assume a third conceptual framework: their framing as multinational corporations (MNCs) or transnational corporations. However, as described in Chapter 5, the development of the MNC as a concept did not carry the same critical edge as monopolies, despite attempts to draw analogies between them. While the MNC gained a critical connotation in the 1970s as a signifier of the great ills of development policies, it was later reconfigured as a vehicle for progress and change in the 1980s. It has remained a contested category ever since. This may reflect the complicated intellectual history of the term and perhaps, also, the extent to which the fight against monopolies is more compatible with the economic order of the twentieth century than the fight against the MNC.

Alongside the gradual rise of an alternative investment regime in the 1970s, this period saw the shift towards international human rights as a central focal point for international regulation.[10] It was within this context that the discussion on the regulation of private business corporations in international law became focused on their *inclusion* as *subjects* of direct international legal responsibility. The term 'MNC', as a critical label for business operations, did not gain sufficient critical traction, amid the continuing dialogue over North/South power relations and the political dynamics of host governments and communities. It would reappear in the 1990s as a mega-subject violating the rights of weaker subjects, reflecting a human rights struggle between two individuals: the natural person (the individual whose rights were violated) and the legal person (the corporation as a subject of responsibility).

Along with the growing influence of international human rights, there emerged the paradox this book has sought to tackle. Human rights campaigns over labour positioned the private business corporation as a neglected subject of international law that should be recognized as a subject of international legal responsibility. Further, human rights campaigns situated this regulatory failure in the context of post-Cold War globalization. Indeed, private business corporations did not occupy the hearts or minds of many international lawyers before the 1990s as they did afterwards. Nor were there any visible efforts to conceive of them *as subjects* of

---

[10] For an influential account on the 1970s as the transitional period towards international human rights as 'the last utopia', *see* SAMUEL MOYN, THE LAST UTOPIA (2010).

international legal responsibility before the very end of the twentieth century. But this does not mean that international legal practices, institutions, and doctrines were immaterial to their emergence or consistently failed in their regulation. In this book, I have argued the contrary. Private business corporations have traditionally been conceived by the most central international legal concepts, such as sovereignty, as entities whose marginality is self-evident. This framing enabled the allocation of costs and responsibilities in ways that proved quite beneficial to the interests of businesses and powerful states. International law also introduced conceptual and institutional opportunities that supported the fight against the negative influence of private business corporations. Similarly, alternative concepts to that of the private business corporation as a *subject of responsibility* (such as businesses as participants, monopolies, and MNCs) were applied at different junctures, to either challenge or further facilitate the regulation of private commercial enterprises through international law. Thus, while private business corporations rarely appeared in the international legal texts as subjects of responsibility or a source of concern during the better part of the twentieth century, this book has exposed the central role international regulation played in their history, and in doing so, has sought to challenge our very understanding of the history of corporations in international law.

Index

Note: *For the benefit of digital users, indexed terms that span two pages (e.g., 52–53) may, on occasion, appear on only one of those pages.*

sovereign prerogative, 174

sovereignty, 10–11, 12, 16, 37, 64, 110, 144–45, 146–47, 153–54, 162–63, 167, 173, 205

sovereign veil, 4, 142–43

Soviet Union, 71–72, 74, 156

Speer, Albert, 85, 87–88n83

spoliation, 74, 86–87n79, 97–98, 99–100, 101–2, 102–3n159, 103, 108, 121–22, 140

Sprecher, Drexler A., 72–73n12, 74n20, 102–3n159, 114–15n4, 115–17n16, 127

SS, 72, 74, 81

Standard Oil, 84–85, 151–52

state capitalism, 78–79

Stokes Mission, 162

Subcommittee on War Mobilization of the Senate Committee on Military Affairs, 115

subsequent trials, 10–11, 72–73, 81, 96, 129

Suez Canal, 184

sugar, 184

sweatshops, 220–21, 224n7

Taylor, Telford, 71–72n4, 73–74n19, 76, 80–81, 98–99, 112, 114–15n4, 135–36, 137–38

Thayer, Russell, 89

Third Reich, 72, 78–79, 81, 90, 95, 96

German industry, 105

Third World Approaches to International Law, 7–8

threat to peace, 162–63

Thyssen, Fritz, 72–73, 114–15n4

totalitarian monopoly capitalism, 79

totalitarian state, 10–11, 70–71, 77–78, 91–92n108, 110, 128

total war, 93, 108

traditional authority, 127, 140

transnational corporations, 208, 209, 226, *see also* multinational corporations (MNC)

code of conduct, 210–11, 217

transnational law, 5, 146, 169–74; *see also* Jessup, Philip

transnational networks, 6–7

transnational regulatory space, 6

Treaty of Versailles, 10–11n30, 137, 157–58n64

Truman, Harry S., 115–17n13, 163

U.N., 12–13, 154, 171, 176

Code of Conduct on Transnational Corporations, 213, 217

Commission on Permanent Sovereignty over Natural Resources, 184–85

Commission on Transnational Corporations, 210, 217

Committee on Restrictive Business Practices, 172

Economic and Social Council, 209

Guiding Principles on Business and Human Rights, 224

information sharing and gathering, 212

investment, 183

U.N. Centre on Transnational Corporations (UNCTC), 217

U.N. Charter, 154, 171

art. 2(7), 162–63, 168, 175

art. 34–35, 162–63

art. 94, 162–63

Chapter VII, 175

UNCTAD (United Nations Conference on Trade and Development), 217

Restrictive Business Practices Set, 213

World Investment Report, 217

Unilever, 25

United African Company, 18–19, 25

United States, 42, 57, 184, 194, 203–4, 205, 211

BIT programme, 215

expropriation, 157–58

Foreign Corrupt Practices Act (FC2A), 214

Office of Military Government. *See* OMGUS (U.S. Office of Military Government)

oil supply, 151, 206–7

security laws, 206

Temporary National Economic Commission (TNEC), 115n7

as world economic leader, 185–86, 187

United States v. Alfried Krupp. See *Krupp* case

United States v. Carl Krauch. See *I.G. Farben* case

United States v. Ernst von Weizaecker, 98n136

United States v. Friedrich Flick. See *Flick* case

unjust enrichment, 156

Vernon, Raymond, 195, 196

von Schnitzler, Georg, 83, 102–3n157

von Wilmosky, Tilo Freiherr, 141

Vorstand. *See* I.G. Farben, Vorstand

war crimes, 74, 99–100, 124, 131

war machine, 90–91

war prisoners, 124

Wartime Economy Leader. *See* Wehrwirtschaftsführer

Watergate investigations, 206

Weber, Max, 92–93, 134–35, 139

Wehrmacht, 74n170, 85–86, 101

Wehrwirtschaftsführer, 128–29

Weimar Republic, 78–79, 94–95, 107–37

Wilkins, Mira, 196–97, 199–200